SPINOZA NOW

SPINOZA NOW

Dimitris Vardoulakis

EDITOR

University of Minnesota Press
Minneapolis
London

A different version of chapter 14 was previously published as Alexander García Düttmann, "Viertes Modell: Leben und Tod," in *Derrida und ich: Das Problem der Dekonstruktion*, 137–50 (Bielefeld, Germany: Transcript, 2008).

Copyright 2011 by the Regents of the University of Minnesota

All rights reserved. No part of this publication may be reproduced, stored in a retrieval system, or transmitted, in any form or by any means, electronic, mechanical, photocopying, recording, or otherwise, without the prior written permission of the publisher.

Published by the University of Minnesota Press
111 Third Avenue South, Suite 290
Minneapolis, MN 55401-2520
http://www.upress.umn.edu

Library of Congress Cataloging-in-Publication Data

Spinoza now / Dimitris Vardoulakis, editor.
    p. cm.
Includes bibliographical references and index.
ISBN 978-0-8166-7280-6 (hc : alk. paper)
ISBN 978-0-8166-7281-3 (pb : alk. paper)
1. Spinoza, Benedictus de, 1632–1677. I. Vardoulakis, Dimitris.
B3998.S745 2011
199'.492—dc22

                        2010032605

The University of Minnesota is an equal-opportunity educator and employer.

Contents

Note on References to Spinoza's Works............ vii

Editor's Note.................................. ix

Spinoza Now: An Introduction xi
    Dimitris Vardoulakis

Part I. Strategies for Reading Spinoza

1. Spinoza and the Conflict of Interpretations 3
    Christopher Norris

2. What Is a Proof in Spinoza's Ethics?............. 39
    Alain Badiou

3. The Joyful Passions in Spinoza's
   Theory of Relations.......................... 51
    Simon Duffy

4. Spinoza's Ass................................ 65
    Justin Clemens

Part II. Politics, Theology, and Interpretation

5. Toward an Inclusive Universalism:
   Spinoza's Ethics of Sustainability 99
    Michael Mack

6. Prophecy without Prophets: Spinoza and
   Maimonides on Law and the Democracy
   of Knowledge............................... 135
    Arthur J. Jacobson

7. Interjecting Empty Spaces: Imagination
   and Interpretation in Spinoza's *Tractatus
   Theologico-Politicus* 161
    Warren Montag

8. Marx before Spinoza: Notes toward
   an Investigation 179
    Cesare Casarino

Part III. Spinoza and the Arts

9. Image and Machine: Introduction to
   Thomas Hirschhorn's *Spinoza Monument* 237
   Sebastian Egenhofer

10. Spinoza, Ratiocination, and Art 263
    Anthony Uhlmann

11. An Inter-action: Rembrandt and Spinoza 277
    Mieke Bal and Dimitris Vardoulakis

Part IV. Encounters about Life and Death

12. Power and Ontology between
    Heidegger and Spinoza 307
    Antonio Negri

13. A Thought beyond Dualisms,
    Creationist and Evolutionist Alike 321
    A. Kiarina Kordela

14. A Matter of Life and Death:
    Spinoza and Derrida 351
    Alexander García Düttmann

Contributors 363

Index 369

Note on References to Spinoza's Works

THE VARIOUS TRANSLATIONS of Spinoza's works offer often significantly different interpretations of the meaning of his original Latin text. For this reason, the contributors have been free to choose their preferred translations or to translate themselves the Latin from the established text of Spinoza's works in the Gebhardt edition of the *Opera*.

In references to the *Ethics*, the Roman numeral indicates the part of the *Ethics* to which the author is referring, e.g., *Ethics* I is *Ethics*, Part I; *Ethics* II is *Ethics*, Part II; and so on. In addition, the following abbreviations are used:

A	axiom
Ap.	appendix
C	corollary
D	definition
L	lemma
P	proposition
Pr.	proof
S	scholium

For instance, *Ethics* II, P7, refers to *Ethics*, Part II, Proposition 7, and *Ethics* IV, P34S, refers to *Ethics*, Part IV, Scholium to Proposition 34.

Editor's Note

Spinoza Now attempts to place Spinoza in a contemporary context. This project started in 2005 at the Centre for Ideas of the Victorian College of the Arts, Melbourne, Australia. A number of the papers published here were first presented at the conference Wandering with Spinoza, held at the Centre for Ideas from September 13 to 15, 2006. The editor would like to thank the director of the Centre for Ideas, Elizabeth Presa, for her unwavering belief in the value of such a project. The editor also thanks Norma Lam-Saw for research assistance.

Spinoza Now: An Introduction

DIMITRIS VARDOULAKIS

THE TITLE of this collection—*Spinoza Now*—highlights the importance Spinoza places on the present moment for any political or cultural investigation. It also includes contributions that are of the present—attempts to think about, on, and with Spinoza in addressing contemporary issues and that are in response to current directions in Spinoza studies. I will address these two aspects of the title in turn.

"For this much is quite certain, and proved to be true in our *Ethics*, that men are necessarily subject to passions." This statement, from Spinoza's *Political Treatise* (1, §5), encapsulates the importance of the present for his philosophy.[1] Even though Spinoza insists on a knowledge from the perspective of eternity or the infinite, communal living is nevertheless permeated with the affects each one feels while living. A desire is always in the present. Thus philosophy for Spinoza is inextricably linked to life, to the now of existence.

Such a position is not a simple vitalism. The thought in *Political Treatise* that emphasizes the now may be better outlined in relation to what it opposes. Spinoza opens the *Treatise* by treating two opposing positions about human interaction: optimism and pessimism. The optimists are discussed in the first paragraph of the *Treatise*. They are those philosophers who look on the passions as vices to be avoided at all cost. "So it is their custom to deride, bewail, berate . . . or execrate" the passions. Thus they construct political theories that seek to eliminate affects. Spinoza is not simply skeptical about such philosophizing because it "borders on fantasy or could be put into effect in Utopia"; he finds such theories so unfounded that they become amusing: "for the most part it is not ethics . . . but satire." The optimist's hope to suppress the present so as to imagine a future that has tamed the passions is entirely devoid of practical significance.

The pessimists are discussed in the second paragraph of the *Treatise*. They are those who are distrustful of politicians. Because politicians know from experience "that there will be vices as long as there are men," they fear people. This leads them to practices that may be construed as cunning or wicked, especially in the eyes of "theologians, who believe that sovereign powers ought to deal with public affairs according to the same moral principles as are binding on the private individual." However, this collapse of the distinction between private and public is yet another unfounded fancy, one that is built on fear—not hope. If past experience points to human vice, there is all the more reason to deal with that fear in contemporary political practice rather than seeking to repress it with moralizing.

As Deleuze has emphasized, Spinoza cannot be understood as a moral philosopher, and this means that Spinoza is mindful of the gap or break between false hope and crippling fear—between a utopian belief in the future and a dread of the past. Between them is located the now. At this space, *ethics* develops.

A brief overview of Spinoza's reception is required to show the second aspect of the title, namely, how Spinoza has emerged as a figure who allows us to think of our contemporary situation.[2] Rejection was the first significant reaction to Spinoza's work.[3] The seed for that reaction was already sown in 1670, when Spinoza's *Theologico-Political Treatise* was published. The book contained a sustained argument against revealed religion by questioning, for example, the existence of miracles. From that moment onward, Spinoza was painted as an atheist, and to be perceived as a follower of Spinoza was indeed a dangerous position in which to find oneself. Consequently, even after the *Opera Posthuma* were published shortly after Spinoza's death in 1677, few actually read Spinoza's works. To compound this, twenty years later Pierre Bayle wrote an article on Spinoza in the *Dictionnaire historique et critique* (1697) that interpreted Spinoza as collapsing the distinction between God and nature—a position that was understood to lead to Spinoza's atheism. For years to come, the philosophical community would get their "Spinoza" from Bayle's summary.

The identification of God and nature received a name at the beginning of the eighteenth century: *pantheism*. Spinoza was seen as recognizing God in everything, which only led to the inference that he identified God in nothing. At the same time, interpreting Spinoza as a vehement atheist attracted the attention of those who were keen to challenge the superstitions of religion and the authority of the churches on revealed religion. Thus Spinoza was becoming aligned with Enlightenment, or at least with a polemical and combative strand of Enlightenment, while at the same time the prominent figures of the Enlightenment did not refer to Spinoza and distanced themselves from what they probably saw as opprobrious attacks on religion. This ambiguity erupted into the famous *Pantheismusstreit*, or Pantheist Controversy, at the end of the eighteenth century. Shortly after Lessing's death, Jacobi contested in 1785 that Lessing had confessed to him that he was a Spinozist. Lessing was one of the figureheads of the Enlightenment in Germany as well as in Europe, and Jacobi's claim amounted to an accusation that Enlightenment deified reason. As Frederick Beiser puts it, "the belief in Spinoza's cosmic God seemed to be the religion of science itself."[4] In other words, Jacobi sought to argue that pantheism, or the identification of God with nature, was the position that any system that places reason over belief is bound to adopt. When Lessing's friend Mendelssohn, himself a leading figure of the Enlightenment, responded to Jacobi, suddenly Spinoza emerged as the métier of the Enlightenment project.

If the Pantheist Controversy implicated luminaries of the Enlightenment and thereby exposed its limitations, Jacobi's second public controversy involving Spinoza had a generative effect. This second controversy related to Fichte's philosophy and unfolded in spring 1799.[5] The transcendental idealist notion of the subject had now become Jacobi's target. Jacobi again argued that there are two options, this time articulated in terms of subjectivity: either the subject is absolute, as Fichte argues, in which case the subject is deified, or there is space for belief and the subject is not commensurate with reason. This controversy played a role in Fichte's losing his position at Jena University, where his students included Hegel and Schelling as well as Novalis, the Schlegels, and Hölderlin—or, in sum, the figures who would effect the transition to romanticism. Thus they were all exposed to Spinoza as the figure who unraveled their professor, Fichte. Paradoxically, their exposure to Spinoza led to a different interpretation of pantheism, which was now seen as positive because it affirmed the importance of nature or what they referred to as the particular. Novalis's designation of Spinoza as "God-intoxicated man," or Hegel's assertion that the whole of Spinoza can be read in relation to Proposition 7 of Book II of the *Ethics* ("the order and connection of ideas is the same as the order and connection of things"), should be understood in this context.[6] The next couple generations of philosophers exhibit a positive receptiveness of Spinoza. For instance, Marx ranked Spinoza as one of his formative influences, whereas Nietzsche saw in Spinoza his only genuine predecessor. Thus, whereas the seventeenth and eighteenth centuries viewed Spinoza with suspicion and hostility, in the nineteenth century Spinoza became the secret conversant of romanticism and its aftermath.

A crucial reason why Spinoza was never addressed in any thorough fashion by the philosophers of the nineteenth century was that there was not much scholarship on which they could build. This was rectified in the twentieth century, which saw an explosion of Spinoza scholarship. It started in the first decades of the twentieth century with the voluminous works appearing mostly in Germany on the context of Spinoza's philosophy. In America, Harry Austryn Wolfson produced a remarkable account of the sources of Spinoza's arguments,[7] and more recently Yirmiyahu Yovel has provided an authoritative account both of Spinoza's context and its impact on subsequent philosophies.[8] Alongside these works that concentrate on the external circumstances of Spinoza's thought, there is another side to this approach to Spinoza in the twentieth century, one that concentrates on the internal structure of Spinoza's argument and, in particular, on the *Ethics*. Perhaps the most prominent example here is Martial Guéroult's *Spinoza*. The two volumes of exegesis of Part I and Part II of the *Ethics* offer a close analysis of the philosophy that directed one toward grasping the architectonics of the book, that is, on presenting the structure or system of the work as a whole.⁹ Edwin Curley has attempted something similar, although less voluminous, in America.¹⁰ In sum, this approach as a whole—in its concentration on both the external or contextual circumstances of Spinoza's philosophy and the internal structure of his work—can be characterized as encyclopedic. The impact of this encyclopedic approach has been that it established Spinoza as a topic of study and disengaged the name "Spinoza" from both impassioned renunciations and their correlative, strategic appropriations.

Another approach to Spinoza emerged in the 1960s and can be characterized as an intensification of the romantic fascination with Spinoza. If, in Novalis's already quoted phrase, Spinoza was a "God-intoxicated man" in the sense that he sought the universal in the particular, this focusing on the particular is now further elaborated, showing its implications for a philosophy of power. The two instrumental figures in this new approach to Spinoza were Louis Althusser and Gilles Deleuze. Even though Althusser did not publish a lot on Spinoza, as Warren Montag has shown, his notion of the structure is indebted to Spinoza's notion of the immanent cause, that is, a cause present only through its effects. Thus Spinoza gave the means to Althusser to evade a teleological or scientific Marxism that sought reality in an inexorable and analyzable chain of causal relations of production. At roughly the same time, Deleuze's book *Expressionism in Philosophy* argued that expression in Spinoza undoes traditional representationalism in philosophy. According to Deleuze, the question that motivates Spinoza's ethics is "what can a body do?"; that is, what kind of relations produce and are produced by the individual?¹¹ Althusser's and Deleuze's interpretations of Spinoza inspired a subsequent generation of scholars, such as their respective students Étienne Balibar and Antonio Negri.¹² Warren Montag and Ted Stolze's edited volume *The New Spinoza*, also published by the University of Minnesota Press, offers the best collection of the rich range of views of this approach.¹³ We can summarize this approach by saying that it builds on the encyclopedic scholarship of the previous approach to present Spinoza as a philosopher of power, that is, as a philosopher who concentrates on immanence and particularity. In this sense, Spinoza is mobilized in the move against structures of transcendence and universalism—or what has come to be understood as modernity.

In the past few years, a new direction has started developing that could predominate in Spinoza studies in the twenty-first century. This approach assumes the centrality of Spinoza's thought in modernity—not merely as a figure who leads to modernity but moreover as a figure whose thought is modern. Thus Michael Hardt and Antonio Negri's influential critique of modern sovereignty, *Empire*, is permeated with Spinoza's influence.[14] This is also evidenced by its sequel, *Multitude*, because the title-term's provenance is Spinoza's *Political Treatise*.[15] Even though Spinoza is not referred to continuously in these two works by Hardt and Negri, still the Spinozan insistence on immanence is utilized in understanding current issues. There are several other examples of this approach. For instance, Moira Gatens and Genevieve Lloyd also use Spinoza's philosophy to address philosophical and political issues of the present in *Collective Imaginings*.[16] In addition, works in neighboring disciplines, such as Antonio Damasio's *Looking for Spinoza*, attempt a theoretical approach to neuropsychology based on Spinoza's theory of affects.[17] This third direction characteristically uses Spinoza to think about issues related to the present. Spinoza's thought participates in current debates. Maybe this new approach is philosophy's way of catching up with other practices, such as literature, which, at least since Alexander Pope and George Eliot, has seen Spinoza as a source of inspiration.[18] There are also important examples of a Spinozan influence in the arts, notably the *Spinoza Monument* by Thomas Hirschhorn (Amsterdam, 1999). There Spinoza becomes a contemporary, a participant in cultural and intellectual production, the figure who allows us to think of our modernity.

The encyclopedic approach to Spinoza that started at the beginning of the twentieth century is still valuable today because it provides a basis for further scholarship. The approach that presents Spinoza as a philosopher of power and hence aligns him with modernity can be seen as setting the foundations of the third approach: only after establishing Spinoza's import for postmetaphysical thought would it have been possible to bring Spinoza to the now. *Spinoza Now* takes the challenges faced by this latter approach seriously. It includes as broad a variety of approaches as possible. All the contributions actively engage with Spinoza, making his thought relevant today. The chapters seek to pursue Spinoza's thought by thinking with Spinoza.

The two aspects of the title—Spinoza's own emphasis on the now and the new approach in Spinoza studies emphasizing his present relevance—should be seen as interlaced. What characterizes them both is a dynamic conception of production. For Spinoza, the past and the future are both productive of, and produced by, the present. The immutability of the static substance is only a formal principle to guarantee the infinite unfolding of being and thought. The new approach to Spinoza reproduces this dual direction of production in explicating Spinoza. But in so doing, it is also producing a Spinoza of the "now," a Spinoza who participates as a productive force in cultural formation.

The first four chapters offer different ways of understanding the reception of Spinoza's thought as well as forging new ways for thought through an understanding of that reception history. In the opening chapter of the volume, Christopher Norris conducts a critical overview of the way Spinoza has been received by various philosophical traditions. Norris starts by observing the great conflict in the interpretation of Spinoza, namely, that Spinoza has been viewed either as a mystic or as an atheist, either as a spiritualist or as a materialist. Tracing some aspects of this variegated history, Norris argues that its latest incarnation is the divided interpretation of Spinoza between analytic and continental philosophers. Something unites the two approaches, however, namely, the thrust to overcome dualism, either in its Cartesian or Kantian manifestation. From that point of view, Spinozan monism emerges as standing beyond the analytic–continental dichotomy. Norris does not argue that Spinoza bridges the gap between the two philosophical schools but rather that Spinoza's metaphysics necessitates a rapprochement between analytic and continental philosophy that will be mutually beneficial.

Alain Badiou concurs with Christopher Norris about the conflict of interpretation generated by Spinoza, and especially his *Ethics*, and proposes a solution to this problem. Departing from the observation that even though the *Ethics* are written *more geometrico*—in a geometrical order—very little of the literature on Spinoza has actually paid close attention to this mathematical methodology. Examining a single proposition—*Ethics* I, P28—Badiou shows that the way the proof of the proposition is related to previous propositions, definitions, axioms, and so on, is indispensable in understanding the *Ethics*.

The geometrical order creates a web of relations that structure the *Ethics*. This mirrors Spinoza's insistence in Definition 2, at the very beginning of the *Ethics*, that the distinction between the infinite and the finite is strictly relational. The ratiocination and the order of being are, therefore, correlated. Spinoza, argues Badiou, propounds a mathematics of Being—an ontology according to which thinking or the intellect is action as such.

The implicit targets of Badiou's argument, according to which Spinoza's theory of relations can only be read in parallel with the mathematical nature of proofs in the *Ethics*, are the attempts to read the theory of relations through the theory of passions. Simon Duffy discusses the two most prominent exponents—Gilles Deleuze and Pierre Macherey—in locating the theory of relations in the third part of the *Ethics*. By exploring Deleuze's and Macherey's different interpretations of the relation between active or joyful and passive or sad affections, Duffy shows two ways of constructing a politics departing from the theory of passions. Duffy concentrates on the elusive "joyful passions," which are neither properly active nor purely passive and therefore forge a relation between joyous and sad affections.

Is there a way of mediating between the mathematical and the affective approach? Justin Clemens's chapter, in locating the emergence of the political in *in*-action, and in showing that inaction is a matter of the mathematics of Being and of affective disposition, suggests a possible mediation. This chapter presents a genealogy of the Buridan's ass paradox (*Ethics* II, P49S)—the donkey that cannot decide between two equidistant bales of hay. Clemens argues that the paradox has two ostensible targets: Descartes's separation of will and understanding and Hobbes's exclusion from the covenant with the sovereign of all those who cannot decide. As such, Buridan's ass shows the tight connections between Spinoza's ontology, epistemology, and politics. From this perspective, argues Clemens, Buridan's ass demonstrates Spinoza's materialism.

All the different approaches explored in the first four chapters have one thing in common: the insistence that Spinoza's ontology is linked to his politics. This insistence can take another, more specialized guise: the link between theology—broadly conceived to include any notion of universalism—and the political. This link is possible because of the process of interpretation—the biblical exegesis that

Spinoza proposes in the *Theologico-Political Treatise* or the notion of expression in the *Ethics* that Deleuze emphasizes. The four chapters of Part II deal with this theme.

Like Clemens, Michael Mack also addresses Descartes's and Hobbes's influence on Spinoza, but shows how it is possible to eschew an absolute universalism in favor of an inclusive universalism. Mack shows that Spinoza is not arguing against religion or theology per se but rather against the politics of domination to which Cartesian dualism of necessity leads. The reason for this is that there is a line connecting theology with teleology and anthropomorphism, which only leads to the possibility of one group claiming superiority and domination over another. Mack describes this as a self-destructive or autoimmune process. This is juxtaposed to the intellectual love of God from *Ethics* V, which Mack interprets as instating a communality, in the sense that it describes a plurality of individual minds, an affirmation of singularities. Only this communality, argues Mack, gives us a chance for a nonviolent politics.

Arthur J. Jacobson turns to the *Theologico-Political Treatise* to examine the status of prophets. It is well known that for Spinoza, there are no miracles, and in this sense prophesy is part of natural knowledge, its distinctive characteristic being that it helps in the formation of community. Jacobson further complicates this standard account of Spinoza's prophets by pointing out a paradox, namely, that if prophesy is natural knowledge, then everyone, in principle, even if not in fact, can be a prophet. This structure, as Jacobson demonstrates, can also be found in Maimonides. The effect of this structure in Spinoza is that knowledge, then, is shareable by everyone—there is a democracy of knowledge.

Warren Montag looks at scripture itself to make a related point to that raised by Jacobson. Montag points out the correlation between ontology and politics expressed in "God, or Nature" from the *Ethics* has its equivalent in the *Theologico-Political Treatise*, in which Spinoza writes, "Scripture, or the mind of the Holy Spirit." This indicates that interpretation is also a partner in ontology and politics. But this is only possible, as Montag demonstrates, if interpretation presupposes that any work does not exist prior to its effects. There is no independent space of reason that remains outside a causality that includes the imagination and all the faults that characterize the human's mind and actions. This crucial Spinozan insight is missing, argues Montag, from Jonathan Israel's image of Spinoza as the prime representative of "radical Enlightenment" that supposedly demystified knowledge, emptying it of all superstition. Conversely, Montag shows that scripture is equivalent to the *mind* of the Holy Spirit because it is the palimpsest of the interaction, inevitably and invariably at fault, of imagination and reason. Furthermore, if scripture, like Nature, is perfection, then the Bible is, paradoxically, no longer an exemplary or singular text but rather the manifestation of interpretation's role in the interplay between ontology and politics. To recall the distinction about the prophets drawn by Arthur Jacobson, scripture, in principle, has no superiority over any other text; it is more important than other texts only in fact, through the influence it exercised in the conceptualization of law and norm.

Like Montag, Cesare Casarino also departs from a close reading, in this case, a passage that refers to the "concatenation of all things" (*Ethics* I, Ap.). Casarino first points out that Spinoza uses the notion of concatenation to explicate the argument of the first part of the *Ethics*. Such an explication is rare, if not unique, in the *Ethics*. Casarino shows that this is not accidental. Concatenation is interlinked with Spinoza's understanding of interpretation that requires two simultaneous procedures: the positing of a totality, on one hand, and, on the other, the signification and performance of meaning. This dual aspect is precisely what Deleuze has termed *expression* or *sense*. But there is also a second, political consequence of this move. Concatenation and the totality it implies present Spinoza as a genuine theorist of globalization—the *Ethics* appears as a response to capital and its totalizing imperative. According to Casarino's argument, the explication that signifies and performs its meaning is not commensurable with representation in the sense that it activates potentiality in the process of interpretation: the knowledge of an object is not subjective but a feature of the object itself. This allows for singularity. As Marx showed, it is possible to think of the ontological function of God as absolute immanence. But in Spinoza, that absolute immanence is accompanied by the concatenation of all beings, which retains being's singularity. Thus Spinoza emerges as a theorist of capital and globalization who comes—anachronistically and yet all the more poignantly—after Marx.

Part III takes up the issues discussed in the previous chapters to present them in relation to Spinoza's relevance for the arts. Such an unusual approach aims not only to present Spinoza from a novel perspective that can be illuminating but in addition to demonstrate that Spinoza's thought can be applied to a variety of contexts and issues of contemporary relevance.

Sebastian Egenhofer also tackles the Marxist legacy of Spinoza's thought, concentrating on how the notion of production is indispensable in understanding the art of the twentieth century. There is an increasing shift from the imagistic to the economic aspect of production—from Mondrian's abstractions, whose process of material production is secondary, to Judd's minimalism, which makes the material manifestation the focal point, to Asher's works, operating with and against their own economic genesis. Egenhofer suggests a next stage indicated by the "precarious materiality" of Thomas Hirschhorn's *Spinoza Monument*. Here the two aspects of production are inseparable—or, even more emphatically, they allow for the conceptualization of this inseparability. The work of art is both the experience and the thought that structures that experience. In this way, Hirschhorn's work manifests that the Marxian notion of production unfolds in a Spinozan matrix, as the various ways in which the infinite can be expressed in its finite modes. In other words, only when the Spinozan link between ontology and politics is imbued with the Marxian notion of production can Hirschhorn's originality come to the fore.

Anthony Uhlmann combines issues discussed in earlier chapters—the theory of relations in Badiou and Duffy, the notion of the necessity of a gap in interpretation in Montag, and the concomitance of production and its idea in Egenhofer—to show that it is possible to develop a Spinozist understanding of the arts. Departing from Beckett's fascination with Spinoza, Uhlmann acknowledges that, at first blush, the parallelism between thought and experience, the infinite and finite, or substance and its modes poses a problem for art. But this is only so if art is under the sway of representation. Spinoza, as Uhlmann shows, had already moved beyond representation by insisting that the parallelism does not suggest a lack of contact; rather, infinite knowledge is of necessity related to its finite modes—the first kind of knowledge is implicated in the third kind of knowledge.

This theory of relations enacts gaps between its different parts. The presence of these gaps is also indispensable for the arts. A work of art does not convey a message; rather, a work of art establishes relations whose message is the (ethical) imperative to fill the gaps that, of necessity, persist. This means that, just as in Spinoza's relation of substance and its modes, modern art is both the unfolding of material relations and the thinking that accompanies them.

Mieke Bal and Dimitris Vardoulakis explore the relation between thought and matter from a different perspective, emphasizing the rupture that makes their relation possible. Spinoza addresses this by drawing the distinction between essence and existence. As Bal and Vardoulakis note, this distinction is drawn with recourse to examples from art. This is not accidental. As an analysis of three different versions of Rembrandt's depiction of Joseph, Potiphar, and his wife demonstrates, Rembrandt's work makes possible a similar distinction between image and words. The complex interpretations that arise when the image is denied an immediate meaning echo Spinoza's insistence that there is no immediate connection between thought and matter, essence and existence. From this perspective, the link between Rembrandt and Spinoza is not based on the fact that they were neighbors in Amsterdam's Jewish quarter but rather is based on adopting a similar attitude to the creation of art and culture. Thus Spinoza emerges not so much as an aesthetician as a philosopher whose ontology reverberates with an understanding of the arts precisely because the distinction of essence and existence allows for creation and production.

The last three chapters provide encounters between Spinoza and other philosophers. These encounters are not primarily comparative analyses, nor are they merely the impetus for exploring current philosophical issues; rather all three encounters stage the importance of the Spinozan ontology's privileging of life over death.

Antonio Negri begins his analysis by pointing out that modern philosophy is characterized by the Hegelian move to unite essence and existence. As Bal and Vardoulakis discussed in the previous chapter, and as Negri emphasizes here again, essence and existence are never united in Spinoza. Negri further observes that Heidegger's ontological difference rests on the same premise. The disjunction between essence and existence makes Heidegger and Spinoza both antimodernist philosophers, yet here the similarities end, for ultimately they construct contradictory, even antithetical, ontologies. Heidegger proposes an ontology of the void, emphasizing the nothingness of being, which is achieved through the projective aspect of care, the destiny that subjugates being in being-toward-death. This is, argues Negri, a totalizing move, whose reactionary political overtones are clear to see. Conversely, Spinoza's ontology understands being as plenitude, and instead of an emptiness, there are relations of power. The result is radically different from Heidegger, Negri insists. Instead of the totalizing impulse of death, we have in Spinoza the singularity of life, which articulates itself in love, the construction of being through affect. This constructive aspect makes the escape from destiny through freedom possible and, consequently, is a genuinely democratic impulse.

A. Kiarina Kordela shows that the way that death is conceived is crucial for Spinoza's political stance seen from a psychoanalytic perspective. For this to come to the fore, argues Kordela, it is important to avoid two interrelated premises that structure Antonio Damasio's interpretation of Spinoza. These are, first, that Spinoza performs an inversion of Cartesian dualism by privileging the body over the mind, and second, that consequently Spinoza's is solely a philosophy of life, one that indicates homeostasis, self-preservation, and the pleasure principle. Kordela shows that such an inversion of Cartesianism only leads to a new dualism—a dualism that can only conceive of death as a biological occurrence. As Kordela demonstrates, however, death is never solely biological for Spinoza. Instead, as the discussions of suicide evidence, Spinoza's conception of death is indispensable in social and political critique. Thus Spinoza emerges as having recourse to the death drive alongside the pleasure principle. This political dimension, then, allows Spinoza's ontology to reverberate with psychoanalysis. Like Negri, Kordela shows that this dimension emerges in Part V of the *Ethics*, in the discussion of the intellectual love of God.

Alexander García Düttmann explores the relation between life and death by staging a dialogue between Spinoza and Derrida. Düttmann begins his chapter with Spinoza's assertion that a free man fears death least of all. This entails that freedom requires a liberation from the affect of fear and, more generally, liberation from the bondage of affect—which also means the attainment of wisdom. In Spinoza's construal, freedom as an affirmation of life is nothing other than the acceptance of the law's necessity—a freeing oneself from that necessity even though that necessity persists. Derrida's notion of the law is never articulated in terms of necessity but always in terms of indecision. The absence of certain or adequate criteria precludes any certainty of the law's validity. Derrida also sides with life, but here life is understood as the infinite deferral of the law, as the suspension of its necessity. From that perspective, the Spinozan position about freedom being the acceptance of the necessity of the law appears thoroughly incompatible with Derrida. Yet the matter is not as simple as that. For though Derrida can refute Spinoza on the grounds that it is merely idealism to impute the liberation over affect—that is, to tame being or reality by subsuming it to the law of the substance—still Spinoza can respond that Derrida's own assertion of the impossibility of grasping necessity can be conceived as a law in itself, as the ultimate affirmation of necessity. Despite their differences, their mutual affirmation of life makes it at least possible for them to say that they understand each other.

Janouch mentions the following comment that Franz Kafka made to him:

> "Accident is the name one gives to the coincidence of events, of which one does not know the causation. But there is no world without causation. Therefore in the world there are no accidents, but only here . . ." Kafka touched his forehead with his left hand. "Accidents only exist in our heads, in our limited perceptions. They are the reflection of the limits of our knowledge. The struggle against chance is always a struggle against ourselves, which we can never entirely win."[19]

Kafka unwittingly expresses himself as a true Spinozist here. There is, on one hand, an unshakeable necessity. However, on the other hand, that necessity is not subject to a law, or at least to a law that can be discovered. This necessity persists despite us—and yet, simultaneously, it can exist only because of us, because of our struggles to bridge the gap that separates us from that necessity.

The insistence on the now in Spinoza's philosophy is about this gap and this struggle. Their effects are so deep that they bring disparate categories into contact, from ontology to politics and from ethics to aesthetics. What has to be remembered, however, is that the gap can never be filled, the struggle can never completely succeed or, in Kafka's words, "we can never entirely win." This must apply to Spinoza himself. Thus "Spinoza now" is not so much a statement about a truth that Spinoza's writings can reveal to us in our present situation; rather, it is the injunction to adhere to the attitude that affirms both necessity and its impossibility. It is hoped that this will lead to an engaged thought that strives to rediscover that struggle in the past and to ensure that it continues in the future.

Notes

1. Baruch Spinoza, *Political Treatise*, in *Complete Works*, trans. Samuel Shirley, ed. Michael L. Morgan (Indianapolis: Hackett, 2002), 1, §5.
2. Given that Spinoza's biographical details are well known, I will mention here only the nodal points. Spinoza's family had emigrated to Amsterdam, the most liberal city of its time, from the Iberian Peninsula owing to the persecution of Jews. He was born there in 1632. Spinoza's life changed dramatically when he was excommunicated in 1656 and was forced to leave the Jewish community of Amsterdam. Nobody knows the exact reason for the excommunication, but it is certainly related to Spinoza's free thinking and his study of philosophy. These endeavors led to the publication of Spinoza's first book, *Principles of Cartesian Philosophy*, in 1663. By then, Spinoza was leading a relatively quiet and solitary life, although he had faithful disciples or admirers in the Netherlands and was in correspondence with the best minds of his time in Europe, including Leibniz. Responding to contemporary political events, Spinoza stopped writing his magnum opus, the *Ethics*, to compose the *Theologico-Political Treatise*, which was published anonymously in 1670. The reaction was ferocious, and it meant that Spinoza was not confident enough to publish anything else in his lifetime. After his death in 1677, his friends collected and published his writings, including the *Ethics*, his unfinished *Political Treatise*, and his

correspondence. The best biography of Spinoza is Steven Nadler's *Spinoza: A Life* (Cambridge: Cambridge University Press, 1999).
3. The best overview of Spinoza's reception up to the beginning of the twentieth century is Pierre-François Moreau's "Spinoza's Reception and Influence," in *The Cambridge Companion to Spinoza*, ed. Don Garrett (Cambridge: Cambridge University Press, 1996), 408–33. I refer the interested reader to Moreau's essay for a more detailed overview.
4. Frederick C. Beiser, *The Fate of Reason: German Philosophy from Kant to Fichte* (Cambridge, Mass.: Harvard University Press, 1987), 60. See also Beth Lord, *Kant and Spinozism* (London: Palgrave, 2011).
5. See Anthony J. La Vopa, *Fichte: The Self and the Calling of Philosophy, 1762–1799* (Cambridge: Cambridge University Press, 2001).
6. For the complex relation between Spinoza and Hegel, see Pierre Macherey's classic *Hegel ou Spinoza* (Paris: Maspero, 1979); published in English as *Hegel or Spinoza*, trans. Susan M. Ruddick (Minneapolis: University of Minnesota Press, 2011).
7. Harry Austryn Wolfson, *The Philosophy of Spinoza: Unfolding the Latent Process of His Reasoning*, 2 vols. (New York: Schocken, 1969 [1934]).
8. Yirmiyahu Yovel, *Spinoza and Other Heretics*, 2 vols. (Princeton, N.J.: Princeton University Press, 1989).
9. The first volume of Guéroult's book *Spinoza* was titled *Spinoza I: Dieu*, and the second was titled *Spinoza II: L'Âme*; they were published in 1968 and 1974, respectively. A third volume that was going to treat Parts III–V of the *Ethics* was barely started at the time of Guéroult's death.
10. Edwin Curley, *Behind the Geometrical Method: A Reading of Spinoza's Ethics* (Princeton, N.J.: Princeton University Press, 1988).
11. Gilles Deleuze, *Expressionism in Philosophy: Spinoza*, trans. Martin Joughin (New York: Zone Books, 1992).
12. See Étienne Balibar, *Spinoza and Politics*, trans. Peter Snowdon (London: Verso, 1998), and Antonio Negri, *The Savage Anomaly: The Power of Spinoza's Metaphysics and Politics*, trans. Michael Hardt (Minneapolis: University of Minnesota Press, 2002).
13. Warren Montag and Ted Stolze, eds., *The New Spinoza* (Minneapolis: University of Minnesota Press, 1997).
14. Michael Hardt and Antonio Negri, *Empire* (Cambridge, Mass.: Harvard University Press, 2000).

15 Michael Hardt and Antonio Negri, *Multitude: War and Democracy in the Age of Empire* (New York: Penguin, 2004).
16 Moira Gatens and Genevieve Lloyd, *Collective Imaginings: Spinoza, Past and Present* (London: Routledge, 1999).
17 Antonio Damasio, *Looking for Spinoza: Joy, Sorrow, and the Feeling Brain* (Orlando, Fla.: Harcourt, 2003).
18 George Eliot even translated the *Ethics*. See Benedict de Spinoza, *Ethics*, trans. George Eliot, ed. Thomas Deegan (Salzburg, Austria: Institut für Anglistik und Amerikanistik, Universität Salzburg, 1981). See also Isaac Bashevis Singer's remarkable short story "Spinoza in the Market Street," in *The Spinoza of Market Street and Other Stories*, 7–25 (New York: Bard Books, 1970). Another more recent but fascinating example is Norma Cole's poetry collection *Spinoza in Her Youth* (Richmond, Calif.: Omnidawn, 2002).
19 Gustav Janouch, *Conversations with Kafka: Notes and Reminiscences*, trans. Gononwy Rees, with an introduction by Max Brod (London: Derek Verschoyle, 1953), 55.

PART I
Strategies for Reading Spinoza

1

Spinoza and the Conflict of Interpretations

CHRISTOPHER NORRIS

IF THERE HAS ALWAYS been a "new Spinoza," this is no doubt because his thinking so strongly resists assimilation on any of the terms laid down by every mainstream school of European philosophy from Descartes to the present. Thus his work has very often been taken up by radicals or dissidents—those who approach it with a view to transforming the discourse of ontology, metaphysics, epistemology, ethics, politics, or aesthetics—while always leaving something unaccounted for, or something that is consequently thought to require a likewise radical critique.[1] This pattern of response goes a long way back—historically as well as philosophically speaking—to the earliest stages of Spinoza's reception, when his writings became a chief zone of engagement in the struggle for freedom of conscience and belief or for emancipation from the dictates of religious (whether Christian or Jewish) orthodoxy.[2] Later on, it assumed the same kind of salience for the quarrel between idealism and materialism or—at its most extreme—between the romantic (German and English) idea of Spinoza as a "God-intoxicated" mystic and his underground reputation as an out-and-out determinist, materialist, and atheist.[3]

Perhaps the most remarkable thing about this reception-history was that both parties to each dispute could cite chapter and verse from Spinoza's texts and moreover buttress their respective readings with a good show of exegetical care and argumentative rigor. It is the same with those recent or present-day schools of Spinoza interpretation that are often sharply at odds with each other on basic points of method, doctrine, and principle yet that likewise manage to put up a strong textual-documentary as well as philosophical case. Thus, for instance, thinkers such as Althusser and Balibar—"structural Marxists," as the label went—could very plausibly appeal to Spinoza by way of support for their rationalist account of the relationship between lived experience, ideology, and the process of "scientific" concept formation,[4] while others, like Gilles Deleuze, could just as plausibly invoke him as the chief source or elective precursor for a kind of radical process metaphysics grounded in the notions of desiring-production and molecular or deterritorialized energy flows.[5] More than that, the impact of his work was clearly visible across a swathe of developments in hermeneutics, critical theory, and the human and social sciences, where Spinoza's philosophicohistorical critique of revelation and scriptural warrant was among the most crucial early contributions to the project of secular Enlightenment thought.[6]

Some years ago, I wrote a book about Spinoza that put the case for his pervasive yet underacknowledged influence and tried to sort out some of these multiple, often closely intersecting, yet sometimes wildly divergent lines of intellectual descent.[7] In particular, I traced the conflict of interpretations that started out with his double role as archheretic or vilified atheist, on one hand, and on the other, purveyor of a knowledge—a mystical-intuitive mode of comprehension—beyond all the limits and endemic shortcomings of plain-prose reason. This conflict has been repeated in various displaced or surrogate forms over the past three centuries of often intense and heated debate around Spinoza's thought. Nowadays it appears in the clash of priorities between those in the analytic camp, who regard him as having some useful (if often misleadingly formulated) things to say about issues in metaphysics, epistemology, or philosophy of mind,[8] and those of a so-called Continental persuasion, who tend more often to emphasize Spinoza's politics or what they see as the basically political nature of Spinozist ethics, ontology, and psychology.[9] Even so, this fails to capture the full complexity of the situation because there is something in common—philosophically if not politically speaking—between the analytic drive for conceptual clarity and precision and Althusser's claim for Spinoza (in company with Marx) as having achieved a decisive epistemological break with the currency of commonsense or ideological belief.[10] Indeed, the very fact of his having spawned so diverse and complex a reception-history is one measure of Spinoza's extreme singularity and his way of holding out against classification according to such ready-made categories. French thinkers in the wake of structuralism, Deleuze especially, have on the whole been more concerned to emphasize this aspect of Spinoza's thought as a part of their campaign against the grip of conceptual abstraction or "totalizing" systems of whatever kind, not least Althusserian Marxism.[11] However, it has also left a strong impression among his analytical commentators through their sense of his standing quite apart from—and posing a sizeable challenge to—some of the most rooted assumptions of mainstream philosophic thought.

Thus, for all their marked, even drastic differences of interest, idiom, and dominant agenda, the two traditions are, at any rate, largely agreed in their perception of Spinoza as a thoroughly anomalous and (to say the least) provocative thinker. Though to some, this has been cause for unqualified celebration—in particular those, like Deleuze, who enlist him on the side of radical difference or heterogeneity—in others, it has provoked a very mixed response and sometimes taxed their exegetical patience to the limit and beyond. Here I am thinking chiefly of Jonathan Bennett's approach, in the mode of Russell-style rational reconstruction, whereby he offers a patient, detailed, and often admiring account of Spinoza's *Ethics* until he gets to the "third kind of knowledge"—*scientia intuitiva*—achieved through the "intellectual love of God," at which point, all this patience suddenly runs out and his commentary gives voice to a sense of bafflement and downright exasperation.[12] Thus, picking out a phrase from the more indulgent Stuart Hampshire, "I contend that instead of implying that Spinoza has brought us 'beyond the limits of literal understanding' and that this is acceptable because it is inherent in his chosen topic, we should say openly that Spinoza is talking nonsense and that there is no reason to put up with it."[13] As for Frederick Pollock and his claim that these passages are "among the most brilliant endeavors of speculative philosophy," and moreover, that they "throw a kind of poetical glow over the formality of [Spinoza's] exposition," Bennett is quite unable to contain his indignation. Thus, "when a commentator as shrewd as Pollock is reduced to such babbling by his desire to praise the final stretch of the *Ethics*, that is further evidence that this material is worthless. Worse, it is dangerous: it is rubbish that causes others to write rubbish."[14] Still, as I say, even these sharply conflicting valuations bear witness to the sheer singularity of Spinoza's thought and its power to solicit uncommonly intense and deeply felt modes of response, whether as an unprecedented challenge or a scandal to received ideas. In this context, we might recall Derrida's etymologically pointed use of *solicit* (from the Latin *solicitare*) with the sense of challenging and summoning forth but also of shaking to the very foundations.[15] What unites these otherwise disparate approaches is their willingness—albeit very often within certain clearly marked limits—to accept the possibility of a thinking at odds with those dominant conceptions that have shaped the self-image of reputable philosophic discourse.

If commentators once joined battle over the issue of Spinoza as atheist and radical materialist versus Spinoza as nature-mystic and proto-Wordsworthian pantheist, they now more often take sides over matters of ontology, epistemology, or philosophy of mind and language. Or again, they divide with respect to the question of whether these are indeed (as analytic philosophers would have it) the core issues in Spinoza's thought or whether—on the dominant Continental view—they must ultimately take second place to his ethicopolitical concerns. Thus, as things stand at present, it is hard to imagine (say) followers of Althusser, Balibar, or Deleuze entering into some kind of constructive dialogue with philosophers whose main points of reference are the commentaries offered by analytic thinkers like Bennett, Donald Davidson, or Alan Donagan.[16] Yet, in truth, the Spinoza who emerges through Althusser's structuralist–Marxist reading bears a closer resemblance to Bennett's Spinoza—the rationalist thinker of "adequate ideas" as opposed to the delusions of imaginary commonsense belief—than to anything that finds room in Deleuze's (for want of any better description) radical–empiricist account. And again, despite obvious differences of idiom, what Deleuze has to say about Spinoza's doctrine of the affects and his notion of *conatus* as the inbuilt drive toward self-preservation and fulfillment on the part of every living organism finds a close parallel in readings from a very different quarter that likewise place chief emphasis on his treatment of the positive and negative emotions as the basis for any rational account of knowledge as conducive to human well-being. Among the latter can be counted Antonio Damasio's recent book, which comes at these issues—that is to say, questions concerning the relationship between cognitive and passional components of the human psyche—from a neurophysical and cognitive-psychological angle but which nonetheless adopts a broadly analytic rather than Continental approach.[17] My point is that Spinoza's thinking resists any adequate classification in terms of the standard, textbook account of how philosophy has developed over the past four centuries. For if Spinoza is undoubtedly a full-fledged rationalist who maintains that true wisdom can only be achieved through a reasoned critique of commonsense notions or intuitive, self-evident ideas, then he is just as much a radical empiricist (more aptly, a radical naturalist and materialist), according to whom such wisdom consists in a due recognition of the various physical, causal, and sociopolitical factors that bear on human knowers in their quest for more adequate self-understanding.

Of course, the mere fact that he cannot be placed on either side of these deep-laid philosophic rifts doesn't mean that he manages to bridge them effectively or achieve the ultimate reconciliation between subject and object, mind and world, reasons and causes, or free will and determinism that has eluded philosophers from Descartes down and continues to preoccupy analytic and Continental thinkers alike. However, it does provide a telling reminder of just how anomalous a figure Spinoza must appear by the light of any orthodox historiography or any attempt to assimilate his thought to this or that certified line of descent. Where responses do tend to divide in fairly predictable ways is by reacting to the scandal that Spinoza represents either in downright celebratory terms—as a salutary challenge to the norms and pieties of orthodox philosophic thought—or with various degrees of suspicion, mistrust, or hostility. Thus Bennett, as we have seen, has a high opinion of the *Ethics* just so long as it remains on analytically respectable ground, that is, just so long as Spinoza is concerned with the corrective capacity of adequate ideas when applied to the various confusions thrown up by the realm of sensory appearances or ideas of imagination. However, this attitude switches very sharply to one of disappointment or shocked incredulity when Spinoza moves on, in Part V, to expounding the third kind of knowledge, that which involves a direct apprehension of the nature or essence of things somehow conceived as present to thought without any form of conceptual mediation. Such claims can only strike Bennett as amounting to a quasi-mystical doctrine whereby the mind is taken to possess something very much like the power of intellectual intuition that Kant likewise denounced, that is, a capacity to pass beyond the realm of phenomenal appearances where sense data are brought under adequate concepts and thus lay claim to an immediate knowledge of ultimate, noumenal reality.[18]

Yet it is hard to see the point of any rational reconstruction in the analytic mode that adopts so partial or selective a view of those elements in Spinoza's thought that are deemed to merit serious attention by present-day analytic standards. For what drops out of sight in this process is also what constitutes the singular challenge of a thinking that runs directly counter to the whole tradition of epistemological enquiry that began with Descartes, found its systematic high point in Kant, and is still very much a part of the present-day analytic agenda. That is to say, it is the radically monistic approach that typifies not only Spinoza's claims with regard to *scientia intuitiva* but also his entire conception of knowledge or, more precisely, his entire ontology of mind and nature conceived as twin aspects or attributes of a single, indivisible substance.

It seems to me that analytic philosophy has long been striving to escape or overcome this Kantian legacy while in fact coming up with nothing more than a series of minor variations on it.[19] Spinoza alone, among the great thinkers of philosophical modernity, goes so far in his rejection of the dualist epistemological paradigm and his embrace of a radically monist ontological alternative as to provoke bewilderment not only among his goodwilled exegetes but also among those analytic types who are themselves in quest of some such (albeit less radical) alternative. As I have said, this contrasts with the positive, even celebratory response to Spinoza's thinking in the recent Continental—mostly French—reception-history where he has been recruited to a range of philosophical causes whose main (in some cases sole) point of contact is the link they propose between issues of ontology and issues of an ethical or sociopolitical nature.[20]

Not that this dimension is altogether ignored by analytic commentators, forming, as it does, a crucial component of Spinoza's case for the role of philosophy in achieving a clearer, more distinct idea of the various factors (causal and social) that operate either to expand or to contract our scope for the exercise of human creative and emancipatory powers.[21] They have also shown some interest in pursuing the relation between Spinoza's more formal or logically articulated procedures of argument in the *Ethics* and the kinds of concern that animate those other portions of that work in which he discusses the affective or passional aspects of human knowledge and experience, along with more overtly *engagé* writings such as the *Tractatus Theologico-Politicus*.[22] After all, any serious attempt to make sense of Spinoza's project as a whole will have to find some plausible way of explaining how the exercise of reason may contribute to a better, more enlightened understanding of the factors that make for psychological, social, and political well-being through a wise acceptance of our place in the natural order of things. More than that, it will have to offer an account of this process that ties in convincingly with Spinoza's critique of religious revelation and his arguments concerning the complex background of historical and cultural conditions that alone provide an adequate contextual basis for reading the scriptures in a critically informed and nondogmatic way.

So of course, the broadly analytic reception has included some work on this aspect of Spinoza's thought and on relevant details of his own sociopolitical background as one much involved in the various debates—as well as the frontline struggles for power and influence—within the Dutch Republic of his time.[23] However, it has not shown anything like the commitment of thinkers like Althusser, Balibar, Deleuze, or (most strikingly) Antonio Negri to produce a reading of the new Spinoza that brings these multiple aspects together in a strictly inseparable fusion of politics, life-history, and work.[24] What unites these various Continental approaches—despite their otherwise large divergences of aim—is a shared conviction that Spinoza's thought cannot be understood except through a reading that takes due account of both its immanent ("purely" philosophical) modes of argument and its close imbrication with the various historical, social, and political events that made up its formative background. That is, they start out by rejecting the analytic principle that requires a clear distinction between context of discovery and context of justification, or the kind of strictly second-order research that has to do with matters of cultural–historical or psychobiographical interest and the kind of first-order investigation that pertains to the assessment of philosophic claims in accordance with distinctly philosophical criteria of truth and validity.[25] For an *echt*-analytic commentator like Bennett, this distinction is so very basic—so definitive of what properly counts as philosophy rather than intellectual or cultural history—that the worth of Spinoza's intellectual achievement is to be judged solely with reference to the context of justification, which for him means in keeping with present-best ideas of conceptual rigor and precision.[26] For others of a broadly similar but somewhat less hard-line analytic persuasion (among them Alan Donagan), the distinction holds in matters of conceptual exegesis or strictly philosophical content but doesn't prevent such extraneous interests from making some (albeit very limited) contribution to our better understanding of Spinoza's thought.[27] However, this allowance doesn't go so far as to invoke a contingent, that is, historical, geographically specific, and sociopolitically emergent context for his central philosophic concerns, that is to say, his monist ontology and metaphysics, along with whatever implications they might hold for current debates in epistemology, philosophy of mind, or cognitive psychology.

Nor is it surprising that this should be the case, given both the analytic premise that issues in philosophy cannot be reduced to second-order questions of history, politics, or psychobiography and also—reinforcing that belief among his analytic commentators—Spinoza's commitment to the idea of philosophy as aimed toward an order of truth transcending any mere particularities of time and place. Yet, of course, there is another whole dimension of Spinoza's thought that is inescapably rooted in the social conditions and political events of his time and that cannot be understood without reference to those same conditions and events.[28] Moreover, it is one that touches so directly on his chief metaphysical concerns—especially the issue of free will versus determinism that lies at their very heart—that any attempt to apply the two-contexts principle and distinguish clearly between life and work is sure to end up by offering a highly partial, not to say distorted, view of those concerns. This is where his Continental readers have an edge because they reject that principle—at least in its more doctrinaire form—and make a point of relating life to work not just as a matter of more-or-less relevant psychobiographical or sociohistorical background but as offering the only adequate means to grasp what is most distinctive and uniquely challenging about Spinoza's project. For it is a main part of that project to explain how we can think of human beings *both* as belonging to an order of causal necessity that allows no appeal to some imaginary realm of purely autonomous agency or choice *and yet* as possessing the capacity to transform passive into active modes of experience. This capacity comes about—so he maintains—through the achievement of adequate ideas, which in turn make possible some measure of freedom from the realm of unknown and hence blindly operative causal forces.

Of course, this way of putting Spinoza's case—like his own formulations in the *Ethics* and elsewhere—is very far from resolving the free will–determinism issue and might well be seen as merely restating it in a sharpened or more intransigent form. Yet it is the merit of readings like those of Balibar, Deleuze, Macherey, and Negri to insist that he alone among the great thinkers of early philosophical modernity faced up to that issue without taking refuge—like Descartes before and Kant after him—in a dualist metaphysics of subject and object, mind and body, or a noumenal domain wherein reason gives the rule for its own autonomous exercise and a phenomenal realm wherein everything is subject to the dictates of causal necessity. Moreover, they do so most often with specific reference to that complex background of historical, political, religious, and sociocultural events that exerted such a crucial formative influence on Spinoza's thinking about issues of free will and determinism. Of course, this may be said to beg the question yet again because, after all, there is a prima facie contradiction—or at any rate, a sharp clash of priorities—between the claim for Spinoza as one who possessed a sufficient degree of intellectual autonomy to think the issues through in a novel, creative, and independent-minded way and the claim that his ideas were crucially affected by the distinctive pressures and specific challenges of the time. Indeed, these commentators might be seen as going out of their way to emphasize the problem and ensure that Spinoza's readers have to face it fair and square rather than seeking a convenient escape route or evasive compromise solution that would purport to bring him out as a moderate determinist and upholder of free will in some likewise moderate, qualified, or compatibilist form.

Thus the main thrust of interpretations like those mentioned earlier is to insist—contra such face-saving or emollient accounts—that Spinoza's was an outlook radically opposed to any notion that the problem might be assuaged by adopting a sensible line of least resistance midway between those strictly unthinkable extremes. For instance, they stress that he took time off from composing the *Ethics* and before proceeding to those parts of Part V in which, if anywhere, his doctrine of freedom might attain its definitive statement to write the *Tractactus Theologico-Politicus* as an urgent and topical contribution to debates about politics, religion, and the future of the Dutch Republic.[29] That work was primarily concerned with explaining how the supposed timeless truths of scriptural revelation should rather be understood as products of their own historical, cultural, and sociopolitical locale, along with the motives of those various, far-from-disinterested parties who first wrote them down and then engaged in the process of editing, transmission, and selective deployment to overt or covert manipulative ends. That is to say, the *Tractatus* was a thoroughgoing exercise in the mode of materialist, causal-explanatory, sociodiagnostic, protosecular, and demythologizing critique that would emerge to full view only after another two centuries of largely underground, since often forcefully repressed or persecuted, life.[30] Of course, one reason for this, quite apart from its explosive theologicopolitical content, was the fact that Spinoza here seemed to adopt a thoroughly determinist approach that purported to demonstrate the false and illusory character not only of religious truth-claims but also of our cherished, theologically sanctioned self-image as believers whose faith—or lack of it—could properly be ascribed to our own God-given capacity for autonomous belief formation. What the *Tractatus* drives home to painful effect for anyone who wishes to retain such faith is both the logical impossibility of squaring this latter pair of requirements and the extent to which that entire belief system, along with its various doctrinal, scriptural, and institutional props, can be seen to rest on a basis of merely contingent historical events. Thus it leaves no room for such imaginary ideas as those of revelation, divine intervention, or miracles, all of which Spinoza treats (like Hume after him) as resulting from a mixture in various proportion of natural, historical, and psychological causes joined to the effects of ignorance, fear, and predisposed or passive credulity.

In short, as these commentators acknowledge, the free will–determinism issue is by no means resolved or quietly laid aside but is in some ways rendered all the more intractable by Spinoza's decision to interrupt work on the *Ethics* and devote several years of intensive research under often very difficult personal and social circumstances to composing the *Tractatus*. Their point, like his, is to wean us away from any idea that thinking might achieve a genuine—as distinct from merely notional—margin of autonomy or freedom by claiming to rise above the conditions of its physical or causally constrained, as well as its historically situated, time and place. Yet their commentaries would surely miss something crucial if they didn't all the same make allowance for the strong countervailing tendency in Spinoza's thought, that is, his commitment to a doctrine of adequate ideas that affirms the power of intellect to criticize false beliefs and pass beyond them to a knowledge no longer in the grip of illusory common sense or ideological notions. This is what lends a degree of credibility to the sorts of analytical approach, like Bennett's, that pretty much ignore any background matters of historical, cultural, or sociopolitical context, or again, the attitude summed up by Donagan when he remarks that "generally [Spinoza's] life was of a piece with what he wrote: discoveries about its details—apart from facts about his intellectual exchanges—bear dubiously on disputed questions about what he thought."[31] It is also the aspect of his thinking that most captivated Althusser and the early Macherey when they recruited certain pregnant formulations from Spinoza as a prime exhibit in their structuralist–Marxist case against Hegelian, Lukacsian, or other such "expressive" ways of figuring the link between socioeconomic base and politicocultural superstructure.[32] Rather we should try to conceive it as a complex, decentered, and overdetermined mode of relationship wherein there exist certain "structures in dominance" but wherein economic forces should be taken to predominate only "in the last instance," or just insofar as they are assigned that role by the entire existing conjuncture.

This is not the place for anything like a critical exposition of Althusserian Marxism. It is sufficient to say—in the present context—that Spinoza's influence is often plain to see in its emphasis on structural (as opposed to expressive or totalizing) modes of explanation and on the crucial role of philosophy as a form of theoretical practice aimed toward resisting or breaking the hold of intuitive, self-evident, or commonsense (i.e., ideological) beliefs. Thus, according to Althusser and Balibar,

> effects are not outside the structure, are not a pre-existing object, element, or space in which the structure arrives to imprint its mark; on the contrary, the structure is immanent in its effects, a cause immanent in its effects in the Spinozist sense of the term, that the *whole existence of the structure consists in its* effects, in short that the structure which is merely a specific combination of its peculiar elements, is nothing outside its effects.[33]

Moreover, Spinoza should also take credit for having pioneered the mode of critical or symptomatic reading that enabled commentary to go beyond its traditional, fideist attitude in matters of textual (especially scriptural) warrant and thereby reveal those moments of unresolved aporia, strain, or contradiction that signaled the effect of some repressed yet disruptive ideological content. Clearly what Althusser and Balibar have in mind is the *Tractatus Theologico-Politicus* and its precocious combination of textual exegesis with a range of approaches—hermeneutic, source-critical, historical-reconstructive, cultural-materialist in no very stretched sense of the term—that would have to wait a good two centuries before they were taken up and developed. Hence their very striking claim in *Reading Capital*:

> The first man ever to have posed the problem of *reading*, and in consequence, of writing, was Spinoza, and he was also the first to have proposed both a theory of history and a philosophy of the opacity of the immediate. With him, for the first time ever, a man linked together in this way the essence of reading and the essence of history in a theory of the difference between the imaginary and the true.[34]

So there is another side to the recent reception-history, one that has more to do with adequate ideas and with the power of thought to criticize and thereby transcend its own formative context or background conditions than with the need to recall theory to a sense of its own inescapable enmeshment in those same conditions.

However, it is worth recalling once again how urgent were the social and political circumstances that bore on Spinoza when his main concern—and a chief motive for writing the *Tractatus*—was to stave off the threat of religious dogmatism and the warring factions whose claim to exclusive possession of scriptural truth looked set to destroy the Dutch Republic. Nor is the *Ethics* by any means free of such turbulence, since—as must strike the attentive reader—there is a notable contrast between the order of numbered axioms, propositions, and corollaries with their appearance of impassive, (quasi-) geometrical precision and the various interpolated scholia in which Spinoza finds room for some powerful expressions of positive and negative affect. This is why, as Deleuze puts it, there is need for

> a double reading of Spinoza: on the one hand, a systematic reading in pursuit of the general idea and the meaning of the parts, but on the other hand and at the same time, the affective reading, without an idea of the whole, where one is carried along or set down, put in motion or at rest, shaken or calmed, according to the velocity of this or that part.[35]

Thus it was always very much on the cards that the high theoreticist "moment" epitomized by Althusserian Marxism would at length give way to a reactive trend—in Spinoza scholarship and also in the wider context of post-1980 French philosophical debate—that mounted a vigorous challenge to it. That challenge took shape among thinkers like Deleuze in the name of difference, intensity, "desiring-production," "molecular" versus "molar" forces, "deterritorializing" lines of flight versus "reterritorializing" modes of control, and other such attempts to evoke or connote what lay intrinsically beyond the grasp of adequate conceptualization.[36] Along with this went a drastically changed estimate of Spinoza's significance, one that located the potentially transformative and liberating power of his thought not so much in the process of conceptual critique, whereby confused or imaginary ideas yielded place to their clear or adequate counterparts, but rather in those passages from the *Ethics* that affirmed the priority of positive over negative or joyous over sad affects and emotions. Thus the image of Spinoza that predominates in Althusser's work—that of an elective precursor to Marx who somehow manages to construct (or discover) in advance the main theoretical apparatus of Marxist *Ideologiekritik*—now yields place to the image of one who adopted a simulacrum of rationalist method to impart a certain order to his otherwise unmanageably prolix and tumultuous thoughts.[37] What is so remarkable is that both these conflicting accounts find warrant not only in a few, carefully selected passages from Spinoza but on the basis of readings that adduce large amounts of highly relevant textual evidence, and that do so moreover with consistent and well-defined interpretative ends in view.

I should perhaps make it clear that I am not for one moment presenting Spinoza as some kind of textual Rorschach blot into whom various parties can read—or onto whom they can readily project—whatever meanings or messages they choose. On the contrary, as I have said, these variant readings each have a claim to exegetical rigor and fidelity that redeems them from any such charge. More to the point is Derrida's remark that certain thinkers—maybe all great thinkers, or those who have given rise to a significant reception-history—tend to generate sharply opposed interpretations that cannot be reconciled or subject to settlement one way or the other because they can both cite chapter and verse in their own support and can both very plausibly assert their credentials as the authorized version.[38] Very often, these debates fall out between left and right lines of intellectual descent, as can be seen in different ways—so Derrida observes—with philosophers from Aristotle to Kant, Hegel, Nietzsche, and (not least) Marx. He also provides a useful metaphor by which to think about this curious feature of intellectual history, namely, that of the tape-recording machine with multiple playback heads, such that any given segment of tape (or passage of text) may be decoded in different ways yet without this necessarily entailing any dropouts or distortions (interpretative oversights, errors, or symptoms of gross ideological bias).

Thus philosophers and literary theorists tend to distort the issue by constructing a false *tertium non datur*, that is, by supposing it to fall out between defenders of a strict intentionalist or single-right-reading position and those who adopt an attitude of anything goes or total hermeneutic license. However, this is merely to sidetrack attention from the more challenging question as to *just what it is* about certain passages in certain authors that somehow gives rise to such instances of deep-laid scholarly–critical dispute, given that there do exist certain constraints on the range of admissible readings. For if one thing is clear from Derrida's work on thinkers from Plato and Aristotle to Rousseau, Kant, Nietzsche, Husserl, and J. L. Austin, it is that (as he puts it) interpretation cannot develop in just "any direction at all" or "authorize itself to say almost anything" but rather requires "all the instruments of traditional criticism"—of philology, textual scholarship, and a due regard for authorial intent—as an "indispensable guardrail" in the process of critical exegesis.[39] On the other hand—crucially—this guardrail "has only ever *protected*, it has never *opened* a reading," so that criticism has to go beyond "the effaced and respectful doubling of commentary" to reveal how "the writer writes *in* a language and *in* a logic whose proper system, laws, and life his discourse cannot dominate absolutely." And again, "the reading must always aim at a certain relationship, unperceived by the writer, between what he commands and what he does not command of the patterns of the language that he uses."[40]

It is Nietzsche who provides one of Derrida's most striking examples since in no other case have the divergent left and right interpretations run to such extremes and been able to cite such a range of good (or, at any rate, highly plausible) warrant in the text. But there is also a sense in which Nietzsche lends himself too easily to Derrida's purpose because his writings contain such a mass of provocative, willfully extreme, and often downright contradictory remarks assembled with such scant regard for all the normal (to his way of thinking, inertly conformist) protocols of rational discourse. Spinoza offers a more interesting test case insofar as his thinking manifests a high degree of logical consistency, even if his style of reasoning *more geometrico* in the *Ethics* is apt to make it seem more rigorously argued and tightly structured than it is. So where left and right Nietzscheans can always point to different, often conflicting passages in the text that provide support for their likewise divergent interpretations, it is not so easy to explain how Spinoza could have spawned such a multifarious reception-history. This challenge becomes yet more acute when one considers that his was the most resolutely monist and hence—one might expect—most unambiguous, clearly stated, and multiple-reading-proof philosophic system to have appeared in Western philosophy since the great monists of antiquity such as (at opposite extremes) a metaphysician such as Parmenides and radical materialists such as Democritus or Epicurus. And yet, as I have said, it is the utterly unqualified or uncompromising character of Spinoza's monist ontology that has given rise to this likewise extreme pattern of contrasting interpretations. Thus his reputation has always been a battleground between those who considered him a pantheist, a mystic, a well-nigh saintly figure, or (in the famous words of Novalis) a "God-intoxicated" thinker and, on the other hand, those—including the vast majority of his contemporaries—who deemed him an out-and-out materialist, atheist, and wicked subverter of every last moral value.

Of course, the terms of this controversy have changed, and one is nowadays unlikely to find Spinoza either praised or vilified for any such reasons. All the same, it is not too hard to discern the legacy of those old battles in the more restrained and philosophically specialized yet nonetheless sharp divergences of view that continue to attend his present-day reception-history. For there is just as great a difference between, say, Althusser's high-structuralist or rationalist reading and Deleuze's take on the prophet of unbridled desiring-production as any that arose in his own time or during the subsequent two centuries when *Spinozism* was a watchword—and a dangerous charge to bring or to face—in various philosophical, theological, and sociopolitical disputes. Or again, there is just as much at stake in doctrinal terms between those who take Spinoza to be offering intimations of a new and radically distinct mode of cognition in Part V of the *Ethics* (where he talks about the "third kind of knowledge," or *scientia intuitiva*) and those, like Bennett, who come at it from a strongly analytic or rational-reconstructive angle and who tend to throw up their hands in despair at just this point.[41] What unites them, all the same, is a strong sense that Spinoza is venturing into strange seas of thought where established philosophical distinctions break down, among them most obviously those between mind and body, subject and object, or self and world. Hence, no doubt, his renewed appeal to philosophers of otherwise diverse persuasion who see in Spinoza's radical monism—or something very like it—the hope of achieving a clean, conceptually unencumbered break with the whole bad legacy of Cartesian dualism and its various, for example, Kantian and present-day (whether analytic or Continental) successor movements.

Thus Donald Davidson cites Spinoza as the one early-modern philosopher who managed to think his way through and beyond the Cartesian impasse and who thereby prefigured the current turn toward a thoroughly naturalized or nonmetaphysical yet also (just as crucially) nonreductionist account of the mind–body relationship.[42] What Davidson puts forward, briefly stated, is a theory of "anomalous monism" that seeks to maintain the following principles: (1) that for any mental event, there is a corresponding physical (brain) event in the absence of which the mental event would not have occurred; (2) that this correlation, though strict, is non-law-governed or anomalous since it is construed as holding only between event-tokens rather than event-types; and (3) that although the mental supervenes on the physical, there is no prospect of reducing the former to the latter—of pushing right through with any radical behaviorist, eliminativist, or central-state-materialist program—because they involve altogether different descriptive or conceptual registers. Where the one requires a discourse (like those of neurophysiology or cognitive science) adequately stocked with causal-explanatory terms and predicates, the latter requires a language equipped with just the sorts of vocabulary that figure in our everyday as well as philosophical talk of human meanings, motives, reasons, intentions, beliefs, desires, attitudes, and so forth. On Davidson's account—and on Spinoza's as Davidson reads him—we can enjoy the full benefits of both while preventing any possible conflict between them by keeping in mind the central tenet of anomalous monism, that is, the lack of any nomic (i.e., any fixed, invariant, or type-type) connection that might lend credence to the strong reductionist or physicalist case. This theory Davidson takes to be implicit in Spinoza's idea of mind and body as two different attributes of the self-same substance, and likewise in his cautiously coded talk of *deus sive natura*—"god or nature"—as two distinct yet compatible ways of referring to a single ultimate reality whose various modes (or particular instantiations) could just as well be conceived under one or the other attribute.[43]

It is obvious enough why Davidson should look to Spinoza not only as a thinker who arrived at some strikingly similar ideas about the mind–body relationship but also as one who went a long way toward Davidson's closely connected views on the nature of actions and events. Thus he cites a well-known passage from the *Ethics* in which Spinoza sets out his cardinal distinction between active and passive powers: "Our mind does certain things and undergoes other things, viz. Insofar as it has adequate ideas, it necessarily does certain things, and insofar as it has inadequate ideas, it necessarily undergoes other things."[44] He might just as well have cited a range of other passages to similar effect, as when Spinoza states that "whatsoever increases or diminishes, helps or hinders the power of activity in our body, the idea thereof increases or diminishes, helps or hinders the power of thought in our mind," or—by the same token—that "the mind, as far as it can, endeavors to conceive those things, which increase or help the power of activity in the body."[45] Davidson is clearly attracted to this as a way of reconceiving the free will–determinism issue that would seem to overcome that old and (on its own terms) strictly insoluble antinomy by locating the distinction between active and passive affects in the degree to which the self-realizing powers of this or that particular mind–body have attained their fullest scope of expression or exercise. Thus "on the positive side, Spinoza gives analyses of volition, perception, and the emotions consistent with his thoroughgoing naturalism and determinism. Perhaps the most striking feature of his concept of action is that it differs from being acted on just to the extent that its causes and effects lie within rather than outside us, and that this in turn is a matter of the extent and character of our knowledge."[46] However, he goes straight on to remark that this notion "follow[s] directly from [Spinoza's] objective view of human beings as integral parts of the causal chain of events" and that "even to us to whom this attitude comes perhaps more naturally than to [his] contemporaries, it is a sobering perspective."[47] Yet, after all, that perspective is one that Davidson must surely be taken to share if his monism is not to appear as just a notional concession to the science-led intellectual climate of our time and his use of the qualifying term *anomalous* (i.e., his rejection of psychophysical laws) as a somewhat shifty device for avoiding the nemesis of a hard-line physicalist, central-state materialist, or downright determinist creed.

In fact, it seems to me that Davidson's approach is not so much an answer or a working solution to the problem of Cartesian dualism as a conceptual sleight of hand or finessing of the issue that leaves that problem very firmly in place. This emerges in the following passage, where his usual, briskly problem-solving tone gives way to a flat restatement of the old puzzle and what sounds very much like an outlook of resigned acceptance that it cannot be resolved. "I confess," Davidson writes,

> that I do not see how even the most complete understanding of human psychology can avoid essential reference to the material forces that impinge on us. Nor do I see how psychology, as long as it deals with concepts such as those of action, intention, belief, and desire, can either be reduced to the natural sciences or made as exact and self-contained as physics. As I suggested, we may even take Spinoza as having shown why such a psychology is impossible; the nomological irreducibility of the mental to the physical can be taken to point in this direction.[48]

So it seems that Davidson's theory of anomalous monism is not so much clarified or rendered more plausible as it is pushed even further out on a limb by this analogy with Spinoza on the dual, self-subsistent, and causally isolated attributes of mind and body. That is to say, it becomes even harder to conceive how the theory could amount to a genuine or working monism, as distinct from a self-defeating attempt to reconcile two contradictory or, at any rate, mutually exclusive claims. Moreover, although his appeal to Spinoza has a certain prima facie plausibility, it gives a similar impression of evading the radical implications of Spinoza's thought and reducing what is truly exorbitant about it—not only in the view of his more orthodox-minded contemporaries but also, as we have seen, in that of many present-day admirers—to little more than a convenient façon de parler adopted by way of heading off certain otherwise intractable philosophic problems. Thus one gets little sense from Davidson's account of what opponents at the time—and for a good two centuries thereafter—were wont to denounce as Spinoza's cryptoatheism, or his promotion of a thoroughgoing determinist and materialist creed under cover of a vaguely mystical or pantheist rhetoric.

That sense comes across far more powerfully in Deleuze, Balibar, and other voices from the recent Continental reception-history who emphasize both the uncompromising nature of Spinoza's ontological monism and the fact that it cannot be understood—at least without massive distortion—unless one interprets it in equally uncompromising naturalistic and materialist terms. This is no doubt one reason, as Althusser and Balibar remark, why "the history of philosophy's repressed Spinozism unfolded as a subterranean history *at other sites*, in political and religious ideology (deism) and in the sciences, but not on the illuminated stage of visible philosophy."[49] For despite all philosophy's periodic claims, more than ever during the past few decades, to have moved decisively beyond any form of Cartesian mind–body dualism, that idea still exerts so strong a residual hold that any truly radical break with it—such as Spinoza represents—is apt to strike many as un-, pre-, or downright antiphilosophical.[50] This applies especially to his doctrine of the positive and negative (or joyful and sad) affects, one that finds room for freedom of will and the notion of autonomous agency only insofar as these can be squared with the single most basic Spinozist precept, that is, the indivisible unity of mind and body or the claim that they must always be conceived as two attributes of the one, self-identical substance. From this it follows that the process whereby passive dispositions take on an active character or sad affects are converted into their joyful, affirmative, life-enhancing counterparts cannot consist in some conscious effort of will or deliberate exercise of mind over matter such that the one (mental) attribute would assert its claim to freedom and self-fulfillment independently of—or in isolation from—the other. What we have to envisage, rather, is the activity of jointly mental and physical striving (Spinoza's *conatus*) through which every sentient being endeavors to persist in its own proper and distinct mode of existence, this latter conceived as a development toward its state of maximum possible flourishing. What we are *not* to suppose—at least if convinced by Spinoza's radically monist ontology—is that the process might occur (as philosophers have often thought) through the bending of our will or the summoning of mental, intellectual, or moral resources that somehow belong to a realm quite apart from that of our physical or bodily movements and affects.

So there are certain caveats that need to be entered before going along with Davidson's case for viewing Spinoza as a champion of anomalous monism avant la lettre. On this account, his strongest elective affinity in present-day terms is with the broadly compatibilist or "no problem" thesis that physicalism and mentalism or brain-talk and mind-talk can perfectly well be reconciled just so long as one assigns them to different languages or conceptual-descriptive registers and thus heads off any conflict between them.[51] From the same distinctly modern standpoint, there is nothing to be lost—and a good deal to be gained—by translating Spinoza's ontological claims out of their original, overly scholastic and metaphysically otiose idiom into one that sheds all that surplus baggage through a careful restatement in more up-to-date, that is, analytic and linguistic terms. Thus it looks as if the Spinozist doctrine of substance and attributes can be rendered acceptable by present-day standards of intelligibility and yet retain everything distinctive about it through a straightforward process of assimilation to something like Davidson's theory of anomalous monism. Yet this does entail certain significant losses or—from a standpoint not so much in sympathy with the governing interests of analytic philosophy after the linguistic turn—a tendency to opt for the line of least resistance with regard to Spinoza's most challenging claims. That is, it has recourse to a linguistified version of the double-aspect theory that no doubt succeeds in outfacing the threat of hard-line physicalist or central-state-materialist arguments but only at the cost of so far reinterpreting Spinoza's doctrine as to render it consistent with Davidson's studiously noncommittal (not to say somewhat evasive or shuffling) view of these matters.

Of course, there is a sense in which Spinoza's writings lend themselves to just this kind of revisionist treatment insofar as they adopt a systematically equivocal language or a trick of constantly playing on phrases—such as *deus sive natura* (god or nature) or the mind as "an idea of the body"—that leave commentators hard-pressed (or perhaps gratefully unobliged) to decide between rival interpretations. All the same, this ignores several points that bear directly on the question as to what counts as a valid understanding of crucial Spinozist concepts and categories. One is the fact that Spinoza would have seen absolutely no merit in the notion that those concepts and categories made sense only to the extent that they played an accepted role in some existing (whether everyday or specialized) linguistic register.[52] On the contrary, he thinks of natural language and its various (supposed) imperfections—vagueness, ambiguity, metaphor, referential opacity, and so forth—as among the chief obstacles to philosophic progress and hence as standing in need of treatment through an "emendation of the intellect" that would lead from confused or "imaginary" notions to clear and distinct concepts.[53] In this respect, Spinoza agrees with his contemporaries—rationalists and empiricists alike—that language is, at best, an efficient (i.e., transparent or nondistorting) means for the conveyance of ideas from one mind to another and, at worst, a continual source of error and mutual misunderstanding.[54] Thus, "since words are a part of the imagination—that is, since we form many conceptions in accordance with confused arrangements of words in the memory, dependent on particular bodily conditions—there is no doubt that words may, equally with the imagination, be the cause of many and great errors, unless we keep strictly on our guard."[55] David Savan spells out the implications of this in a passage that leaves no doubt as to the distance that separates Spinoza from many of his present-day (including his best-willed or most sympathetic) exegetes. According to Spinoza, he writes:

> An idea is not an image and does not consist of words. A true idea can neither arise from experience of words and images nor can it be verified through such experience, for experience can give no knowledge of essences.... Whereas an idea is certain, words are uncertain.... And whereas it is of the nature of reason to consider things as necessary and under a certain form of eternity, words are connected with contingency and time.[56]

It is only from our own ensconced position on this side of the recent though nowadays near-ubiquitous linguistic turn that such a notion might seem philosophically naive, and then only insofar as we adopt a Wittgensteinian rather than a Frege-Russell view of such matters.[57] At any rate, Spinoza would have had little time for any argument that construed his central doctrine—the mind–body identity thesis—in such a way as to empty it of all substantive content by lopping off its ontological claims, espousing a linguistified version of the double-aspect theory, and thereby allowing us to carry on talking in the same old dualist terms.

That is to say, if Spinoza is indeed to be recruited in the name of anomalous monism without resorting to a strong-revisionist (or grossly inaccurate) account, then the monism needs to be taken at full strength and the anomaly interpreted not as an absence of real, objectively existent nomic regularities or causal laws but rather as a frank admission that they are—and may forever remain—beyond our utmost powers of comprehension. Although Davidson's position sometimes lends itself to glossing along these lines, he is more often to be found insisting that because mind-events and brain-events are "under different descriptions," it is pointless (or strictly nonsensical) to advance any strong, ontologically committed version of the mind-brain identity thesis.[58] And again, because causes and reasons must likewise be thought of as falling under different descriptions—because they make sense only as playing a role in (respectively) the physical or natural and the human or social sciences—therefore, on Davidson's account, we shall go badly wrong and risk summoning the twin specters of reductionism and determinism if we allow ourselves to mix them up. Yet, of course, it was precisely Spinoza's willingness to raise those specters and to do so, moreover, without having recourse to any such strategic or cryptodualist fallback stance that prompted his expulsion from the Jewish community of Amsterdam and thereafter drew the wrath of orthodox religionists against him and anyone brave or incautious enough to earn the label "Spinozist."[59] Nor can Davidson's reading gain much in the way of added plausibility from Spinoza's other reputation as a mystically inclined pantheist thinker or—its close equivalent in psychophysical terms—from his notion of mind as "an idea of the body," thus seeming to reverse the order of priority and suggest some kind of mentalist (even panpsychist) view of how their ultimate identity is best understood.[60] What disappears in Davidson's account is once again the extremity—by any "normal" philosophic standard—of Spinoza's monist doctrine. For those alternative idioms don't so much soften or defuse its determinist impact as insist (like the phrase *deus sive natura*) on the need for all divine, supernatural, and suchlike deluded or imaginary terms to be read metaphorically or allegorically and thereby rendered consistent with a thoroughly naturalized worldview.

It is this aspect of the radical Spinoza—the philosophically exorbitant character of his thought—that comes across to more singular and striking effect in the recent Continental (mainly French) reception than among his analytically minded commentators. One reason, no doubt, is that the Continentals have fewer inhibitions about pursuing metaphysical themes, or pursuing them (so to speak) in a full-bloodedly metaphysical way rather than in the scaled-down descriptivist or semantic mode that has been the hallmark of most recent work in the analytic tradition. Another is the way that commentators such as Balibar, Macherey, Deleuze, and (most conspicuously) Negri have shown a far greater willingness to integrate their often highly speculative theses concerning Spinoza's philosophic thought with a detailed interest in the various historical and political events that left a visible, sometimes decisive mark on the course of his life and work.[61] The great exception here is Althusser, who himself claimed Spinozist (as well as Marxist) warrant for insisting on a sharp conceptual distinction between ideology and science, or on one hand the realm of commonsense, confused, or imaginary notions and on the other hand the realm of adequate ideas arrived at through a process of rigorously theorized rectification and critique. By the same token—and taking a lead from Gaston Bachelard's method of applied rationalism in philosophy of science—Althusser assumes that any interest attaching to Spinoza's life and its sociopolitical context may well be legitimate for the purposes of intellectual biography or the history of ideas but must always give way to quite different, altogether more demanding standards of accountability when it comes to issues of knowledge and truth.[62] Thus Althusser's approach, premised on Spinoza's distinction between the first (confused or imaginary) and the second (adequate) kinds of knowledge, to this extent has more in common with those analytic modes of thought that likewise make a cardinal point of distinguishing context of discovery from context of justification, or the background conditions of emergence for this or that scientific hypothesis and the validity-conditions that properly apply when it is subject to the rigors of empirical testing and further theoretical analysis. In Althusser, this went along with the notion of a Marxist theoretical practice—or labor of conceptual critique—whereby we might achieve an adequately theorized grasp of how ideology exerted its otherwise ubiquitous power to interpellate subjects and their various modes of commonsense knowledge and experience.[63]

As I have said, there was good Spinozist warrant for Althusser's claims in this regard, whatever the well-known problems with them from a practical-political as well as philosophical standpoint. It is also fairly clear how Spinoza could be read as offering support for Althusser's argument—in opposition to the humanist, Hegel-influenced readings of Marx dominant in France at the time—that a chief prerequisite for the better understanding of Marx's thought was to break with such anthropocentric residues through a form of theoretical antihumanism that sought to reveal its underlying conceptual or epistemocritical structures. Yet just as this involved a highly partial and selective reading of Spinoza—one premised exclusively on the doctrine of adequate versus inadequate or imaginary ideas—so Althusser's larger project ran aground (or so it has seemed to many commentators) on its failure to explain how this ascetic imperative could possibly provide any motivating impulse for political agency and change.[64] Indeed, it was largely in reaction against that high structuralist or theoreticist project that thinkers like Deleuze, Balibar, and Negri—albeit in different ways—set out to make their case for the other Spinoza, that is, the thinker whose undoubted commitment to the rationalist way of ideas went along with an equal (and by no means opposite) commitment to the maximization of active over passive or joyful over sad affects. This is why the recent Continental reception has typically managed to find room for a range of Spinozist themes and concerns that tend to be excluded—or to figure only marginally—in most analytic accounts. Or rather, it manages to take simultaneous account of those various aspects of Spinoza's work that more often receive separate treatment by specialists in different quarters of the Anglophone academic community.

Thus, for instance, there has been some groundbreaking work by intellectual and cultural historians who have uncovered far more than was previously known about the sociotheologicopolitical contexts of Spinoza's thought and its later reception. Most notable of these is Jonathan Israel's study of Spinoza as the central figure in that radical enlightenment that emerged among certain dissident factions in the seventeenth-century Dutch Republic and whose critical-emancipatory character was tamed or repressed by the mainstream (bourgeois) enlightenment that flourished in France and then Germany a century later.[65] Israel's work belongs very much to a tradition of Spinoza commentary in which detailed scholarship has often coexisted with a strong sense of political partisanship or a marked sympathy for just those motivating values—secularism, tolerance, republican beliefs, freedom of thought and expression, cosmopolitanism in the political, legal, and juridical spheres—for which he stood as an emblematic figure. It is a tradition that goes back, via champions like Lewis S. Feuer, to the centuries-long history of his underground reputation, when Spinozist (i.e., atheist, materialist, and politically subversive) ideas were subject to vigorous church-and-state repression in many parts of Europe and beyond.[66] Then again, recent developments at the interface between neuroscience and cognitive psychology have led some admirers—like Damasio—to hail Spinoza as a thinker far ahead of his time in his outright rejection of Cartesian dualism, his recognition of the strictly indissoluble tie between mind and body or thought and emotion, and moreover, his having set forth these prescient ideas in a way that falls square with some of the most advanced current thinking in the field.[67] Yet there is a strong sense throughout Damasio's book that he sees this approach as one that holds the promise of rescuing Spinoza from the dead hand of philosophy and granting him the favor of a reading informed by the latest scientific knowledge. In Israel's narrative likewise, the richness and sophistication of historical scholarship goes along with a fairly routine treatment of Spinoza's philosophical ideas and a relative lack of concern with their specific rather than general bearing on that ferment of radical ideas that his book brings so vividly to life. In fact, one has to look elsewhere—to the French reception and its complex interweaving of metaphysical or speculative with historical, political, and sociocultural themes—to gain a more adequate (i.e., philosophically informed and integrated) view of Spinoza's galvanizing role.

My point is not to suggest that we should reconcile these diverse claims on Spinoza's behalf in some kind of grand synthesis. Such a prospect is neither realistic nor even desirable, given what we surely should have learned from Spinoza and his best exegetes, that is, that his thinking stubbornly resists assimilation to any of the ready-made concepts or categories by which philosophers, no less than intellectual historians, try to keep things safely under control. This is no doubt why the many attempts to recruit Spinoza to this or that philosophic cause—for free will or determinism, pantheism or atheism, compatibilism vis-à-vis the mind–body issue or a hard-line physicalist position—have always and inevitably run into problems when striving to square these doctrines with a properly attentive, impartial reading of his work. Indeed, a chief lesson of the modern French reception, and one that could only have resulted from its greater degree of speculative license, is the strange copresence in Spinoza's thought of a rationalism aimed toward removing or correcting all the causes and effects of the mind's enslavement to the passions and a countervailing will to intensify those passions to the point where they are no longer merely suffered but actively promoted and enjoyed. Thus the compact history of visions and revisions that leads from Althusser to Deleuze and that takes in the shift of focus exhibited by thinkers like Balibar and Macherey is one firmly grounded *at every stage* in a detailed engagement with Spinoza's texts and *in no way* contravening the letter or the spirit of those texts. Rather it is a faithful reflection that Spinoza remains the great exception—in Negri's phrase, the "savage anomaly"—whose thinking is able to solicit and support (if not fully accommodate or reconcile) such a range of conflicting interpretations.

All the same, there is something distinctly unsatisfactory about the way that historians, philosophers, critical theorists, and lately cognitive psychologists have tended each to go their own way and stake their claim to the new or radical Spinoza without much sign of either knowing or caring what the others have to say. This is not, I think, just because they come at his ideas from such divergent and specialized angles of interest but also because the philosophers—who might be expected to mediate these various concerns—are themselves so deeply at odds with regard to the nature, import, and present-day significance of Spinoza's work. That is to say, there exists such a gulf between the two philosophical cultures and their respective ideas of what constitutes a valid or worthwhile contribution to debate that it is hard for people in other disciplines to get any confident purchase on the issues involved. Thus there is reason to suggest that Jonathan Israel might usefully have looked to Deleuze and Balibar by way of philosophic support for his conception of Spinoza as a seminal thinker of the radical enlightenment. Moreover, Damasio might likewise have drawn on Deleuze—on his detailed working-out of the Spinozist idea of active versus passive affects—as offering a line of approach very much to his own neuroscientific and cognitive-psychological purposes. What has so far got in the way of such productive exchange is that most workers in those other fields tend to take their philosophic bearings from a received, often analytically filtered account of Spinoza's thought that finds no room for such suspect—hermeneutically venturesome—approaches. This is not so much a matter of tough-minded analytic commentaries in the mode of rational reconstruction descending from Bertrand Russell and taken up with comparable vigor by Jonathan Bennett.[68] In their case, the treatment is so frankly selective and the ideas they can't accept so forcefully denounced that readers are left in no doubt regarding the dominant agenda. Rather it is the more moderate descriptivist program—of which Stuart Hampshire is the best-known exponent—that has exerted such a deep and pervasive influence on the way that Spinoza is typically read by Anglophone philosophers and also by those (intellectual historians among them) who take their cue from that same dominant tradition.[69] Here the main object—with Spinoza, as likewise with Leibniz, Kant, and others—is to coax these thinkers down from the heights of metaphysical or speculative thought and lead them back to a sensible acceptance that, in truth, philosophy can do no more than describe or map the conceptual geography of our various, whether everyday or scientific, modes of knowledge and experience.[70]

Yet if there is one thing that Spinoza stands up for contra this whole way of thinking, it is the need for philosophy to challenge, criticize, and—where necessary—amend or rectify such taken-for-granted notions. Moreover, as again emerges very strongly from the recent French reception, this applies just as much to Spinoza's radically heterodox thinking about ethics and politics as to his thinking on matters of ontology, epistemology, and philosophy of mind. In my book, I put the case for Spinoza as the single most important, albeit underrecognized, source for many then current or lately emergent ideas in critical and literary theory. What I have sought to do here is make a similar case for the potential of a close engagement with Spinoza's thought to revitalize large areas of present-day philosophic discourse by cutting across their more restrictive and narrowly specialized concerns. Above all, it brings out the impossibility of addressing such core topics—even after the much-heralded linguistic turn—without raising substantive metaphysical issues that go well beyond the scaled-down descriptivist conception that marks the outer bound of acceptability for most analytic thinkers. In this respect, Spinoza poses a greater challenge than Kant, despite the latter's role in a good deal of recent analytic philosophy as representing either the kinds of metaphysical temptation that we have nowadays thankfully laid to rest or else (more in keeping with Kant's self-estimate) a means of putting philosophy back on its feet by precisely defining its operative scope and limits.[71] For that role has much to do with the clear continuity—pointed out by recent commentators—between Kant's epistemological project and the analytic enterprise that took shape largely as a linguistic (or logicosemantic) transposition of central Kantian themes.[72]

Thus one way of writing the history of analytic philosophy is as a series of attempted and loudly proclaimed breaks with Kant—especially with his subject-centered epistemology and his doctrine of synthetic a priori knowledge—that have then periodically given way to various attempts at a partial reconciliation along descriptivist, naturalized, or other such revisionist lines.[73] What has led to this oscillating pattern of rejection and qualified acceptance is the presence within analytic philosophy of just the same chronically unstable dualisms—subject and object, mind and world, concept and intuition—that Kant claimed to resolve in his first *Critique* but that have nonetheless continued to vex thinkers from the German post-Kantian idealists to John McDowell. It is the same with those recent efforts to "dismount from the seesaw" (McDowell's phrase), or at any rate to damp down its movements, whether by following Sellars and Davidson in their attack on the empiricist "myth of the given," along with its attendant scheme-content dichotomy, or else by invoking some naturalized (or detranscendentalized) version of Kant.[74] That these efforts have failed—that the dualism always crops up again in a more-or-less covert, displaced, or surrogate form—is a case borne out (as I have argued elsewhere) by a good many episodes in recent analytic debate.[75] My point now, by way of conclusion, is that Spinoza's radically monist understanding of mind and body or mind and world offers by far the most effective counterinstance to this whole way of thinking and its hold on philosophers from Descartes down. Moreover, it constitutes a standing reproof to that other tenacious dualism that has had such a damaging effect on recent philosophical debate, namely, the split—however one perceives it—

between the analytic and Continental traditions of thought. For there is no hope that philosophy will rise to the Spinozist challenge unless it puts away some of the fixed preconceptions that have so far acted as a strong disincentive for taking that challenge at its full philosophic, that is, ontoepistemological as well as ethicopolitical force.

Notes

1. See, e.g., from various philosophic and political perspectives, Etienne Balibar, *Spinoza and Politics* (London: Verso, 1998); Lewis Samuel Feuer, *Spinoza and the Rise of Liberalism* (Boston: Beacon Press, 1958); Jonathan Israel, *Radical Enlightenment: Philosophy and the Making of Modernity, 1650–1750* (Oxford: Oxford University Press, 2002); Christopher Norris, *Spinoza and the Origins of Modern Critical Theory* (Oxford: Blackwell, 1991); Gideon Segal and Yirmiyahu Yovel, eds., *Spinoza* (Aldershot, U.K.: Ashgate, 2002); Paul Wienpahl, *The Radical Spinoza* (New York: New York University Press, 1979); Yirmiyahu Yovel, *Spinoza and Other Heretics*, vol. 1, *The Marrano of Reason*, and vol. 2, *The Adventures of Immanence* (Princeton, N.J.: Princeton University Press, 1989).
2. See esp. Stephen Nadler, *Spinoza's Heresy: Immortality and the Jewish Mind* (Oxford: Oxford University Press, 2002); Samuel J. Preuss, *Spinoza and the Irrelevance of Biblical Authority* (Cambridge: Cambridge University Press, 2001); Steven B. Smith, *Spinoza, Liberalism, and the Question of Jewish Identity* (New Haven, Conn.: Yale University Press, 1997); Theo Verbeek, *Spinoza's Theologico-Political Treatise: Exploring "The Will of God"* (London: Ashgate, 2003); Yovel, *Spinoza and Other Heretics*, 2 vols.
3. See various entries under n. 1 and 2; see also Frederick C. Beiser, *The Fate of Reason: German Philosophy from Kant to Fichte* (Cambridge, Mass.: Harvard University Press, 1978); Moira Gatens and Genevieve Lloyd, *Collective Imaginings: Spinoza Past and Present* (London: Routledge, 1999); Leszek Kolakowski, "The Two Eyes of Spinoza," in *Spinoza: A Collection of Critical Essays*, ed. Marjorie Grene, 279–94 (Garden City, N.Y.: Anchor Books, 1973).
4. Louis Althusser, *For Marx*, trans. Ben Brewster (London: New Left Books, 1969), and Althusser, "Elements of Self-Criticism," in *Essays*

in *Self-Criticism*, 101–61 (London: New Left Books, 1976); Louis Althusser and Etienne Balibar, *Reading Capital*, trans. Ben Brewster (London: New Left Books, 1970); Etienne Balibar, *Spinoza and Politics*; Pierre Macherey, *Hegel ou Spinoza?* (Paris: Maspero, 1979), and Macherey, *In a Materialist Way: Selected Essays*, ed. Warren Montag, trans. Ted Stolze (London: Verso, 1998).

5 See esp. Gilles Deleuze, *Spinoza: Practical Philosophy*, trans. Robert Hurley (San Francisco: City Lights Books, 1988), and Deleuze, *Expressionism in Philosophy: Spinoza*, trans. Martin Joughin (New York: Zone Books, 1992); see also the various references to Spinoza in Gilles Deleuze and Félix Guattari, *A Thousand Plateaus: Capitalism and Schizophrenia*, trans. Brian Massumi (Minneapolis: University of Minnesota Press, 1987).

6 Spinoza, *Theologico-Political Treatise*, trans. Samuel Shirley (Indianapolis, Ind.: Hackett, 2001). See entries under n. 2; also Israel, *Radical Enlightenment*; Robert J. McShea, *The Political Philosophy of Spinoza* (New York: Columbia University Press, 1968); Richard H. Popkin, *The History of Scepticism from Erasmus to Spinoza* (Berkeley: University of California Press, 1979); Leo Strauss, *Spinoza's Critique of Religion*, trans. E. M. Sinclair (New York: Schocken Books, 1965); Silvain Zac, *Spinoza et l'interpretation de l'écriture* (Paris: Presses Universitaires de France, 1965), and Zac, *Philosophie, Théologie, Politique dans l'oeuvre de Spinoza* (Paris: Vrin, 1979).

7 Norris, *Spinoza and the Origins of Modern Critical Theory*.

8 See esp. Jonathan Bennett, *A Study of Spinoza's Ethics* (Cambridge: Cambridge University Press, 1984), and Bennett, *Learning from Six Philosophers*, vol. 1, *Descartes, Spinoza, Leibniz* (Oxford: Clarendon Press, 2001); also Donald Davidson, "Spinoza's Causal Theory of the Affects," in *Truth, Language, and History*, 295–313 (Cambridge: Cambridge University Press, 2005); Alan Donagan, *Spinoza* (Chicago: University of Chicago Press, 1988); Grene, *Spinoza: A Collection of Critical Essays*; Stuart Hampshire, *Spinoza* (Harmondsworth, U.K.: Penguin, 1951); G. H. R. Parkinson, *Spinoza's Theory of Knowledge* (Oxford: Clarendon Press, 1953). Two anthologies that offer a useful conspectus of past and present scholarship, commentary, and criticism are Genevieve Lloyd, ed., *Spinoza*, 4 vols. (London: Routledge, 2001) and Don Garrett, ed., *The Cambridge Companion to Spinoza* (Cambridge: Cambridge University Press, 1996).

9   See n. 4 and 5.
10 See n. 4 and 8.
11 For further discussion, see Norris, *Spinoza and the Origins of Modern Critical Theory*.
12 Spinoza, *Ethics*, in *The Collected Writings of Spinoza*, vol. 1, trans. Edwin Curley (Princeton, N.J.: Princeton University Press, 1985).
13 Bennett, *A Study of Spinoza's Ethics*, 373.
14 Ibid., 374.
15 See Jacques Derrida, "Différance," in *Margins of Philosophy*, trans. Alan Bass, 3–27 (Chicago: University of Chicago Press, 1982).
16 See entries under n. 8.
17 Antonio Damasio, *Looking for Spinoza: Joy, Sorrow, and the Feeling Brain* (London: Heinemann, 2003). See also Jerome Neu, *Emotion, Thought, and Therapy: A Study of Hume and Spinoza, and the Relationship of Philosophical Theories of the Emotions to Psychological Theories of Therapy* (London: Routledge Kegan Paul, 1978).
18 Immanuel Kant, *Critique of Pure Reason*, trans. N. Kemp Smith (London: Macmillan, 1964).
19 For further argument to this effect, see Christopher Norris, *Minding the Gap: Epistemology and Philosophy of Science in the Two Traditions* (Amherst: University of Massachusetts Press, 2000); Norris, *Truth Matters: Realism, Anti-realism, and Response-dependence* (Edinburgh: Edinburgh University Press, 2002); Norris, *Philosophy of Language and the Challenge to Scientific Realism* (London: Routledge, 2004); Norris, *On Truth and Meaning: Language, Logic, and the Grounds of Belief* (London: Continuum, 2006).
20 See n. 4 and 5.
21 See n. 6.
22 See, e.g., Edwin M. Curley, *Behind the Geometrical Method: A Reading of Spinoza's* Ethics (Princeton, N.J.: Princeton University Press, 1988).
23 See n. 6.
24 Antonio Negri, *The Savage Anomaly: The Power of Spinoza's Metaphysics and Politics*, trans. Michael Hardt (Minneapolis: University of Minnesota Press, 1991).
25 See esp. Hans Reichenbach, *The Rise of Scientific Philosophy* (Chicago: University of Chicago Press, 1938).
26 Bennett, *A Study of Spinoza's Ethics*.

27 Donagan, *Spinoza*.
28 See esp. Israel, *Radical Enlightenment*; also Margaret Gullan-Whur, *Within Reason: A Life of Spinoza* (London: Jonathan Cape, 1998), and Steven Nadler, *Spinoza: A Life* (Cambridge: Cambridge University Press, 1999).
29 See esp. Balibar, *Spinoza and Politics*, and Negri, *Savage Anomaly*.
30 See n. 1–3 and 6.
31 Donagan, *Spinoza*, 10–11.
32 See n. 4.
33 Althusser and Balibar, *Reading Capital*, 188–89.
34 Ibid., 16.
35 Deleuze, *Spinoza: Practical Philosophy*, 129.
36 Deleuze and Guattari, *A Thousand Plateaus*, and Gilles Deleuze and Félix Guattari, *The Anti-Oedipus: Capitalism and Schizophrenia*, trans. Robert Hurley, Mark Seem, and Helen R. Lane (Minneapolis: University of Minnesota Press, 1977).
37 See n. 1, 3, 5, and 22.
38 Jacques Derrida, *The Ear of the Other: Texts and Discussions*, trans and ed. Christie V. McDonald, Claude Lévesque, and Peggy Kamuf (New York: Schocken Books, 1985).
39 Jacques Derrida, *Of Grammatology*, trans. Gayatri C. Spivak (Baltimore: Johns Hopkins University Press, 1976), 158.
40 Ibid.
41 Bennett, *A Study of Spinoza's Ethics*.
42 Davidson, "Spinoza's Causal Theory of the Affects."
43 For further elucidation of these arguments, see Davidson, *Essays on Actions and Events* (Oxford: Clarendon Press, 1980).
44 Spinoza, *Ethics* III, P1.
45 Spinoza, *Ethics* II, P2n.
46 Davidson, "Spinoza's Causal Theory of the Affects," 310.
47 Ibid.
48 Ibid., 312.
49 Althusser and Balibar, *Reading Capital*, 102.
50 See esp. Tim Crane and Sarah Patterson, eds., *A History of the Mind–Body Problem* (London: Routledge, 2000); also D. M. Armstrong and Norman Malcolm, *Consciousness and Causality: A Debate on the Nature of Mind* (Oxford: Blackwell, 1984); Cynthia Macdonald, *Mind–Body Identity Theories* (London: Routledge, 1989); G. N. A. Vesey, ed.,

Body and Mind: Readings in Philosophy (London: Allen and Unwin, 1964).

51 For further discussion, see entries under n. 50; also Margaret Donaldson, *Human Minds: An Exploration* (Harmondsworth, U.K.: Penguin, 1992); Stephen Priest, *Theories of the Mind* (Harmondsworth, U.K.: Penguin, 1991); David M. Rosenthal, ed., *The Nature of Mind* (New York: Oxford University Press, 1991).

52 See esp. Ludwig Wittgenstein, *Philosophical Investigations*, trans. G. E. M. Anscombe (Oxford: Blackwell, 1959); also Richard Rorty, ed., *The Linguistic Turn: Recent Essays in Philosophical Method* (Chicago: University of Chicago Press, 1967), and—from a dissenting standpoint—C. W. K. Mundle, *A Critique of Linguistic Philosophy* (Oxford: Clarendon Press, 1970), and Norris, *Philosophy of Language.*

53 Spinoza, *On the Improvement of the Understanding*, in *The Chief Works of Benedict de Spinoza*, ed. and trans. R. H. M. Elwes, 2:3–41 (New York: Dover, 1951).

54 For some highly relevant commentary, see Ian Hacking, *Why Does Language Matter to Philosophy?* (Cambridge: Cambridge University Press, 1975); also Norris, *Spinoza and the Origins of Modern Critical Theory*, 103–42; G. H. R. Parkinson, "Language and Knowledge in Spinoza," in Grene, *Spinoza: A Collection of Critical Essays*, 73–100; David Savan, "Spinoza and Language," in *Studies in Spinoza: Critical and Interpretative Essays*, ed. S. Paul Kashap, 236–48 (Berkeley: University of California Press, 1972).

55 Spinoza, *On the Improvement of the Understanding*, 33.

56 Savan, "Spinoza and Language," 239.

57 See the essays collected in Rorty, *The Linguistic Turn*, for a representative sampling of work in both these traditions, i.e., the Frege-Russell, or *echt*-analytic, and the Wittgenstein-Austin, or ordinary-language, lines of descent.

58 See n. 43.

59 See n. 1, 2, and 6.

60 For the most recent and controversial statement of this position, see David J. Chalmers, *The Conscious Mind: In Search of a Fundamental Theory* (Oxford: Oxford University Press, 1996).

61 See n. 6, 24, and 28.

62 See esp. Gaston Bachelard, *The Philosophy of No*, trans. G. C. Waterston (New York: Orion Press, 1969), and Bachelard, *The New*

Scientific Spirit, trans. Arthur Goldhammer (Boston: Beacon Press, 1984); also Mary Tiles, *Bachelard: Science and Objectivity* (Cambridge: Cambridge University Press, 1984).

63 See n. 4; also Althusser, "Ideology and Ideological State Apparatuses," in *"Lenin and Philosophy" and Other Essays*, trans. Ben Brewster, 121–73 (London: New Left Books, 1977).
64 See esp. Ted Benton, *The Rise and Fall of Structural Marxism* (London: New Left Books, 1984), and Gregory Elliott, *Althusser: The Detour of Theory* (London: Verso, 1987).
65 Israel, *Radical Enlightenment*.
66 See Feuer, *Spinoza and the Rise of Liberalism*, and other entries under n. 1, 2, 6, and 24.
67 Damasio, *Looking for Spinoza*.
68 Bennett, *A Study of Spinoza's Ethics*.
69 Hampshire, *Spinoza*.
70 For classic examples of this approach, see P. F. Strawson, *Individuals: An Essay in Descriptive Metaphysics* (London: Methuen, 1959), and Strawson, *The Bounds of Sense: An Essay on Kant's "Critique of Pure Reason"* (London: Methuen, 1966).
71 For representative surveys, see Graham Bird, ed., *A Companion to Kant* (Oxford: Blackwell, 2006); Paul Guyer, ed., *The Cambridge Companion to Kant* (Cambridge: Cambridge University Press, 1992).
72 See esp. Robert Hanna, *Kant and the Foundations of Analytic Philosophy* (Oxford: Oxford University Press, 2001).
73 See Norris, *Minding the Gap*; also J. Alberto Coffa, *The Semantic Tradition from Kant to Carnap: To the Vienna Station* (Cambridge: Cambridge University Press, 1991).
74 John McDowell, *Mind and World* (Cambridge, Mass.: Harvard University Press, 1994); see also Christopher Norris, "McDowell on Kant: Redrawing the Bounds of Sense," and Norris, "The Limits of Naturalism: Further Thoughts on McDowell's *Mind and World*," in Norris, *Minding the Gap*, 172–96, 197–230, respectively.
75 Norris, *Minding the Gap*.

2

What Is a Proof in Spinoza's Ethics?

ALAIN BADIOU

AS WE KNOW from all the literature on Spinoza, the question of the unity of Spinoza's philosophy is a very difficult one, as is the question of the nature of his work. I completely agree with Christopher Norris, who writes in the previous chapter of the conflict of interpretations. I don't know of any other philosopher who has been a fundamental reference for so many completely opposed philosophical trends. This point is particularly striking in the recent French philosophy. Louis Althusser proposes to read Spinoza as the greatest materialist philosopher in the genealogy of Marx, in which Spinoza plays the role of the dialectical contradictory term of Hegel. Pierre Macherey, in the same line, concludes that Spinoza is the only true pre-Marxist philosopher. With Martial Guéroult, we have a purely constructive vision of Spinoza, as the complete achievement of classical rationalism. For Gilles Deleuze, Spinoza is the philosopher of the close relationship between the creative power of life and the expressive power of concepts. For many thinkers in the tradition of Jewish theology, Spinoza is an example of pure spirituality, whereas for some others of the same tradition, like Benny Levy, Spinoza is a terrible and negative example of the way in which the letter of the Law was corrupted and became a sort of fetishism of the scientific deduction. For Jean Cavaillès, Spinoza advocates the perfect identity between a logical framework in ontology and the necessity of positive action in ethics. For the followers of Antonio Negri, Spinoza represent nothing less than the first philosophical communism, for all the followers of Deleuze, Spinoza wrote the greatest book in favor of a qualitative and intensive conception of nature, whereas Charles Ramond sustains with strong arguments that Spinoza promotes a strictly extensive and quantitative vision of the real world—and so on.

In this context, it seems impossible to hope for the discovery of a true Spinoza, perhaps because Spinoza is not reducible to philosophy, or more precisely, because his work is something that composes the strange unity of three different intellectual creations: conceptual, spiritual, and artistic. We can read his *Ethics* as a radical attempt to create a purely immanentist ontology, but we can also read it as a book of wisdom, in which some sentences are much more important than the deductive framework.

Spinoza writes, for instance, in *Ethics* IV, P67, that "a free man thinks of nothing less than of death, and his wisdom is a meditation not of death but of life"; in *Ethics* IV, P71, that "only free men are truly grateful one to the other"; and in *Ethics* V, P62, which is also the final proposition of *Ethics*, that "blessedness is not the reward of virtue, but virtue itself." Aren't all these like some beautiful and poetic aphorisms of a master of wisdom?

But we can also read *Ethics* as a pure artistic construction, in which, like in Wittgenstein's *Tractatus*, the deductive transparency is the sensible, the musical medium that leads to a pleasure with no other destination than itself. And the famous "intellectual love of God" is then, in fact, the love without object that we feel when we enjoy the reading of *Ethics*.

So Spinoza is a philosopher of immanence, but he is something else besides, maybe something greater: a master of spirituality and an abstract artist. And that's why the question of Spinoza's style is so important. But we find once more that the question of style, or more precisely, the question of the different styles of Spinoza, constitutes in itself a battlefield of interpretations. For some of them, there is a constant unity of style, but for some others, there are evident ruptures. Antonio Negri, for example, would like to demonstrate that the style of the first two parts is the style of a metaphysical rationalism, concerning the fixed Substance, but that the style of the last three books is something completely new, a "savage anomaly or novelty" that envelops a thinking of potency as such, a thinking of ontological creativity. Gilles Deleuze distinguishes the deductive style of appendices and scholia. For him, the difference of styles is a sort of symptom for the complex interplay between a theory of multiplicities and a theory of expressivity.

My own access to Spinoza will also be a formal one. I will begin with a paradoxical remark: in fact, the great majority of readings of Spinoza do not care at all about the most extensive part of the text of the *Ethics*, as this most extensive part consists in the proofs of the propositions. And though you have many commentaries about the 257 propositions (the Latin word is *propositio*), many commentaries about appendices and about notes *(scholium)* or explanations *(explicatio)*, there are very few commentaries about the near 300 proofs *(demonstratio)*.

I think that this in itself proves empirically a very important point concerning the huge field of interpretations. That is to say, that the really exceptional form of *Ethics*, the mathematical form, as well as that Spinoza writes just under the title *Ethics* that this ethics is *ordine geometrico demonstrate* (proved in geometrical order), all these things have, for the great majority of interpretations, either a purely symbolic signification or no importance at all.

My approach is here, on the contrary, to take seriously in consideration the "geometrical order." I intend to read all the details of the proofs, to accept without restriction the fundamental idea of Spinoza himself: we can go mathematically from a mathematics of being to a mathematics of eternal love and intellectual blessedness. The secret of freedom lies in the full understanding of the logical necessity, and the political consequences are that the secret of victory of weakness and poverty over power and wealth does not lie in a negative revolt but in a positive discipline, or that the force of equality does not resemble the natural force of a storm but the mental inflexibility of a proof. With Spinoza's *more geometrico*, we learn that we have to act, not within the violent disorder of the chaos, but within the cold quietness of the stars, because in the most radical action, we have to persist in the most important positive emotion, positive affect, which is *acquiescentia in se ipso*, "welcoming of oneself," or, if you accept this translation, "self-welcoming." This affect is defined by Spinoza in the "Definitions of the Affects" (E III) as *"laetitia, orta ex eo, quod homo se ipsum, suamque agendi potentiam contemplatur"* (pleasure arising from the fact that man regards himself and his power of acting).

To find the pleasure of contemplating our "power of acting" in the action itself, we have to be as quiet and cold as the action is violent and confusing. We have not to be swayed by the anxiety for the result of our action but rather carried by its immanent discipline. We have to exist not only in the emotions of our bodies but in the eternal knowledge of these emotions: "*Mens nostra, quatenus se et corpus sub aeternitatis specie cognoscit*" (EV, P30, the human mind insofar as it knows itself and its body under the species of eternity). In this reading of Spinoza, we have to exist as much as possible, not only in the propositions as results but in the process of the proofs, because the proofs are the true knowledge of the necessity of the result.

The latest translator of *Ethics* in French, Bernard Pautrat, gives us a clear maxim to read Spinoza. In the foreword of his translation, he writes, "We have to read Spinoza's *Ethics* as a book of mathematics, the contents of which is composed of proved truths, more as a book of philosophy disguised in a book of mathematics."

Insofar as *Ethics* is really a mathematics of being, it is also the book of an artist and of a master of wisdom. Since Plato's *Republic*, we know that without geometry, it is impossible to find an access to justice, and we know since Aristotle, in *Metaphysics Beta*, that it exists a fundamental artistic disposition of mathematical objects. Spinoza himself, in the appendix to the first part of *Ethics*, writes, "The truth might have lain hidden from the human race through all eternity, had not mathematics, which deals not in the final causes, but the essence and properties of things, offered to men another standard of truth." Only mathematics offers to us an "other standard of truth," and this "other standard" is simultaneously conceptual, ethical, and artistic. It is truth, but truth as action and beauty. So to read Spinoza is to read not only propositions, explanations, scholia, and appendices but also to read proofs, and to read proofs as proofs. It is the only way to constitute *Ethics* as a book of mathematics—a mathematics of Being.

It is naturally impossible to explain here all the consequences of this reading. Among these consequences, we discover a great number of new reasons for admiring Spinoza, and also some new reasons for criticizing him, when the consistency of the proof is dubious. For a proof that is not a proof is, in the framework of Spinoza's philosophy, a kind of blindness of the human mind. In *Ethics* V, P23S, Spinoza writes something striking: "The eyes of the mind by which it sees things and observes them are proofs." The relationship of our mind with the real things is made of proofs. A false proof is the destruction of this relationship. Therefore we have to explore, proposition after proposition, proof after proof, the clarity of the vision of the real by this exceptional mind that lies and acts under the name of Spinoza. I have done this exercise concerning Part I of *Ethics* and some parts of Part II. You can find some fragmentary results of this reading in one chapter of my *Being and Event* and in the chapter of my *Theoretical Writings* titled "Spinoza's Closed Ontology."

Here I want to propose a new, limited, and more formal exercise concerning one proof, a complex one. It is the Proof of Proposition 28 of Part I. The skeleton of this proof can be found below. I will begin by explaining two points: first, why I have chosen this special proposition for our methodological exercise, and second, what is exactly the skeleton of a proof.

In the first part of *Ethics*, Proposition 28 has a strategic function concerning the immanent distinction between finite and infinite. This distinction is immanent by Proposition 15: "Whatever is, is in God, and nothing can exist or be conceived without God." So a finite thing is in God and an infinite one also. We cannot distinguish between finite and infinite things by the very nature or the true being of these things, for the being of everything is God, who is the only substance, or, as Spinoza says in Proposition 18, *"Deus est omnium rerum causa immanens, non vero transiens"* (God is the immanent and not the transient cause of all things). So we can only distinguish between finite things and infinite things by their relationship to other things. It is clear from Definition 2, at the very beginning of the book, that, ontologically, the distinction between finite and infinite is only a relative one: "That thing is said to be finite in its kind [*in suo generi finite*] which can be limited by another thing of the same kind. For example, a body is said to be finite because we can conceive another larger than it." The distinction is not intrinsic but relational.

Proposition 28 extends this idea to the most important relationship between all things that exist in God, or in Nature, that is, causality. Exactly as a finite thing must be limited by another finite thing, a finite thing must be the transient cause of another finite thing.

You have on one side God as the immanent cause of all things, finite or infinite, that exist in Him. On the other side, you have the transient cause of a thing, its immediate cause. But here the problem is more complex. Certainly an infinite thing cannot have, as its immediate cause, a finite thing. It is a fundamental idea of Descartes, and it is the heart of his first proof of the existence of God. I have in my mind the Idea of an infinite being, the formal dimension of this idea is the infinite, but my mind is finite. So the cause of this idea cannot be my mind or a finite idea in my mind. Only an infinite being was able to create this idea and put it in my mind. Spinoza, in a certain sense, reverses the proof. For him, it is properly impossible that an infinite thing would be directly the cause of a finite one. It would be a miracle, and for Spinoza, there are no miracles in Nature or in God. A finite thing is certainly created by God and in God, but the means of the creation, the immediate or transient cause, is another finite thing that is created by God and in God by the means of another finite thing, and so on. Finally, the causality organizes in God all finite things in infinite chains along the line of immediate causality. In this sense, there is a sort of self-sufficiency of the realm of finite things. The substantial reality of this realm is the infinite God, but from the point of view of immediate determination, a finite thing is in relationship only with other finite things. And that's why we can hope to construct a positive science of the immediate determination inside the finitude of our mind. That is the strategic function of Proposition 28. "Every individual thing, or whatever thing that is finite and has a determinate existence, cannot exist nor be determined for action, unless it is determined for action and existence by another cause which is also finite and has a determinate existence; and again, this cause also cannot exist nor be determined for action unless it be determined for existence and action by another cause which also is finite and has a determinate existence: and so on to infinity." We can say that this proposition asserts something like the closure of the finite in respect to the relation of immediate causality.

Now, what is the skeleton of a proof? In Figure 2.1, you have the skeleton of Proposition 28. It is the deductive genealogy of the proposition, and here "P" stands for "proposition," "A" for "axiom," "C" for "corollary," and "D" for "definition." In the last column on the right, column 8, you find the proposition itself, as the result of the proof.

I	II	III	IV	V	VI	VII	VIII
						A1 D3 D5	
				D8	P20	C20	
			D4	P19			
					D2	P21–P22	
				A7	P11		
			D1	P7			
D3	P2–*P5	P6	C6				
A4 A5	P3						
				D1	P4	C24	
				D6	P14		P28
			D3 D6	P5–*P11			
		A1 A4	P4				
		D3 D5	P1				
					D5		
				A4	P25	C25	
				*P15			
				D3 D5 A1	P15		
				*P14			
					*P25	P26	
				Obvious	P16		
I	II	III	IV	V	VI	VII	VIII

FIGURE 2.1. Skeleton of proof of *Ethics* I, P28.

For a proof, you can use, first, any proposition that has been proved before, in this case, six propositions: 21, 22, 26, and Corollaries to Propositions 20, 24, and 25. Second, you can use some of the initial axioms, in this case, Axiom 1. And third, you can use some of the initial definitions, here, Definitions 3 and 5.

In column 6, you find all that is necessary to have proofs of all the propositions used in the Proof of Proposition 28. For example, to prove Propositions 21 and 22, we must use Definition 2 and Proposition 11. To prove the Corollary to Proposition 24, we must use Proposition 14 itself and Proposition 4. Why do we have, at the bottom of column 6, a star before P25? It is because Proposition 25 has been used before, and so its skeleton is already inscribed in column 5.

So, in a column, we have all that is necessary to prove all propositions of the following column. The process ends when we have a column without any proposition, that is, a column with only initial axioms or initial definitions. This is the case in our first column, with only Definition 3 and the two Axioms 3 and 5.

You understand that the extent of the skeleton is a measure of the complexity of the proof, and in philosophical matters, the complexity of a proof is a measure of the difficulty of the problem or a measure of the strength of the proposition in the conceptual field. We can say that the extent of the skeleton of a proof is linked to the synthetic power of that proposition.

In fact, the skeleton of Proposition 28 is the most extensive skeleton in Part I of the *Ethics*. It utilizes seventeen propositions, seven definitions, and four axioms. We have here a formal proof of the strategic function of this proposition: its deductive machinery mobilizes practically all the conceptual means of the Spinozan ontology. The reason is that the law of the relative independency of the finite things has a double use: a negative one and a positive one. Negatively, this law destroys the religious claim of a direct and transient relationship between the infinite Being and the becoming of the finite things. This negative result means that there is no creation of the world ex nihilo, and there are no miracles. Positively, the law asserts the possibility of a complete and scientific knowledge of the determination of finite things. This "yes" to positive science, and this "no" to miracles, explain why Spinoza was, during the eighteenth century, something like the scandalous and essential specter of reason—in the same light that Marx saw communism as the specter of politics during the nineteenth century. And Proposition 28 of Part I of *Ethics* is the conceptual framework for this specter.

But the skeleton of the proof is also a sort of spectral analysis of the entire ontology of Spinoza. Through the machinery of the proof, we directly see what is really crucial in the statements of this ontology. For example, we noticed that Definitions 3 and 5 are used repeatedly: four times in the skeleton of one proposition! But what are these definitions? Definition 3 is the definition of the substance, so the definition of Being qua Being, and Definition 5 is the definition of what is a modification of a substance or of what is, not in itself, but in something else. But we know that nothing else exists as the unique Substance, the name of which is God, and its modifications. This is the content of Proposition 30: "Intellect, finite or infinite in actuality, must comprehend the attributes of God and the modifications of God and nothing else." So the Proof of Proposition 28 indicates already, by its form, the very essence of Spinoza's ontology.

I give you another example. We observe in the skeleton of the proof that Proposition 11 is used twice (in the Proof of Propositions 21 and 22 and in the Proof of Proposition 14). But in fact, it is used once more, for it is in the skeleton of Proposition 14, which is itself used twice. Just from its use, we can imagine that this proposition has a strategic significance—and it has indeed, for Proposition 11 asserts the existence of God: "God, or a substance consisting of infinite attributes, each of which expresses eternal and infinite essence, necessarily exists." So important is this proposition that Spinoza gives us no less than three different proofs. We clearly understand the strategic function of this proposition, and this strategic function is immediately visible in the disposition of the Proof of another strategic proposition, Proposition 28.

Finally, we can propose a sort of parody of one of the most famous statements of Spinoza, which we find in *Ethics* II, P7: "The order and connection of ideas is the same as the order and connection of things." We can also say that the order and connection of sentences in the skeleton of a proof is the same as the order and connection of the concepts that are presented by the proposition that is proved by this proof.

That's why the *more geometrico* is not at all a pure form or an artificial disposition imposed on a conceptual movement. The mathematical form is appropriate to the mathematical contents. As we have seen, proofs are the eyes of the mind. That's why what the mind sees is of mathematical nature. For we have only God and all sorts of immanent modifications of God, exactly as we have an infinite geometrical space and all sorts of figures and transformations in it. And the reality of figures and transformations is made of points in space, is made of space itself, exactly as the reality of modes is made of substance. And finally, the result of a transformation applied to a finite figure is another finite figure, exactly as the cause of a finite thing is an other finite thing. This is precisely the content of our Proposition 28. In fact, the most secret, and simultaneously explicit, proposition of Spinoza is that Being is a geometrical order. Being is the geometry of all possible geometries. And the geometry has to be exposed in geometrical order, *more geometrico*, not by choice but by necessity. The geometrical order is the only language worthy of God, God who is the space of all things.

In fact, it is the only eternal language. The true being of our mind is, as says *Ethics* V, P40S, "*aeternus cogitandi modus*," an eternal mode of thinking. The only possible way to inscribe this eternal mode of thinking is the totally universal language of mathematics, a language that is, as Jacques Lacan said, a complete transmission, a transmission without rest.

This is a sufficient reason to reject all interpretations of Spinoza based on potency in terms of virtuality, on action in terms of actualization, or on desire in terms of creativity of life. In the geometrical order, which expresses the divine geometry or the mathematics of Being, nothing is virtual, and everything is actual. Nothing is a creation, and everything except God is a consequence. Even the act of thinking has no relation with a virtual disposition. In *Ethics* I, P31, Spinoza speaks of "the intellect in actuality." But immediately after, in a scholium, he specifies, "The reason why I speak here of intellect in actuality is not that I concede that intellect in potentiality can be granted." If, in our reading, we respect Spinoza's style, it becomes properly impossible to interpret his vision as a kind of classical Nietzscheism. For Spinoza, "action" is not a name for life. "Action" is a name for truth or for adequate ideas. This appears clearly, first, in the proof *Ethics* III, P3, "the actions of the mind arise from adequate ideas alone," and second, in the Proof of Proposition 40, "the property of intellect through which alone we are said to act." So "action" is a property of the intellect, and this property arises from adequate ideas only. So only the actual existence of an adequate idea is active, and virtuality is always confusing and passive. Therefore "intellect in potentiality" cannot be granted; nothing "in potentiality" can be granted. All that exists is an active process, is actual in the global geometrical space, of which we can write only in the partial but exact geometric order. The eyes of the mind are proofs because the light of God expresses forever what the French poet Lautréamont names the "strict mathematics," or perhaps more precisely, the "harsh mathematics." Philosophy, as a masochist lover, has to accept this harsh mistress. The Spinozan reward is that *"laetitia concomitante idea sui"*—pleasure accompanied by the idea of iself—which is nothing less than eternal love. Is there something better? It is up to you to decide.

3

The Joyful Passions in Spinoza's Theory of Relations

SIMON DUFFY

THE THEME OF THE CONFLICT between the different interpretations of Spinoza's philosophy in French scholarship, introduced by Christopher Norris in this volume and expanded on by Alain Badiou, is also central to the argument presented in this chapter. Indeed, this chapter will be preoccupied with distinguishing the interpretations of Spinoza by two of the figures introduced by Badiou. The interpretation of Spinoza offered by Gilles Deleuze in *Expressionism in Philosophy* provides an account of the dynamic changes or transformations of the characteristic relations of a Spinozist finite existing mode, or human being.[1] This account has been criticized more or less explicitly by a number of commentators, including Charles Ramond.[2] Rather than providing a defense of Deleuze on this specific point, which I have done elsewhere,[3] what I propose to do in this chapter is provide an account of the role played by "joyful passive affections" in these dynamic changes or transformations by distinguishing Deleuze's account of this role from that offered by one of his more explicit critics on this issue, Pierre Macherey.[4] An appreciation of the role played by "joyful passive affections" in this context is crucial to understanding how Deleuze's interpretation of Spinoza is implicated in his broader philosophical project of constructing a philosophy of difference. The outcome is a position that, like Badiou in the previous chapter, rules out "intellect in potentiality" but maintains a role for the joyful passive affects in the development of adequate ideas.

The Distinction between Joyful Passive Affections and Sad Passive Affections

In his interpretation of Spinoza's theory of relations in *Expressionism in Philosophy*, Deleuze assigns a specific role to joyful passions. They are characterized as a significant determinant in the dynamic changes or transformations of the characteristic relations of finite existing modes. The theme of joyful passions is pivotal in distinguishing Deleuze's reading of Spinoza's theory of relations from that offered by Macherey in *Introduction à l'Ethique de Spinoza, la cinquième partie*.

While discussing the General Definition of the Affects at the end of Part III of the *Ethics*, Macherey formulates the problem that effectively distinguishes his interpretation of this aspect of the *Ethics* from that of Deleuze.[5] He raises the following question: "Can the soul be completely active, without at all being passive, or does it rather find itself permanently placed between the two extremes of passivity and activity, following regimes which make it lean sometimes to the side of activity, sometimes to that of passivity? And then what are the thresholds which swing one of these regimes into the other?"[6] Each of the two interpreters approaches this problem differently.

Macherey and Deleuze are in accord with regard to the fixity of singular essence, but their interpretations differ with regard to the transformations of the characteristic relations determinative of singular things. According to Macherey, the affective life of a singular thing is constituted by its ideas or passions, which are expressed as an "uninterrupted affective flux."[7] The transformations of the characteristic relations of a singular thing correspond to the varying degrees to which the uninterrupted affective flux hinders or limits the active expression of a mode's power to act within the range of a maximum and a minimum. All a mode's power to act is expressed, however, according to the uninterrupted affective flux; it is simultaneously expressed both actively and passively. The passive affections, or the passions, are the mark of a negation, and inversely, the active affects, or actions, are the active expression, or affirmation, of a singular thing's power to act. Macherey considers passion, with its logical mark of "negativity," to be that "which is found most naturally in man." The question for Macherey is therefore "to know whether man can ever completely escape this logic and engage in actions which are not marred by such a limitation?"[8]

Deleuze, however, considers the transformations of the relations characteristic of modal existence to implicate a mode's capacity to be affected. A mode's capacity to be affected is constituted by its active affections. Passive affections, on the contrary, function only to limit its capacity to be affected. This limit functions within the range of a maximum and minimum; that is, a mode's capacity to be affected, which is affirmed by its *conatus* as the expression of its power to act, is open to variation within the "general limits" of this range.[9] According to Deleuze, the variation of a mode's power to act is directly limited by the passive affections to which it is subjected, rather than proportionally limited, as Macherey proposes.

The difference between Macherey's and Deleuze's reading of Spinoza's theory of relations rests with their respective interpretations of the role of passive affections. According to Macherey, they remain an integral part of the existence of a singular thing, being expressed by its *conatus* even though hindering its capacity to actively, or more perfectly, express its fixed power to act. According to Deleuze, on the contrary, only active affections function integrally as part of modal existence. Passive affections function rather to limit the existence of a finite mode, that is, of the active affections constitutive of its capacity to be affected, which is affirmed by its *conatus* as the expression of its power to act.

This, however, does not exhaust the differences between their respective interpretations of passive affections but rather prepares for a further distinction. Deleuze argues that "the opposition of actions and passions should not conceal the other opposition that constitutes the second principle of Spinozism: that of joyful passive affections and sad passive affections."[10] Spinoza first introduces the notions of joy and sadness in the *Ethics* II, P11S, by making explicit reference to them as passions: "By joy, therefore, I shall understand in what follows that passion by which the mind passes to a greater perfection. And by sadness, that passion by which it passes to a lesser perfection." The other reference that Deleuze cites is from the *Ethics* III, P58, where Spinoza introduces joys and desires whose active character sets them apart from those joys and desires that are passions because they are determined by external encounters. Spinoza writes, "Apart from the joy and desire that are passions, there are other affects of joy and desire that are related to us insofar as we act." These are the only two explicit references to passions which are joys to be found in the *Ethics*. In *Expressionism in Philosophy*, Deleuze characterizes these joyful passions as "joyful passive affections," and it is from this starting point, with joyful passive affections, that Deleuze begins his account of the transformations of the characteristic relations of finite existing modes.

Macherey concedes that "the notion of a 'joyful passion' is not in fact entirely absent from Spinoza's text, at least at first glance."[11] However, when he offers an account of the transformations of the characteristic relations of singular things, the notion of a joyful passion does not retain the same significance that Deleuze assigns it in *Expressionism in Philosophy*. In fact, "joyful passions" are implicated quite differently in Macherey's reading of the *Ethics*. However, before developing Macherey's account of what he calls "passionate joys," the role played by joyful passive affections in Deleuze's account of the transformations of the characteristic relations of finite existing modes needs to be explicated.

The Role of Joyful Passive Affections in Deleuze's Account of Modal Existence

Deleuze actually prefigures his discussion of joyful passive affections at the beginning of chapter 15 of *Expressionism in Philosophy*, when he argues that "our passive joy is and must remain a passion: it is not 'explained' by our power of action, but it 'involves' a higher degree of this power."[12] What does Deleuze understand by correlating a passion with an increase in a mode's power to act? This would seem to contradict his concept of the role of passive affections in the determination of a finite existing mode, that is, insofar as they function solely to limit its existence. This suggestion of a contradiction is reinforced by the fact that Deleuze follows his introduction of the distinction between joyful passive affections and sad passive affections by the statement that "one increases our power, the other diminishes it."[13]

Deleuze seems to be arguing that although joyful passive affections are passions, they function more or less actively and therefore can be seen to occupy an intermediate place between passions and actions, or in effect, to mediate between them. However, a closer reading of *Expressionism in Philosophy* reveals that a different logic is being developed, one according to which joyful passive affections mediate not between active and passive affections but rather solely between different active affections. To explicate the mechanism by means of which this logic operates, it is necessary to determine exactly what the relation is, then, between a joyful passive affection and the increase in power to which Deleuze relates it.

Deleuze suggests that we "come closer to our power of action" insofar as we are affected by the joy of a joyful passive affection.[14] He argues that "passive joy is produced by an object that agrees with us, and whose power increases our power of action, but of which we do not yet have an adequate idea."[15] However, he maintains that "it never increases enough for us to become the adequate cause of the affections that exercise our capacity to be affected."[16] The initial affect is a passion because we are affected from the outside by an external object; however, this object agrees with our nature and, consequently, is not harmful to us. We therefore do not experience the passive affection as the passion of sadness because our power to act is not diminished by the encounter. One would expect a feeling of ambivalence to be experienced because at this stage, our perfection has been neither augmented nor diminished. Yet, insofar as the external body "agrees" or "has something in common with our nature," the potential for the combination of the power to act of the external body with our own, and therefore the increase in power that this would involve, promotes the feeling of joy that allows the overall affect to be described as a joyful passive affection. What Deleuze understands by an object that "agrees" or "has something in common with our nature" is one with which we can be further integrated. Each relation "agrees" solely insofar as it can be further integrated in relation to another, thus generating a new, more composite relation. Therefore the concept of finite existing modes or individuals whose natures agree corresponds to the potential for their complication or integration in a more composite relation. Insofar as the effect of this external body on our own is experienced as an affection that is explained by the external body, it remains an inadequate idea of the imagination, and therefore a passion. To distinguish passive joys from active joys, Deleuze argues that an "active joy we produce by ourselves, it flows from our power of action itself, follows from an adequate idea in us."[17]

According to Deleuze, joyful passive affections are passions because they limit the expression of our power to act and yet correspond to a feeling of joy because they are somehow implicated in an increase of that power. This can only work if joyful passive affections are understood to function at the limit imposed by passive affections. The joy of a joyful passive affection can therefore be understood insofar as it affirms that limit while simultaneously announcing the potential for positive transformation, that is, the surpassing of the limit or an increase in the power to act, rather than functioning solely as a limit marking the point beyond which a finite existing mode ceases to exist, as do sad passive affections.

Only to the extent that this initially inadequate relation results in the production of active joys, and therefore in an increase in our power of acting, are joyful passive affections implicated in the transformative process. Joyful passive affections indicate a partial or inadequate idea of something common to both our own body and an external body that affects it. They indicate the potential for an increase in our power to act but are not themselves directly related to that increase in power. It is rather the active affections that follow from joyful passive affections that are directly associated with the increase in power. The suggestion of a contradiction between joyful passive affections as passions and the increase in our power associated with them is therefore unfounded. Deleuze's use of the concept of joyful passive affections should rather be understood to be the articulation of the process of transformation, or increase in power, that actually takes place in the generation of active joy by means of the accumulation of joyful passive affections.

The Simplest of Common Notions

Spinoza maintains that the ideas that we generally have of ourselves, and of external bodies, are only inadequate ideas or passive affections that indicate an encounter between some external body and our own. A joyful passive affection, because it is a passion, is always the result of an external cause and is thus always indicated by an inadequate idea. However, because it is a joyful passive affection, it indicates that there is something common to an external body and our own or that it has a nature compatible, or potentially convergent, with our own.

According to Deleuze, the experience of a joyful passive affection can induce the formation of the corresponding common notion. The first common notions formed by an individual are those that apply to its body and to another whose nature agrees directly with its own and therefore affects its body with joy. When our mind forms an idea of what is common to the external body and our own, it forms a common notion. The joyful affection then ceases to be passive and becomes active. By indicating that there is something common, that there is a connection between the bodies, a joyful passive affection can initiate the formation of a common notion. A common notion is an adequate idea of the relation, which therefore incorporates the cause of the affection within the very idea of that affection. Deleuze maintains that Spinoza describes an affection that expresses its cause in this way as no longer passive but active. The joy of a joyful passive affection no longer indicates an inadequate idea of an object that agrees with us but the necessarily adequate idea of what is common to that object and ourselves. An adequate idea of the affection is formed when the cause of the affection is attached to what is common to the bodies involved, that is, when the potential for the integration of their natures is actualized. This is the "leap," of which Deleuze speaks, from inadequate to adequate ideas, from joyful passive affections to active joys, from passions to actions.

The Relation between Passivity and Activity in the Affective Life

Macherey does not agree with the division of passive affections into joyful passive affections and sad passive affections. In "The Encounter with Spinoza," he claims "rather bluntly that for Spinoza all passions, without exception, are sad—even those that are or appear to be joys. Or that they are all ultimately sad, in a sort of passionate entropy."[18] Macherey distinguishes what he considers Spinoza to be referring to in the *Ethics* II, P11S, and the *Ethics* III, P58, as "passionate joys" from that which Deleuze characterizes as "joyful passive affections." Contrary to what he considers to be Deleuze's point of view, Macherey maintains that passionate joys, "which are in fact imaginary joys linked to encounters with external bodies, cannot be assembled into a coherent stable group, but rather tend inevitably to conflict, tending not towards composition but towards decomposition."[19]

In the *Ethics* III, P17, Spinoza introduces the theme of the *fluctuatio animi* in the case of a sadness that doubles as a joy. Macherey explains this case in the following manner: Spinoza "starts by presenting a sad affect attached ordinarily to an object . . . then he shows how, by contamination, because the object in question appears to resemble another object which ordinarily gives us joy, this joy is artificially transferred onto the first object, which is then the cause 'by accident' of this affect."[20] Therefore the *fluctuatio animi* permanently exposes the joy associated with this affect to the risk of reversing to sadness. This is why Macherey considers all passions, "including joys that are passions," to have a "sad destiny," which cannot somehow be transformed into something active, which Macherey accuses Deleuze of attempting to do with joyful passive affections. Macherey maintains that a joyful passive affection, as characterized by Deleuze in *Expressionism in Philosophy*, is "a contradiction in terms, corresponding at best to a passing, unstable and literally non-viable state of our constitution."[21]

The first common notion that we can have, according to Macherey, is *amor erga Deum*, whereas for Deleuze, the first common notions that we can have are the simplest common notions, which represent what is common to our body and to certain external bodies by which we are effected. Macherey does not deny that there are the simple common notions of which Deleuze speaks; however, he does deny that from them we can deduce adequate ideas without first having attained the love toward God, which he therefore considers to be the first common notion capable of leading to adequate ideas. Macherey considers the love toward God to establish the basis for the regulation of the affective life and therefore to be the first step in the production of the second kind of knowledge, whereas for Deleuze, the love toward God represents one step in the transition from the second kind of knowledge to the third kind of knowledge. The idea of God as the cause of all things, that is, the general common notion of the love toward God, is, for Macherey, the primary point of reference for adequate ideas. All adequate ideas without exception therefore include, by means of the love toward God, the idea of God as their cause. According to Deleuze, however, adequate ideas are constituted locally by means of the simplest of common notions or the shared knowledge that each involved idea or body is the common cause of the adequate idea. An adequate idea for Deleuze is therefore determined in direct relation to the bodies or ideas that interact with one another as causes of the adequate idea, without necessarily requiring reference to the general common notion of the love toward God. It is on the basis of this argument for the deduction of adequate ideas from simple common notions that Deleuze's understanding of joyful active affections is distinguishable from the account of "passionate joys" offered by Macherey.

A Joyful Passive Affection Can Be Reversed to Sadness

The difference between the "passionate joys" of Macherey and the joyful passive affections of Deleuze is brought out effectively by the discussion of the *fluctuatio animi* in "The Encounter with Spinoza." In fact, Macherey argues that the *"fluctuatio animi . . .* completely undermines the notion of joyful passions" presented by Deleuze.[22] Macherey understands a "passionate joy" to be a joy "by accident," that is, a sadness that is doubled as a joy, and he maintains that Spinoza chose this case, "and not that where a joy is impaired by becoming tinged with bitterness," to determine the theme of the *fluctuatio animi*.[23] The joy of a passionate joy is a joy whose cause remains unknown; it is therefore associated with a passion and, according to Macherey, must reverse to being sad. Macherey contends that Deleuze's interpretation of a "joyful passion" as a joyful passive affection presents a joy that does not reverse as expected, which leads him to ask "if there is in joy something stronger and more stable than in sadness, which protects it against this risk of reversal?"[24] Macherey can be understood to be suggesting with this question that Deleuze's response would be yes, because for Deleuze, the sadness of a sad passive affection simply limits the existence of an existing finite mode, whereas the joy of a joyful passive affection not only affirms the limit but simultaneously announces the potential for positive transformation, that is, to go beyond the limit imposed by the passive affections in general. In this way, Deleuze does seem to interpret joy as being stronger and more stable than sadness, which could therefore protect it against the risk of reversal. Macherey responds to the question by arguing that "the extremely condensed way in which the content of this question is exposed in proposition 17 and in its scholium, only permits the question to be posed, but hardly gives any means to respond to it."[25] In fact, Spinoza only gives the example of a sadness that doubles as a joy in his explication of the *fluctuatio animi*.[26] Macherey therefore argues that such "a harmful pleasure, whether inflicted or suffered, would clearly for Spinoza be a passion imbued with *fluctuatio animi*, ineluctably producing a negative legacy of sadness."[27] By referring to a joyful passion as "a harmful pleasure," or simply a sadness that doubles as a joy, Macherey reduces the Deleuzian concept of a joyful passive affection to that of a passionate joy.

Deleuze, on the contrary, considers the ethical view to provide a means of responding to the question raised by Macherey. Deleuze does not deny that "passionate joys," as described by Macherey, are experienced by finite existing modes, nor that such a joy can be doubled or reversed to sadness and therefore be lost to the *fluctuatio animi*. And Deleuze in no way guarantees that every joyful passive affection will always produce an active joy. According to Deleuze, a joyful passive affection "may always . . . be interrupted by destruction, or even simply by the sadness of the loved object itself."[28] In other words, insofar as a joyful passive affection is a passion, its cause can be confused with another external cause or image of an object or body, which effaces the joy and renders the joyful passive affection sad. There is therefore nothing inherently stable or coherent in a joyful passive affection that stops it from falling prey to the *fluctuatio animi*. Instead, Deleuze is arguing that despite the difficulty in distinguishing a passionate joy from a joyful passive affection, the joy of a joyful passive affection can be isolated before it becomes prey to the *fluctuatio animi* and in this way contributes to the formation of a common notion. Macherey does not at all agree with Deleuze on this point. Macherey argues, on the contrary, that nothing can turn a passionate joy into an action because, being a passion, it necessarily tends toward a *fluctuatio animi*; that is, for him, "all passions without exception . . . [tend] towards a *fluctuatio animi*."[29]

Deleuze's concept of a joyful passive affection is the concept of a joy that can be reversed to sadness or, conversely, that can contribute to the formation of common notions. The uncertainty of a joyful passive affection is carried over into the common notions that can be formed from it when Deleuze maintains that the isolation of a joyful passive affection does not bypass the need for common notions "to be formed, and formed either more or less easily, and so being more or less common to different minds."[30] Macherey is in agreement with Deleuze on this point when he writes that "that which distinguishes the souls of different men, is the place occupied by those common notions in relation to other ideas, inadequate ideas."[31] However, the theme of joyful passions remains one of the points around which their respective interpretations of Spinoza's theory of relations diverge.

Deleuze's position can be presented as follows. According to Deleuze, the "natural situation" of our existence as human beings is such that we are filled with inadequate ideas and passive affections. This is so because, according to Spinoza, we "are continuously affected by external bodies" (*Ethics* II, P47S). Before we can form common notions, we must learn to distinguish sad passions from joyful passions, what Deleuze describes as "a starting point in joyful passions."[32] Sad passions are inadequate ideas that arise from the experience of random encounters with external bodies, whereas joyful passions are inadequate ideas that arise from the encounters with external bodies that have something in common with our own. The immediate idea that we have of these external bodies that have something in common with our own is partial and therefore imaginary. Insofar as this encounter is associated with the experience of joy, we can form an idea of there being something common to the external body and our own. We desire to increase this initial joy by striving to determine or to form an idea of what it is that is specifically common to our body and the external body by means of the simplest of common notions. Our chances of achieving this, which is in no way guaranteed by the joyful passive affection, are improved to the extent that we relate or imagine several things at once as similarly common to our body and the external body, thereby increasing the number of affections associated with the joy of the joyful passive affection—what Deleuze describes as "the accumulation of joyful passive affections."[33] Although joyful passive affections are inadequate ideas of the imagination and, as such, involve privation of the knowledge of their cause, they are at the same time affections that 'involve,' or implicate, that cause.[34] The imagination is composed of inadequate ideas that, through an understanding of their cause, by means of the mechanism of joyful passive affections and the simplest of common notions, may be transformed into adequate ideas, thereby constituting reason. In this way, the joyful passive affection is the mechanism by which the mind moves from an inadequate idea to an adequate idea and by which the body moves from experiencing a passion to an action. Deleuze argues therefore that "the active joys that flow from common notions find as it were their occasional causes in passive affections of joy,"[35] and according to Deleuze, the only way of reaching an adequate idea is by means of the mechanism of joyful passive affections.

Notes

1. Gilles Deleuze, *Expressionism in Philosophy: Spinoza*, trans. Martin Joughin (New York: Zone Books, 1992).
2. Charles Ramond, *Qualité et quantité dans la philosophie de Spinoza* (Paris: Presses universitaires de France, 1995), 189–231.
3. See Simon Duffy, *The Logic of Expression: Quality, Quantity, and Intensity in Spinoza, Hegel, and Deleuze* (Aldershot, U.K.: Ashgate, 2006), chap. 6.
4. Pierre Macherey, *Introduction à l'Ethique de Spinoza, la troisième partie* (Paris: Presses universitaires de France, 1995). All citations quoted from this text are my translations from the French. See also Pierre Macherey, "The Encounter with Spinoza," trans. Martin Joughin, in *Deleuze: A Critical Reader*, ed. Paul Patton, 139–61 (Oxford: Blackwell, 1996).
5. Baruch Spinoza, *Ethics*, in *The Collected Works of Spinoza*, vol. 1, trans. Edwin Curley, 408–617 (Princeton, N.J.: Princeton University Press, 1985).
6. Macherey, *Introduction à l'Ethique de Spinoza*, 20.
7. Ibid., 121.
8. Ibid., 71.
9. Deleuze, *Expressionism in Philosophy*, 225.
10. Ibid., 246.

11 Macherey, *Introduction à l'Ethique de Spinoza*, 153
12 Deleuze, *Expressionism in Philosophy*, 240.
13 The whole passage reads, "The opposition of actions and passions should not conceal the other opposition that constitutes the second principle of Spinozism: that of joyful passive affections and sad passive affections. *One increases our power, the other diminishes it.* We come closer to our power of action insofar as we are affected by joy"(Deleuze, *Expressionism in Philosophy*, 246; emphasis added).
14 Deleuze, *Expressionism in Philosophy*, p. 246.
15 Ibid., 274.
16 Ibid., 241.
17 Ibid., 274.
18 Macherey, *Introduction à l'Ethique de Spinoza*, 153.
19 Ibid., 154.
20 Ibid., 162–63.
21 Ibid., 154.
22 Ibid., 156.
23 Ibid., 166.
24 Ibid.
25 Ibid.
26 Spinoza, *Ethics* III, P17: "If we imagine that a thing which usually affects us with an affect of Sadness is like another which usually affects us with an equally great affect of Joy, we shall hate it and at the same time love it." *Ethics* III, P17S: "This constitution of the Mind which arises from two contrary affects is called vacillation of mind [*fluctuatio animi*], which is therefore related to the affect as doubt is to the imagination (see *Ethics* II, P44S); nor do vacillation of mind and doubt differ from one another except in degree. But it should be noted that in the preceding Proposition I have deduced these vacillations of mind from causes which are the cause through themselves of one affect and the accidental cause of the other. I have done this because in this way they could more easily be deduced from what has gone before, not because I deny that vacillations of mind for the most part arise from an object which is the efficient cause of each affect."
27 Macherey, *Introduction à l'Ethique de Spinoza*, 156.
28 Deleuze, *Expressionism in Philosophy*, 244.
29 Macherey, *Introduction à l'Ethique de Spinoza*, 155.

30 Deleuze, *Expressionism in Philosophy*, 307.
31 Pierre Macherey, *Introduction à l'Ethique de Spinoza, la seconde partie* (Paris: Presses universitaires de France, 1997), 291.
32 Deleuze, *Expressionism in Philosophy*, 307.
33 Ibid., 283.
34 For an account of this "involvement" according to the logic of different/ciation, see Duffy, *Logic of Expression*, chaps. 6–8.
35 Deleuze, *Expressionism in Philosophy*, 307.

4

Spinoza's Ass

JUSTIN CLEMENS

Clement made irresolution a policy. He carried thought to excess and mistook it as a substitute for action instead of its guide. He could find a hundred reasons for the decision, and a hundred against it; it was as if Buridan's ass sat on the papal throne.
—Will Durant, *The Renaissance*

The Montagne thus decided the issue. It found itself in the position of Buridan's ass, not, indeed, between two bundles of hay with the problem of deciding which was the more attractive, but between two showers of blows with the problem of deciding which was the harder. On the one hand, there was the fear of Changarnier; on the other, the fear of Bonaparte. It must be confessed that the position was no heroic one.
—Karl Marx, *The Eighteenth Brumaire of Louis Bonaparte*

Spinoza's Passing Remark

Proposition 49 in Part II, "Nature and Origin of the Mind," of Benedict de Spinoza's *Ethics* reads as follows: "There is in the mind no volition or affirmation and negation, save that which an idea, inasmuch as it is an idea, involves." As we know, for Spinoza, there is "no absolute or free will; but the mind is determined to wish this or that by a cause, which has also been determined by another cause, and this last by another cause, and so on to infinity" (*Ethics* II, P48).[1] It is only the weakness of our imaginations overwhelming our reason that leads us to "consider things, whether in respect to the future or the past, as contingent" (*Ethics* II, P44C1). As such, "will and understanding are one and the same" (*Ethics* II, P49C), not independent faculties but bound up with particular ideas, which, as particulars, cannot permit the idealizing division of the mind.

Whereas for Descartes, there is a crucial distinction between apprehending a fact and affirming its truth, this very distinction is one of the targets of Spinoza's critique. Error cannot be dependent on the will for Spinoza, as John Cottingham reminds us: "Firstly, the will is not distinct from the intellect; secondly, the will is not endowed with the kind of freedom that Descartes postulated."[2] Rather Spinoza's famous dictum about the understanding should induce us to affirm that the understanding is integrally affirmation. Rather than considering will as an infinite faculty that mimics that of a projected, transcendent God, Spinoza refuses the very traces of such a division for his ontology, which integrally depends on the constrained affirmation of the true.

This radical fusion of the will and understanding in the face of particular ideas by Spinoza immediately leads him to entertain in the scholium to the corollary of *Ethics* II, P49, possible objections to his new doctrine. Is it not the case that "the will has a wider scope than the understanding" (i.e., that we can assent to things that we do not perceive), that we can suspend our judgments before assenting to things that we do perceive, and that we do not need "any greater power than for affirming, that what is false is true"? Finally, Spinoza says, "it may be objected, if man does not act from free will, what will happen if the incentives to action are equally balanced as in the case of Buridan's ass? Will he perish of hunger and thirst?" It is this apparently passing invocation of the sophism that is of interest here.[3]

The canonical scenario of Buridan's ass is deceptively simple. A starving ass wanders into a barnyard, where it is confronted with two equally appealing bales of hay. Because these bales are identical in all respects (size, shape, smell, distance), the poor creature is unable to make a decision and starves to death between them. Spinoza's invocation of the ass emerges at a crucial point in his argument and directs us toward an entire sheaf of questions. Is such a state of perfect equilibrium actually possible? If so, does the very possibility of decision considered as an act of free will itself necessarily founder?

Is there even an adequate idea of such a suspension? To answer such questions, let us first turn to some key elements of the mazy discussions by commentators of this scenario before returning to Spinoza and to the specifically political implications of his account.

In the Name of Nominalism

First of all, it seems that Spinoza has misattributed this paradox to the French scholastic Jean Buridan (ca. 1295–1356), a professor at the University of Paris and one of the key figures in the introduction of impetus physics into medieval Europe.[4] The paradox, however, has never been located as such in Buridan's own extant published works. As Peter King notes:

> Buridan is best-known to philosophers for the example of "Buridan's Ass," starving to death between two equidistant and equally tempting bales of hay, who appears in Spinoza, *Ethica* II, scholium to prop. 49. But this poor fragment of Buridan's great reputation is as apocryphal as his supposed amorous adventures with the Queen of France, famous from François Villon's poem *"La [sic] testament,"* or his founding of the University of Vienna: Buridan's ass is not to be found in Buridan, though his examples are studded with asses.[5]

In fact, forms of the sophism are much older than Buridan; none of them have asses, either. Authorities often trace its origins to Aristotle's critique of Anaximander's cosmology, where Aristotle posits the immobilization of a hungry and thirsty man caught between food and drink—and so its abiding link with Buridan seems now to be substantially due to Spinoza's own misattribution.

Second, this paradox has been extraordinarily insistent in the history of thought, as Nicholas Rescher's reconstruction shows. Versions of the paradox can be found in Anaximander, Aristotle, Al-Ghazali, Averroes, Aquinas, Peter John Olivi, Dante, Duns Scotus, William of Ockham, Khodja Zadeh, Rabelais, Montaigne, Thomas Gataker, Spinoza, Leibniz, Christian Wolff, Thomas Reid, Kant, Schopenhauer, Augustus de Morgan, and Lewis Carroll, among many others.[6] Accounts of the paradox persist today, not just in analytic philosophy's lemon-squeezing discussions of the complexities of decision, but also in disciplines such as politics, marketing, and economics. Joseph Schumpeter, for example, calls the ass "perfectly rational," and the ass is often belabored as an example by Amartya Sen.[7] I will return to this phenomenon in a moment.

Third, and despite this insistence, it is most often the case that Buridan's ass (or its alleged equivalents) appears in passing, as a suggestive figure or handy example, before being banished again in favor of other arguments, other figures. Its insistent recurrence is thus notable for its resolutely marginal status.

Fourth, although there are indeed an extraordinary number of variants of the scenario usually considered functionally or logically identical by commentators (e.g., a hungry and thirsty man equidistant between food and drink, a man choosing between two dates, a cord equally strong at all points), the figure of the ass in the canonical, post-Spinozan version of this fable evidently has a broad and sustained appeal. Despite, then, the clear situational influences on the specificities of the scenario, whether these are linked to the context of intraphilosophical argumentation or public demonstration, there has, in modernity, been something about the ass that particularly fires the philosophical imagination. In a way, this fourth point links the others: the presence of an ass renders the scenario at once allegorical and analogical.

It is rendered allegorical because the ass clearly functions as a parodic figure of sovereignty: King Ass. Just as in the fables of Aesop or La Fontaine, Scholasticism or Nietzsche, the ass itself has often provided an exemplary conceptual figure for thought.[8] The monotheistic religions and classical myth, philosophy, politics, and literature establish a tradition that runs to the present, for which a few choice examples should suffice to designate here. As the arbiter of a musical competition between Pan and Apollo, Midas gave the palm to Pan, whereon Apollo punished the hapless judge by giving him ass's ears. Antisthenes allegedly asked the Athenians why they didn't vote in donkeys as horses when they were prepared to elect candidates who bore as much resemblance to generals as donkeys did to horses. In the *Nicomachean Ethics*, Aristotle quotes Heraclitus to the effect that "donkeys prefer rubbish to gold," which has usually been understood either as underlining the asses' inability to make proper evaluations or, quite to the contrary, as showing that evaluation itself is relative, differing between creatures on the basis of use or taste.⁹ In Shakespeare's *A Midsummer Night's Dream*, the fairy queen Titania is punished by her husband, Oberon, by having her fall in love with the hapless weaver Bottom, whose head has been transformed into that of an ass. Heinrich Heine, the great German poet and friend of Karl Marx, was a big fan of asses, which appear throughout his work.¹⁰

These allegorical or parabolic aspects of the sophism have analogical correlates as well. In addition to its allegorical qualities, the scenario constitutes a model for staging the disjunction of law and its application, or to put this another way, it proposes that the transition between deliberation and decision is in fact obscure and is itself in need of explanation. In such cases, the scenario functions as an emblem of what is regularly called "choice without preference"; that is, it poses the problem of a decision that can be founded on no objective criteria to propose, further, whether a decision is really at stake. It moreover foregrounds the problematic links between reason and action, "the necessity of indifference" and the "liberty of indifference." This, once again, ties it directly to the problem of sovereignty in political thought.

In other words, Buridan's ass poses as an analogical conundrum, in the most reduced possible form, the problem of how to account for the fact that people can die for a principle that isn't a proposition or that has no possible propositional or empirical justification. Yet it is also the case that the problem of life that this scenario pinpoints has often not been seen by the tradition of commentary as indeed a real *problem*. What it also underlines, in the absence of any social reference, is the central place uncertainty, undecidability, indecision, and indecisiveness play, not just in a psychological or logical frame, but in a political one as well. As Walter Benjamin puts it in a famous passage:

> The antithesis between the power of the ruler and his capacity to rule led to a feature peculiar to the *Trauerspiel* which is, however, only apparently a generic feature and which can be illuminated only against the background of the theory of sovereignty. This is the indecisiveness of the tyrant. The prince, who is responsible for making the decision to proclaim the state of emergency, reveals,

at the first opportunity, that he is almost incapable of making a decision. Just as compositions with restful lighting are virtually unknown in mannerist painting, so it is that the theatrical figures of this epoch always appear in the harsh light of their changing resolve. What is conspicuous about them is not so much the sovereignty evident in the stoic turns of phrase, as the sheer arbitrariness of a constantly shifting emotional storm in which the figures of Lohenstein especially sway about like torn and flapping banners.[11]

Benjamin—who is here, not coincidentally, speaking about a peculiar form of modern Baroque drama—thereby stages the face-off between personal capacity and position as a key aspect of the problem of political tyranny. The sovereign is an ass that cannot decide, and this is, therefore, more than an allegory: it speaks directly to problems of will, reason, thought, decision, act, consequences, law, life, and death. The perennial philosophical problems of the indiscernible and the undecidable are therefore also integrally practical problems, problems of and for pragmatics and politics.

In other words, the paradoxes of Buridan's ass propose very serious and very central problems to thought. Indeed, philosophy as a discourse and the phenomenon of paradox are foundationally, historically, conceptually, and pragmatically indissociable. There is and can be no philosophy without some relation to paradox and paradoxes; the latter consistently function as an inspiration, gateway, motor, and limit to philosophy. As Gilles Deleuze insists, "the force of paradoxes is that they are not contradictory; they rather allow us to be present at the genesis of the contradiction."[12] Paradoxes are often deliberately concocted by logicians and philosophers to direct attention toward the constitutive failure of reason to think through its own presuppositions, consequences, and limits or, at the very least, toward the pretensions of certain forms of rationality. One needs to think only of Epimenides's liar paradox or Zeno's paradoxes of motion to get a sense of just how untimely—in every sense of the word—such paradoxes are. They arrive out of time, as a shock or surprise, and compel a response that needs, at the very least, to have something novel about it. Such paradoxes are also untimely insofar as they transmit an atemporal or transsituational force, retaining their import for thinkers in wildly different times and places. The proposed solutions, moreover, invariably produce new problems, often of an entirely unexpected kind, and these new problems exemplarily take the form of new or adapted paradoxes. To put this another way, paradoxes force philosophy to rethink the stakes of truth and the true, reason, and being. As such, paradoxes have regularly led to major transformations of the philosophical field itself.

It seems to me that this is also the case for Spinoza, for whom the ass exemplifies a certain sort of post-Cartesian conundrum—which forces him to rethink the nature of ontology, reason, and the political at once. Indeed, Spinoza's genius is evident in his refusal to treat the problems raised by Buridan's ass as simply empty, a game, or an easily resolved dilemma; at the same time, he ultimately considers whatever demonstrative force the scenario has as founded on a confusion. But let us first examine the stakes of the sophism in more detail.

Pandering to the Ass

I have already briefly sketched the key elements in the drama of Buridan's ass, which rest, as should now be evident, on the abyssal nature of accounting for decision. The ass's simplicity is, in other words, extremely complex. What are some of the complexities of this little fable, and what solutions have been proffered to resolve it?

Above all, Buridan's ass is the most reduced form of a paradox of decision. The ass has to decide or it will die. It cannot hold off forever; there is an *urgency* to make the decision. The ass *knows* all the variables in the situation precisely (i.e., there is no ignorance or lack of knowledge at stake). Yet, if it is truly making a decision—and not simply driven by (causal) necessity—then it must truly find some *basis* for such a decision, that is, some kind of difference, however infinitesimal, in the objects. So the sophism presents compulsion to decide, urgency to decide, total knowledge of the variables, and a requirement to find a motivation for the decision.

If this scenario may seem to have inextricably psychological overtones—different versions hinge on the different relations possible between sense, desire, reason, and volition and emphasize differently the ass's immobilization through such different affects as anxiety or confusion—the history of the scenario shows that it has also been brought to bear on problems in cosmology and logic.[13] In fact, one of the suggestive aspects of Buridan's ass is that it is precisely an instance in which the problem of the transition between decision and action, fact and interpretation, proves to be an uncircumventable problem, *no matter the conceptual framework in which it arises.* And once Buridan's ass or one of its avatars has arisen, then some solution clearly has to be found.

One favored kind of solution can be found in Mark Skousen and Kenna C. Taylor's *Puzzles and Paradoxes in Economics,* in which they claim, against Schumpeter, that:

> In fact, there is no animal that could be less rational. From a logical point of view, there are actually three choices, the third being to starve where he is. Clearly, this third choice of starvation will be ranked lower in the donkey's revealed preferences than the other two on the donkey's value scale. If both left and right bales are equally preferable, the donkey will allow pure chance to decide on either one.[14]

Note the use of the word *clearly,* which shows that Skousen and Taylor have clearly failed to take the force of the paradox properly. For the paradox suggests that in the taking of a decision, there is either no clear ranking possible or, when a calculus can (and therefore *should*) be applied, there is no real decision to be made—other than to apply the calculus, of course. But the *possibility* of application of *any* calculus is precisely what is put in question by the ass.

In a similar but not identical vein, Amartya Sen makes a distinction between "maximization" and "optimization," the former involving selecting for "a better," the latter for "the best." Sen can thus write:

> Buridan's Ass, as a vigorous optimiser and a great believer in complete orderings, could not choose either haystack (since neither was shown to be clearly the best), and it thus died of starvation. It starved to death since it could not rank the two haystacks, but of course each would have generated a better consequence than starvation. Even if the donkey failed to rank the two haystacks, it would have made sense—good cost–benefit sense—for it to choose either rather than neither. Cost–benefit analysis does need maximization, but not completeness or optimisation.[15]

This solution also presupposes that the decision here is not *between the objects* themselves but between the *ways in which objects can be ranked*. The possibility of discriminating between *ways to decide* proves crucial here; that is, if the objects cannot be distinguished, they can be taken as a class in themselves, and one can then decide about the class itself, as now opposed to another class. Moreover, it suggests that if there is any decision to be made by the ass, an integral component of the decision to be made is that there is no decision to be made at the level of presentation itself and that it is precisely the couplet of the indifference of the objects and the necessity to choose one of them that forces a metadecision of some kind (in this case, that maximization is better than optimization). The real decision would not then be a choice *between* objects but an *acceptance* of the ungroundedness of such a (non)-choice, the *recognition* that the selection cannot be totally ordered, and a de facto *commitment* to a pragmatic selection that does not make any assertions about the specificity of the object chosen over the other. This solution basically proposes that better is better than best. Note that this proposed solution introduces the motif of a radical nonsimplicity of decision; rather the process of decision must itself involve a multiplicity of shifts between different cognitive registers.

In yet other accounts, the fundamental matrix of the dispute is reduced to the following: either affirmation of necessity or recourse to auxiliaries (to which a rationalist might respond, then there is no *decision* to be made); either the binding together of necessity and decision or recognition of their irremediable separation (in which case, there is no decision to be made, or decision is indistinguishable from pure spontaneity, in which case, there is no decision to be made); we then desultorily conclude with either a rationalism of the concept or a pragmatism of the world. So we find that, for certain rationalists, there is no real decision in the ass's case, or that such a decision is really ungrounded: it cannot be told apart from pure chance on the objective side or from irrationality (madness, pure spontaneity, sovereign exceptionality) on the subjective side. By the way, it is then no surprise that Jacques Derrida, in his own resolute hesitations, often cites Kierkegaard's "The Instant of Decision Is Madness."[16]

Either way, the subject vanishes, at the very moment that knowing and deciding, cause (hunger) and motivation (reason for deciding), come apart. Into the bargain, the problem of the incommensurability of indiscernibles arises: it is not just that the bales are identical (they may just as well be differences-without-distinction or whose distinctions are themselves unevaluable) but that indiscernibility must be excluded to ensure the grounded application of a calculus of any kind (this is why Leibniz argues so strenuously for the principle of the "identity of indiscernibles"). Hence *the problem of contingency emerges as indissociable from the problem of decision.*[17]

For certain pragmatists, as we know, the concept of decision is *necessarily* fuzzy (perhaps to be subjected to a Wittgensteinian-type language-game analysis) or is to be supplemented by auxiliary means. One might discern a kind of spectral equation of choice and life in some of these solutions: even if there are no real choices to be made in life, at least life offers the possibility of such choices (even if unactualizable), and that is better than death, conceived as the absolute impossibility of choice. This still presumes, however, that the decision is linked to a metadecision (e.g., choosing life is better than choosing death because choosing life is also choosing to continue to have the possibility of choosing)—a decision that is precisely put in question by the paradox. After all, part of the difficulty posed by the scenario is precisely this: if reason needs a minimum to decide on, this very minimum eradicates the need for decision (i.e., there is only one right option). To choose is not really to choose; but not choosing is choosing not to be, which is a less choice form of not-choosing than not-really-choosing.

Commentators then worry about whether there is even a decision to be made about whether there is a decision to be made—not just between particular objects, between possible consequences of choosing an object, between possible criteria to apply in choosing an object, between whether there is even any point in bothering to choose between these objects, how fast such a choice needs to be made, and whether one is even really choosing even if one does decide that there is a choice to be made. Yet one cannot simply buy out of decision making. Does someone or something else, then, decide for you? The questions go on and on. What has been affected in this barrage of questions implicates the objects, consequences, criteria, ends, places, timing, reality, affects, and subjects of decision.

It places the enigma qua pure barrier without content at the heart of the problem of reason's default in the face of decision.

Yet what remains of the problem in almost all of the proposed solutions is its status as a *problem*: what subsists unexplained, perhaps inexplicable, in the commentaries is how the ass might effect the transition from recognizing the problem to recognizing that there is no problem. This is where the *hesitation* of the ass is crucial: how long does it take to make a decision? Does it happen all at once? Over a period of time? What sort of agencies are involved in such a decision? The problem of the temporality of decision making has to be reintroduced here, perhaps on the basis of singular situations, not global descriptions. The scenario also points to a peculiar spatial dislocation: absolute equidistance entails paralysis.

Keeping these remarks in mind, let me give the major genres of proposed solutions (note that they are not necessarily all mutually exclusive):

1. The real decision is not *between* b_1 or b_2, but *for* (b_1 or b_2), or, in the terms of the scenario itself, between death or life: "pick a bale, any bale!"[18] Of course, this still leaves us with some sticky questions: is this really a decision or rather is the decision to be made that there is no decision to be made? Moreover, this solution does not take Buridan's ass as an impetus to philosophy but rather just as a kind of puzzle of not much import, one that can be solved and resolved and whose major benefit is its illumination of logicoeconomic details.
2. The aporia the ass presents can only be resolved by recourse to auxiliaries. As Rescher puts this type of solution, historically, one of the most popular, "*random selection is the rationally appropriate procedure for making choices in the face of symmetric preference.*"[19] Or, what perhaps comes to the same thing, the recourse to auxiliaries (e.g., custom, a coin toss, expert advice) does not of itself vitiate the concept of decision.[20]
3. There is a genuine "liberty of indifference," that is, that decision is entirely independent of knowledge about the object or the ontological status of the object.
4. The sophism alerts us that there can be no such thing as real indifference between objects or any real lack of motivation

but rather that motives "incline but do not necessitate" (as Leibniz maintains with his doctrine of the identity of indiscernibles and little perceptions).
5. The scenario is itself misconceived—a concomitant of illicit hypostatization, of "language going on holiday"—such that, in the very irresolvability (or triviality) of the problems it expresses, it ought to make us rethink the philosophical method in toto. One could even parody Wittgenstein here: "we find decision puzzling, because we don't find the whole business of deciding puzzling enough."
6. The freedom or action of a subject is not linked to a concept of decision qua act of will (which is founded on an insufficient representation of reality) but rather to the affirmation of necessity through the understanding (the Stoics, Bergson, and, as we shall see, Spinoza).[21]

To rephrase this list in a way that brings out some of the fundamental dissensions in the variations, (1) no intrinsic mark in the objects is necessary for a decision, which can nonetheless still locate *some* reason, say, in the consequences (i.e. a particular reason *can* always be found); (2) a decision can be automated or contingent (i.e., no particular reason *needs* to be found); (3) the power of decision making is radically free (i.e., there is *never* a *real* reason); (4) if the reasons for a decision cannot be fully explicated, as the outcome of infinitely complex weighing processes, they are never without reason (i.e., there is *always* a *real* reason); (5) the concepts of decision, will, and so on, are themselves irremediably flawed because they have no ties with whatever the real might be (i.e., a demonstration of the falsity of problems of decision); and (6) indecision or indecisiveness is not real when freedom is intellectual affirmation (i.e., there is *only* a *real* reason).

Though such a summary can only be dissatisfactory and perhaps misleading, its benefit here is simply to underline the sophism's extraordinary power to polarize the philosophical field and thus to stage, in an extreme and stark fashion, the complexity of the problems of decision. Yet, in this polarization, the very complexities start to reintricate the divergent positions with each other again. It's surely notable that these divergent-yet-implicated responses emerge from the most minimal possible scenario, in which the *objects* on which the decision is to be exercised are utterly inert; the *injunction* to choose derives from a compulsion for the subject itself (necessity); the *urgency* of the decision is pressing (there's not "all the time in the world"); and the *outcome* of the decision is certain (death or survival). The tradition, in fact, does not resile from just how preposterous the thought-experiment is, although it cannot, as we have seen, ever leave it entirely alone.

Behind Buridan's Ass Lurks Hobbes's Beast

Spinoza himself, unlike so many of the aforementioned commentators, and despite the mention of Buridan's ass apparently merely in passing, takes the force of the sophism with a seriousness rarely equaled in the tradition. There are a number of reasons for this seriousness. Above all, Spinoza's novel conception of ontology is calibrated to undermine all possible applications of the sophism—to suggest how its very presuppositions about the nature of choice, its staging of the problematic, are due to fundamental misunderstandings. At the same time, Spinoza remains careful to link his response to the tradition, undoubtedly as part of the pedagogical aspects of his program.

Indeed, the geometrical means of presentation of the *Ethics* are not due to a stylistic or literary decision, and Spinoza's position can only be falsified if it is treated as such. Harry Wolfson's claim, then, that there are two Spinozas—the first, the explicit axiomatizer, the other, a secret medievalist—is not only false in itself but, in inducing Wolfson to minimize the radical novelty of Spinoza's method, forces him to miss both the true targets of Spinoza's critique and the true source of the latter's authorization: the staged progression of axiomatic deductive reasoning that, for Spinoza as for Hobbes, can, in its clarity, distinctness, order, and rigor, be doubted by no rational creature.[22] Just as the doctrine of an ontological difference between will and understanding misconceives the status of the subject, the presumption of a gap between presentation and argument misconceives method and falsifies the demonstration.[23] Hence the crucial Proposition 7 of Part II: "The order and connection of ideas is the same as the order and connection of things." The *Ethics* not only provides a model for the order and connection of ideas but is *the* model for philosophy's suture of ideas and things, knowing and being, indeed, a model without any possible copy. Yet there is indeed a real sense to Wolfson's remarks, as we shall see.

Spinoza also wishes to combat the commonplace belief that we are free only regarding things we "moderately desire," that is, those things that seem to give us some space for vacillation, not compelling us by force or passion or indubitability. This is also why Buridan's ass is a site where the risk of contingency could seem most pressing for Spinoza, or to put this another way, it is where necessity (the ass *must* choose or die) seems to require a doctrine of volition bordering on some kind of "liberty of indifference."

Spinoza's response is found in the long scholium to the proof of the corollary of *Ethics* II, P49:

> I am quite ready to admit, that a man placed in the equilibrium described (namely, as perceiving nothing but hunger and thirst, a certain food and a certain drink, each equally distant from him) would die of hunger and thirst. If I am asked, whether such a one should not rather be considered an ass than a man; I answer, that I do not know, neither do I know how a man should be considered, who hangs himself, or how we should consider children, fools, madmen, etc.[24]

John Caird, in a classic work, offers the following gloss: "Spinoza's reply virtually is, that the supposed conflict of motives is, when we examine what we mean, only a conflict of ideas, and that ideas never really conflict save when one idea is adequate and another confused and imperfect; that in the latter case reason is the true umpire, and that suspense or inaction would prove, not that reason fails to decide, but that the non-deciding agent is a fool or a madman."[25] This, a standard reading, is astute and accurate as far as it goes. Spinoza unhesitatingly affirms that such a situation is entirely possible but that it has no rationally founded correlate. Once again, note how seriously Spinoza takes the problem and how radical is his response: will and understanding cannot be separated, given that they are always and only true when they are particular affirmations of particular ideas, themselves the expressions of necessity.[26] As he states in "On the Improvement of the Understanding," "an idea is in itself nothing else than a certain sensation; but doubt will arise through another idea, not clear and distinct enough for us to be able to draw any certain conclusion with regard to the matter under consideration; that is, the idea which causes us to doubt is not clear and distinct."[27] It is thus the confusion of perceptions—not the affirmation of ideas—that might lead to such a deleterious situation as exemplified by Buridan's ass.

So it is further necessary to emphasize that Spinoza's epistemological doctrine cannot be separated from his ontology, an ontology that also founds and implies a politics: the infinite attributes and modes of God are not submitted to a transcendent One but to an immanent oneness that is the cause of all things, and that, being all on a sole and single plane, things *are* so in their multiplicity. This also entails, as Alain Badiou has argued, Spinoza's foreclosure of the void, the banishment of contingency, the indistinction of "inclusion and belonging," and the opening of a symptomatic gulf between the finite and the infinite.[28] But it also means that we are confronted with an ethics of ideas that is fundamentally also a politics of equality *because* it is an ontology of immanence.[29]

It is at this point that I want to return to the ass and, moreover, to the linkages that Spinoza immediately makes with suicides, children, fools, and madmen. Many commentators identify a Talmudic origin for this list, thereby placing it in the sphere of religious beliefs that Spinoza has himself personally left behind and that he criticizes as he historicizes. At the same time, one must also recognize that any such allusion cannot simply be to misguided theological beliefs but must have a direct political import as well. Spinoza was not the notoriously atheistic author of a *Theologico-Political Treatise* for nothing, a book famously denominated by Pierre Bayle as "a pernicious and a hateful book."[30]

In fact, the allusion is not simply—if at all—to Jewish sacred texts and rabbinical interpretation but to another, very specific text, much more contemporary, powerful, pressing, and virulent in the context of the later seventeenth century at large and for Spinoza in particular. For, in chapter XXVI of his *Leviathan*, titled "Of Civil Laws," Thomas Hobbes has recourse to precisely the same sequence of dupes: "Over natural fools, children, or madmen there is no law, no more than over brute beasts; nor are they capable of the title of just or unjust, because they had never power to make any covenant or to understand the consequences thereof, and consequently never took upon them to authorize the actions of any sovereign, as they must do that make to themselves a commonwealth."³¹ If the animus against the Cartesian hyperbole of the will is clear here—Buridan's ass is certainly Descartes's donkey—we must also stress the ethical and political animus of Spinoza's ass against Hobbes. For Spinoza, there is no real division between natural and civil right, no representation, no One to rule the Multitude as transcendent exception. It is not a social covenant as artificial rupture with the state of nature that orders politics but rather nature itself that ultimately orders the political realm, and it is therefore Spinoza's radical naturalism that induces him to invoke Buridan's ass here against the Hobbesian assault. If, for Spinoza, Descartes has attempted to protect "revealed theology from the intrusion of philosophy"³² through a transcendental division of dominion, Hobbes, too, has given way on his own naturalism to the benefit of a revivified division between sovereign and subject.

It is not simply that fools, children, and madmen are incapable of making a covenant that places them outside the necessarily artificial laws of a commonwealth—such a law for Hobbes requiring their active submission to a sovereign³³—but that their freedom is curtailed precisely by their inability to be active, to *affirm*, in Spinoza's specific, intellectual sense: "he, who, as in the case of an infant or a child, has a body capable of very few activities, and depending, for the most part, on external causes, has a mind which, considered in itself alone, is scarcely conscious of itself, or of God, or of things" (*Ethics* V, P39S). It is therefore not the case that fools, children, and madmen remain irremediably prepolitical or, more precisely, unable to enter into a true political commonwealth. On the contrary, they are barely political *because* they are insufficiently natural: they are separated from their own power, restricted in their affirmation of adequate ideas, not simply incapable of compacting with a sovereign.³⁴ Crucially, too, these figures are not all restricted in the same way, for "all men are born completely ignorant of everything," and they, too, affirm insofar as their right enables them.³⁵

For such a separation does not compromise their natural right, and this fact has immediate political consequences. We might turn here to chapter 16 of the *Theological-Political Treatise*, titled "On the

Foundations of the State, on the Natural and Civil Right of Each Person, and on the Authority of Sovereign Powers," to verify this. The chapter explores consequences of two of Spinoza's principles: first, the problem of how far free thinking can be extended in the best kind of state, and second, the problem of sovereign power in general, especially regarding the sovereignty of individuals. For Spinoza, of course, "each individual thing has the sovereign right to do everything that it can do, or the right of each thing extends so far as its determined power extends."[36] Moreover, "we recognize no difference between human beings and other individual things of nature, nor between those human beings who are endowed with reason and others who do not know true reason, nor between fools or lunatics and the sane."[37] Beasts, too, cannot be very far away: Spinoza at once invokes the right of big fish to eat smaller ones.

One consequence is that, in a commonwealth, then, *promises are never enough*: force must always be added to ensure compliance. Yet this force is not that which reduces men to slavery or infancy but rather that which helps induce to reason insofar as reason will show that obedience to a sovereign has more benefits than following one's pleasures.[38] Such obedience involves an increase, not a decrease, in power. Yet this reason will also show the limits of all and any practical sovereignty, for, as Spinoza adds in the following chapter:

> No one will ever be able to transfer his power and (consequently) his right to another person in such a way that he ceases to be a human being; and there will never be a sovereign power that can dispose of everything just as it pleases.[39]

Aside from anything else, this simple—yet far from anodyne—statement emphasizes that the state or the sovereign can be neither total nor totalizing, nor can their putative "willing" be understood outside the immanence of nature. If the state goes as far as its power can extend, then, we will end up in a democratic republic, not a Hobbesian state—and this state itself can only affirm our further powers for transformation ("everyone is allowed to think what he or she wishes and to say what he or she thinks") as long as they do not contravene the necessities of obedience.

For Spinoza, a slave is not a child is not a citizen. But this is also why affect proves so crucial for the Spinozan ontology, to explain how one can become other than one is through experience; such experience, moreover, cannot ultimately be founded on any real undecidability; any experience of the undecidable can only be a function not of freedom but of ignorance; such ignorance is therefore directly mortificatory, as opposed to life affirming; yet such an experience is also precisely educative.[40] Hence Deleuze will say that, as a Spinozist, "you will define an animal, or a human being, not by its form, its organs, and its functions, and not as a subject either; you will define it by the affects of which it is capable. Affective capacity, with a maximum threshold and a minimum threshold, is a constant notion in Spinoza."[41] Quite right: affect in Spinoza is such a profound notion *because* it must have an ontological bearing, and I think this is ultimately what separates Spinoza from the rest of the tradition of commentary on Buridan's ass.

One speculative point remains: why did Spinoza call the sophism "*Buridan's* ass" at all? Is this attribution simply an accident or mistake, of no real consequence? I do not believe so. I have already implied that "Buridan's ass" is a covert, distance-taking denomination of "Hobbes's beast," whether one thinks of that beast as the wolf-that-is-man in the state of nature or of Leviathan itself as the greatest of artificial beasts on earth: an ass-in-wolf's-clothing, wreathed in the fear of death. Perhaps we can go further still. Jean Buridan's impetus physics was precisely directed against the well-known failures of the Aristotelian system and was explicitly presented as such. As Alexandre Koyré puts the problem with Aristotle's physics in a classic essay, "movement which is *contra naturam* requires throughout its duration the continuous action of an external mover conjoint to the moved. Remove the mover, and the movement will equally stop." As Koyré further notes, "Aristotelian physics thus forms an admirable and perfectly coherent theory which, to tell the truth, has only one flaw (besides that of being false): that of being contradicted by everyday practice, by the practice of throwing."[42] So Buridan's posthumous reputation at least partially derived from his insistence, with the other partisans of impetus physics, that the mover also, in moving, transmitted some kind of further force to what was moved and, in so doing, produced "the movement as its cause." If it is no longer a process of actualization, movement is still conceived according to a rudimentary form of common sense.⁴³ It is not until Galileo, Descartes, Beeckman, and others that the real nature of motion can be properly formalized—and it can only be so under the conditions of a mathematical physics. What the seventeenth century is therefore capable of, it is capable of because of its mathematics and its materialism, indeed, its sewing together of the two—and this is precisely Spinoza's position in the wake of Descartes and Hobbes. In other words, impetus physics was incapable of surmounting or resolving the Aristotelian problems of movement because there was no way for Buridan to be a modern natural philosopher. Yet Buridan, at the same time, is someone who correctly recognized the problems.

Significantly, though, Buridan's own peculiar compromise between voluntarism and rationalism—that intellect is not enough to determine the will in any simple way but that some other cause must be available that the deferral or suspension of the act of willing will be explicable—has recently been read as, in fact, a strictly intellectualist position, one that hinges on a specific doctrine of not-willing as deferral.⁴⁴ Buridan's proposal can therefore only be made, in Spinoza's terms, on the basis of a superadded principle (a peculiar doctrine of not-willing) *at the very same moment* that it takes a valuable step in the right direction (no real separation of reason and will).

Spinoza's very nomination of the sophism as "Buridan's ass" can be read it as follows: "Buridan's ass" specifically denominates the philosophical failures of both Descartes, with his idealizing division of substance and hyperbole of the will, and Hobbes, who gives way on his own materialism through an idealizing division of nature and commonwealth and through the hyperbole of the sovereign's will. Descartes and Hobbes fail because they split substance and consecrate volition—if in their apparently very different ways—and thereby remain theologians. Hobbes, despite his attempts to resolve the problems of political commonwealth, succumbs to an asinine solution by attempting to "save the appearances" of political tyranny (also supported by traditional discourses of, e.g., divine right) by superadding a theory of antinatural sovereign exceptionality. The real solution is, at least on Spinoza's own account, a truly mathematical and materialist one that affirms immanence, multiplicity, univocity, and necessity. The radical doubt of the ass, its suspension of action, is not due to its rationalistic philosophical motives or its genuine empiricism but rather to its inability to affirm ideas. For Spinoza, the problems of decision raised by the ass are false problems, based on the imaginative confusion of those who separate will from thought. The only solution can be given in and by the active affirmation of true ideas, for which "no love save intellectual love is eternal."

Notes

1. All references to the *Ethics* are from B. de Spinoza, *Ethics, Including the Improvement of the Understanding*, trans. R. H. M. Elwes (New York: Prometheus, 1989).
2. John Cottingham, "The Intellect, the Will, and the Passions: Spinoza's Critique of Descartes," *Spinoza: Critical Assessments*, vol. 2, *The Ethics*, ed. G. Lloyd (London: Routledge, 2001), 221.
3. In what follows, I will be referring to Buridan's ass as, alternatively, a "sophism," a "scenario," a "drama," etc. In my opinion, very little hangs on these variant denominations; I deploy them in context when emphasizing one or another aspect of the ass, but they are ultimately not determining for the logic of my argument. If I prefer the term *sophism*, however, it is for a couple reasons: (1) the term *sophism* has a notable extraphilosophical history (on which, see Barbara Cassin's brief note in *L'effet sophistique* [Paris: Gallimard, 1995], 505–6) and (2) it is Jacques Lacan's term for his own scenario of the prisoners and "logical time," about which he says it is "a remarkable sophism, in the classical sense of the term—that is, a significant example for the resolution of the forms of a logical function at the historical moment at which the problem these forms raise presents itself to philosophical examination." Lacan, *Ecrits*, trans. B. Fink with H. Fink and R. Grigg (New York: W. W. Norton, 2006), 163. Following Lacan's lead, I propose that Buridan's ass becomes a significant sophism for the seventeenth-century thinkers in particular—precisely because of the problematic of the will that Descartes establishes—although it has, as we will see, a much longer philosophical history.
4. Buridan is usually considered a nominalist inheritor of William of Ockham, against whom he later turned. The fifteenth-century French poet (and career criminal) François Villon wrote a famous

poem in which Buridan appears, "Ballade des Dames du Temps Jadis," embedded in the great longer poem "Le testament" (ca. 1461). The poem has been translated into English by a number of reputable poets, perhaps most influentially by Dante Gabriel Rossetti, as "The Ballad of Dead Ladies." The relevant stanza runs: "Where's Héloise, the learned nun, / For whose sake Abeillard, I ween, / Lost manhood and put priesthood on? / (From Love he won such dule and teen!) / And where, pray you, is the Queen / Who will'd that Buridan should steer / Sew'd in a sack's mouth down the Seine? / But where are the snows of yester-year?" The "Queen" of this verse is Jeanne of Navarre, and the reference to Buridan being thrown in the river is presumably a triple scholastic joke at his expense: (1) Buridan was renowned for being a ladies' man, who, in the course of his adventures, had an encounter with Queen Jeanne, who, as was allegedly her wont, would subsequently have her lovers thrown into the Seine; Buridan allegedly saved himself from being drowned by having a barge filled with hay sail past just as he was being defenestrated by the Queen's henchmen. (2) As F. C. T. Moore points out, in one of the paradoxes treated in his *Sophismata*, under *Insolubilia* in chapter VIII, Buridan gives this title for Sophism XVII: "You Will Throw Me in the Water." The sophism itself concerns Socrates and Plato. Plato, guarding a bridge, tells Socrates that the latter can cross if the first proposition he utters is true; if not, Plato will throw Socrates in the water. Socrates immediately responds, "You will throw me in the water." If what Socrates says is indeed true, then Plato cannot throw Socrates in the water, which renders the statement immediately untrue; if it is false, then Plato will not throw Socrates in the water, which of course makes it true. One might immediately object that the statement is therefore neither true nor false, i.e., not simply true, which means Socrates should indeed end up in the water. (3) There is a third joke, on the problems raised and allegedly resolved by Buridan's impetus physics itself (of which more later).

5   Peter King, "John Buridan: Life and Times," in *John Buridan's Logic: The Treatise on Supposition; The Treatise on Consequences*, trans. and with an introduction by P. King (Dordrecht, Netherlands: D. Reidel, 1985), 3. See also S. M. Kaye's speculations in "Buridan's Ass: Is There Wisdom in the Story?" *Dialogue and Universalism*, no.

3–4 (2005): 137–46, that Buridan's fable is best understood in the context of Ockham's philosophy. Note, too, that if one wants to play this Scholastic game, Duns Scotus would be another important interlocutor. For Scotus, the freedom of the will is such that, in willing X, the will could always also have been able to will not-X at the same time, suggesting a kind of pre-Leibnizian "garden of forking paths" (to invoke J. L. Borges's fable).

6 See Nicholas Rescher, *Scholastic Meditations* (Washington, D.C.: Catholic University of America Press, 2005).

7 Joseph Schumpeter, *History of Economic Analysis* (New York: Oxford University Press, 1954), 94, 1064, cited in Mark Skousen and Kenna C. Taylor, *Puzzles and Paradoxes in Economics* (Cheltenham, U.K.: Edward Elgar, 1997), 117.

8 "Pons asinorum" ("Bridge of asses") was traditionally the epithet given to Proposition 5, Book 1 of Euclid's *Elements* of geometry: "In isosceles triangles the angles of the base equal each other, and, if the equal straight lines are produced further, then the angles under the base equal one another."

9 "And it is thought that every animal has its own special pleasure, just as it has its own special function: namely, the pleasure of exercising that function. This will also appear if we consider the different animals one by one: the horse, the dog, man, have different pleasures—as Heraclitus says, an ass would prefer chaff to gold, since to asses food gives more pleasure than gold." Aristotle, *Nichomachean Ethics*, trans. H. Rackham (Cambridge, Mass.: Harvard University Press, 1934), X, v. 8.

10 Indeed, Buridan's ass reemerges directly in Heine's writings but figures as a problem of sexual desire: should he sleep with the mother or the daughter? *"In welche soll ich mich verlieben, / Da beide liebenswürdig sind? / Ein schönes Weib ist noch die Mutter, / Die Tochter ist ein schönes Kind."* "Verschiedene," in H. Heine, *Historisch-kritische Gesamtausgabe der Werke: Neue Gedichte*, Band II, ed. E. Genton (Hamburg, Germany: Hoffman and Campe, 1983), 49. As Claudio Magris notes in his superb travel book on the Danube, "ever since Apuleius, the ass has been honoured for its sexual potency. This potency, on which even Buffon dwelt, is not the arrogance of the bull, all very fine for purposes of machismo, nor the disagreeable satyriasis of the cockerel, but is part and parcel of its humble

patience, the unruffled strength of the way it faces life." Magris, *Danube*, trans. P. Creagh (London: Harvill, 2001), 109. I would like to thank Gert Reifarth for drawing Heine's poem to my attention.

11 Walter Benjamin, *The Origins of German Tragic Drama*, trans. J. Osborne, with an introduction by G. Steiner (London: Verso, 1977), 70–71. As Benjamin adds, "indecision" is "the complement of bloody terror" (71). Because the problematic of a sovereign decision will be at stake later in this chapter, it is of interest to note that Carl Schmitt found Benjamin's theses worthy of a serious response and that, in doing so, he had recourse to Hobbes: "The exoteric dossier of this debate, which took place in various forms and at differing levels of intensity between 1925 and 1956, is not very large: Benjamin's citation of *Political Theology* in *The Origin of German Tragic Drama*; the curriculum vitae of 1928 and Benjamin's letter to Schmitt from December 1930 (both of which attest to an interest in and admiration for the 'fascist public law theorist' and have always appeared scandalous); and Schmitt's citations of and references to Benjamin in his book *Hamlet or Hecuba*, written when the Jewish philosopher had been dead for sixteen years. This dossier was further enlarged with the publication in 1988 of the letters Schmitt wrote to Hansjörg Viesel in 1973, in which Schmitt states that his 1938 book on Hobbes had been conceived as a 'response to Benjamin [that has] remained unnoticed.'" Giorgio Agamben, *State of Exception*, trans. K. Attell (Chicago: University of Chicago Press, 2005), 52. And since Schmitt's name has been raised, it is also pertinent to note the now-extensive discussion about "forced choices" that national socialism inflicted on its victims and that Primo Levi ultimately denominated as occupying a "gray zone." William Styron's *Sophie's Choice* (New York: Random House, 1979) proffers one novelistic variant of such a decision.

12 Gilles Deleuze, *The Logic of Sense*, trans. M. Lester with C. Stivale (New York: Columbia University Press, 1990), 74.

13 As Rescher, *Scholastic Meditations*, 43, notes: "1. Its Greek context in cosmological discussion of the Earth's place in the physical universe (Anaximander, Plato, Aristotle). 2. Its Scholastic context in ethico-theological discussion of man's freedom of will (Aquinas, probably Buridan, and others). 3. Its medieval Arabic context in epistemo-theological discussion of the amenability of God's choices

to reason and to human rationalization, that is, the possibility of explaining God's actions in ways acceptable to reasoning men (Ghazali, Averroes)."

14 Skousen and Taylor, *Puzzles and Paradoxes in Economics*, 119. One problem with this proposed solution is that it misses the possibility that giving chance such a role precisely undermines what choice is allegedly about (e.g., selecting between possibilities on a basis that is not simply randomized), and it presumes that life is unquestionably better than death in the application of the metacalculus.

15 Amartya Sen, "The Discipline of Cost-Benefit Analysis," *Journal of Legal Studies* 29, no. 2 (2000): 940–41. Sen cites Bourbaki and set theory for support for this distinction.

16 Indeed, Derrida deploys it as an epigraph for "Cogito and the History of Madness," in *Writing and Difference*, trans. and with notes by A. Bass (Chicago: University of Chicago Press, 1978), 31. In this context, Gilles Deleuze's comments on the problem of choice are of extreme interest: "A fascinating idea was developed from Pascal to Kierkegaard: the alternative is not between terms but between the modes of existence of the one who chooses. There are choices that can only be made on condition that one persuades oneself that one has no choice, sometimes by virtue of a moral necessity (good, right), sometimes by virtue of a physical necessity (the state of things, the situation), sometimes by virtue of a psychological necessity (the desire that one has for something). The spiritual choice is made between the mode of existence of him who chooses on the condition of not knowing it, and the mode of existence of him who knows that it is a matter of choosing. It is as if there was a choice of choice *or* non-choice. If I am conscious of choice, there are therefore already choices that I can no longer make, and modes of existence that I can no longer follow—all those I followed on the condition of persuading myself that 'there was no choice.'" Deleuze, *Cinema 1: The Movement-Image*, trans. H. Tomlinson and B. Habberjam (London: Continuum, 2005), 117. It is, moreover, no surprise, then, that a cinematic ass quickly raises its head: "Bresson adds yet a fifth type, a fifth character—the beast or the ass in *Balthazar* possessing the innocence of him who does not have to choose" (119).

17 This gives us the peculiar situation in which, as Rescher, *Scholastic Meditations*, 47, puts it, "it is surely a contingent fact that random

processes and devices exist in the world: it is logically feasible to conceive of a possible universe without them. Now the problem of choice without preference is, in its abstract essentials, a theoretical and not a practical problem. It seems curious that the solution of this theoretical problem hinges upon the availability of an instrumentality (viz., random choice) whose existence is contingent. Surprisingly, it is thus possible to conceive of circumstances (specifically, symmetric choice situations) in which the possibility of rational action depends upon an otherwise wholly extraneous matter of contingent fact: the availability to rational agents of random selection methods." But isn't it precisely the case that the scenario implies that logic cannot totalize its own field—that logical operators are also necessarily implicated with modal categories?

18 Moore, in fact, thinks the real thrust of Averroes's case is the following: "that the difficult case could occur, but that it was one in which the person should be represented as having a desire or preference for a disjunction—a wants (p or q). But the desire for a disjunction can be fulfilled *without* there being any desire for one disjunct over the other." F. C. T. Moore, "Rome Inferences and Structural Opacity," *Mind* 99, no. 396 (1990): 606. Moore continues, "In these cases it is the *logical operators* which become opaque in the neighbourhood of propositional attitudes, in the sense of failing to license the usual inferences" (607).

19 Rescher, *Scholastic Meditations*, 42.

20 "In practice, of course, an ass would have inherited enough horse-sense to eat one bale and then the other. One of the reasons that Buridan's Ass is a silly ass, then, is precisely that he interpreted choice too strictly. Non-rational or arbitrary choice is not self-contradictory nor is it irrational. In some instances non-rational choice has a rational application, e.g. resolving the ass's dilemma, starting a game, drawing a ticket, arbitrating a dispute and deciding a tied vote. In others, it would be used irrationally, e.g. selecting a bride, electing a pope, judging a man on trial for his life and grading examinations. But whether it is applied rationally or irrationally it is still a genuine type of choice." James I. McAdam, "Choosing Flippantly or Non-rational Choice," *Analysis* 25, suppl. 3 (January 1965): 136. Or, "in the absence of reasons, must Buridan's Ass starve? . . . In the absence of grounds for preference, it is reasonable to use a

randomising instrument of selection such as a coin toss." Robert G. Burton, "Choice," *Philosophy and Phenomenological Research* 42, no. 4 (1982): 585.

21 As F. C. T. Moore writes in *Bergson: Thinking Backwards* (Cambridge: Cambridge University Press, 1996), 112, "to the extent that the branching diagrams purport to represent a sequence of events which leaves room for freedom, they create fertile ground for paradoxes such as Buridan's Ass, by putting into the diagram or its interpretation the notion of the two branches being equally open, while leaving out the fact that one of them is the one which has been, or will be taken." Furthermore, "branching diagrams are a way of representing a *given* sequence of events, together with a representation of alternative sequences which could have occurred if things were not as they were. They cannot capture *real* hesitation" (113).

22 See H. A. Wolfson, *The Philosophy of Spinoza: Unfolding the Latent Processes of His Reasoning* (Cambridge, Mass.: Harvard University Press, 1948), e.g., 24: "In its concentrated form of exposition and in the baffling allusiveness and ellipticalness of its style, the *Ethics* may be compared to the Talmudic and rabbinic writings upon which Spinoza was brought up, and it is in that spirit in which the old rabbinic scholars approach the study of their standard texts that we must approach the study of the *Ethics*." Deleuze offers another account: "The *Ethics* is a book written twice simultaneously: once in the continuous stream of definitions, propositions, demonstrations, and corollaries, which develop the great speculative themes with all the rigors of the mind; another time in the broken chain of scholia, a discontinuous volcanic line, a second version underneath the first, expressing all the angers of the heart and setting forth the practical theses of denunciation and liberation." Gilles Deleuze, *Spinoza: Practical Philosophy*, trans. R. Hurley (San Francisco: City Lights Books, 1988), 28–29. See also the essay "Spinoza and the Three 'Ethics,'" in *Essays Critical and Clinical*, trans. D. W. Smith and M. A. Greco (Minneapolis: University of Minnesota Press, 1997), e.g., 138: "This book, one of the greatest in the world, is not what it seems at first glance: it is not homogenous, rectilinear, continuous, serene, navigable, a pure language without style."

23 Hence Pierre Macherey casts aspersions on those who conceive of

the *Ethics* as "a collection of separate treatises—briefly stated, an ontology or a theology, an epistemology together with a physics, and a physiology, politics and, finally, an ethics—that have been collected and arranged in a certain order for publication. Spinoza, however, expressly states that these are successive 'parts' of a whole." Spinoza, "From Action to Production of Effects: Observations on the Ethical Significance of *Ethics* I," in *God and Nature: Spinoza's Metaphysics,* vol. 1, ed. Y. Yovel (Leiden, Netherlands: E. J. Brill, 1991), 162.

24 It would presumably be surprising to Spinoza that at least two of the twentieth century's greatest thinkers seem to have starved themselves to death, if according to very different logics: Kurt Gödel and Simone Weil. As Jacqueline Lagrée remarks, "one significant example has to do with suicide. We know the extent to which all of *Ethics* IV, which Spinoza aptly calls 'On Human Bondage,' is aimed at demonstrating that philosophy is a meditation on life and not on death. Thus, in his opinion, 'those who kill themselves are weakminded and completely conquered by external causes contrary to their nature' (*Ethics* IV, P18, S§3). To him, then, suicide represents the very highest degree of alienation or human bondage." Spinoza, "From External Compulsion to Liberating Cooperation: A Reply to Macherey," in Yovel, *God and Nature,* 184.

25 John Caird, *Spinoza* (Edinburgh: William Blackwood, 1888), 242–43. Or, as Cottingham, "The Intellect, the Will, and the Passions," 231, puts it, "Spinoza insists that the Buridanian man would indeed perish of hunger and thirst. The reasoning appears to be this: if the premise is that there is absolutely nothing impinging on the man's perceptions but the feelings of hunger or thirst and the equally distant food and drink, then on this assumption there will indeed be no decision.... A being whose perceptions were limited strictly to these immediate stimuli and nothing else would not be anything recognizable as a human being in the sense of a normal rational agent."

26 Spinoza, "The Improvement of the Understanding," in *Ethics,* 27. Hence Spinoza's response to the other possible objections he raises, in order, (1) will is a universal that essays to explain all particular volitions but, as such, fails to recognize that such particulars must each and all be affirmations; (2) we can indeed suspend our

judgment, but "suspension of judgment is . . . strictly speaking, a perception, and not free will"; (3) "the will is something universal which is predicated of all ideas, and that it only signifies that which is common to all ideas, namely, an affirmation, whose adequate essence must, therefore, in so for [sic] as it is thus conceived in the abstract, be in every idea, and be, in this respect alone, the same in all, not in so far as it is considered as constituting the idea's essence: for, in this respect, particular affirmations differ one from the other, as much as do ideas." Hence the singularity *and* the equality of ideas; hence the impossibility of suspension in the realm of free will; and hence the bond between freedom and necessity forged by affirmation.

27 Moreover, "doubt is only a suspension of the spirit concerning some affirmation or negation which it would pronounce upon unhesitatingly if it were not in ignorance of something, without which the knowledge of the matter in hand must needs be imperfect. We may, therefore, conclude that doubt always proceeds from want of due order in investigation." Spinoza, "On the Improvement of the Understanding," 28.

28 See Alain Badiou, *Being and Event*, trans. O. Feltham (London: Continuum, 2005), 112–20. See also "Spinoza's Closed Ontology," in *Briefings on Existence: A Short Treatise on Transitory Ontology*, trans. and ed. N. Madarasz (Albany: State University of New York, 2006), 73–87. Significantly, in this latter essay, Badiou remarks that "the real problem is: How? How does the finite intellect have true ideas, given that it does not have adequate knowledge of the body-object whose idea it is?" (83). On Badiou's reading of Spinoza, see S. Gillespie, *The Mathematics of Novelty: Badiou's Minimalist Metaphysics* (Melbourne: re.press, 2008), 25–42.

29 On this point, in addition to Gilles Deleuze's indispensable work, *Expressionism in Philosophy: Spinoza*, trans. M. Joughin (New York: Zone Books, 1990), see the excellent study of Etienne Balibar, *Spinoza and Politics*, trans. P. Snowdon (London: Verso, 1998).

30 Why would Bayle express such distaste for the book in such terms? As Jonathan Israel puts it in his introduction to a new English translation of the text, "progress in understanding the history of human thought and belief, and Man's ancient texts, depends on combining a particular set of naturalistic philosophical criteria with new rules

of text criticism which supplement the philology of the past with the strict elimination of all supernatural agency and miracles and a constant stress on reconstructing historical context. The general principles guiding Spinoza's text criticism are identical to those he applies to the study of nature." B. de Spinoza, *Theological-Political Treatise*, ed. J. Israel, trans. M. Silverthorne and J. Israel (Cambridge: Cambridge University Press, 2007), xvi. In other words, the "atheist Jew" has been so blasphemous as to organize an account of the "two books"—the Book of the World, and the Book of Scripture—as if they were both subject to the *very same* rationalist principles, thereby, as commentators have noted, rendering both religion and theology the *effect* of inadequate ideas.

31 Thomas Hobbes, *Leviathan*, ed. A. P. Martinich (Peterborough, Ont., Canada: Broadview, 2002), 202. Although it is uncertain whether Spinoza had access to *Leviathan* when writing the *Theological-Political Treatise* (which he had begun in 1665), as Noel Malcolm reminds us, "the main outlines of the political theory in that book are drawn not from debates within Judaism but from the Dutch Hobbesian-republican tradition. Even the lengthy discussions of the Old Testament in that book may also owe something directly to Hobbes: although Spinoza did not read English, he was a friend of the man who was translating *Leviathan* into Dutch in the period 1665–7, and he may also have had time to benefit from the Latin translation of *Leviathan* (1668) before finishing the *Tractatus theologico-politicus* in 1670." Malcolm, *Aspects of Hobbes* (Oxford: Oxford University Press, 2004), 47.

32 Theo Verbeek, *Spinoza's Theologico-Political Treatise: Exploring "the Will of God"* (Aldershot, U.K.: Ashgate, 2003), 151. As Verbeek continues, "it is likely that Spinoza aims at lifting the epistemological obstacles Cartesians had erected to prevent philosophy from interfering with theology and faith" (151).

33 Hobbes, *Leviathon*, 197, defines *civil law* in this manner: "CIVIL LAW is to every subject those rules which the commonwealth hath commanded him (by word, writing, or other sufficient sign of the will) to make use of, for the distinction of right and wrong, that is to say, of what is contrary and what is not contrary to the rule."

34 As Deleuze, *Expressionism in Philosophy*, 263–4, says in his negotiations of this dicey point, "the state of reason, in its initial aspect,

already has a complex relation to the state of nature. On the one hand the state of nature is not subject to the laws of reason: reason relates to the proper and true utility of man, and tends solely to his preservation; Nature on the other hand has no regard for the preservation of man and comprises an infinity of other laws concerning the universe as a whole, of which man is but a small part. But the state of reason is not, on the other hand, of another order than the state of nature itself. Reason, even in its 'commandments,' demands nothing contrary to Nature: it demands only that everyone should love themselves, seek what is useful to themselves, and strive to preserve their being by increasing their power of action. There is thus no artificiality or conventionality in reason's endeavor. Reason proceeds not by artifice, but by a natural combination of relations; it does not so much bring in calculation, as a kind of direct recognition of man by man." For a good short account of the relation between Spinoza and Hobbes on this point, see A. Armstrong, "Some Reflections on Deleuze's Spinoza," in *Deleuze and Philosophy: The Difference Engineer*, ed. K. A. Pearson (London: Routledge, 1997), esp. 46–48.

35 Spinoza, *Theological-Political Treatise*, 196.
36 Ibid., 195.
37 Ibid., 196.
38 As Spinoza puts it in the *Ethics* IV, P37S§2, "an emotion can only be restrained by an emotion stronger than, and contrary to itself, and that men avoid inflicting injury through fear of incurring a greater injury themselves. On this law society can be established, so long as it keeps in its own hand the right, possessed by everyone, of avenging injury, and pronouncing on good and evil; and provided it also possesses the power to lay down a general rule of conduct, and to pass laws sanctioned, not by reason, which is powerless in restraining emotion, but by threats."
39 Spinoza, *Theological-Political Treatise*, 208.
40 In her book *Surplus: Spinoza, Lacan* (Buffalo: State University of New York Press, 2007), 8, A. K. Kordela identifies a torsion in Deleuze's and Spinoza's argument against final causes precisely in regard to the exemplary event that introduces life and death into human existence: "As Deleuze, who obviously accepts Spinoza's distinction between scientific and moral truths, puts it in his paraphrase

of Spinoza's argument: '[B]ecause Adam is ignorant of causes, he thinks that God morally forbids him something, whereas God only reveals the natural consequences of eating the fruit.' This distinction, however, remains untenable as far as Adam's subsequent action is concerned. For, God's explanation why Adam should not eat of the tree of knowledge is simply that 'in the day that you eat of it you shall die.' Nothing in this statement indicates whether Adam should prefer to live rather than die, and this preference in itself presupposes an end (to live) as better than another end (to die)." While this is, to some extent, true, is it not the Spinozan–Deleuzian point that Adam will learn only through *affect* and not through fiction?

41 Deleuze, *Spinoza: Practical Philosophy*, 124.
42 Alexandre Koyré, "Galileo and Plato," *Journal of the History of Ideas* 4, no. 4 (1943): 411.
43 This matters here insofar as medieval scholars tended to forge a particular relation between physics and psychology. As Jack Zupko notes, "like most medieval commentators on Aristotle, Buridan conceives of psychology as that branch of physics whose proper subject is mobile, animate being." Zupko, "John Buridan on the Immateriality of the Intellect," *Proceedings of the Society for Medieval Logic and Metaphysics* 1 (2001): 5.
44 On this, see Fabienne Pironet, "The Notion of 'non velle' in Buridan's Ethics," in *The Metaphysics and Natural Philosophy of John Buridan*, ed. J. M. M. H. Thijssen and J. Zupko (Leiden, Netherlands: Brill, 2001), 199–219. Following Zupko, Pironet demonstrates that "no one should hesitate to say that Buridan is an intellectualist, and even a strict intellectualist" (199). The demonstration hinges on a difference between the Scotistic and Buridanian doctrines of "notwilling."

PART II
Politics, Theology, and Interpretation

5

Toward an Inclusive Universalism: Spinoza's Ethics of Sustainability

MICHAEL MACK

Spinoza and the Critique of Hierarchy

Does the ethology Spinoza advanced in his *Ethics* have singular significance for the formulation of a viable contemporary social theory? Spinoza's presence in the thought of divergent twentieth-century thinkers from Louis Althusser via Etienne Balibar and Gilles Deleuze to Antonio Negri's recent critique of twenty-first-century forms of imperialism (as well as Martha Nussbaum's work on the intelligence of the emotions) indicates his peculiar contemporaneousness.[1]

This is not to claim that Spinoza anticipated the social problems that haunt our seemingly inclusive global society. Instead of dislocating Spinoza's thought from his particular historical setting, this article analyzes how his *Ethics* delineates the project of a kind of modernity that offers an alternative to the current Kantian approach toward defining the modern. Within the latter part of the eighteenth century—under the immense influence of Kant's transcendental philosophy—history came to represent modernity: the future of humanity seemed to promise its immanent perfectibility. I have shown elsewhere how these attempts at constructing a "perfect" otherworldly world within this one were premised on the exclusion of worldly imperfections.[2] Judaism and the Jews represented these bodily remainders of contingency and political as well as ethical deficiency. It was thought that with the progress of history, worldly imperfections would vanish from the world just as Jews and Judaism would cease to exist in the perfect modern state of the future.

For writers who critically confronted this demotion of naturalistic contingency and embodied life, Spinoza's antiteleological thought became an inspiration for their literary revision of Kant's idealism. This chapter therefore discusses Spinoza's writings on politics and ethics as an alternative to a Kantian conception of modernity. It analyses the ways in which Spinoza's *Ethics* delineates the blueprint for a nonhierarchical and nonexclusive understanding of human sociability. Accordingly, it takes issue with a recent trend in scholarly literature that attributes a hierarchical framework to Spinoza's understanding of ethics.[3] Recently, Steven B. Smith has thus argued that the *Ethics* radicalizes Descartes's divide between the biological, namely, the natural realm of the body, and the intellectual sphere of the mind.[4]

There is some scholarly disagreement as to how radical the divide was that Descartes established between mind and body. Susan James has taken some critics to task who overemphasize this divisiveness: "By treating *The Meditations on First Philosophy* as Descartes's philosophical treatment, scholars have created a one-sided interpretation of Cartesianism in which the division between body and soul is overemphasized and sometimes misunderstood."[5] John Cottingham has abstained from overemphasizing Descartes's divide between body and mind,[6] but he nonetheless acknowledges Spinoza's striking departure from a Cartesian mind–body dualism: "When Spinoza himself speaks of the mind and body as being 'united,' or of their 'union,' he emphatically rejects the Cartesian idea of union as an intermingling or joining together; what is meant, rather, is that mind and body are *unum et idem,* one and the same."[7] Recently, Steven Nadler has confirmed this crucial difference between Descartes's and Spinoza's philosophy in relation to their respective writings about mind and body: "For Spinoza, there is a fundamental identity between mind and body—and thus a fundamental unity to the human being—that goes much deeper than any difference there may be between them."[8] According to Smith, however, Spinoza seems to emphasize the difference rather than the unity between the corporal and the cerebral.

Instead of critically questioning this binary opposition between nature and intellect, Spinoza here appears to reaffirm the supremacy of the latter over the former. This hierarchy of values results from imputing a certain teleological agenda to the underlying conception and structure of the *Ethics*. On this view, Spinoza's denial of teleology on the part of both nature and God only paves the way for his enthronement of humanity as the agent of moral progress in the universe. In this way, Nadler has recently argued that Spinoza's *conatus* (i.e., Spinoza's understanding of self-preservation) is through and through teleological: "Thus, *all* individuals have a basic kind of teleological behavior, in so far as they strive to do what best preserves their being."[9] Clearly Spinoza's critique of a certain kind of theology is directed against the elevation of human teleology into a quasi-divine sphere—what Spinoza calls *anthropomorphism*. This anthropomorphic conception of God–Nature renders absolute human conceptions of teleology that are intrinsically egoistic. According to some strands within recent Spinoza scholarship (i.e., Smith and, to some extent, Nadler), the *Ethics* ultimately extols rather than questions humanity's egoistic and teleological superiority over the heteronomy of God–Nature. No wonder, then, that Spinoza emerges as a Kantian avant la lettre.[10] We will see that this Kantian view of Spinoza's *conatus* is based on a reading of Spinoza as a Hobbesian thinker.

This view argues that the *Ethics* reaffirms the centrality and superiority of human agency that the Copernican revolution had threatened to overturn. The earth might no longer be the center of the universe. Human epistemology and morality, however, vouch for the supremacy of man's rational constitution over anything that might be subsumed under the category of the merely natural (the body) or irrational (God). Smith thus argues that Spinoza only undermined teleology to debunk the role of God or nature in the life of the world: "The denial of any sort of natural teleology or divine providence has an ethical corollary. The *Ethics* deflates the idea that our moral judgments of approval and disapproval have any counterpart in nature."[11] From the perspective of this interpretation, Spinoza indeed anticipates Kant's further development of Descartes mind–body divide. Spinoza does not question this divide. "Rather," writes Smith, "Spinoza maintains that there are at least two different and irreducible conceptual vocabularies, a language of bodies in motion and a language of minds with reasons and purposes."[12] Smith conflates Spinoza's approach with a Cartesian hierarchy that subjects the assumed irrationality of the body to the purported purposefulness of the mind to challenge contemporary thought and scientific inquiry.[13]

Instead of marshalling Spinoza as a bulwark for the defense of an antiquated conception of what should constitute rationality, this chapter follows the approach of the neurologist Antonio Damasio. While having previously discussed the scientific inadequacy of the Cartesian mind–body divide in his study *Descartes' Error,* Damasio, in *Looking for Spinoza,* argues that Spinoza's *Ethics* develops a social theory that dovetails with recent scientific findings about the homeostatic relationship between the mind and the body.[14] According to Damasio, Spinoza's antiteleological thought helps advance a nonhierarchical understanding of humanity's place within nature. In what sense does Spinoza criticize teleology? His philosophy is antiteleological insofar as it refuses to recognize a purposeful design in nature. As a corollary of his critique of teleology, Spinoza abandons a prioritization of the mind over and above the body. This nonhierarchical stance moves his thought into close vicinity of that of Darwin and Freud.[15] Following Damasio's approach, this chapter focuses on Spinoza's attempt to abandon a mind–body dualism. It is this element in Spinoza's thought that accounts for his centrality in twentieth-century philosophical discussions such as those of Nussbaum, Negri, and Deleuze.

Not only did Spinoza align the working of the mind with the working of the body; he also established an invariable link between the equilibrium of the individual and that of the society to which he or she belongs. This connection between the biological and the epistemological on the individual scale thus prepares the ground for the larger sphere of intersubjective relations that connect the preservation of the self to the survival of the other. As a neurologist, Damasio emphasizes the scientific validity of Spinoza's social philosophy. "The biological reality of self-preservation," writes Damasio, "leads to virtue because in our inalienable need to maintain ourselves we must, of necessity, help preserve *other* selves."[16] The two related expressions *perfection* and *virtue* within the *Ethics* serve to amplify the signifying field of that concept that describes the future viability of life's ongoing existence, namely, the central word *conatus.*

This article thus interprets Spinoza's notion of perfection not in terms of teleology but in terms of sustainability on both an individual and a social scale. The main social significance of this undertaking consists in analyzing how a Spinozan vision of society aims at the prevention of various defensive reactions, which constitute the main cause of racism and other prejudices.[17] An analysis of Spinoza's biological approach toward social theory paves the way for a novel account of human agency that does not prioritize the concerns of the mind over those of the body; rather both entities emerge as being intrinsically interconnected. Bringing a contemporary scientific perspective to bear on philosophical issues does not only help diminish the often assumed divide between the humanities and the sciences; this hybrid approach also has significant repercussions for a novel conception of the relationship between philosophy and social criticism. The aims of this undertaking are accomplished through an analysis of how different communities may come to realize that their respective truth claims are not absolute but rather have a certain narrative element to their foundation. Toward this end, this chapter analyzes Spinoza's attempt at building a society in which the self and the other are not in competition but are instead dependent on each other. Does this narrative notion of identity deserve to be called relativist? Rather than being a relativist, Spinoza is a realist. He is antirelativist because he criticizes an epistemology that trims down reality to its conception of the world.

A skeptic might, however, object that Spinoza's philosophy only had revolutionary impact within the self-enclosed field of biblical hermeneutics. The innovative force of Spinoza's thought was, however, not confined to the realm of Bible criticism. It had a much larger reach. As Jonathan I. Israel has recently pointed out, Spinoza's revolution "overtly challenged the three principal pillars of medieval and early modern society—monarchy, aristocracy, and the Church—going some way to overturning all three."[18] For an accurate discussion of the religious critique of theology as politics, it is therefore necessary to discuss Spinoza's ontological critique of all kinds of epistemological mediations, be they theological, economic, sociopolitical, or scientific. At this point, he breaks with Cartesianism. It is therefore worth presenting a brief account of Spinoza's departure from the epistemological foundations that Descartes inherited from Plato.

Spinoza's Critique of an Absolutist Epistemology

The middle of the seventeenth century witnessed the emergence of a new age. This new era set out to introduce philosophy as the master discourse that would from then on increasingly shape the outlook of Western European society on an all-encompassing level. It would not only have an impact on academic matters but would saliently contribute to new developments in divergent fields such as the applied sciences and economics. In short, from the mid-seventeenth century onward, philosophy attempted to dethrone theology as an intellectual tool that was providing the ideological basis for critical inquiry into all kinds of areas within society.

Whereas Descartes affirmed the validity of the established order in both political and theological matters (as he preeminently did at the opening of his *Meditation on the First Philosophy* of 1641), Spinoza's *Tractatus Theologico-Politicus* (1670) advocated the application of a scientific method to the study of biblical texts. In the *Ethics* (which was published posthumously in 1677), Spinoza would extend Descartes's rationalist approach from the field of Bible criticism to that of theology, anthropology, politics, and social analysis.

While emphasizing the distinction between philosophy, on one hand, and theology as well as politics, on the other, the metaphorical description with which Descartes characterizes the novelty of his philosophical method nevertheless implies the totalizing potential of his undertaking. In what ways does Descartes's use of metaphor undercut his seemingly humble self-limitation of philosophy as a self-enclosed entity that pays its respect to the spiritual and worldly powers that be? In his *Discourse on Method* (1663), Descartes compares his philosophical approach to the pulling down of an old house: "And just as in pulling down an old house we usually preserve the debris to serve in building up another, so in destroying all those opinions which I considered to be ill-founded, I made various observations and acquired many experiences, which have since been of use to me in establishing those which are more certain."[19] The destruction of the old building serves as the foundation for the construction of the new, which promises a more all-encompassing sense of certainty.

A house, however, symbolizes a unified whole made up of particular entities. Descartes is thus at pains to emphasize that the abolition at work in his philosophy does not threaten the theological foundations of the body politic. Scholars have in fact analyzed the ways in which Descartes's writing supports rather than undermines the cultural and social relevance of the Roman Catholic Church. He supports the status of the Church through his adherence to Suarez's novel theological argument, according to which there is a radical divide between the world of nature and the sphere of divine grace. This theology has been dubbed a theology of pure nature to distinguish it from Augustine's and Thomas Aquinas's conception of nature as being capable of receiving the divine gift of grace.

Descartes's philosophical dualism between body and mind may be the offspring of the theological divide between the realms of pure nature and grace. According to Jean-Luc Marion, Descartes in fact radicalized Suarez's theology of pure nature. How did he do so? By erasing a certain semantic meaning from the term *capacitas*: Augustine and Aquinas used this expression not to denote nature's and humanity's autonomous capabilities (i.e., nature's/humanity's independent power) but its openness toward the receipt of the gift of divine grace. Marion argues that Descartes pushed "the semantic variation until *capacitas* was de facto understood as a strict synonym of *potentia*."[20] *Potentia*, however, describes a purely natural sphere: the realm of nature's autonomy that Suarez and, following him, Descartes strictly separate from the workings of divine grace. Could it be that Descartes's rationalist approach is in fact a theological one, one that radically departs from Augustine's and Aquinas's theology of grace but nonetheless develops and radicalizes Suarez's "modern" theology of pure nature?

Descartes endeavored to sever the union between theology and philosophy, as illustrated by his immanent use of the traditionally theological term *capacitas*. Has his undertaking been successful? Marion polemically asks, "Could Descartes be an unacknowledged theologian of pure nature?"[21] This seems to be the case. Marion points out that "starting with Descartes, the relation between man and God is apprehended by modern metaphysics in terms of power (*pouvoir*) and capacity (*puissance*),"[22] and he argues that this Cartesian development "is in large part thanks to the theology of pure nature."[23] What are the implications of this discussion for a better understanding of Descartes's revolution? It may well be that Descartes attempts to demolish one theological dwelling space (the one built by Augustine and Aquinas when they formulated a theology that allows for nature's openness toward the gift of divine grace). He preserves its debris, however, to have the necessary materials for the construction of a new one.

Indeed, Descartes avers that the house he is in the process of tearing down has nothing to do with the societal architectonics of both an absolutist monarchy and the Roman Catholic Church's claim to infallible truth. At the opening of his *Meditations on First Philosophy,* he thus takes great care to depict the philosophical as a self-enclosed field of inquiry whose critical potential stops short at questioning the political and theological powers that be. He then proceeds to emphasize that his mind–body divide serves as an epistemological bastion in the support of Leo X's orthodoxy. "As regards the soul," Descartes argues, "although many have considered that it is not easy to know its nature, and some have even dared to say that human reasons have convinced us that it would perish with the body, and that faith alone could believe the contrary, nevertheless, inasmuch as the Lateran Council held under Leo X (in the eighth session) condemns these tenets, and as Leo expressly ordains Christian philosophers to refute their arguments and to employ all their powers in making known the truth, I have ventured in this treatise to undertake the same task."[24] The supremacy of the mind over the body proves the immortality of the soul and thus reaffirms the social order that divides those who work menially from those who are engaged in nonmental work.

By 1660, however, Spinoza (no doubt spurred by his expulsion from the Jewish community in 1656) abandoned Descartes's purported differentiation between philosophical discovery, on one hand, and religious as well as social life, on the other. To improve the welfare of humanity, Spinoza argued, the philosopher cannot avoid addressing human issues in their entirety. He thus did away not only with the traditional philosophical–theological dualism between body and mind but also with philosophy's self-restriction to a limited field of social influence. Spinoza attempted to make philosophy relevant for the life of the people. It was therefore no longer the occupation of a privileged group. Instead, philosophy became a democratic endeavor.[25]

By arguing that the mind cannot fully control the life of the body, Spinoza in fact undermined the societal force of various ideologies that have their foundation in specific epistemological assumptions (be they theological, philosophical, scientific, or economic). In this manner, he opened the way for an understanding of humanity that does not force abstract standards on the specific contexts of human minds and bodies. He therefore did not merely differentiate theology from philosophy. If he had done so, he would simply have followed in Descartes's footsteps. Crucially, Spinoza marked off philosophical strivings and scientific claims to epistemological certainty from the inevitable uncertainties of embodied social life. Had he only driven a wedge between theology and philosophy, Spinoza would have been close to replacing the monolithic assumptions of the former with those of the latter. Instead, Spinoza questioned the validity of all kinds of human epistemologies, thus affirming the mind's lack of control over both the individual body and the body politic.

The Spinozan critique of various kinds of intellectual endeavors (not just those of "theology") thus resulted in a blurring of the boundaries that demarcate the realm of sensuous enjoyment from the realm of cerebral work: "All these things [relating to both bodily enjoyment and cerebral work]," Spinoza argues, "indeed, show clearly that both the decision of the mind and the appetites and the determination of the body by nature exist together—or rather are one and the same thing, which we call a decision when it is considered under, and explained through, the attribute of thought, and which we call determination when it is considered under the attribute of extension and deduced from the laws of motion and rest" (*Ethics* III, P2).[26] As a corollary, Spinoza reveals that "the decisions of the mind" are "nothing but the appetites themselves" (*Ethics* III, P2). In this way, purposeful, namely, teleological, thought emerges as nothing else but appetitive: "By the end [*finem*] for the sake of which we do something [*facimus*] I understand appetite [*appetitum intellego*]" (*Ethics* IV, D7). Unpacking this short sentence helps us understand the relationship between Spinoza's critique of teleology and his deconstruction of the Cartesian mind–body divide. The telos of the final (*finem*) aim itself constitutes the motif force of the appetitive (*appetitum*). To be able to do something (*facimus*), we rely on the bodily function of the visceral (*appetitum*). The geometrical method thus serves as an instrument for the self-reflection of the mind *(intellego)* on its dependence on bodily desire. Self-consciousness can therefore not do without desire, precisely because it is desire's self-awareness. Spinoza's philosophical inquiry into the dependence of the mind on the body has crucial consequences for a reanimation of his social and cultural theory. This issue will be discussed in the following section.

The Theological Foundations of Teleological Thought

Critics have so far not sufficiently discussed how Spinoza's critique of theology works as social criticism. Why does Spinoza broach the issue of anthropomorphism? What exactly is the target of his critical inquiry? He takes issue with the teleological thought inherent in anthropomorphic conceptions of God. According to Spinoza, neither philosophy nor theology exists in a self-enclosed sphere of influence. Rather, any type of epistemology that plays a dominant role in a particular society at a particular time inevitably shapes specific social relations. Significantly, Spinoza discusses theological anthropomorphism in the context of prejudices that permeate different societal fabrics. He analyzes how social prejudices "depend on this one: that men commonly suppose that all natural things act, as men do [*homines . . . ut ipsos*], on account of an end; indeed, they maintain as certain that God himself directs all things to some certain end, for they say that God has made all things for man, and man that he might worship God [*Deum . . . ut ipsum*]" (*Ethics* I, Introduction to Ap.). Here Spinoza criticizes not so much the worship of God but human self-adulation. The parallelism between the phrases *homines . . . ut ipsos* and *Deum . . . ut ipsum* serves to emphasize precisely this point: humans attribute human forms of behavior to God's nature because they perceive themselves as divine. Spinoza thus reveals religious worship of God as deification of the self.

This adulation of the self by the self hinges on the espousal of teleology as the sine qua non for the definition of what distinguishes the human from the nonhuman and thus the divine from that which lacks divinity. Everything that belongs to the order of nature, as perceived in terms of God's creation, supposedly strives toward a telos, toward an end. Various social prejudices gain momentum, thanks to the philosophical positing of teleology as the certain criteria by means of which we have to distinguish between logical, namely, theological, forms of life and those that are illogical and thus excluded from the order of God's creation. In this way, social prejudices result from the equation of the rational (and thus Godly) with teleology. Those forms of life alone are worthy of sustenance and evince a goal-oriented structure. The teleological thus functions as the linchpin around which the anthropomorphic conception of God and nature revolves.

Spinoza's *Ethics* focuses on how dichotomous ways of thinking are an outcome of perceiving the divine from the perspective of teleology. By enthroning the finality of the goal as the main criterion of rational action, society intellectually justifies all kinds of exploitative power relations. Under Spinoza's scrutiny, teleology emerges as a cover-up for the pursuit of self-interest that disregards the well-being of the other. The end of purpose-driven action coincides with the single-minded pursuit of one's advantage in the present, without paying attention to the disadvantageous consequences that might accrue in the future. The anthropomorphic conception of a goal-directed God thus provides theological justification for man's domination over nature:

> It follows, *second*, that men act always on account of an end [*finem*], namely on account of their advantage [*utile*], which they want.... Hence they [humans] consider all natural things [*omnia naturalia*] as means to their own advantage.... For after they considered things as means, they could not believe that the things had made themselves [*Nam postquam res, ut media, consideraverunt, credere not potuerunt, easdem se ipsas fecisse*]; but from the means they were accustomed to prepare for themselves, they had to infer that there was a ruler, or a number of rulers, of Nature [*aliquos naturae rectores*], endowed with human freedom who had taken care of things for them, and made all things for their use. (*Ethics* I, Ap. 1)

The end *(finem)* of human action describes that which the self conceives of as being useful *(utile)* for itself. Spinoza does not, of course, devalue self-advantage. What he thus criticizes in teleological thought is not self-interest per se; rather he excoriates those modes of perception that represent the self as the center of life. According to Spinoza, it is certainly not wrong that humanity lives on the fruits of nature. He criticizes certain teleological modes of thought, then, for divinizing a utilitarian relationship toward the external natural world. Though it is worth emphasizing that Spinoza does not take issue with utilitarianism as such, it is equally important to show how he excoriates both the loss of perspective and the logical fallacies that go along with a self-inflation of humanity. The target of Spinoza's critique of anthropomorphism is not theology as such but Descartes's conception of pure nature that subjects the merely mechanical natural world to the power and will of God's representative on earth: humanity.

Countering the anthropomorphism within the theology of pure nature, Spinoza makes clear how humanity's will and power (as manifested in teleology) self-destroys itself at the point where it loses track of human limitations. It thus sacrifices the sustainability of life to the quasi-divine power of redemption that posits in the future the attainment of its goals. Spinoza's rationalism is not hostile to theology as such. Why is this so? Because Spinoza understands by reason a faculty that limits the unlimited reign of the passions and thus curbs the exhilarating presumptions of humanity's omnipotence and omniscience.[27] What Spinoza thus criticizes as theology is that element that endows humanity with the domination over nature. The natural world does not have an independent existence. Instead, nature *(omnia naturalia)* serves exclusively as means *(media)* for the self-preservation of humanity. Spinoza therefore unmasks Suarez's and Descartes's theology of pure nature as anthropomorphism and teleology.

At this point, self-preservation appears in a rather ambiguous light. Crucially, teleology instantiates an irrational kind of *conatus*: here the self preserves itself to the detriment of those circumstances and forces that enable the survival of the other, but this exclusive strategy has the potential to hit back, mirroring the flight trajectory of a boomerang. Does Spinoza's notion of the *conatus* adumbrate a critique of societal self-destruction? Theodor Adorno has implicitly raised this question while discussing Elias Canetti's response to the Nazi genocide.[28] In an important conversation with Canetti, Adorno has drawn attention to Spinoza's thought on self-preservation:

> Horkheimer and I have in fact analysed the problem of survival in the *Dialectic of Enlightenment*. In so doing we came upon the realisation that this principle of survival, which you [i.e., Canetti] in your terminology call the moment of survival, namely the situation of

survival in the succinct sense—as it was for the first time, one could say in a classical manner, formulated by Spinoza—that this motive of survival, transforms itself into a destructive force, into the destructive and always at the same time into the self-destructive force if it turns wild, as it were, if it thus abandons the relationships to those others which stand opposed to it.[29]

Adorno here astutely points out that Spinoza is careful to emphasize that the will to survival is a social phenomenon. It has to be inclusive of others. If it turns exclusive, it will pave the way for self-destruction, and then the immunity of the individual will disintegrate into autoimmunity. Adorno underscores this point when he says that "this motive of survival, transforms itself into . . . the destructive and always at the same time into the self-destructive force if it . . . abandons the relationships to those others which stand opposed to it." Adorno's interpretation of Spinoza's *conatus* has an illuminating bearing on an accurate understanding of the autoimmunity or self-destruction inherent in some aspects of our contemporary global society. Thus Derrida has recently discussed how autoimmune processes such as "the strange behaviour where a living being, in quasi-*suicidal* fashion, 'itself' works to destroy its own protection"[30] invariably refer back to their opposite: to Spinozist attempts at self-preservation. These self-destructive processes result from triumphal declarations of moral, epistemological, military, and spiritual superiority of one societal formation over the one that poses, or is seen to pose, as its enemy. This awareness of one's own triumph accompanies the perceived increase of one's power. Spinoza shows how proclamations of one's own superiority often go hand in hand with a loss of reality.

What causes this societal drift toward unreality? A given society that seeks to establish its supremacy over and above other societies' claims to significance attempts to make reality conform to its epistemological standards. An inability to engage with epistemologies that differ from that of one's own conception thus does not evince realism. On the contrary, it indicates relativism, precisely because it does not come to terms with the differing and always changing complexities of diverse social realities. The denial that the external world exists as an inviolable entity—as formulated by Descartes in his radicalization of Suarez's theology of pure nature—justifies political actions that are based on the principle of domination *(aliquos rectores)*.³¹ This hegemony deprives nature of animation (i.e., Descartes's mechanical understanding of the nonhuman world), turning it into a zombielike means that does not have a life of its own *(nam postquam res, ut media, consideraverunt, credere non potuerunt, easdem se ipsas fecisse)*.

The anthropomorphic, namely, teleological, conception of God does not only give rise to the ruthless and self-destructive exploitation of nature; it also lays the foundation for violence and ethnocentric discrimination within society itself. Teleological thought pitches the telos of one community against that of another. The difference in religious worship thus furthers war between different social units, each of which deifies its specific way of life that goes along with its specific (anthropomorphic) conception of God. Under this teleological–theological constellation, particularity comes into conflict with universality. Self-preservation mutates to self-destruction at the point at which goal-directed behavior turns exclusive. Within this process, the self ignores that the pursuit of perfection does not coincide with the single-minded attainment of a goal that it set for itself as a self-enclosed entity; rather, perfection has to do with that which enables the sustainability of life, that is to say, with the avoidance of social exclusion and the abandonment of defensive reactions that aim to affirm one's superiority over another.

Critique as the Self-Reflexive Awareness of Subjective Fictions

A particularity that seeks to realize its goals while defending itself against the aspirations of other particular social as well as cultural units endangers its own survival precisely by focusing exclusively on its own telos. As Etienne Balibar has pointed out, Spinoza employs the term *ingenium* to denote the singularity not only of individuals but also of ethnic groups.³² The deification of the specific teleology that structures the life of a particular social group eventuates in the war of all against all. Spinoza thus argues, contra Hobbes, that violence does not originate within the state of nature; rather, it is the outcome of confusing those intellectual constructs that serve to represent a singular entity with the expression of reality as such. The real, however, is not only singular but also diverse.

Teleological constructions about "all final causes are nothing but human fictions [*figmenta*]" (*Ethics* I, Ap. 2). Spinoza does not want to abolish these fictions. If he did, he would be hostile to diversity because it is exactly in the figuration of these *figmenta* that the imagination shapes the singular cultural formations of different ethnic groups. Instead, Spinoza critiques an inability to detect the fictional elements that underpin human modes of reasoning. He makes teleological forms of thought responsible for a lack of self-awareness. Self-reflexivity makes the self aware of the fictional foundations of what it takes to be the truth (be that nature or God). A social unit that makes absolute its specific teleological conception of the world deifies itself and thus loses self-consciousness of the nonabsolutist, namely, limited, and thus desire-based texture of its epistemes: "So it has happened that each of them [individuals as well as ethnic groups] has thought up from his own temperament different ways of worshiping God, so that God might love him above all the rest [*ex suo ingenio excogitaverit, ut Deus eos supra reliquos diligeret*], and direct the whole of Nature according to the needs of their blind desire and insatiable greed" (*Ethics* I, Ap. 1). Here Spinoza analyzes how the teleology qua theology that justifies man's domination over nature has an immediate impact on the way in which different communities interact with each other. Instead of recognizing the fictional character of their specific social imaginings, each group claims superiority over other groups *(ut Deus eos supra reliquos diligeret)*. This touting of supremacy refers to theology to back up the accuracy of its statements with the absolute authority that only the name of deity seems to be able to provide.

Significantly, Spinoza focuses on the mind *(excogitaverit)* as the source of this confusion of particular inclination *(ex suo ingenio)* with the absolute truth value issuing from God. Rather than providing an accurate account of reality as it could be, here the mind will transform potentially peaceful interactions between humanity and nature as well as potential types of cooperation between different ethnic groups into violent encounters in which particular entities destroy themselves while fighting for their predominance.

Critics have so far ignored the way in which Spinoza's critique of theology as teleology and thus anthropomorphism ironically relates to Descartes's and Hobbes's voluntarism. A notable exception is Jerome B. Schneewind, who has drawn attention to the fact that Spinoza's philosophy restored the split, perpetrated by voluntarist natural lawyers, between politics (prefigured by Duns Scotus's view of God's unlimited and arbitrary power) and ethics. Spinoza replaced Descartes's will with a notion of wisdom that strives for both the joyful and the virtuous: "Each increase in perfection is an increase in both our joy and virtue."[33] In contrast to Descartes, Spinoza maintained that virtue was not superimposed on nature by reason, God, or political power; rather, the virtuous coincides with the joyful fulfillment of each individual's different natural potential.[34] This appreciation of an infinite variety of different forms of life makes for the *differentia specifica* of his understanding of self-preservation (*conatus*) from that of Hobbes.

Hobbes's political philosophy is based on a dualism between the state of nature, on one hand, and the politics of reason, on the other. It is this dualistic paradigm that will later form the basis of Kant's idealism.[35] Kant transforms Hobbes's dualism between *status naturalis* and *status civilis* into one between the state of nature and the state of freedom. By freedom, however, Kant understands a radical independence from any reliance on the goods of this world. Kantian rationality, with its unbridgeable gulf between the realms of freedom and nature, sets out to demonstrate the worthlessness of bare life (as pure nature). He thus adheres to Suarez's and Descartes's theology of pure nature. Reason dominates and overcomes nature by humiliating desires for objects in the external world. Kant deemed these desires "pathological." Kant's famous law of autonomy helped enact such subjugation of the forces of the body to the body politic. Here Hobbes clearly meets Kant.

Both Kant and Hobbes attempt to distill a moral kernel out of the Christian heritage. This moral essence should thus form the basis of their respective political philosophies. Both emphasize, as Leo Strauss has shown, conscience over and against action: "In believing that the moral attitude, conscience, intention, is of more importance than the action, Hobbes is at one with Kant as with the Christian tradition."[36] Spinoza's ethology, by contrast, focuses on actions and their outcome rather than on the inward sphere of conviction.

In his work on politics and religion, Spinoza, as Leo Strauss has shown, is heavily indebted to Averroes in that he does not completely disqualify the religious dimension within political life.[37] Why does Spinoza abstain from secular radicalism? He values that aspect in different forms of religion that give rise to actions that are supportive of what he understands by ethics. Hobbes and Kant, however, do not allow for a religious element that would contradict their conviction about the absolute supremacy of the secular state. In this way, Spinoza's "break with the immediately preceding tradition was much less radical than that of Hobbes."[38] It is to some extent due to Spinoza's nonhostile attitude toward religion that his understanding of the *conatus* differs from that of Hobbes. In contrast to Hobbes, Spinoza argues that the self-preservation of a given human community depends on the preservation of the whole of humanity and nature. Spinoza's is thus a holistic approach. Unlike Hobbes, he does not divide humanity into different groups, differentiating between a state of nature and a state of civilization or between religious communities and those who have attained the state of Hobbes's rational absolutist monarchy.

Spinoza appreciates a plural world consisting of different social and religious ways of life. As Schneewind put it, "knowledge of God is the highest good, and one person's possession of that knowledge obviously does not lessen another's share. We need not compete for the true good. We would not be led into conflict if we all understood this."[39] Spinoza critiques teleology on account of its exclusivity. The mind turns passionate and thus prone to violence if it focuses on the exclusive rather than on the inclusive. By combining virtue with joy, Spinoza bridges the gulf between the universal and the singular as well as the apparent gap that lies between the ethical and the political. Descartes perpetuates this separation between politics and ethics. This is squarely in line with his conception of philosophy as a self-enclosed entity, as discussed earlier.

Whereas Schneewind analyzes the differences between Descartes and Spinoza, Michael Allen Gillespie tends to see both philosophers as representative of the voluntarist heritage with which modernity had to come to terms at its inception in the seventeenth century. As Gillespie (following Hans Blumenberg) has shown, Descartes idealizes the power of the human will to create a bastion that could prove capable of fending off God's deleterious interference with the workings of the mind.[40] The feared *potentia absoluta* that had been a divine prerogative in the voluntaristic theology of Ockham and Duns Scottus became a human attribute in Descartes's confirmation of the will's or mind's superiority over the body:

> *Ego cogito ergo sum* is the bulwark that Descartes raises up against the omnipotent God and the radical skepticism that he engenders. It is his bastion for the defense of human reason and freedom. This principle, however, is not merely a bastion or refuge—it is also the Archimedean point upon which Descartes stands in his attempt to move the world, the basis for the universal science with which he seeks to win back the earth for man by dethroning this arbitrary and irrational God and making man the master and possessor of nature.[41]

Whether it is the human mind as will or the absolute power of God within teleological constructions, nature always figures as that remainder of imperfection that has to be overcome. Only the subjugation of nature under the willful agency of either the divine (Ockham's and Scott's voluntarism) or the human (Descartes's rationalism) guarantees the implementation of a purposeful scheme of things. Spinoza analyzes the subjective and thus fictional element within either theological or philosophical types (or both) of teleology that profile themselves as objective proofs of nature's deficiency. His critique of theology thus amounts to a critical inquiry into the fallacy of the mind that takes itself to be absolute and affirms its supremacy over that from which it sees itself separated: be it the body or the external material world.

Spinoza subjects the affects to this style of geometric analysis not to discard the affective. He clearly knows that this would be impossible.[42] Instead, the point of his dissection of feelings consists in showing how they are closely tied to the workings of the mind. He thus addresses those who "prefer to curse or laugh at the affects and actions of men, rather than to understand them" (*Ethics* III, Preface). Anthropological research has shown that laugher functions as symbolic transposition of a feeling of superiority in precisely those contexts in which the one who laughs abandons a relationship of empathetic understanding that can be found in enlightened and thus enlightening forms of humor.[43] Laughter at affections in a way that precludes comprehension amounts to an assumption of supremacy, which, as we have seen, Spinoza criticizes in anthropomorphic conceptions of God. This touting of superiority accompanies defensive reactions as regards perceived threats either in nature or in the intrahuman social sphere. The effects of these actions are equal to those of aggressive offences: they appear to be defensive to the one who perpetrates them, but they are clearly offensive to the one who has to endure them.

Voluntarism as the Autoimmunity of Teleology

Descartes's voluntaristic rationalism reinforces the defensive strategies that an anthropomorphic conception of God justifies theologically. Spinoza emphasizes the originality of his appraisal of the affects. Descartes did not pay much attention to the emotive aspects of humanity:

> But no one, to my knowledge, has determined the nature and powers of the affects.... The celebrated Descartes, although he too believed that the mind has absolute power over its own actions, nevertheless sought to explain human affects through their first causes, and at the same time to show the way in which the mind can have absolute dominion [*absolutum ... imperium*] over its affects. But in my opinion, he showed nothing but the cleverness of his understanding, as I will show in the proper place [*sui ingenii acumen ostendit, ut suo loco demonstrabo*]. (Ethics III, Preface)

Spinoza reveals Descartes's declaration of the absolute dominion *(absolutum imperium)* of the mind over the affects as nothing else but a sign of subjective preference rather than objective analysis. In a subtle move, he contrasts his perspective *(mea sententia)* with Descartes's confirmation of the mind's absolute domination over arbitrary and merely subjective emotions. The polite style of the preceding excerpt does not diminish the force of its ironic tone. This becomes abundantly clear if one reads the original Latin text. The showiness *(ostendit)* of Descartes's intellectualism mirrors the imperial *(imperium)* gesture with which the mind affirms its supremacy *(absolutum)* over the affects that it associates with the body. Spinoza praises Descartes's intellect *(acumen)* while in the same breath belittling it as a sign of a temperamental attitude *(sui ingenii)* rather than an instrument to be employed in the quest for objective knowledge.

To be sure, Spinoza does not excoriate individual inclinations and idiosyncratic preferences. What he takes issue with is the endeavor to dress up particular opinions as if they were universally valid truths that make everything that contradicts them or opposes them appear intellectually inferior. As he shows in its proper place *(ut suo loco demonstrabo)*, namely, at the opening of Book V, Descartes's enthronement of the will as the mind's absolute control over the body radicalizes a Stoic belief in the intellectual control over the life of the emotions.[44] In a quasi-objectivist mode, Descartes locates the headquarter of the mind's, namely, the will's, empire in a specific anatomical point, the pineal gland, "by whose aid the mind is aware of all the motions [*cujus ope Mens motus omnes*] aroused in the body and of external objects, and which the mind can move in various ways simply by willing" (*Ethics* V, Preface). By pinpointing the source of the will's power in the specific cerebral location of the pineal gland, Descartes objectifies his subjective theory of voluntarism. Here the brain (of which the pineal gland forms a part) serves as a concrete location by which we can quasi-experimentally fathom the anatomical mechanism that enacts the omnipotent working of the mind *(cujus ope Mens motus omnes)*. In Spinoza's account, Descartes's objectivist method mirrors that which it describes: the will's absolute domination over the inclinations of the body.[45] Spinoza characterizes the salient point of his own originality as precisely the abandonment of any teleological opposition between that which is to be dominated and the dominant, the inferior and the superior, the perfect and the imperfect, the goal and the goalless.

By employing a nonprejudicial approach in his analysis of the emotions, Spinoza sets out to question a hierarchical divide between superiority and inferiority that structures philosophical, scientific, and theological forms of teleology. He thus detects in the teleological the structural kernel that shapes superstitious kinds of actions and thoughts. According to Deleuze's interpretation of the *Ethics*, "superstition is everything that keeps us cut off from our power of action and continually diminishes it."[46] What, however, is the superstitious in Spinoza's view? As the preceding discussion has shown, Spinoza defines teleology as the deification and thus universalization, namely, objectification, of subjective thoughts and opinions. This making absolute of one's own will and desire characterizes the anthropomorphic conception of God, which Spinoza criticizes as both theology and superstition. In this way, he unmasks the superstitious foundations of Descartes's voluntaristic rationalism, which in turn is a secular (i.e., philosophical) translation and transmutation of Ockham's and Duns Scott's theological discourse about a voluntaristic God.

Like the teleological, the superstitious thrives on the hierarchical divide between superiority and inferiority. That which opposes the willing subject becomes demoted to the inferior. Countering such supposition of a divide in the sublunar world between what is faulty and what is perfect, Spinoza does away with a terminology that aligns embodied life along a hierarchical horizon. Rather than arguing that particular objects have particular shortcomings, Spinoza affirms the flawless character of each living being. Spinoza makes this point clear in his letter of January 5, 1665, to William van Blyenbergh when he writes that "everything that is, considered in itself, and without regard to anything else, includes perfection, which always extends in each thing as far as does the essence of the thing itself."[47] What may strike us as imperfect amounts in reality to nothing else but an organism's vulnerability to specific internal as well as external effects. In this way, there is nothing in nature that is evil or poisonous as such. The deleterious effects of any particular substance do not make up its constitutional core; rather, an individual proves destructive not through his or her existence, which we might construe abstractly as the essence of his or her character, but rather by the particular violent turn his or her actions take in any given situation. Likewise, a mushroom is not poisonous as such; otherwise, it would poison itself. Spinoza tries to persuade us that we distinguish between abstract concepts and our understanding of ever-changing particular entities that form a substantial part of our everyday lives. We might be harmed by eating a poisonous mushroom, but Spinoza warns us of taking this effect it has on us as the static character of the plant itself.[48] The mushroom in question proves deleterious to our digestive system. It does not, by contrast, damage our sense of eyesight while observing it.

As it is, nature has already come into being within a state of perfection. "But my reason is this [*Sed mea haec est ratio*]," Spinoza affirms, "nothing happens in Nature that can be attributed to any defect in it, for nature is always the same, and its virtue and power of acting are everywhere one and the same, that is, the laws and rules of Nature, according to which all things happen, and change from one form to another, are always and everywhere the same [*ex unis formis in alias mutantur, sunt ubique & semper eadem*]" (Ethics III, Preface). Thus differentiating his thought from that of Descartes, Spinoza draws the reader's attention to sociological, political, and medical and psychological factors that vitiate both the well-being of individuals and the welfare of entire societies. Significantly, Spinoza does not frame his analysis in an objectivist style. On the contrary, he opens his remarks by paying attention to the subjective position of his argument *(sed mea haec est ratio)*. There is an apparent paradoxical tension between the subjective formulation of his reasoning and the content of the reasoning itself. For what Spinoza advances in this dense paragraph is not an argument for the separateness of individual subject positions but an affirmation of their intrinsic interconnectedness, of their underlying unity *(& ex unis formis in alias mutantur, sunt ubique & semper eadem)*.

A hierarchical form of teleological thought denies this interrelationship between different subject positions. For it attributes a praiseworthy goal to a single and thus specific entity, whose telos it contrasts with the faultiness of purpose within another social foundation. Teleology as superstition thus sheds light on the destructive passions of the mind. The mind operates via affects at precisely the point at which it turns exclusive. This exclusivity is only seemingly rational. In fact, it not only undermines the welfare of the other, which it sees as either a threat or a competitor; in the end, it destroys the self together with the other because both are intrinsically interconnected. This is why calculation and friendship cannot be separated from each other in Spinoza's account of intersubjectivity.

From the perspective of self-interest, the defensive reaction of warlike behavior is not an option; rather friendship truly instantiates the dictates of self-preservation *(conatus)*. In striking contradiction to Hobbes's anthropology, according to which man is a wolf to man, Spinoza argues that we are in need of each other as if we depended on the help of a deity. Once the anthropomorphic conception has been abandoned, which gives rise to the exclusivity of teleological thought, we realize that not one of us is able to survive independently. We are all in need of each other. The anthropomorphic conception of God attempts to cover up this needfulness by endowing a specific social and ethnic group with a redemptive teleology (and thus with quasi-divine backing), which it posits as a lack in other human communities.

In this way, Spinoza's dictum that "man is a God to man" (*Ethics* IV, P35S) only attains its full significance if one bears in mind Hobbes's proclamation that man is a wolf to man.[49] Spinoza does not deny that humanity sometimes tends to act in a self-destructive manner, as if it were its own carnivore (i.e., a wolf). However, he emphasizes the as-if factor. Destructive, and therefore self-destructive, behavior does not come naturally. Unlike Hobbes, Spinoza does not posit a state of nature that is characterized by unrestrained violence. He does not share Hobbes's conception of the state of nature as the war of all against all.[50] The reason for this is that his understanding of nature is different from Hobbes's understanding. According to Spinoza, nature is a force that connects rather than divides. Spinoza emphasizes his holistic and nonviolent conception of nature in his letter of October 1665 to Henry Oldenburg: "I do not think it right for me to laugh at nature, much less to weep over it, when I consider that men like the rest, are only part of nature, and that I do not know how each part of nature is connected with the whole of it, and how with the other parts."[51] Rather than being the product of the state of nature, violence is the offspring of a specific cultural formation that shapes a social world in which war and social exclusion are accepted as anthropological givens.

How does it come, then, that human society revolves around violence and exclusivity? In his answer to this crucial question, Spinoza focuses on the autoimmunity of teleology. The telos of a specific group turns, over time, into the cause of its own destruction. Spinoza's work on the relation between the passions of the mind and the medical phenomenon of autoimmunity has a special significance in the context of contemporary cultural and social theory. Gilles Deleuze has drawn attention to Spinoza's discussion of autoimmunity in Part IV of the *Ethics*. Deleuze's analysis of Spinoza and autoimmunity focuses on death:

Death is all the more necessary because it always comes from without. To begin with, there is an average duration of existence: given a relation, there is an average duration in which it can be realized. But, further, accidents and external affections can interrupt its realization at any moment. It is death's necessity that makes us believe that it is internal to ourselves. But in fact the destruction and decomposition do not concern either our relations in themselves or our essence. They only concern our extensive parts which belong to us for the time being, and then are determined to enter into other relations than our own. This is why the *Ethics*, in Part IV, attaches a good deal of importance to the apparent phenomenon of self-destruction; in reality what is involved is always a group of parts that are determined to enter into other relations and consequently behave like foreign bodies inside us. This is what occurs with the "autoimmune diseases." A group of cells whose relation is disturbed by an external agent, typically a virus, will be destroyed by our characteristic (immune) system.[52]

Deleuze focuses on the way in which autoimmunity blurs the boundaries between self and other and between good (food) and bad (poison): "poison or food?—with all the complications, since a poison can be food for part of the thing considered."[53] According to Deleuze, Spinoza's discussion of autoimmunity in Part IV of the *Ethics* thus illustrates the blurring of the subject–object distinction that characterizes Deleuze's nonsupplementary plane of immanence, where there is "no longer a form, but only relations of velocity between infinitesimal particles of unformed material," and where there "is no longer a subject, but only individuating affective states of an anonymous force."[54] Spinoza's discussion of autoimmunity thus questions the existence of autonomous individuals: hidden forces within the self that destroy the self. Clearly this view undermines the commonsense understanding of a distinctly delineated boundary that separates the self from others.[55]

Spinoza reveals self-destruction as a wish for the destruction of others. The medical boundaries between self and other are fluid, as are the emotional–affective boundaries. Spinoza illustrates this in Part IV of the *Ethics* when he discusses the case of envy and hate between Peter and Paul (*Ethics* IV, P34S). This discussion illustrates how the affects (i.e., envy and hate) bring about a division between self and other (i.e., between Peter and Paul) in the first place. Without the quasi-autoimmune influence of the affects, Peter's self-preservation could be identical with that of Paul, and vice versa. According to Spinoza, we are only opposed to each other when we are torn by affects–passions. Spinoza foregrounds his discussion of self-preservation via an analysis of autoimmunity and self-destruction to bring to the fore the potential coincidence of the two elements. In doing so, Spinoza wants to sensitize his readers to the deleterious and truly irrational consequences of such coincidence. At this point, self-preservation mutates into its opposite: into autoimmunity. Derrida has recently analyzed the political and ethical consequence of self-preservation, which has become self-destruction.

As has been discussed in section 3, Derrida has defined "an autoimmunitary process" as "that strange behavior where a living being, in quasi-*suicidal* fashion, 'itself' works to destroy its own protection, to immunize itself *against* its 'own' immunity."[56] Significantly, Derrida put the terms *itself* and *own* into quotation marks, thus pointing to the unstable character of this self that tries to preserve itself while working against itself. In his reading, autoimmunity is not only a medical but also a social, political, and economic process that is one-dimensional and that, in its one-dimensionality, furthers precisely that *against* which it sets out to work.

The linearity of teleological reason thus becomes explosive. In this way, "autoimmunitary movements . . . produce, invent, and feed the monstrosity they claim to overcome."[57] Offering an alternative to social practices that turn suicidal (i.e., autoimmune), Spinoza shows how teleological conceptions of perfection contrast with the perfected state of sustainability. Politicians as well as religious leaders who attempt to set their society on the path toward the establishment of some transcendent and thus nonembodied ideational construct often do so with the concomitant aim of proving the imperfections of neighboring states, depicting these in terms of the devalued body and the merely material. By proclaiming the purported superiority of their own society, they work, however, for its destruction. The insistence on the supremacy of one's own telos does not only potentially justify the employment of violent means for the attainment of this aim. It also provokes the resentment, if not hate, of those over whom one seeks to triumph.

This becomes abundantly clear in Spinoza's discussion of the passions and, in contrast to them, the third kind of knowledge. Crucially, in his account of the human affects that forms the heart of the discussion of Part IV, Spinoza analyzes the mind's abstraction in terms of a given society's passion to triumph over another. Here hierarchy emerges as the tyranny of universal ideas. The mind as driven by passions for distinction and exclusivity constructs an ideal of universality by means of which it passes judgment on nature's deficiency. Here the end justifies the employment of violent means. Everything that deviates from the model of the universal constitutes imperfection. The term *sin* describes this deviation. According to Spinoza, the moralistic language of sinfulness gives rise to the hierarchical dichotomy that values that which is perceived as perfect and devalues that which appears as imperfect:

> But after men began to form universal ideas, and devise models [*exemplaria excogitare*] of houses, buildings, towers, and the like, and to prefer some models of things to others, it came about that each one called perfect what he saw agreed with the universal idea he had formed of this kind of thing, and imperfect what he saw agreed less with the model he had conceived [*cum concepto*], even though its maker thought he had entirely finished it. Nor does there seem to be any other reason why men also commonly call perfect and imperfect natural things, which have not been made by human hands. For they are accustomed to form universal ideas of natural things as much as they do of artificial ones. They regard these universal ideas as models of things, and believe that Nature (which they think does nothing except for the sake of some end) looks to them, and sets them before itself as models. So when they see something happen in Nature which does not agree with the model they have conceived of this kind of thing, they believe [*credunt*] that Nature itself has failed or sinned, and left the thing imperfect. (*Ethics* IV, Preface)

As in his critique of theology, in his analysis of teleological reason, Spinoza focuses on the fictional fallacy to which an epistemology that takes its ideational constructs as absolute invariably falls prey.

The preceding extract opens with human cognition and ends with the uncertainty of belief systems. Societies as well as individuals construct particular models *(exemplari excogitari)* that give shape to their peculiar preferences and idiosyncratic inclinations. Here again, Spinoza does not take issue with subjectivity as such. Instead, he excoriates a cognitive fallacy that elevates an individual construct into an absolute assessment of reality as it should be. The conceptual *(concepto)* turns out to be a matter of belief *(credunt)*. Spinoza detects a theological opposition between sin and immaculateness behind the cognitive value judgment that contrasts perfection with imperfection.

The preceding important extract shows how Spinoza analyzes the ways in which theology and teleology meet. Teleological reason in a crucial respect coincides with the anthropomorphic construction of God, which Spinoza critiqued at the opening of the *Ethics*. Both teleology and Spinoza's understanding of theology inflate the sense of power with which any given society sees itself endowed. According to teleological reason, a future goal sets those who subscribe to it apart from the rest of the human community in terms of moral and intellectual superiority. This sense of cognitive superiority could then serve as justification for the use of unrivalled military force that could in turn pave the way toward the attainment of a redemptive future.

In a related manner, anthropomorphic conceptions of God commingle the spiritual with the political. In this way, the God of a specific community functions as a device that separates this group from other groups in terms of superiority and inferiority. According to Spinoza, theological conceptions thus serve to trump up rather than to critically reflect on a sense of human omnipotence. The self here merges with the deity it worships. Spinoza sees in this kind of self-preservation turned wild the ultimate cause of different forms of violent conflict. Bloodshed results from the self's touting of superiority. The self who revels in his or her own supremacy derives joy from the inferiority of the other:

> For whenever anyone imagines his own actions, he is affected with joy (by P53), and with greater joy, the more his actions express perfection, and the more distinctly he imagines them, that is (by

II40S1) the more he can distinguish them from others, and consider them as singular things. So everyone will have the greatest gladness from considering himself, when he considers something in himself which he denies concerning others. (*Ethics* III, P55S)

True perfection, by contrast, does not separate between the self and the other. This is exactly what Spinoza means by the intellectual love of God, namely, the third kind of knowledge, which guarantees the immortality of the soul:

> This love toward God is the highest good which we can want from the dictate of reason [*Deum Amor summum bonum est, quod ex dictamine rationis*] (by IVP28), and is common to all men [*omnibus hominibus commune*] (by IVP36); we desire that all should enjoy it (by IV37). And so (by Def. Aff. XXIII), it cannot be stained by an affect of envy, nor (by P18 and the Def. of jealousy, see IIIP35S) by an affect of jealousy. On the contrary (by IIIP31), the more men we imagine to enjoy it, the more it must be encouraged, q.e.d. (*Ethics* V, P20Pr.)

Here Spinoza explains why the truly rational love of God represents the highest good. The *deum amor ex dictamine rationis* (the love of God out of the instruction obtained from rational inquiry) enables social and political interactions that are free from violence precisely because they are not accompanied by feelings of envy and jealousy, which, as the previous discussion has shown, arise from touting teleological claims of superiority. The *summum bonum* thus coincides with that which is common rather than exclusive to the diversity of all peoples *(omnibus hominibus commune est)*.

Communality as the Immortality of the Soul

As corollary of the discussion advanced in this chapter, it becomes clear that it is exactly this communality that Spinoza understands by the eternity of the mind. Critics have often asked why Spinoza subscribed to the concept of the soul's immortality while at the same time affirming the parallelism between mind and body. How can the soul be immortal if it is intrinsically tied to the decay of the body? "'To deal with this mess," Aaron V. Garret has recently argued that according to Spinoza, "only a *part* of the mind is eternal."⁵⁸ This statement might reconcile the apparent contradiction of Spinoza's writing on the parallelism of body and mind, on one hand, and the immortality of the soul, on the other.

Yet, at the same time, it gives rise to another paradox. How does the separation of the mind into an inferior and thus perishable part and into a superior and thus immortal essence square with Spinoza's focus on communality and interconnectedness (an element that Garret otherwise emphasizes in his study)?⁵⁹ Spinoza defines reason as that aspect of the mind that proves capable of understanding the necessary causes of various experiences the body undergoes in communal life. It can thus only operate as part of a bodily entity. What happens if the body to which the mind belongs has perished? As we have seen, the mind, as the rational love of God, does its work in a communal manner. There is not a single body that can rationally claim reason as its exclusive possession; rather it forms part of the whole of humanity in every aspect of its diversity.

The mind, as reason (rather than as affect), asks us to look out for our self-interest. But the "us" in question here does not denote a singular and exclusive group. On the contrary, it describes humanity in its entirety. The mind's eternal nature thus introduces a novel conception of what it means to be a unity. As unified form, the eternity of the mind at the same time constitutes a plurality. Once a particular body perishes, the mind keeps on living in relation to the diversity of other bodies that are still alive. As unity, it thus inhabits plurality. Rather than being linear and one-dimensional, the mind as rational love of God is ever changing. This continuity of change makes for its eternity. We "live in continuous change," Spinoza affirms (*Ethics* V, P39S). Spinoza's notion of the mind as a plural, sustainable, and ever-changing unity could thus serve as a blueprint for an inclusive universalism that would be truly beneficial for the nonviolent solving of problems that global societies are facing at the dawn of the twenty-first century.

Notes

1. See Louis Althusser, "The Only Materialist Tradition, Part I: Spinoza," trans. Ted Stolze, in *The New Spinoza*, ed. Warren Montag and Ted Stolze (Minneapolis: University of Minnesota Press, 1997), 3–19; Etienne Balibar, *Spinoza and Politics*, trans. Peter Snowdown (New York: Verso, 1998); Gilles Deleuze, *Expressionism in Philosophy: Spinoza*, trans. Martin Joughin (New York: Zone Books, 1992), and Deleuze, *Spinoza: Practical Philosophy*, trans. Robert Hurley (San Francisco: City Lights Books, 1988); Antonio Negri, *The Savage Anomaly: The Power of Spinoza's Metaphysics and Politics*, trans. Michael Hardt (Minneapolis: University of Minnesota Press, 1991), and more recently, Negri, *Subversive Spinoza: (Un)contemporary variations*, ed. Timothy S. Murphy, trans. T. S. Murphy, M. Hardt, T. Stolze, and C. T. Wolfe (Manchester, U.K.: Manchester University Press, 2004); Martha C. Nussbaum, *Upheavals of Thought: The Intelligence of Emotions* (Cambridge: Cambridge University Press, 2001).
2. Michael Mack, *German Idealism and the Jew: The Inner Anti-Semitism of Philosophy and German Jewish Responses* (Chicago: University of Chicago Press, 2003).
3. Cf. Don Garrett, "Teleology in Spinoza and Early Modern Rationalism," in *New Essays on the Rationalists*, ed. Rocco J. Gennaro and Charles Huenemann, 310–35 (Oxford: Oxford University Press, 2003).
4. Stephen B. Smith, *Spinoza's Book of Life: Freedom and Redemption in the Ethics* (New Haven, Conn.: Yale University Press, 2003).
5. Suzan James, *Passion and Action: The Emotions in Seventeenth-century Philosophy* (Oxford: Clarendon Press, 1997), 106.
6. John Cottingham provides the following nuanced account of Descartes's writings about the relationship between mind and body: "Descartes, though insisting that mind and body are distinct, frequently stresses the unavoidable fact of their interaction: they are 'so closely conjoined and intermingled as to from a unity,' he wrote in the *Meditations* (AT VII. 81; CSM II. 56); and in the correspondence with Princess Elizabeth of Bohemia, he spoke of the idea of the union of mind and body as one of the fundamental notions 'on which all our other knowledge is patterned' (AT III. 665; K 457). Spinoza acknowledges that 'man consists of a mind and

body,' and that the 'human mind is united to the body' (G II. 96; c. 457). But what he means by this 'union' is very different from what Descartes meant. In the preface to Part V of the *Ethics* he pours scorn on the notion of any sort of 'interaction' between mind and brain, of the sort which Descartes envisaged in his account of the role of the pineal gland"; Cottingham, *The Rationalists* (Oxford: Oxford University Press, 1990), 131.
7   Cottingham, *Rationalists*, 132.
8   Steven Nadler, *Spinoza's Ethics: An Introduction* (Cambridge: Cambridge University Press, 2006), 135.
9   Ibid., 199.
10 In this way, Spinoza's *Ethics* seems to anticipate the austerity of Kant's categorical imperative: "Like Kant's categorical (moral) imperative, the dictates of reason transcend personal differences and make universal demands on human behaviour." Ibid., 227.
11 Smith, *Spinoza's Book of Life*, 52.
12 Ibid., 80.
13 In the preface, Smith makes clear that this is the agenda of his inquiry: "I am not interested in the *Ethics* because it helps to confirm contemporary opinions and points of view, but because it challenges them." Ibid., xii.
14 Antonio Damasio, *Descartes' Error: Emotion, Reason, and the Human Brain* (New York: Grosset/Putnam, 1994), and Damasio, *Looking for Spinoza: Joy, Sorrow, and the Feeling Brain* (London: Harcourt, 2003).
15 "Darkly, through the glass of his unsentimental and unvarnished sentences, Spinoza apparently had gleaned an architecture of life regulation along the lines that William James, Claude Bernard, and Sigmund Freud would pursue two centuries later. Moreover, by refusing to recognize a purposeful design in nature, and by conceiving of bodies and minds as made up of components that could be combined in varied patterns across different species, Spinoza was compatible with Charles Darwin's evolutionary thinking." Ibid., 13.
16 Ibid., 171.
17 For an analysis of racism in terms of defense mechanisms, see Michael P. Levine, "Philosophy and Racism," in *Racism in the Mind*, ed. M. P. Levine and T. Pataki, 78–96 (Ithaca, N.Y.: Cornell University Press, 2004).

18 Shmuel Feiner, *The Jewish Enlightenment*, trans. Chaya Naor (Philadelphia: University of Pennsylvania Press, 2004), 714.

19 René Descartes, *Discourse on Method and Meditations on First Philosophy*, ed. David Weissman, with essays by William T. Bluhm, Lou Massa, Thomas Pavel, John F. Post, and Stephen Toulmin (New Haven, Conn.: Yale University Press, 1996), 19.

20 Jean-Luc Marion, *Cartesian Questions: Method and Metaphysics* (Chicago: University of Chicago Press, 1999), 91.

21 Ibid.

22 Ibid., 95

23 Ibid.

24 Descartes, *Discourse on Method*, 50.

25 Jonathan Israel as well as Steven Nadler rightly emphasize Spinoza's democratic outlook. Nadler argues that Spinoza's support of democracy is one of the reasons why he originally set out to ensure that a Dutch translation of the *Ethics* was available: "Despite the difficulties of the book [i.e., the *Ethics*], Spinoza clearly believed that anyone—and we are all endowed with the same cognitive faculties—with sufficient self-mastery and intellectual attentiveness can perceive the truth to the highest degree. This is probably the reason why he seems from the start to have wanted to make sure that a Dutch translation of the *Ethics* was available, so that 'the truth' would be accessible for many. For it is our natural *eudaimonia*, our happiness or well-being, that is at stake, and for Spinoza this consists in the knowledge embodied in the propositions of the *Ethics*." Steven Nadler, *Spinoza: A Life* (Cambridge: Cambridge University Press, 1999), 226–27.

26 The English edition of the *Ethics* used here is *Spinoza, Ethics*, ed. and trans. Edwin Curley, with an introduction by Stuart Hampshire (London: Penguin, 1996). I have also consulted the original Latin in Spinoza, *Opera*, vol. 2, ed. Carl Gebhardt (Heidelberg, Germany: Carl Winter, 1925).

27 As Philip Goodchild has recently argued, this sense of human limitation is rational: "For to be rational today is to pay attention to the universal limits of human experience. The truth of common experience is the ecological limit, the suffering of the planet. The truth of the cause of this suffering is the socio-economic limit, the capture of piety by uncontrolled global free-market capitalism."

Goodchild, *Capitalism and Religion: The Price of Piety* (London: Routledge, 2002), 252.

28 For a detailed discussion of this topic, see Michael Mack, *Anthropology as Memory: Elias Canetti's and Franz Baermann Steiner's Responses to the Shoah* (Tübingen, Germany: Niemeyer, 2001).

29 Elias Canetti, "Gespräch mit Theodor W. Adorno," in *Aufsätze, Reden, Gespräche* (Munich, Germany: Hanser, 2005), 141.

30 Giovanna Borradori, *Philosophy in a Time of Terror: Dialogues with Jürgen Habermas and Jacques Derrida* (Chicago: University of Chicago Press, 2003), 94.

31 Cf. Michael Mack, "The Metaphysics of Eating: Jewish Dietary Law and Hegel's Social Theory," *Philosophy and Social Criticism* 27, no. 5 (2001): 59–88.

32 Balibar thus points out that "the concept which is used here to differentiate between the individual's singularity and the singularity of a historically constituted group is *the same* as that which was earlier used to express the essence of the individual's singularity *(ingenium).*" Balibar, *Spinoza and Politics*, 37.

33 Jerome B. Schneewind, *The Invention of Autonomy: A History of Modern Moral Philosophy* (Cambridge: Cambridge University Press, 1998), 221.

34 This Spinozan understanding of virtue as not opposed to but as emerging from nature has special significance with respect to the globalization conflict within the twenty-first century. The ideology of morality that governs the discourse of Islamic fundamentalism performs the violent imposition of "the good and thus Godly" onto the perceived depravity of the West's naturelike materialism.

35 As Leo Strauss convincingly argues, Hobbes's political philosophy presupposes dualism: "The idea of civilization presupposes that man, by virtue of his intelligence, can place himself outside nature, can rebel against nature. This dualism is transparent all the way through Hobbes' philosophy, not least in the antithesis of *status naturalis* and *status civilis.*" Strauss, *The Political Philosophy of Hobbes: Its Basis and Its Genesis*, trans. Elsa M. Sinclair (Chicago: University of Chicago Press, 1952), 168.

36 Ibid., 23.

37 "Whereas Spinoza, who is in this respect fully in line with the Averroist tradition, indeed takes the trend of this tradition to the ultimate

conclusion, could not but recognize religion as an essential means for the maintenance of the state, in Hobbes' theory of the sate there is no point of union which could serve for a similar defense of religion." Leo Strauss, *Spinoza's Critique of Religion*, trans. E. M. Sinclair (Chicago: University of Chicago Press, 1997), 101.

38 Ibid.

39 Schneewind, *Invention of Autonomy*, 222.

40 Blumenberg argues that the nominalism of late Scholasticism distances itself from a biblical understanding of God. It subscribes to Aristotle's understanding of an "unmoved mover," whereas the Bible depicts God as always being engaged with humanity. According to Blumenberg, Descartes turns this view of a transcendent absolute into the sphere of immanence. The cogito ergo sum thus instantiates the emergence of the human as the immanent unmoved mover. Against this background, Blumenberg accounts for the two-faced character of the Enlightenment. It is at once teleological (thus clinging to a great design theory that inhabits a certain theological sphere) and atheistic: "The provocation of the *transcendent* absolute at the point of its extreme radicalization transmutes into the discovery of the *immanent* absolute.... The Janus face of the Enlightenment—its renewal of a teleological optimism, on the one hand, and its atheistic inclination, on the other—loses its contradictoriness, if one understands it as the unity of the attempt at both human self-affirmation and the rejection of its role in the system of the late Middle Ages." Hans Blumenberg, *Säkularisierung und Selbstbehauptung* (Frankfurt, Germany: Suhrkamp, 1974), 209–11; my translation.

41 Michael Allen Gillespie, *Nihilism before Nietzsche* (Chicago: University of Chicago Press, 1995), 33.

42 Cf. Warren Montag, *Bodies, Masses, Power: Spinoza and His Contemporaries* (New York: Verson, 1999), and Moira Gatens and Genevieve Lloyd, *Collective Imaginings: Spinoza, Past and Present* (New York: Routledge, 1999).

43 For a detailed discussion of this point, see Mack, *Anthropology as Memory*, 25–29.

44 In the Preface of Book V of the *Ethics*, Spinoza emphasizes this philosophical trajectory that connects Descartes with the Stoics as follows: "Here, then, as I have said, I shall treat only of the

power of the mind, or of reason, and shall show, above all, how great its dominion over the affects is and what kind of dominion it has for restraining and moderating them: For we have already demonstrated above that it does not have an absolute dominion over them: Nevertheless, the Stoics thought that they depend entirely on our will, and that we can command them absolutely: But experience cries out against this, and has forced them, in spite of their principles, to confess that much practice and application are required to restrain and moderate them. . . . Descartes was rather inclined to this opinion."

45 As Damasio has shown, the identification of the brain with the mind in direct opposition to the merely bodily has until recently been the accepted creed as regards the perception of human intelligence: "And so, perhaps for most scientists working on mind and brain, the fact that the mind depends closely on the workings of the brain is no longer in question. . . . Uncovering a causative nexus from brain to mind, and a dependence of mind on brain, is good news, of course, but we should recognize that we have not yet elucidated the mind–body problem satisfactorily, and that the enterprise faces several hurdles, large and small. At least one of those hurdles could be overcome with a simple change of perspective. The hurdle relates to a curious situation: While the modern scientific coupling of brain and mind is most welcome, it does not do away with the dualistic split between mind and body. It simply shifts the position of the split. In the most popular and current of the modern views, the mind and the brain go together, on one side, and the body (that is, the entire organism minus the brain) goes on the other side." Damasio, *Looking for Spinoza*, 190.

46 Deleuze, *Expressionism in Philosophy*, 270.

47 Spinoza, *The Correspondence of Spinoza*, trans. and ed. with introduction and annotations by A. Wolf (London: George Allen and Unwin, 1928), 147.

48 This is why Deleuze, with his Nietzschean opposition between good and bad, might partially reinstate the hierarchical structure that Spinoza critiqued in his analysis of the dichotomy between good and evil. In Deleuze's account of Spinoza, evil seems to reemerge with the abstract and universal concept of badness: "All evil comes down to badness, and everything that is bad belongs to the category

that includes poison, indigestion, intoxication." Deleuze, *Spinoza: Practical Philosophy*, 72.

49 As Nadler has pointed out, Spinoza studied "Hobbes' political writings, especially the Dutch (1667) or Latin (1668) translation of *Leviathan*" in the early 1670s. Nadler, *Spinoza's Ethics*, 244.

50 Nadler has argued that "like Hobbes's state of nature, Spinoza's prepolitical condition is one of unrestrained pursuit of self-interest." Ibid., 245. It is with such an interpretation of Spinoza's notion of nature that the current chapter takes issue.

51 Spinoza, *Correspondence of Spinoza*, 205.

52 Deleuze, *Spinoza: Practical Philosophy*, 42.

53 Ibid., 126.

54 Ibid., 128.

55 As Philip Goodchild has pointed out, this is why Deleuze "attributed to Spinoza the discovery of an unconscious of thought: there is always a thought that acts or thinks, but does not know itself." Goodchild, *Capitalism and Religion*, 157.

56 Borradori, *Philosophy in a Time of Terror*, 94.

57 Ibid., 99.

58 Aaron V. Garret, *Meaning in Spinoza's Method* (Cambridge: Cambridge University Press, 2003), 195.

59 Thus Garret defines interconnectedness as the hallmark of Spinoza's philosophical approach: "That this is the case, i.e. that apparently unrelated concepts are interconnected in often surprising ways is itself one of the hallmarks of Spinoza's method." Ibid., 18.

6

Prophecy without Prophets: Spinoza and Maimonides on Law and the Democracy of Knowledge

ARTHUR J. JACOBSON

AT TWO DIFFERENT POINTS in his *Tractatus Theologico-Politicus,* Spinoza takes what appear to be contrary positions on the status of the "propagators" of "natural knowledge." He asks whether they might fairly be called prophets. In chapter 1, "Of Prophecy," Spinoza takes care to deny that they are prophets, though the knowledge they propagate surely is prophecy, according to Spinoza's definition of prophecy at the beginning of the chapter. In chapter 7, "Of the Interpretation of Scripture," he takes a position apparently unrelated to the propagators of natural knowledge that forces us, by implication, to consider whether they may be prophets of a kind after all. This essay explores the tension between these positions and a comparable tension in Maimonides's writings on the laws of prophecy.

In chapter 1 of the *Tractatus,* Spinoza denies that the propagators of natural knowledge are prophets.[1] He has just finished arguing that natural knowledge itself can indeed be called prophecy, according to the definition of prophecy as "the certain knowledge of some thing revealed by God to a human being."[2] From this definition, it follows, he says, "that natural knowledge can be called prophecy. For that which we know by natural light depends solely on the knowledge of God and his eternal decrees. . . . The nature of God, insofar as we participate in it, and God's decrees dictate, as it were, [natural knowledge] to us."³ In the same way, God, according to rabbinic tradition, dictated the Five Books to Moses. The revelation of natural knowledge, Spinoza believes, is no different. Furthermore, natural knowledge is certain; we can know whether we know. "For the idea of God (in the manner I have indicated) and nature dictates to us all that we clearly and distinctly understand, certainly not in words but in a far more excellent manner, one that agrees exceedingly well with the nature of mind, as everyone who has tasted intellectual certainty has doubtless experienced on his own." The only difference between natural knowledge and other sorts of prophecy is the means by which it is conveyed, through "natural light" rather than in a vision or by direct, face-to-face communication with God.

But this one difference, the means of conveyance, defies our usual ideas about prophets. Because God conveys natural knowledge to us through natural light, and because natural light is "common to all human beings,"⁴ then natural knowledge, unlike any other sort of prophecy, must be common to all human beings as well. Here Spinoza must confront the question, given that natural knowledge is divine and its communication to human beings prophecy, must we consider every human being a prophet?

Yet Spinoza immediately draws back from the question, seeming to deny his assertion that natural knowledge is "common to all human beings." Instead of asking whether all human beings are prophets— the question he must be asking if natural knowledge is indeed to be common to all—he asks whether the *propagators* of natural knowledge are prophets.⁵ By posing this question narrowly, and by not asking the more general question that the argument requires, Spinoza implicitly denies that *all* human beings receive natural knowledge as a direct communication from God. Only some do: only those who propagate (or are capable of propagating) natural knowledge. The others, who do not (and cannot) propagate, must not be able to receive natural knowledge directly, as a divine communication. Otherwise, if they could receive natural knowledge directly, they either would or could also propagate that knowledge and thus be included in the class of propagators. And if no one were in the class of those who lack direct access to natural knowledge, then none could be in the class of propagators: no one could propagate because propagation entails the dissemination of knowledge by those who have it to those who don't—it assumes the simultaneous existence of both those who lack direct access and those who have it.

But Spinoza's implicit division of all humanity into two classes this way—those who receive natural knowledge directly from God and those who don't—poses a question in answer to which Spinoza stakes out a clear and unequivocal position: are those who can't receive natural knowledge directly from God able to know whether the knowledge that the propagators communicate to them is indeed natural knowledge, or whether it is knowledge of another sort, or whether it is even knowledge? For these indirect recipients of natural knowledge have no direct access to God, no certain template against which to measure the verity and accuracy of the propagators' knowledge. Even worse, they have no way of telling who is an authentic propagator, someone genuinely receiving direct communications from God, and who is not—one who either deceives himself into thinking that he is an authentic propagator or deceives others into thinking that he is, knowing full well that he is not.

Spinoza's answer to this question is that the "rest of humanity"—the recipients of natural knowledge indirectly through propagators rather than directly from God—"are able to perceive and consider what [the propagators] teach with a certainty and dignity equal to theirs, and this not only through faith."[6] That is to say, they are able to tell whether the knowledge they receive at second hand is or is not genuine natural knowledge, despite the fact that the knowledge they receive from propagators is in words and images, unlike the form in which the propagators receive knowledge, as divine intuition.[7] Moreover, the rest of humanity has this ability as against propagators, even though they do not have it as against God. In other words, they are able to tell what is and what is not genuine natural knowledge when propagators present it to them in the form of a report—in words and images—but they are unable to form an intuition of the knowledge apart from the report. They have the intuition against which to judge the verity and accuracy of a propagator's report, but not otherwise. They are handicapped in their access to natural knowledge but not in their certainty about its truth.

Whether this portrait of the variable relationship of human beings to natural knowledge is either attractive or accurate, it does, in Spinoza's view, settle the question whether the propagators of natural knowledge can be considered prophets. They cannot.[8] For Spinoza, direct access to divine intuition does not mark one off from the rest of humanity as a prophet. The rest of humanity can "perceive and consider what they teach with a certainty and dignity equal to theirs, and this not only through faith." Only if the rest of humanity could not perceive and consider the teachings of propagators, only if the relationship between the rest of humanity and the propagators were a relationship of faith, would it be proper to call the propagators prophets. Prophecy requires faith; natural knowledge does not.

Then later, in chapter 7, Spinoza criticizes Maimonides's view on the proper method of scriptural interpretation and defends his own view against it. Spinoza's view, which I shall not elaborate, is that "the method of interpreting Scripture is no different from the method of interpreting nature."[9] The interpreter must treat the text as a mass of data, just as the scientist looks at nature. The interpreter understands a text, just as the scientist understands laws that make sense of data. The text creates its own laws, its own peculiar nature, and these laws need have nothing whatsoever to do with the laws of nature, the laws of reason, or the laws of any other text or any possible world. The text may be understood, nonetheless, just the way one understands nature—looking at the text as it is, taking the text on its own terms, grasping the laws the text lays down just as one would grasp the laws that the orbits of the planets lay down, or the growth of a plant, or the combustion of a wick exposed to fire. It is the natural light and no other that illuminates these laws of the text, just as it illuminates the laws of physics, or biology, or chemistry.[10]

Against his own method, Spinoza arrays a host of difficulties that he acknowledges to be genuine. He then presents and criticizes opposing views. Chief among these is Maimonides's view, which subjects every passage of scripture to the test of reason: "For he thought every passage of Scripture to admit various—indeed contrary—senses, and us not to be certain about the truth of any, unless we know that passage, exactly as it is interpreted, to contain nothing which does not agree with reason or is incompatible with it."[11] Subjecting the text to the laws of reason, however, prevents one from using natural light to understand the text. For a text not designed specifically according to the laws of reason but according to a different set of laws does not and cannot yield to the laws of reason on their own terms. A light other than the natural light (*"alio praeter lumen naturale"*[12]) would have to be the route to understanding.

But then, the signal quality of the natural light, that it is "common to all human beings," would be lost. No other light has that quality. Every other light is artificial, not natural. The reasoning appropriate to every other light is artificial reason. Its proofs are artificial proofs according to artificial criteria of truth. It requires demonstrations (*demonstrationes*) rather than immediate intuitions. Every other light must be cultivated and transmitted in a costly program of research and education. Basing interpretation on a light other than the natural light, therefore, has the following consequence:

> If this opinion were true [that the passages of scripture must agree with reason], then, it would follow that the vulgar, who are for the most part ignorant of demonstrations, or lack the leisure for them, would be able to accept nothing concerning Scripture but from the sole authority and testimony of the philosophers, and consequently will have to assume that philosophers are unable to err in their interpretations of Scripture, which certainly would be novel authority for a church and an extraordinary class of priests or pontiffs, which the vulgar would rather ridicule than venerate.[13]

Spinoza's method, at least in principle, requires none of this:

> And although our method requires knowledge of the Hebrew language, for the study of which the vulgar are likewise unable to be free, yet they can make no similar objection to us. For the vulgar of the Jews and Gentiles, for whom the prophets and Apostles once preached and wrote, understood the language of the prophets and Apostles, from which they actually perceived the mind of the prophets, but not the justifications of the things they preach, which according to the opinion of Maimonides they ought to understand as well. From the justification of our method it does not necessarily follow that the vulgar submit to the testimony of interpreters. For I display a people [*vulgus*] that is skilled in the

language of the prophets and Apostles, but Maimonides displays no people that understands the reasons of things.[14]

The importance of this last passage is structural. Its structure is the same as the structure of Spinoza's argument in chapter 1 about the propagators of natural knowledge. The vulgar today cannot in fact understand the language of the prophets and the Apostles because the prophets and Apostles spoke Hebrew,[15] which is not the language today. The only people today who can understand the language of the prophets and Apostles are the few who have adequate leisure and incentive to master Hebrew. So, in fact, the vulgar today must rely on interpreters to learn the message of the prophets and Apostles. In fact, they are as if Maimonides's opinion concerning the interpretation of scripture were true: they "would be able to accept nothing concerning Scripture but from the sole authority and testimony of" an intermediary between them and the text. Whether the intermediary is a philosopher or a translator makes no difference. In both cases, the intermediary claims an expertise—one in philosophy, the other in translation—that opens the door to a meaning inaccessible without that expertise. Nevertheless, there is this difference: the vulgar cannot ridicule the authority of a translator in the same way they can ridicule the authority of a philosopher. The translator is not open to the objection that confounds the philosopher, that neither prophets nor Apostles could possibly have been speaking philosophically because they were speaking to the vulgar, and the vulgar in their day would have understood philosophy no better than the vulgar in ours. Because the message of the prophets and Apostles was once accessible to the vulgar, it must in principle be accessible to them today—they would understand the message if they knew the language in which it was written. But the message is not accessible because they don't. That is the structure presented by Spinoza's description of the relationship between biblical text and the vulgar. The vulgar must, in principle, be able to understand biblical text, but in fact, they cannot. A translator must mediate their relationship to the text.

Putting aside once again the merits of Spinoza's argument, notice instead the similarity of this structure—understand in principle, require mediators in fact—to the structure Spinoza sets up in chapter 1.

There the "rest of humanity"—those to whom the propagators of natural knowledge propagate—have complete access to natural knowledge in principle. In fact, they do not. With respect to at least some part of natural knowledge, they are forced to rely on the report of propagators, who do have complete access. The propagators of natural knowledge have an expertise, just like Maimonides's philosophers or Spinoza's translators. The beneficiaries of that expertise, like all beneficiaries of all expertise, are forced to submit to the propagators' "authority and testimony."

In Spinoza's account at least, the sole difference between the propagators and the philosophers and translators is that Spinoza assumes that those with an incomplete knowledge of God are able to distinguish a false from a true report as adequately as if they had a complete knowledge of God. The reader of a translation who does not know the language from which the text has been translated, in contrast, cannot tell whether the translation is faithful or faithless. Translators themselves could not necessarily agree what a faithful translation would be in the first place. The same holds true for the work product of the philosopher. How could the philosophically illiterate know whether a philosopher's interpretation of a passage in the Bible is philosophically sound? Would philosophers ever agree, after all, on what philosophical soundness entails?

In the end, the difference is an illusory one. Given enough time and motivation, the reader of a translation could master the original's language and then be in a position to judge, or at least have an opinion about, the adequacy of a translation. A philosophical illiterate, assuming enough raw intelligence, could become adept in the ways of philosophy and be able to assess the adequacy of a philosopher's interpretation. The disability for both is a disability of circumstance only. It is not a profound disability. Nothing stops either from getting up to speed. The matter stands quite differently for the propagators' audience, those without complete access to natural knowledge. Their disability is hard-wired into their natures: "The nature of God, insofar as we participate in it, and God's decrees dictate, as it were, [natural knowledge] to us."[16] Their disability is one of God's laws. Like certain students of philosophy, they cannot, even in principle, get up to speed. What rescues them from utter dependence on the propagators is Spinoza's assumption that they "are able to perceive and consider what [the propagators] teach with a certainty and dignity equal to theirs, and this not only through faith."[17] Avoiding mastery and subjection depends on this assumption alone.

Spinoza's attack on Maimonides's doctrine of interpretation is thematic for the entire *Tractatus*. The argument of the *Tractatus* is a rejection of Maimonides's insistence on reconciling scripture with the best opinions in science. It is this insistence—that a text whose pitch and pith are ethical also establishes the foundations of philosophy and the sources of science—that causes all the trouble. It is this insistence that leads governments to tell philosophers what to think and philosophers to shrink from the truths of science. It did not ameliorate Maimonides's error, in Spinoza's view, that his intentions toward philosophy were as benevolent as his own. Maimonides was setting up his stand in the wrong market, and in the end, his efforts to reconcile scripture with philosophy could cause only mischief to both. Spinoza's project, therefore, was to defeat Maimonides's endeavor in all its manifold variations, whether benevolent or not, by forever (he vainly hoped) severing the connection between scripture and science. The greater the wonder, then, that the ambivalent structure of Spinoza's thinking about prophecy had its origin—or if not its origin, then its original—in Maimonides's own writings.

In the first part of his *Mishneh Torah* (Repetition of Torah)—*Hilchot Yesodei HaTorah* (Laws That Are Foundations of the Torah)—Maimonides describes the laws of prophecy (in chapter 7). (His *Guide of the Perplexed* describes the philosophy of prophecy.)[18] Commenting on the first law *(halachah)*,[19] Maimonides reviews the physical and spiritual preconditions for prophecy. One who would be a prophet must, first of all, be a very wise sage. He must have a strong character, in the sense that he is never overcome by natural inclinations.[20] He must be physically sound. He must have a "broad and correct" perspective to understand the "great and sublime" concepts of spiritual knowledge. If so, he will become holy. "He will advance and separate himself from the masses who proceed in the darkness of the time." He must train himself not to have thoughts about "fruitless things or the vanities and intrigues of the times."

> Instead, his mind should constantly be directed upward, bound beneath [God's] throne [of Glory, striving] to comprehend the

holy and pure forms and gazing at the wisdom of the Holy One, blessed be He, in its entirety, [in its manifold manifestations] from the most elevated [spiritual] form until the navel of the earth, appreciating His greatness from them. [After these preparations,] the spirit of prophecy will immediately rest upon him.[21]

Commentary to the first *halachah* closes with an explanation of "spirit of prophecy." When the spirit of prophecy rests on someone, his soul becomes "intermingled" with the lowest order of angels, the *ishim*. He will be transformed into a different person, understanding with a knowledge different from what it was previously. He is already "above the level of the other wise men"[22] and "separate . . . from the masses,"[23] even before he has uttered a single prophecy.

For he is not yet a prophet, even though the spirit of prophecy rests on his soul. He is only "a disciple of the prophets," one who aspires to prophecy, a candidate prophet. Once the spirit of prophecy rests on them, disciples must in addition concentrate their attention if they wish to prophesy. They must "seclude themselves, [waiting] in a happy, joyous mood, because prophecy cannot rest upon a person when he is sad or languid, but only when he is happy. Thus, the prophets' disciples would always have a harp, drum, flute, and lyre [before them when] they were seeking prophecy."[24] Even then, prophecy is not guaranteed: "Even though [the disciples] concentrate their attention, it is possible that the Divine Presence will rest upon them, and it is possible that it will not rest upon them."[25]

This was not the case for only one prophet. Moses could elect when to prophesy, without preparation:

> Whenever he desired, the holy spirit would envelop him, and prophecy would rest upon him. He did not have to concentrate his attention to prepare himself [for prophecy], because his [mind] was always concentrated, prepared, and ready [to appreciate spiritual truth] as the angels [are].[26]

Moses's prophecy differs from that of all the other prophets in other ways. Other prophets received prophetic insight in the form of a dream or a vision. Moses prophesied while standing awake. The others prophesied through the medium of an angel. Moses spoke with God "mouth to mouth."²⁷ The others received prophecy in the form of an allegory or metaphor, together with the meaning. For Moses, says Maimonides, "there was no metaphor. Rather, he would perceive the matter in its fullness, without metaphor or allegory."²⁸ The other prophets were terrified as they prophesied. God spoke to Moses as a man speaks to a friend. "Moses' mental power was sufficient to comprehend the words of prophecy while he was standing in a composed state."²⁹ The other prophets experienced prophecy as something of a nightmare: "When any of them prophesy, their limbs tremble, their physical powers become weak, they lose control of their senses, and thus, their minds are free to comprehend what they see."³⁰ In contrast, Moses's permanent seclusion allowed him to be permanently in a heightened state of consciousness, ready for prophecy; he never returned to his "tent": "he separated himself from women and everything of that nature forever. He bound his mind to the Eternal Rock. [Accordingly,] the glory never left him forever. The flesh of his countenance shone, [for] he became holy like the angels."³¹

Maimonides thus sets up a contrast reminiscent of Spinoza's in the *Tractatus*: on one hand, Moses, who has unlimited, certain access to divine communication, on the other, the disciples of the prophets, whose access to divine communication is limited and uncertain. The contrast Spinoza sets up is between two groups, both of which have unlimited access to natural knowledge in principle, but only one of which has it in fact. Can the same be said of the disciples of the prophets: that they have unlimited access in principle, even though Maimonides makes it clear that they do not have it in practice? Does, in other words, possession of the spirit of prophecy qualify the disciples of the prophets as having unlimited access in principle?

Maimonides begins to answer this question in Halachah 7, at the very end of chapter 7. In Halachah 7, he describes the uses of prophecy. A prophet may experience prophecy, he says, just to broaden his own perspective and increase his own knowledge. Or he may be sent to a community to tell them what they should do or to stop them from doing evil. In the latter case, where prophecy performs its political rather than its intellectual function, the prophet is always "given a sign or wonder [to perform], so that the people will know that God has truly sent him."³² But fitness for prophecy—

great wisdom, a strong character, a broad and correct perspective, physical soundness—all these must be present beforehand. If they are not, the person who performs the signs or wonders should not "be accepted as a prophet." If, on the other hand, they are present in someone who "follows the paths of prophecy in holiness, separating himself from worldly matters, and afterwards performs a sign or wonder and states that he was sent by God, it is a mitzvah to listen to him."[33] (A *mitzvah* is a "Torah obligation," or alternatively, a "good deed.")

However, even if a person is fit for prophecy, even if he performs signs or wonders, he still may not be a true prophet. "It is possible that a person will perform a sign or wonder even though he is not a prophet—rather, the wonder will have [another cause] behind it. It is, nevertheless, a mitzvah to listen to him. Since he is a wise man of stature and fit for prophecy, we accept [his prophecy as true]."[34] Notice that Maimonides switches here from speaking about signs or wonders, as if it is all the same whether one is dealing with a sign or with a wonder, to speaking about wonders alone. It is only wonders that he describes as potentially having a cause other than true prophecy. (Only in Halachah 1, chapter 8, do we learn just exactly what this other cause may be, and that is magic or sorcery.[35]) Maimonides doesn't say the same about signs. The question that Maimonides's extraordinary switch from signs and wonders to wonders alone begs the reader to ask is whether confinement of the possibility of non-prophetic causation to wonders is significant, that is to say, whether signs are necessarily perfect indicia of prophetic causation and do not suffer from the same defect in trustworthiness as wonders. That question is sufficiently important to justify interrupting the exposition of Halachah 7, chapter 7, with an answer.

What does Maimonides mean by *sign*? What does he mean by *wonder*? We have to read all the way to chapter 10 to find out. There Maimonides suggests, albeit indirectly, that a wonder is an "alteration" in the "natural order" (literally, "customary world"; the examples he gives—Elijah and Elisha reviving the dead and so forth—make it clear that he means *wonder* to be a synonym for *miracle*, so "alteration" in the "natural order" is a suitable translation).[36] But then he suggests a meaning for *sign* entirely unexpected from the perspective of the discussion in Halachah 7, chapter 7. When a prophet tells us that God has sent him, says Maimonides, he does not have to prove himself by performing wonders like those of Elijah or Elisha, which altered the natural order:

> Rather, the sign of [the truth of his prophecy] will be the fulfillment of his prediction of future events.... Therefore, if a person whose [progress] in the service of God makes him fit for prophecy arises [and claims to be a prophet]—if he does not intend to add [to] or diminish [the Torah], but rather to serve God through the mitzvoth of the Torah—we do not tell him: "Split the sea for us, revive the dead, or the like, and then we will believe in you." Instead, we tell him, "If you are a prophet, tell us what will happen in the future." He makes his statements, and we wait to see whether [his "prophecy"] comes to fruition or not.[37]

If his prophecy does not come true, then he is a false prophet and subject to the death penalty. (A salubrious rule, on the whole. We would do well to apply it to our pundits.) Maimonides tells us to test the prophet many times. But if all his statements prove true, he should be considered a true prophet.[38] A prophet who qualifies this way, by predicting the future, is limited to just one purpose in prophesying—predicting the future—and the future may be a political future or a personal future; it doesn't matter which.[39] So the sign coincides with the prophecy: the prophet's ability to predict the future is a sign of his ability to predict the future. A prophet who qualifies in other ways is apparently not so limited.

It is apparent from Maimonides's text that he does not regard predicting the future as the only sort of sign. In Halachah 2, chapter 8, he describes Moses as knowing that one who believes in a prophet because of signs "has apprehension in his heart, and that he has doubts and suspicions."[40] (In Halachah 1, chapter 8, Maimonides had already described wonders that way.) The sign could be the result of magic or sorcery, not prophecy.[41] Moses therefore asked God to release him from his mission—taking the Israelite slaves out of Egypt. God answers that the *wonders* Moses was able to pull off in Egypt were only a temporary expedient. (Note that Moses had complained about doubtful signs, not wonders.) Once out, the people would stand on the mountain and all doubts would be removed: "Here, I will give you a sign," Maimonides quotes God as telling Moses, "so that they will know that I truly sent you from the outset, and thus, no doubts will remain in their hearts."[42] Thus Maimonides takes care to describe the event that will remove all doubt from the people—their witnessing God speaking to Moses at the foot of Mount Sinai—as a sign, not as a wonder.

Furthermore, it is important to compare the two sorts of signs described by Maimonides. The sign in Halachah 3, chapter 10, involves action by candidate prophets: predicting the future. If a candidate predicts the future accurately, that is a sign that he is a prophet. This sign has two prominent characteristics. First, there's no uncertainty about the sign: the candidate predicts the future, and he's either right or wrong. Second, the prediction concerns events in this world: people doing this or that, storms coming up, objects in certain places, and so on. All the events involved in predicting the future can be described in a natural way; they are movements within nature. Thus the prophetic predictions are predictions about nature. They show a heightened level of consciousness about nature, whether physical nature, animal nature, or human nature. Prediction is always premised on nature. That's what *nature* means: predictable. In contrast, the sign that God gives Moses in Halachah 2, chapter 8, involves God's action: speaking to Moses in front of the assembled throng. It is not an action of the prophet. It is the natural manifestation of a supernatural agent, the people experiencing God as a voice that could be heard. Thus, with Moses, they were able to bear witness to a natural event, whose cause, however, could not be attributed to any natural agent but only to a divine agent. In both instances, the sign was part of nature and therefore certain. In the case of the ordinary prophet, certainty means the coming into being of the future; in the case of Moses, it means the coming into being of God's agency.

Unlike wonders, therefore, signs impart certainty, precisely because they follow rather than usurp the ordinary course of nature.[43] Signs are also obvious. They proclaim that for which they are signs. Wonders, in contrast, do not. Thus predicting the future is a sign of success for predicting the future. Talking with God is a sign of talking with God. Signs are the course of nature. Wonders are a departure from it. Wonders and signs thus describe two different routes to prophecy: one a disruption of the natural order, the other an extension of it, either into the future or into the realm of the divine.

We may now return to the exposition of Halachah 7, chapter 7. After describing the uses of prophecy, the qualifications of prophets, and the inherent uncertainty of prophecy qualified by wonders, Maimonides argues for accepting as true the statements of "a wise man of stature and fit for prophecy" who has performed a sign or wonder, even though he may not, in fact, be a prophet. One question we shall have to face is whether each of the arguments applies to both signs and wonders or to wonders alone because Maimonides qualifies the general reference to signs and wonders by saying that wonders may have a cause other than prophecy, without saying the same about signs.

The first argument suggests a legal analogy (we do it there, so we can do it here too: this is not a practice unknown in other parts of the legal system). The Torah commands rendition of a legal judgment based on the testimony of two witnesses. Both may, in fact, be testifying falsely. But if the witnesses are "acceptable," then the law presumes that they are telling the truth.[44] "Each one serves as a witness to his colleague that he is telling the truth."[45] In other words, we know that in a certain number of cases, both witnesses will be lying or may be mistaken. That's just the way things are. But there's nothing the law can do about it, so long as both witnesses are prepared to lie or are mistaken and so long as both are qualified witnesses. The legal system winds up treating false statements as if they were true because it has no way of knowing which statements are false. That's why it insists on two witnesses at a minimum: it's unlikely (although certainly possible) that two people would be prepared to lie in court or would tell unwitting falsehoods.

The two-witness analogy applies to at least one sort of sign because Maimonides himself applies it to that sign at the beginning of Halachah 2, chapter 8: both Moses and the entire people of Israel, he says, were witness to Moses's appointment as a prophet at Mount Sinai.[46] Had we the report of Moses alone, it would be untrustworthy: he could be lying or mistaken. Had we the report of the people alone, it would be equally untrustworthy. Moses himself must experience God as appointing him; he must have the awareness that he has been made a prophet and that he is acting as a prophet. If Moses lacks confidence in his own mission, if he slights or ignores his own prophetic vision, he will either not communicate the prophecies to the people or dissuade them from believing what they think they heard. Remember, the people are witnesses to a phenomenon out of nature, a supernatural phenomenon, a disembodied voice.

The same considerations apply to wonders. They are no different from the sign the people of Israel witnessed at Mount Sinai: both require mutual witnessing. But what of the other sort of sign: predicting the future? Do the same considerations apply in that case as well? After all, the phenomenon that the people (or person in the case of private prediction) are witnessing is an entirely natural phenomenon, a sequence of events or a thing. It requires no belief, no trust, and no suspension of disbelief. Either the prediction turns out or it does not. Of course, *relying* on the predictions of a tested prophet for the future does require some trust. What if he has lost his prophetic powers? What if he's lying to gain some private advantage? But these are the ordinary risks of ordinary life that don't require reference to prophecy, and fitness for prophecy presumably protects against their coming to pass. Furthermore, a tested prophet has a standing in the community that he would be reluctant to throw away.[47] It is not unimportant, then, that Maimonides speaks of this sort of prophecy separately, in chapter 10, and that unlike the discussions in Halachah 7, chapter 7 (applying the two-witness analogy without seeming qualification to all prophets other than Moses), and Halachah 2, chapter 8 (applying the analogy to Moses), he does not mention the analogy. So it is probable that Maimonides did not mean the analogy to apply to prophets who successfully predict the future because for these prophets, the future is its own witness.

The second argument for accepting as true the statements of "a wise man of stature and fit for prophecy" explains why the first argument is necessary: "Considering these matters and the like, [Deuteronomy 29:28] states: 'The hidden matters are for God, our Lord, but what is revealed is for us and our children,' and [I Samuel 16:7] states: 'Man sees what is revealed to the eyes, but God sees into the heart.'"[48] We do not need to see into the heart of the prophet who successfully predicts the future, except to rely on his trustworthiness as a person. But for all other prophets, we need to know who is in communication with God and who is not. If we knew that, however, then we, too, would be prophets, rendering other prophets otiose.

And that is exactly what happened to the Israelites standing with Moses at the foot of Mount Sinai. With Moses, they witnessed God prophetically; they witnessed God communicating with Moses. In that moment, in that limited way, they became prophets. This is Maimonides's argument in chapter 8, concerning the nature of Moses's prophecy. The Israelites believed in Moses, not because he performed wonders, but because they actually witnessed his appointment as a prophet. "Our eyes saw, and not a stranger's. Our ears heard, and not another's. There was fire, thunder, and lightning, He entered the thick clouds; the Voice spoke to him and we heard, 'Moses, Moses, go tell them the following.'"[49] It is at just this moment that Maimonides returns to the legal analogy first used in Halachah 7, chapter 7. He describes Moses and the people of Israel as "two witnesses who observed the same event together. Each one serves as a witness to his colleague that he is telling the truth, and neither has to bring any other proof to his colleague."[50] In the same way, Moses and all Israel were witnesses to God's communication with Moses at Mt. Sinai, and he did not have to perform any further wonders for them. Moses is the only prophet whose appointment as a prophet is absolutely certain. The people of Israel witnessed it and shared in it as prophets. The people believed in it, not because Torah obligation required them to overcome their doubts, but because they saw it with their own eyes and have no doubts.[51]

So Maimonides's answer to the question, "Do the disciples of the prophets have unlimited access to God in principle, even if they don't have it in fact?" is yes. It is our obligation to treat them as prophets if they claim to be prophets and if they can somehow muster the signs or wonders, whether by accident, or because they are magicians or sorcerers, or because they are, indeed, prophets. And we have this obligation precisely because we can never, in fact, know whether any person claiming to be a prophet is or is not a prophet, unless we ourselves share in the act of prophecy. But then we should not need prophets.

Hence the only condition under which the soundness of a claim to prophecy can be established is the condition under which everyone shares in at least a portion of the prophecy. It is a condition of a democracy of knowledge. It is a condition in which the prophet, as a special figure with unique access to prophetic knowledge, is, at least in part, unnecessary. It is, as for Spinoza, a prophecy without prophets. In all other cases, a prophet is necessary because we lack the ability to hear what God wants to tell us. In those cases, prophecy is necessarily uncertain. Then we must look to the prophet's record of wisdom, fineness of character, broad and correct perspective, and physical soundness—all excellent indicia of a likelihood that the prophet's advice is well intentioned and politically reliable, none having anything to do with what we would ordinarily consider divine communication.

Maimonides's sociology of divine knowledge thus contains three groups, in contrast to Spinoza's two. Spinoza's groups are simple enough: those who have direct access to divine knowledge in fact and those who have it only in principle. Those who have it only in principle are, nonetheless, able to recognize whether the knowledge that propagators are propagating is divine. Spinoza thus creates a democracy of knowledge in principle, an aristocracy of knowledge in fact. The democracy tempers and constrains the aristocracy, however, by insisting on the ability to judge the adequacy of the aristocracy's work.

Maimonides's groups are more complex and divide along somewhat different lines. One group comprises the disciples of the prophets—the ones who are candidates for prophecy but who may or may not, in fact, be prophets. Even though it is always doubtful that any given member of this group is a prophet, Torah law obliges one to treat him as a prophet if he lays claim to prophecy and if his statements are followed one way or the other by signs or wonders. The truth of the matter is that any particular member of this group either is or is not a prophet; we just don't know which, and never will know with any certainty.[52] So it would be quite wrong to say of any member of the group that he is, in principle, a prophet. No—he either is a prophet or he isn't a prophet, but there is no sense in which he is, in principle, a prophet. The case is quite different for the group as a whole. We treat the genus "disciple" as made up exclusively of prophets (or at least that portion of the genus "disciple" whose advice is followed by some sort of sign or wonder), knowing full well that it is not (or probably not) so constituted. We treat both species within the genus the same way, as prophets in principle or as a matter of principle. That is to say, we are unjust to the species of prophets because we do not treat them as prophets but rather as prophets in principle, and we are unjust also to ourselves, because we treat the species of nonprophets as prophets in principle, even though they are not, in fact, prophets. We ignore the question of prophecy and turn instead to questions of fitness, on one hand, and signs and wonders, on the other.

A second group is the people in general, who, unlike the disciples of the prophets, stake no claim to prophecy and do not seek it out. Many of them, lacking the requisite character, are undoubtedly unfit for prophecy; some are undoubtedly fit, without wishing to be prophets. Nonetheless, all of them, fit or unfit, became prophets en masse on one occasion, when they heard God speaking to Moses at the foot of Mount Sinai, just before he ascended the mountain for his extended sojourn with God. In a way, too, Moses was not unlike the mass of people. He, like them, did not seek out prophecy. He, like them, had character traits that one can only describe as flaws (his anger, most notably) and that would not befit another prophet. He, like them, was not fully physically sound (his stutter). The greatest of the prophets was most like the people and least like the prophets. So it is no accident that in the supreme prophetic moment in all of Torah, at Mount Sinai, Moses and the people should share at least a fragment of God's revelation: they heard a voice speaking the first two of the Ten Commandments.[53] Other than this supreme moment, the role of the people is to judge who of the many strivers for prophetic accomplishment ought to be accorded the benefit of the prophetic presumption and be treated in principle, or as a matter of principle, as a prophet. With respect to all prophets other than Moses, therefore, it is the people in the end, not God, who make the prophet. Becoming a prophet is an election, not a chrism anointing an elect.

And finally, a group of one: Moses. The people did not elect him. Alone among the prophets, God appointed him, not through signs (at least ordinary signs) or wonders but in public, in open view. Here it is important to distinguish between private and public. The private reality, the inner truth, is that some of the candidate prophets are indeed prophets, some not. Prophecy other than Moses's takes place in private, while the prophet is asleep: "When any of them prophesy, their limbs tremble, their physical powers become weak, they lose control of their senses, and thus, their minds are free to comprehend what they see."[54] It is overwhelmingly a *physical* experience. At the same time, what the prophet sees while he is asleep is a message granted to him in "metaphoric imagery." "Immediately, the interpretation of the imagery is imprinted upon his heart, and he knows its meaning."[55] The prophet knows that he is experiencing prophecy. But we don't, and we can't. Similarly, only the one who is qualified through a sign or wonder knows whether the sign or wonder is a product of prophecy or of magic and sorcery. (The prophet who is qualified by successfully predicting the future may be a sorcerer or a diviner, Maimonides says, and not a true prophet.)[56] The prophet's vision, the real cause of the sign or wonder—these are all private experiences. The prophecy itself is, in allegory or metaphor, inaccessible to the public on its own terms. Only the prophet knows its meaning, and his knowledge is private, in his heart. God gave Moses prophecies, not as visions, but "through open revelations,"[57] revelations open to all, just as they are, without privileging Moses's heart. The greatest of the prophets, the one closest to God, laid the groundwork for the democracy of knowledge.

For Maimonides, as for Spinoza, embracing a democracy of knowledge requires acquiescence in paradox. For Spinoza, the paradox is that people who have imperfect access to God's nature are assumed to be able to assess adequately the access of others whose access may or may not be perfect (or imperfect in different ways). This is the sine qua non of any democracy, the presumption that every citizen is able to assess the validity of a report of knowledge without being able to know that knowledge directly, unmediated by report. For Maimonides, the paradox is that people who cannot know who among a field of candidate prophets is a true prophet, because they cannot know whose signs or wonders are the product of prophecy and whose are the product of magic or sorcery or divination, are nonetheless able to know who is a proper candidate, whose signs or wonders are entitled to the presumption of prophecy even though he may not, in fact, be a prophet. So long as a candidate shows the requisite moral and intellectual and physical qualities, so long as he also presents himself as a prophet, people are obliged to treat him as one—*halachah* presumes that he is a prophet—even though his signs or wonders are the product of magic or sorcery or divination and he has only deluded himself into thinking, with greater or lesser faithfulness, that they are the product of prophecy instead.

Maimonides thus replaces the presence of prophetic communication—a state known with certainty only through divine knowledge—with ordinary judgments about moral, intellectual, and physical condition, together with a legal presumption connecting these judgments to the status, now made legal and no longer directly divine, of prophet. The only prophecy needing certain knowledge of divine origin, therefore, is the prophecy establishing that presumption—the prophecy of the legal system legislated by Moses—for it is the presumption that makes all other prophecy, understood now strictly as a legal status, possible. Certain divine knowledge becomes common knowledge at only one moment and for one purpose only: just before Moses ascends Mount Sinai, to establish him as the prophet of God's law.

The place of divine public knowledge in Maimonides's *Mishneh Torah* thus stands in stark contrast to its place in Spinoza's *Tractatus*. In the *Tractatus,* divine public knowledge is the knowledge of nature, of *God's* nature, of the world intelligible as law or science. It is knowledge that is available to everyone, everywhere and always, in principle, even though it is not available to them in fact. It is law *as principle* rather than law as fact. In the *Mishneh Torah,* in contrast, divine public knowledge is the knowledge of Moses's appointment as prophet. It is the knowledge of the foundation of law, of law as fact. It is not knowledge that is everywhere and always, but only here and only now. No other public knowledge is divine. This is not to deny that divine public knowledge has a place in the world. It may well. But apart from Moses's prophecy, we cannot with certainty know what that place is.

Nevertheless, the legal presumption that obliges us to accept as prophet a person of the proper moral, intellectual, and physical character who successfully predicts the future gives us what may be described as derivative or second-order divine public knowledge, by comparison with direct or first-order divine public knowledge, such as the public's knowledge of Moses's appointment. For the legal system validated by the knowledge of Moses's appointment obliges us to regard as divine successful prediction by disciples of the prophets.

The divinity of a successful prediction is certain only derivatively. Its direct divinity can only be possible, not certain.

A disciple of the prophets who successfully predicts the future may well consider his prediction to be prophecy. But if his predictions are to be predictably successful over a sustained period, what the disciple must in effect be doing is some sort, however intuitive or primitive, of political or moral or natural science, and the judgment by which the people accept or reject the disciple as a prophet is not prophetic but ordinary democratic judgment. What Maimonides describes, then, is no less than the transformation of law into science.

Spinoza says in his *Tractatus* that today, we have, so far as he knows, no prophets.[58] Maimonides would disagree. Certainly there are no miracles and no prophets qualified by wonders or by signs of the sort the people of Israel heard at the foot of Mount Sinai. But there is predicting the future, there is broadening one's own perspective and increasing one's own knowledge. Both of these are prophecy in the hands of the right person. Both are limited to the few. Neither requires miracles. So there are prophets. We just don't call them that anymore. We call them scientists and philosophers instead.

Notes

THE TRANSLATIONS of Spinoza are my own. In addition to citing Carl Gebhardt's standard Latin edition of the *Tractatus*, Spinoza, *Opera*, vol. 3 (Heidelberg, Germany: Carl Winters Universitaetsbuchhandlung, 1972), I cite page numbers for the two most widespread translations of the *Tractatus* into English: Baruch Spinoza, *Tractatus Theologico-Politicus*, trans. Samuel Shirley (Leiden, Netherlands: E. J. Brill, 1991), and Spinoza, *The Chief Works of Benedict de Spinoza*, vol. 1, trans. Robert Harvey Monro Elwes (New York: Dover, 1951). In the Gebhardt edition, I first cite the page number for the text of the *Tractatus*, then, in brackets, the page number for the volume as a whole. I would like to thank Dimitris Vardoulakis for encouragement and my wife, Peninah Petruck, for many excellent suggestions.

1. Gebhardt, 2 [16], ll. 6–7; Shirley, 60; Elwes, 14.
2. Gebhardt, 1 [15], ll. 5–6; Shirley, 60; Elwes, 13.
3. Gebhardt, 1 [15], ll. 18–20, 27–28; Shirley, 59; Elwes, 14.
4. Gebhardt, 1 [15], ll. 21–22; Shirley, 59; Elwes, 13.
5. See n. 2.
6. Gebhardt, 2 [16], ll. 7–9; Shirley, 60; Elwes, 14.
7. "And certainly from the fact that God revealed Himself to Christ or to his mind in a non-mediated way and not as to the prophets, through words and images, we are able to understand nothing other than that Christ perceived or understood revealed things truly. For a thing is understood when it is perceived by the pure mind itself, without words and images." Gebhardt, 50 [64]; Shirley, 107–8; Elwes, 64.
8. Gebhardt, 2 [16], ll. 6–7; Shirley, 60; Elwes, 14. "But, although natural knowledge is divine, its propagators cannot be called prophets. For the rest of humanity are able to perceive and consider what they teach with a certainty and dignity equal to theirs, and this not only through faith."
9. Gebhardt, 84 [98], ll. 16–18; Shirley, 141; Elwes, 99.
10. Spinoza makes this last point clear only indirectly, by characterizing its opposite in hypothetical terms only. See Gebhardt, 100 [114], ll. 17–24; Shirley, 157; Elwes, 116.

11 Gebhardt, 99 [113], ll. 7–11; Shirley, 156; Elwes, 114–15.
12 Gebhardt, 100 [114], ll. 18–19; Shirley, 157; Elwes, 116.
13 Gebhardt, 100 [114], ll. 24–31; Shirley, 157; Elwes, 116.
14 Gebhardt, 100 [114], l. 31; 101 [115], l. 8; Shirley, 157; Elwes, 116.
15 The Apostles were, of course, speaking Aramaic, not Hebrew.
16 Gebhardt, 1 [15], ll. 27–28; Shirley, 59; Elwes, 14.
17 Gebhardt, 2 [16], ll. 7–9; Shirley, 60; Elwes, 14.
18 Maimonides meant his *Guide* to reconcile those troubled by science to religious orthodoxy. Spinoza meant his *Tractatus* to reconcile those troubled by religious orthodoxy to science. Spinoza thus conceived of his *Tractatus* as the anti-*Guide*.
19 "It is one of the foundations of our faith that God communicates by prophecy with man." Chapter 7, Halachah 1, 244.
20 Ibid., 244–46.
21 Ibid., 246. Words in brackets in the translations of Maimonides's text are in brackets in the original translation. They indicate editorial additions in the interests of clarity.
22 Ibid., 248.
23 Ibid., 246.
24 Chapter 7, Halachah 4, 250–52.
25 Chapter 7, Halachah 5, 252.
26 Chapter 7, Halachah 6, 256.
27 Numbers 12: 8. Ibid., 254.
28 Ibid., 256.
29 Ibid.
30 Chapter 7, Halachah 2, 248.
31 Chapter 7, Halachah 6, 258.
32 Chapter 7, Halachah 7, 258.
33 Ibid., 260.
34 Ibid.
35 Chapter 8, Halachah 1, 262.
36 Chapter 10, Halachah 1, 282–84.
37 Ibid., 284.
38 Chapter 10, Halachah 3, 284–86.
39 Ibid., 288.
40 Chapter 8, Halachah 2, 266.
41 Chapter 8, Halachah 1, 262. Maimonides says this explicitly only in the context of wonders. Magic and sorcery as possible causes

of signs are implicit in the argument of Halachah 2, chapter 8, however.
42 Chapter 8, Halachah 2, 266.
43 "Any prophet who arises and tells us that god has sent him does not have to [prove himself by] performing wonders like those performed by Moses, our teacher, or like the wonders of Elijah or Elisha, which altered the natural order. Rather, the sign of [the truth of his prophecy] will be the fulfillment of this prediction of future events." Chapter 10, Halachah 1, 282–84.
44 Chapter 7, Halachah 7, 258.
45 Chapter 8, Halachah 2, 264.
46 Ibid. See text accompanying n. 43.
47 Nonetheless, Maimonides recognizes the risk that a tested prophet may fail for some reason: "Once a prophet has made known his prophecy and his words have proven true time after time, or another prophet has proclaimed him a prophet, if he continues in the path of prophecy, it is forbidden to doubt him or to question the truth of his prophecy." Chapter 10, Halachah 5, 292–94.
48 Chapter 7, Halachah 7, 260.
49 Chapter 8, Halachah 1, 262, 264.
50 Chapter 8, Halachah 2, 264.
51 Chapter 8, Halachah 3, 268.
52 Even disciples of the prophets whose sign is successfully predicting the future can't be known to be prophets with any certainty. The most Maimonides is prepared to say of such a person is that "he should be considered to be a true prophet" (chapter 10, Halachah 2, 286) or that "it is forbidden to doubt him or to question the truth of his prophecy" (chapter 10, Halachah 5, 294). It is telling that Maimonides does not declare the person a prophet in the indicative, only in the normative.
53 So holds rabbinic tradition, with which Maimonides would have been intimately familiar. In rabbinic tradition, the first two commandments are "'I am (the Lord)' and 'Thou shalt not have (. . . before Me).'" See comment on "Moses spoke" in Rabbi Abraham ben Isaiah and Rabbi Benjamin Sharfman, trans., *The Pentateuch and Rashi's Commentary: A Linear Translation into English*, vol. 2, *Exodus* (Brooklyn, N.Y.: S. S. & R., 1950), 19:19, 209.

54 Chapter 7, Halachah 2, 248.
55 Chapter 7, Halachah 3, 250.
56 Chapter 10, Halachah 3, 286–88.
57 Chapter 7, Halachah 6, 254.
58 Gebhardt, 2 [16], ll. 29–30; Shirley, 60; Elwes, 14.

7
Interjecting Empty Spaces: Imagination and Interpretation in Spinoza's *Tractatus Theologico-Politicus*

WARRAN MONTAG

NO SINGLE WORK has contributed more to the resurgence of interest in Spinoza in the English-speaking world in the last decade than Jonathan Israel's *Radical Enlightenment*.[1] By insisting on the existence of an Enlightenment within the Enlightenment, and therefore on the existence of two (or perhaps more) Enlightenments, Israel makes visible the differences and even contradictions that divided the party of reason. We may even attach names to the poles he defines: Locke's complicit and therefore only partial Enlightenment appears in contrast to Spinoza's uncompromising rejection of every form of supernaturalism and superstition. Accordingly, what was radical about the radical enlightenment was not simply or even primarily a matter of the political doctrine or conception of society advanced by its partisans but rather the radicality of the critical attitude itself, the capacity to subject to critique the greatest possible number of ideas, practices, and institutions. Thus Locke's unwillingness to subject the foundations of Christianity to critique allowed a certain form of supernaturalism to contaminate both his philosophical and political theories; in contrast, it was the very "lawlessness" of Spinoza's philosophical enterprise (to use Kant's phrase), Spinoza's refusal to impose limits on his own use of reason, that made his philosophy a pure specimen of Enlightenment thought.

But Israel is not content to confer this status on Spinoza merely on the basis of the content of his texts alone; rather he judges Spinoza the central figure of the radical enlightenment on the basis of the effects his texts produced, and these effects can be measured quantitatively. No philosophical corpus provoked an equal or greater number of responses, critiques, attacks, and legal forms of exclusion and censorship over a longer period of time than Spinoza's. It is these "negative" effects (which overwhelmingly outnumber the few, usually anonymous, defenses of Spinoza) that allow us to determine not only the force of his philosophy but its very meaning. The implications of such an argument for Spinoza are particularly striking. His texts, especially the *Ethics*, present difficulties of such magnitude for readers today that it appears plausible to attribute to Spinoza the intention of writing a work unreadable to a world presumed in advance unprepared for its truth. Israel, following others before him,[2] shows that Spinoza's works presented few difficulties to his contemporaries, who, precisely to denounce them, had first to ascribe to them a meaning incarnate in at least some portions of the text. It is to these critics that Israel turns to discover what in Spinoza's philosophy can be called radical.

What is it that so disturbed Spinoza's critics? Israel's answer not only compels us to ask how radical the radical enlightenment was but, perhaps even more important, forces us to reconsider what we mean by Enlightenment. Spinoza, in his view, takes the side of naturalism against supernaturalism, of reason against both faith and revelation, far more consistently than the wavering and hesitant Locke, whose Christian devotion places severe limits on his commitment to Enlightenment. In the realm of political theory, Spinoza not only deprives every notion of society as a natural order of any claim to divine provenance but replaces it with a conception of humanity as consisting of originally dissociated individuals motivated by self-interest alone, for whom a democratic state would be the most natural form of society. Spinoza, for Israel, is therefore Hobbes without the absolutist afterthoughts that fatally compromise his otherwise powerful efforts at demystification.

To take only these examples, there are a number of objections one might address to Israel's interpretation of Spinoza. Spinoza's supposed "faith in reason and knowledge" would appear incompatible with many of the arguments in both the *Tractatus Theologico-Politicus* and the *Ethics* (especially Parts III and IV). We might well ask whether faith in reason, or a conception of reason that requires faith, is itself rational. In fact, the very notion of "faith in reason" presents one of the dilemmas that Spinoza seeks to investigate in the *Ethics*, which arguably pursues the possibility of reason in the absence of faith of any kind. As far as Spinoza's political thought comprising an early form of methodological individualism and rational choice theory, while there are those who offer such interpretations of his texts (primarily in the English-speaking world[3]), such claims can only be sustained in relation to the actual texts by the very hermeneutic procedures that Spinoza singles out for criticism in chapter 7 of the *Tractatus Theologico-Politicus*. Indeed, the Spinoza scholarship of the last thirty years suggests that there exists a third Enlightenment that is irreducible to either holism or atomism, collectivism or individualism, liberalism or absolutism.[4] This Enlightenment surfaces intermittently in Israel's text, but always at its margins, unrecognized and untheorized.

In the spirit of this critique of *Radical Enlightenment*, I want to examine what is, for Israel, one of the most important components of Spinoza's philosophical radicalism, namely, the critique of revealed religion in its most concrete form, the scripture: "No other part of Spinoza's assault on authority, tradition and faith proved so generally disquieting as his Bible criticism."[5] Drawing from Spinoza's many critics, Israel concludes that Spinoza's treatment of both the scripture itself and biblical commentary is essentially negative and destructive, as if Spinoza's objective is to deprive scripture not only of any authority at all but of its very meaning, hoping thereby to reduce it to letters on paper without significance and therefore without effect. Interestingly, the very uncompromising intransigence that Israel hails as the mark of the radical enlightenment is what for Hegel (in the *Phenomenology of Spirit*) constitutes its limitation, defining precisely the dependence of Enlightenment on the world of faith in relation to which alone it has meaning, if only the meaning of negation. After prejudice and superstition are banished, asks Hegel, what then for Enlightenment? What then, we might ask, for Israel's Spinoza, whose destruction of prejudice and superstition could have no other effect than to render his own philosophy superfluous? It isn't necessary, however, to look outside of Spinoza for an objection to Israel's conception of his radicalism. His philosophy itself compels us to ask not so much whether such a destruction of the idols is desirable but, rather, whether it is possible. And if it is not possible once and for all to banish superstition, then to desire it becomes the very rejection of reality in favor of nonexistent norms that for Spinoza define superstition, in this case, a superstition of reason. Furthermore, from the point of view of Spinoza's own theses in the *Tractatus Theologico-Politicus*, is it possible for him, as Israel claims, to dismiss "the entire corpus of previous Biblical interpretation whether Christian or Jewish,"[6] as if every word written by commentators for well over a thousand years was nothing more than superstition, utterly devoid of reason and therefore without meaning, or to use a more properly Spinozist idiom, effects? Can Spinoza's actual treatment of previous commentary (as determined by his allusion, references, and citations) be described as a rejection? In other words, is that what actually happens in Spinoza's text? Finally, to the extent that we can extract from Spinoza a theory of interpretation—or, as Louis Althusser insisted, a theory of reading[7]—does this theory permit a simple rejection of texts deemed superstitious or supernatural, as if the texts in question contained nothing other than what their authors intended or desired them to contain?

For Spinoza, the practice of scriptural interpretation was dominated by the assumption that the text in one and the same movement stated a meaning and concealed it, presenting to the reader a surface that veiled and protected the truth beneath (the Epistle Dedicatory to Maimonides's *Guide of the Perplexed* offers a privileged example of such an assumption).[8] To read was then necessarily to move from the appearance of disorder (not simply doctrinal but even literal), contradiction, and discrepancy to a hidden order and harmony, and even from the absence of meaning (what Maimonides calls "absurdity") to its dissimulated presence. It is possible to speak of Spinoza's inversion of this procedure in chapters 7–10 insofar as he moves from the unity, order, and presence attributed to the text by the majority of those he terms "theologians" *(theologos)* to inconsistency, disorder, and absence, which are, for him, irreducible? To say that he moves from the former to the latter is not to say, however, that order and harmony constitute properties of the text at all, whether of its surface or its putative depth. For Spinoza, these qualities are not to be found in the text at all. They have instead been added to and imposed on the text from without as an external covering in which the text is always transmitted in a process Spinoza describes as adulteration and contamination. This covering, *praetextum* in Latin, is precisely a pre-text, in the sense that it advances before the text, interposing itself between the text and its readers.

But we might also pause over the term Spinoza applies to those he accuses of having attempted to "extort from Scripture their own arbitrarily invented ideas," the term *theologians (theologos).*[9] Spinoza does not use the term *commentator* or even *interpreter* here, as he does elsewhere, but *theologian,* a pointedly Christian word and idea that suggests a disregard not only for nature, seeking God outside of creation, but even more for scripture in its literal existence. The text of the *Tractatus Theologico-Politicus* shows very clearly that Spinoza does not include in this category two of the most prominent Jewish commentators, Rashi and Ibn Ezra, both of whom are cited in support of his own interpretations of biblical passages. Spinoza goes so far as to refer to Ibn Ezra as "a man of enlightened mind and considerable learning."[10] In a similar way, although disagreeing with Gersonides's account of the chronology of the Pentateuch, even accusing him of "emending rather than interpreting scripture,"[11] Spinoza is careful not to dismiss Gersonides's other commentaries. Thus he tells the reader that Gersonides was "in other respects a man of great learning."[12] These judgments stand in stark contrast to his scornful dismissal not only of kabbalistic approaches to scripture but, more interestingly, even of the Targumim, or Aramaic translations of the scripture. The Targumim, of course, recall the figure who emerges as Spinoza's main adversary in chapters 7–10 of the *Tractatus Theologico-Politicus*: Maimonides, who relies frequently on the Targum Onkelos and the Targum Yonatan to support his devaluation of the literal existence of the text. However indebted to Maimonides Spinoza may be in his account of prophecy and his critique of the anthropomorphism of superstition, when discussing Maimonides's approach to the interpretation of scripture, Spinoza applies such terms as *absurdity, nonsense, rubbish,* and so on. Even here, however, it is possible to argue that Spinoza's critique of Maimonides pertains more to what the latter says than to what he does, to use Althusser's phrase, that is, to the statement of method advanced at the beginning of the *Guide for the Perplexed* rather than the actual reading of scripture in Maimonides's discussion of the incorporeality of God, which may very well deviate in important respects from the project Maimonides appears to have set out for himself.

Thus we can only conclude that rather than "dismissing the entire corpus of previous Bible interpretation,"[13] as Israel argues, it appears that Spinoza has instead drawn a line of demarcation through this corpus, making visible an antagonism internal to it and, moreover, taking the side of one part against the other. It is important to note that this line in no way respects the integrity of textual boundaries or the proprietary rights of authorship but, on the contrary, separates works and authors from themselves. If Spinoza has indeed not rejected Jewish Bible interpretation but drawn a distinction within it, it remains for us to specify the nature of this difference. But we cannot pass on to his arguments without noting that Spinoza's intervention is conducted entirely within the realm of Jewish commentary; not a single Christian theologian or interpreter is named or referred to in any way in the text.

To begin to understand the function of this line of demarcation, we might turn to the precise terms of Spinoza's denunciation of the theologians: "In no other field have they acted with so few scruples and so much temerity as in the interpretation of Scripture, or the mind of the Holy Spirit" (*Scriptura, sive Spiritus Sancti mente*).[14] This is another of those extraordinary moments (which, to my knowledge, no one has noted or discussed before) in which Spinoza employs the Latin conjunction *sive* (or) as an elliptical form of argumentation, suggesting an equivalence or even identity between terms whose relation was normally thought of as one of hierarchical dependence. In the case of *Deus, sive Natura* (God, or Nature) from the preface to Part IV of the *Ethics*, the conjunction *sive* establishes the identity of God and nature to exclude any recourse to transcendence: one does not look beyond God for God, for a God beyond God. God is his creation: all that he can be and do necessarily is. The operation of the *sive* in chapter 7 of the *Tractatus Theologico-Politicus*, however, seems more complicated in certain respects. In this case, the assumption that the scripture is the expression of the Holy Spirit is displaced by the assertion that the scripture is not an expression of anything but is itself the mind *(mente)* of the Holy Spirit, as if this mind is coextensive with the scripture in its actual existence. If scripture is the mind of the Holy Spirit and not one of its expressions—if, to use the language Spinoza employs in the *Ethics*, the mind of the Holy Spirit is the immanent cause of scripture—then, like God in relation to nature, it cannot be said to exist outside of or prior to the written and therefore material form in which it exists. The Holy Spirit, or rather its mind (and it is indeed curious that the *spiritus* possesses a *mente*), no longer exists outside the scripture as a reservoir of meaning to which contradictions might be referred and thus resolved. While to the perplexed, scripture in its literal existence appears contradictory and disordered, Spinoza, by declaring it the mind of the Holy Spirit, reminds us that order and coherence in the apprehension of scripture, as in the case of nature, pertain to the imagination, which compares that which exists to norms that exist nowhere but in the imagination itself.[15] In the case of scripture, as in nature, reality and perfection are the same thing (cf. *Ethics* II, D6).

To contemplate the mind of the Holy Spirit as it is, however, independently of the external coverings that seem always to have accompanied it, is not an easy task. In a very important sense, the scripture as it is only becomes available to us when we draw a line of demarcation separating it from the pre-texts that are woven not only around it but even into it, filling its gaps and covering the seams and joints that mark its composite nature. If we follow Spinoza's arguments carefully, we can draw the inference that there exist two kinds of *praetexta*, or pretexts. The first is characteristic of the translations from Hebrew, translations that (interestingly, even to this day, with very few exceptions) do not so much render the scripture as it actually is in Hebrew as they do corrupt and distort an originally faulty, mutilated, and obviously composite work into consistency and intelligibility. All the difficulties and ambiguities that characterize the Hebrew (the equivocity that is so important in Maimonides's account of scripture), from the inconsistencies of verb tense, noun inflection, and even spelling to the fact that the meaning of certain words is no longer known, disappear in the translations. Furthermore, many translations resolve the frequent inconsistencies that plague the different historical accounts of the same epochs either by addition or omission but always without noting that they have replaced the actual text with another, different text.

Of all the translations Spinoza might single out for criticism, he chooses one that will be unfamiliar to all but a handful of those likely to read a philosophical treatise in Latin: Spinoza will go so far as to describe the Targum Yonatan ben Uzziel (referred to in the *Tractatus Theologico-Politicus* as "the work of the Chaldaen Paraphrast Jonathan") as a rejection of scripture as it actually is (he uses the verb *negare* [to reject, deny, or negate], which he often employs to describe the activity of biblical commentators and interpreters) and a fabrication "of something new out of his own brain *(ex proprio cerebro)*" (he uses the verb *cudo*, a verb used to describe the activity of a metal or blacksmith, rather than verbs like *excogitare*, denoting mental activity, or even *fabricare, facere,* or *fingere,* which denote a physical making).[16] This Targum, of course, is a stand-in for translations far more familiar to his audience (e.g., the Vulgate, an extraordinarily inaccurate translation of many of the passages that Spinoza examines): Spinoza takes as an example the Targum's Aramaic rendering of a passage from Joshua. He cites the Hebrew and the Aramaic and translates them into Latin to show the discrepancy, simultaneously demonstrating that the translation is itself a commentary that "illuminates" the text by altering its meaning and thereby changing it into something it is not. Gebhardt, in the *Opera,* preserves these passages in the original, presenting the Hebrew with Spinoza's Latin translation, followed by the Aramaic of Targum Yonatan and its Latin rendering, whereas in Shirley's translation, they disappear. It is possible, I believe, to assign the citations from an alphabet few readers could decipher a strategic function: perhaps by confronting his audience with a translation of scripture into a language that is not only foreign (one might be tempted to say Other) but non-Christian, Spinoza incites his readers to proceed without further comment to question the Vulgate text, not to mention the vernacular translations.[17]

I want to focus my discussion of Spinoza's critique of the traditional forms of scriptural interpretation by examining in some detail the concluding paragraph of chapter 9 of the *Tractatus Theologico-Politicus*. It is in relation to this passage, which might at first appear to occupy a minor place in the architecture of Spinoza's argument, that he identifies yet another property of scripture in its actual existence that disappears in translation—in this case, not what is present but what is absent. The oldest extant Hebrew texts, while not themselves translations, are nevertheless transcriptions or copies and are not only susceptible to error but based on texts that are themselves copies of originals that have been lost forever. The very fidelity of the scribes led them to note the flaws in the most authoritative texts available to them. "The scribes of old have noted several doubtful readings and also a number of mutilated passages *(loca truncata)*, but not all there are."[18] Just as Spinoza appears poised to suggest that the scripture in its present form is even less coherent than previously thought, even by those whose business it was to guard the authenticity of the text by the counting of letters and words, he declines to continue this discussion: "I shall not at this point discuss the question as to whether the faults *(mendae)* are of such a kind to cause serious difficulty to the reader."[19] The next sentence, however, proceeds to the discussion that Spinoza has just foresworn. He tells us that he is of the opinion that the mutilated passages will not cause serious difficulty or "at least not to the judicious reader."[20] But what distinguishes the judicious from the injudicious reader? He seems here to suggest that the judicious accept the text, simple and limited as it is, offering little more than ethical doctrines that might as well be found among nations utterly ignorant of the God of Abraham, Isaac, and Jacob, and refrain from abandoning the text as it is in search of hidden meaning.

But Spinoza is not merely interested in the *loca truncata* because they limit speculation and restrict the reader to the simple instruction that can indubitably be derived from scripture. Indeed, he returns to the question of mutilated places in the text at the end of chapter 9. He remarks that "scribes have noted a number of cases of mutilated texts by leaving a space in mid paragraph. The Massoretes have counted them, enumerating 28 cases where a space is left in mid-paragraph. . . . There are twenty-eight such spaces left by the scribes, apart from the passages we have already noted. Yet many of these passages would not be recognized as mutilated, were it not for the space."²¹ Of the twenty-eight cases, Spinoza chooses to examine a passage that has not only been a focal point of commentary but has raised questions central to his philosophical project: Genesis 4: 8, the narrative of Cain and Abel. Spinoza's Latin translation differs totally from the Vulgate text and would be unfamiliar to all but those able to read the Hebrew: "And Kain said to his brother Abel . . . and it happened that they went out into the field where Kain, etc." (בשדה ויאמר קין אל הבל אחיו ויהי בהיותם).²²

Spinoza thus, citing the Massoretes, restores to the line the gap or absence that is unmistakable in Hebrew and which, as we shall see, has furnished occasion for a significant quantity of commentary but which has been obscured by translations that impose on the text a coherence that the original does not possess. According to the Vulgate translation, the verse runs, "And Cain said to his brother Abel, let us go out into the field etc." Not only, of course, does the Vulgate obscure the gap, but adds meaning that is not to be found in the Hebrew, increasing Cain's guilt by suggesting that he lured his brother into the fields to slay him out of jealousy at God's favoring Abel's offering. The case of Jewish commentators is somewhat different. The gaps and other difficulties in the text, of course, remain in the original Hebrew, but the edition to which Spinoza refers by name, the Bomberg Bible (the Mikra'ot Gedolo'ot or Rabbinical Bible), surrounds each passage of scripture with a combination of commentaries and Aramaic translations to supply what the text itself lacks and to resolve its apparent contradictions. In the case of Genesis 4:8, the appearance of the gap to which Spinoza refers has necessitated interpretive suturing. The Targum Yonatan supplies a more elaborate (and also more nuanced) content to Cain's utterance than the Vulgate: Cain indeed exhorts his brother to go into the field with him; while there, the two engage in a disputation about whether the good are rewarded and the unjust punished. It is only when Abel claims that his works were "better ordered" than Cain's and thus deserved God's favor that Cain rose against him in anger and killed him. At the other extreme is Rashi's interpretive minimalism. Rashi merely poses the question of what Cain said to Abel, noting the missing text and suggesting that he provoked an argument with Abel to anger him and in this way justify slaying him.

Interestingly, Spinoza says nothing more about the possible significance of this gap for the meaning of the Cain and Abel episode, nor does he say anything more about the significance of gaps in general in the text of the scripture or that they disappear into the continuity invented by translators or are explained away by commentary. In fact, he ends the chapter with a phrase that appears only one other time in his entire corpus: *Sed de his Satis* (but of this enough). It is the phrase with which his last unfinished work, the *Tractatus Politicus*, stops, even if it does not exactly conclude. It suggests that Spinoza has more to say on the topics in question, or perhaps thinks there is more to be said, but either does not want to or cannot say more about them. What more might be said about the empty spaces left by scribes in the middle of paragraphs? We might begin to think about this problem by noting that what translator Samuel Shirley has rendered as "leaving a space in mid paragraph" is, in Spinoza's Latin, "*in medio paragrapho spatium vacuum interponitur.*" The verb *interpono* denotes an action on the part of the scribes, an active placing of a space (Spinoza uses the verb *intericio*, which denotes a similar action, two sentences later), rather than a passive "leaving" of a space that was in some sense already present. I want to ask whether the act of interposing or interjecting (to translate the Latin verbs very literally) empty spaces is not constitutive of Spinoza's theory of the interpretation of scripture, whether the act of interpretation must not begin with the notation of the seams and joints of a composite text and therefore the disruption of its illusory coherence and continuity to open the way to a knowledge of its historical existence.

But does Spinoza's argument pertain to the very unusual, if not unique, case of scripture alone? To take such a position would be to confirm Israel's argument that Spinoza's reading of scripture seeks to devalue it in its very singularity, demonstrating that it, far from being the exemplary book, is markedly inferior to most other works in its coherence, continuity, and consistency, and that the commentaries that attribute to it what it does not possess are as illusory and useless as the text on which they are based. Before we adopt such a position, however, we would do well to consider Spinoza's own statement to the contrary. At the end of chapter 10 of the *Tractatus Theologico-Politicus*, and therefore at the conclusion of his long and detailed demonstration of the inconsistencies, discontinuities, and contradictions that characterize scripture as it is in its actual existence, he recognizes that "perhaps someone will object that I am plainly subverting scripture [*scriptura plane evertere*—which could also be translated as "completely destroying or overturning scripture"], for according to this argument everyone can suspect it of being everywhere faulty."[23] What he has done, he protests, is instead to separate the faulty and corrupt from the clear and pure and prevent the latter from being harmonized with the former in a protocol of reading that sees the reconciliation of apparently discordant and heteronomous elements as the condition of a text's intelligibility. To note the presence of certain faulty passages does not render the entire text suspect and thus, as he puts it, overthrow or destroy it. It is at this point that Spinoza appeals not to the singularity of scripture as an unusually heteroclite text but precisely the contrary: "No book is found without faults" (*nullus enim liber unquam sine mendis repertus est*).[24]

The sentence that follows (*An quaeso ea de causa ubique mendosos aliquis unquam suspicatus est? Nemo sane: preasertum quando oratio est perspicua, & mens authoris clare percipitur* ["Has anyone for this reason suspected that it is everywhere faulty? No one has done so, especially when the meaning is obvious and the author's intention clear"]) demonstrates that by "faults," Spinoza does not mean textual corruption, the errors of printers or scribes, but rather places at which the text deviates from what he calls *mens authoris*, literally, the author's mind or intellect, which can be "clearly perceived" elsewhere in the "oratio."[25] Spinoza's use of the term *oratio* is in turn significant: though Shirley translates it as "book," it in fact suggests that faults, deviations from the author's mind, occur not simply in books, as he suggests in the previous sentence, but in any discourse, whether spoken or written. Such faults, then, appear necessarily to pertain to discourse in general and not merely to a text as unusual in its history and composition as the Bible. Indeed, if we follow Spinoza's argument, it is not too much to maintain that we may thus speak of the empty spaces to be interjected in any text whatever, that is, the space between what the author thought and did not think but wrote anyway, the space between what the author wanted to say and actually did say. The act of interpretation would then begin with a refusal of the principle of the coherence of texts and a recognition of the necessity of drawing a line of demarcation that marks the existence of a fault or fault line. Furthermore, we should note that Spinoza's argument here neither depends on nor even evokes a distinction between the inside and outside of texts or that between the hidden and the manifest; on the contrary, the text displays its divergent meanings on its surface. It is only the imagination of order and harmony that stands in the way of the knowledge of a text.

Even if we developed Spinoza's argument no further than this, we could see the way in which Spinoza's relation to Jewish biblical commentary cannot be reduced to "rejection." The commentators inevitably said more and other than what they wanted to say, offering in the same text, perhaps, conflicting theories of God, nature, and scripture. Regardless of their intentions and beliefs; authors may well produce works that themselves subvert superstition and supernaturalism. But we cannot leave Spinoza's argument at this point: even to speak of a work originating in the intention of the author (irrespective of whether or not it should later deviate, in whole or in part, from that intention) is to ignore Spinoza's own critique of the very notion of intention, the idea that works of art, buildings, paintings, and so on, are the realization of a preexisting intention (*Ethics* III, P2S). Such notions are products of the imagination that invert causes and effects, supposing, in this case, that the work we wrote was determined by our mind alone, whereas, in fact, the intention arose simultaneously with the work produced, the causes of which we remain ignorant, and was projected into the past as an origin, a cause. Just as the coward believes he or she has freely chosen to flee and could have stayed to fight, or the alcoholic that he or she chooses to drink and could just as freely choose not to do so, so those who speak and, let us add, write think they do so by virtue of a "free decision of the mind" (*Ethics* III, P2S). In fact, for Spinoza, authorial intention can never exist outside of or prior to its textual effects and therefore cannot serve as a point around which an otherwise diverse text could be unified. To refer the contradictions, gaps, and discrepancies of a text to the author, as Maimonides does at the beginning of the *Guide,* whether to refer them to the author's cunning or failures, is to divert attention way from the only place where something like intention can be said to exist: in the text itself. We may now appreciate Spinoza's rather disconcerting use of the term *mens*, or "mind," in relation to texts: *Scriptura, sive Spiritus Sancti mente*, together with the idea that one perceives the *mens authoris*, or "author's mind," in the work, not through it or by means of it. As Spinoza argues in the *Tractatus Theologico-Politicus*, we do not know what we think or believe, except by virtue of works.[26] Our intentions do not exist prior to our works, nor can they be without them. It is in this sense that a text in its actual existence can more accurately be described as the mind of the author than any disembodied repository of potential meanings.

It remains, however, to account for the fact that "no work is found without faults," that is, that no work can be found that does not diverge from itself, exhibiting between its dissociated meanings nothing other than the empty space that marks the impossibility of these meanings being reconciled. Moved by conflicting and contradictory forces to a great extent unknown to us, we produce texts that escape us in so many ways, less hollow containers of meanings than full (although always composite) bodies affecting and being affected by other bodies ad infinitum. To follow Spinoza to the letter is to translate mind into text and text into body and to understand meaning as effect. But few are those who can follow Spinoza on this path, a fact that returns us to Jonathan Israel's account of Spinoza. If Spinoza's relation to the history of biblical commentary cannot, as I have argued, be reduced to one of rejection, it is not simply because his conception of the texts of the commentators is more complex than Israel's; it is also, and perhaps even more importantly, because, for Spinoza, there can be no irreversible historical passage from superstition to knowledge or from imagination to reason. In this sense, Spinoza appears closer to Hegel than we might have thought: even Enlightenment can generate its own superstitions, with faith in Enlightenment, faith in the progress of knowledge, being one of its most potent forms. I will conclude by returning to the conclusion of chapter 9 of the *Tractatus Theologico-Politicus*. Can we understand the reference to Cain and Abel, more precisely, to the empty space where what Cain said to Abel "should" have been, as itself an allegory of the relation between imagination and interpretation? I refer here not to the account of Cain and Abel itself but to the unfailing tendency of commentators to supply what they deemed was lacking: the addition of the entire apparatus of free will and responsibility to the determination of bodies. To call scripture with its "faults," empty spaces, contradictions, and corruptions "the mind of the Holy Spirit" is to declare it perfect, that is, to refuse to relate it to any norm in relation to which it could be deemed flawed. Spinoza compels us to reconceptualize these terms in such a way that they cease evoking a norm external to the reality of the work and instead function as markers of the composite and heterogeneous nature even of any body, including texts. It is only from the perspective of the imagination (a perspective not only inescapable for the human individual caught in the infinite flux of causes and effects but also a perspective codified and embodied in the apparatus of superstition and domination) that the determination of bodies by other bodies "lacks" the dimension of will and intention. These apparatus require such a dimension if they are to extract from this flux singular individuals to deem them responsible and subject to punishment; not only those who, like Cain, kill their fellow human beings but also those who, like Spinoza, seek to produce a philosophy adequate to a world without transcendence.

Notes

1 Jonathan I. Israel, *Radical Enlightenment: Philosophy and the Making of Modernity, 1650–1750* (Oxford: Oxford University Press, 2001).
2 See esp. Rosalie L. Colie, "Spinoza and England 1665–1730," *Proceedings of the American Philosophy Society* 107 (1963): 183–219, and Paul Vernière, *Spinoza et la pensée française avant la Révolution* (Paris: Presses Universitaires de France, 1982).
3 See the work of Lee Rice, Douglas Den Uyl, and Steven Barbone.
4 I refer to work strangely absent from Israel's text: Pierre Macherey, *Hegel ou Spinoza* (Paris: Maspero, 1979); Antonio Negri, *The Savage Anomaly* (Minneapolis: University of Minnesota Press, 1991); Pierre-François Moreau, *Spinoza: l'expérience et l'éternité* (Paris, Presses Universitaires de France, 1994).
5 Israel, *Radical Enlightenment*, 447.

6. Ibid.
7. Louis Althusser, *Reading Capital* (London: New Left Books, 1970), 16.
8. Moses Maimonides, *The Guide of the Perplexed*, 2 vols., trans. Shlomo Pines (Chicago: University of Chicago Press, 1963), 1:11: "Now consider the explicit affirmation of the Sages, may their memory be blessed, that the internal meaning of the words of the Torah is a pearl whereas the external meaning of all parables is worth nothing, and their comparison of the concealment of a subject by its parable's external meaning to a man who let drop a pearl in his house which was dark and full of furniture. Now the pearl is there, but he does not see it and does not know where it is. It is as though it were no longer in his possession, as it is impossible for him to derive any benefit from it until, as has been mentioned, he lights a lamp—an act to which an understanding of the meaning of a parable corresponds."
9. Baruch Spinoza, *Tractatus Theologico-Politicus*, trans. Samuel Shirley (Leiden, Netherlands: E. J. Brill, 1991), 140. Spinoza, *Opera*, ed. Carl Gebhardt (Heidelberg, Germany: Carl Winter, 1925), 3:97.
10. Spinoza, *Tractatus*, 161.
11. Ibid., 304.
12. Ibid., 303–4.
13. Israel, *Radical Enlightenment*, 447.
14. Spinoza, *Tractatus*, 140; Spinoza, *Opera*, 3:97.
15. See, e.g., Spinoza's letter to Henry Oldenburgh, November 20, 1665: "I do not attribute to nature beauty, ugliness, order or confusion. It is only with respect to our imagination that things can be said to be beautiful, ugly, well-ordered or confused." Baruch Spinoza, *The Letters*, trans. Samuel Shirley (Indianapolis, Ind.: Hackett, 1995), 192.
16. Spinoza, *Tractatus*, 166 (translation modified); Spinoza, *Opera*, 3:123.
17. For a comprehensive discussion of Spinoza's use of Hebrew, see Philippe Cassuto, *Spinoza hébraisant* (Paris: E. Peeters, 1999).
18. Spinoza, *Tractatus*, 179 (translation modified); Spinoza, *Opera*, 3:141.
19. Spinoza, *Tractatus*, 179 (translation modified); Spinoza, *Opera*, 3:141.

20 Spinoza, *Tractatus*, 179 (translation modified); Spinoza, *Opera*, 3:141.
21 Spinoza, *Tractatus*, 179 (translation modified); Spinoza, *Opera*, 3:141.
22 Spinoza, *Tractatus*, 179 (translation modified); Spinoza, *Opera*, 3:141.
23 Spinoza, *Tractatus*, 194; Spinoza, *Opera*, 3:149.
24 Spinoza, *Tractatus*, 195; Spinoza, *Opera*, 3:149.
25 Spinoza, *Tractatus*, 195; Spinoza, *Opera*, 3:149.
26 "We cannot know anyone except by his works." Spinoza, *Tractatus*, 123; Spinoza, *Opera*, 3:80.

8
Marx before Spinoza: Notes toward an Investigation

CESARE CASARINO

It is indeed the new world system, the third stage of capitalism, which is for us the absent totality, Spinoza's God or Nature, the ultimate (indeed, perhaps the only) referent, the true ground of Being of our own time.
—Fredric Jameson

Prefatory Remarks on the Foundations of Spinozist Marxism
Toward the end of his essay "Lenin before Hegel," Louis Althusser takes his leave of the readers by hurling at them the following italicized provocation: *"A century and a half later no one has understood Hegel because it is impossible to understand Hegel without having thoroughly studied and understood* Capital."[1] The possibly unwitting wit of this pronouncement lies in its casting G. W. F. Hegel in the role of Karl Marx's famous ape. (I am referring to that passage in the *Grundrisse* in which Marx writes, "Human anatomy contains a key to the anatomy of the ape."[2]) My own provocation in this essay may not be as witty but may well end up being just as hyperbolic and perhaps just as questionable. In brief, this essay argues that it is impossible to make sense of Baruch Spinoza without making sense first of Marx. (As we shall see, the term *sense* has specific connotations and crucial import for the arguments of this essay.) In particular, this essay argues that there are aspects of Spinoza's thought that become intelligible for

the first time if and when read through the lens of Marx's thought: I argue that, for better or for worse, Marx has had an irreversible impact on how to read Spinoza.

Such an argument is motivated in part by a puzzling state of affairs: during more than half a century of Spinoza revival—and, in particular, during approximately four decades in which numerous thinkers, from Althusser to Antonio Negri and beyond, have elaborated a Spinozist Marxism as an alternative to the dialectical orthodoxies of Hegelian Marxism—remarkably few attempts have been made to relate Spinoza and Marx to one another in a direct, explicit, and sustained manner.[3] Such a lacuna begs the question of the foundations—or lack thereof—of Spinozist Marxism. It was partly to begin to redress this lacuna and to formulate this question that this essay was born. Elsewhere, I have speculated on one possible way of relating these two thinkers directly to one another by juxtaposing Marx's theory of surplus value and Spinoza's doctrine of the intellectual love of God that arises from the third kind of knowledge.[4] Here I propose to explore the precondition for any possible juxtaposition between the two, namely, that which makes it possible even to write about them in the same sentence. As I will argue in what follows, this precondition consists of the fact that both Marx and Spinoza need to be understood as early theorists of those current and ongoing processes and phenomena to which we now refer as globalization (and this is an argument that will necessitate also an engagement with certain aspects of Gilles Deleuze's thought). Given that the conceit of my claim here is that Marx was the first theorist of globalization, while Spinoza was the second, I will begin accordingly.

God or Concatenation

In a passage that posits globalization at once (1) as structural and synchronic *precondition* (i.e., as immanent cause), (2) as logical and intrinsic *tendency* (i.e., as process, that is, as circuit between the potential and the actual), and (3) as historical and diachronic *result* (i.e., as immanent effect) of the capitalist mode of production, Marx writes:

> The creation by capital of *absolute surplus value* . . . is conditional upon an expansion, specifically a constant expansion, of the sphere

of circulation. The *surplus value* created at one point requires the creation of surplus value at *another* point, for which it may be exchanged. . . . A precondition of production based on capital is therefore *the production of a constantly widening sphere of circulation,* whether the sphere itself is directly expanded or whether *more points within it are created as points of production.* While circulation appeared at first as a constant magnitude, it here appears as a moving magnitude being expanded by production itself. Accordingly, it already appears as a moment of production itself. Hence . . . capital has the tendency . . . at bottom, to propagate production based on capital, or the mode of production corresponding to it. The tendency to create the *world market* is directly given in the concept of capital itself. Every limit appears as a barrier to be overcome.[5]

It is a short leap from this passage in the *Grundrisse* to those pages in *Capital* in which Marx will reconstruct and retrace step-by-step the circular "movement" at "the end of" which "money emerges once again as its starting-point,"[6] namely, the process by which (a certain amount of) money is transformed into (money as) capital, the process by which an "original value" is turned into "surplus-value" through exchange.[7] In the context of this discussion, in fact, Marx articulates the following contrast:

> The simple circulation of commodities—selling in order to buy—is a means to a final goal which lies outside circulation, namely the appropriation of use-values, the satisfaction of needs. As against this, the circulation of money as capital is an end in itself, for the valorization of value takes place only within this constantly renewed movement. The movement of capital is therefore limitless.[8]

For Marx, "capital" is the name of a "constantly renewed" and ever-expansive "movement" of exchange relations whose structural necessity is to envelop the whole planet, as well as to mediate and relate everything in it, through the production of surplus value. As Kojin Karatani puts it succinctly in his *Architecture as Metaphor,* when commenting on related passages in *Capital,* "the movement of capital socially connects people from all over the world."

Crucially, Karatani adds, "Yet because this sociality is mediational, we are not conscious of it. Though we are actually connected to each other, we are unaware of it."⁹ In short, the limitless movement of capital is not immediately available to consciousness—and this implies that the open-ended totality produced by such a movement cannot enter the field of representation as such. Such, at any rate, is the conclusion reached by Fredric Jameson, following from the same premises. In *Postmodernism; or, The Cultural Logic of Late Capitalism*, for example, Jameson writes:

> Structural coordinates are no longer accessible to immediate lived experience and are often not even conceptualizable for most people. There comes into being, then, a situation in which we can say that if individual experience is authentic, then it cannot be true; and that if a scientific or cognitive model of the same content is true, then it escapes individual experience. . . . At this point an essentially allegorical concept must be introduced—the "play of figuration"—in order to convey some sense that these new and enormous global realities are inaccessible to any individual subject or consciousness . . . which is to say that those fundamental realities are somehow ultimately unrepresentable or, to use the Althusserian phrase, are something like an absent cause, one that can never emerge into the presence of perception. Yet this absent cause can find figures through which to express itself in distorted and symbolic ways: indeed, one of our basic tasks . . . is to track down and make conceptually available the ultimate realities and experiences designated by those figures, which the reading mind inevitably tends to reify and to read as primary contents in their own right.¹⁰

I will leave aside the vexing question of the allegedly "allegorical" nature of the concept—namely, "the 'play of figuration'"—which is introduced here as the solution to the problem of reading the unrepresentable in representation; I would like to focus, rather, on the fact that in this passage, (1) totality is posited as structure in the Althusserian sense, namely, as that absent cause immanent in its own effects which is the mode of production itself, and (2) a clear distinction is made between (reifying) representation and (dereifying) conceptualization.

Jameson seems to imply that just because that totality which is the mode of production is not representable as such—or, in any case, just because this totality may enter the field of representation only in a necessarily distorted manner—it does not follow that it cannot be conceptualized or known. Undoubtedly, Jameson's project of "cognitive mapping" constituted an attempt to address this problem, that is, the problem of the definitional nonrepresentability of a planetary totality thus conceived. This means, among other things, that cognitive mapping needs to be understood as having indexed for Jameson a fundamentally nonrepresentational kind of knowledge all along. In an admirably candid moment of self-criticism, for example, we read:

> What I have called cognitive mapping may be identified as a more modernist strategy, which retains an impossible concept of totality whose representational failure seemed for the moment as useful and productive as its (inconceivable) success. The problem with this particular slogan clearly lay in its own (representational) accessibility. Since everyone knows what a map is, it would have been necessary to add that cognitive mapping cannot (at least in our time) involve anything so easy as a map; indeed, once you knew what "cognitive mapping" was driving at, you were to dismiss all figures of maps and mapping from your mind and try to imagine something else. But it may be more desirable to take a genealogical approach and show how mapping has ceased to be achievable by means of maps themselves.[11]

Such a "genealogical approach," however, is bound to show also how this type of mapping was *never* "achievable by means of maps" in the first place. The problem with cognitive mapping, according to Jameson, was not that it was too difficult to conceive, to figure, to imagine—in short, that it was too remote from and inaccessible to representation. On the contrary, the problem was that it was not nonrepresentational enough. Indeed, what Jameson retains and defends in that "more modernist strategy" which went by the name of "cognitive mapping" is only its nonrepresentational kernel, namely, the "impossible concept of totality." (It is precisely by putting emphasis on such a kernel that Jameson, in a slightly later work—*The Geopolitical Aesthetic*—can eschew any residual representational connotations in his strategy and can state unequivocally that, when it comes to "a totality," it is always a question of "mapping [it] out . . . rather than perceiving or representing [it].")[12] But if the strategy of cognitive mapping was specifically modernist, its nonrepresentational conceptual kernel, as well as the problem necessitating the latter, was much older than modernism as such. For if Marx was correct in identifying such an imperative to totality as "directly given in the concept of capital itself," then the problem of its nonrepresentability, as well as the attempts to solve this problem (conceptually or otherwise), ought to be at least as old as capital itself—and hence their genealogy may be traceable all the way back to the early modern era. This was an era that, on one hand, witnessed an extraordinary proliferation of maps and mappings of all sorts and, on the other hand, witnessed also the fulgurant materialization of an exquisitely mapless mapping.

Baruch Spinoza begins the appendix that ends *Ethics* I with a six-point précis of the preceding arguments regarding God or substance understood as immanent rather than transitive cause of itself and of modes.[13] This précis constitutes the springboard from which Spinoza launches into a trenchant and unsparing critique of teleological and anthropomorphic thought in all its forms—a critique that comprises the remaining part of the appendix. I am concerned here neither with the précis nor with the following critique per se. I intend to zero in, rather, on the transitional passage that connects the two. Between a powerful affirmation of absolute immanence and a radical negation of transcendence in its twin forms of teleology and anthropomorphism, Spinoza writes:

> Further, whenever an opportunity arose, I have tried to remove prejudices that could hinder the perception of my demonstrations. But since there still remain many prejudices which have had, and still have, the power to constitute a major obstacle to men's understanding of the concatenation of all things as I have explicated it [*rerum concatenationem . . . , quo ipsam explicui, . . .*], I have thought it worth while to summon these [prejudices] to the court of reason.[14]

The reason why I have thought it worthwhile to summon this seemingly unremarkable passage to the court of the reader's attention is that it includes an atypical and possibly unique instance of explicit declaration of intent in the entire *Ethics*. For in this passage—on which, to my knowledge, nobody ever has remarked—Spinoza makes it possible to catch a fleeting glimpse not of the signification but of the significance, not of the meaning but of the sense, of the *Ethics*. The sense of the *Ethics* is expressed here and nowhere else, in the locution *rerum concatenationem*—the concatenation of all things (where, by "things," we need to understand all modes of extension and all modes of thought).[15]

An excursus on sense is necessary here. The backbone of Spinoza's *Ethics* consists of a series of propositions. I follow Gilles Deleuze's account within *The Logic of Sense* in understanding any proposition (1) as consisting of four different yet strictly immanent dimensions or functions, namely, denotation, manifestation, signification, and sense; (2) as functioning primarily as a continuous relay or loop of relations among its first three dimensions, which necessitate and refer to one another ad infinitum; and (3) as positing sense as that which at once presupposes, enables, and breaks the proposition's otherwise triangular, closed, and self-referential circuit. Of signification, in particular, Deleuze writes:

> Here it is a question of the relation of the word to *universal or general* concepts, and of syntactic connections to the implications of the concept. From the standpoint of signification, we always consider the elements of the proposition as "signifying" conceptual implications capable of referring to other propositions, which serve as premises of the first. Signification is defined by this order of conceptual implication where the proposition under consideration intervenes only as an element of a "demonstration," in the most general sense of the word, that is, either as premise or as conclusion.[16]

Sense, on the other hand, is for Deleuze *"the expressed of the proposition"*—namely, that *"aliquid"* which is "irreducible to individual states of affairs [i.e., the thing, object, or objects, and relations among objects, which the proposition denotes], particular images and personal beliefs [i.e., that which the proposition manifests as the lived experience of its speaking subject], and universal or general concepts [i.e., that which the proposition signifies or demonstrates]."[17] Sense, in other words, is irreducible not only to the three other functions of the proposition but also to all that the proposition indexes through those functions. Importantly, sense does have nonetheless a special relation to things and to their relations—that is, to states of affairs—which constitute the indexed object of the proposition's first and denoting function. Of sense, in fact, Deleuze writes:

> On the one hand, it does not exist outside the proposition which expresses it; what is expressed does not exist outside its expression. This is why we cannot say that sense exists, but rather that it inheres or subsists. On the other hand, it does not merge at all with the proposition, for it has an objectness [*objectité*] which is quite distinct. What is expressed has no resemblance whatsoever to the expression. Sense is indeed attributed, but it is not at all the attribute of the proposition—it is rather the attribute of the thing or state of affairs. The attribute of the proposition is the predicate—a qualitative predicate like green, for example. It is attributed to the subject of the proposition. But the attribute of the thing is the verb: to green, for example, or rather the event expressed by this verb. It is attributed to the thing denoted by the subject, or to the state of affairs denoted by the entire proposition. Conversely, this logical attribute does not merge at all with the physical state of affairs, nor with a quality or relations of this state. The attribute is not a being and does not qualify a being; it is an extra-being. . . . Sense is both the expressible or the expressed of the proposition, and the attribute of the state of affairs. It turns one side towards things and one side towards propositions. But it does not merge with the proposition which expresses it any more than with the state of affairs or the quality which the proposition denotes. It is exactly the boundary between propositions and things.[18]

Sense names the impossible point of tangency between *les mots et les choses*, the relating nonrelation between the expression of words and the attribution of things. It might be more accurate, then, to define the fourth dimension of the proposition as expression rather than as sense per se. Through expression, the proposition yields its own impassable threshold onto that which it denotes—a threshold of sense that is also an "extra-being," an addition to being, an ontological surplus. At once excessive surplus and unbridgeable abyss, more than a plus and less than a minus, sense is expressed by the proposition just like event is attributed to the state of affairs. In both cases—which constitute the very same case considered from two different sides—something occurs that defies yet marks representation: the virtual sense-event that makes the world go round, that agitates words and things alike, that makes them both glow from the inside, thereby surrounding them both from the outside, as it were, with a halo.[19] I will return to these and other luminous passages of *The Logic of Sense*. Here I would like to conclude provisionally this excursus by putting forth the following claim (to which I will return): the first two dimensions of the proposition (denotation and manifestation) correspond to the two components of Spinoza's first kind of knowledge (i.e., inherently inadequate representational knowledge based solely on sensory perceptions and semiotic systems), whereas its third dimension (signification or demonstration) corresponds to Spinoza's second kind of knowledge (i.e., inherently adequate conceptual knowledge based on common notions), and its fourth dimension (expression) corresponds to Spinoza's third kind of knowledge (i.e., inherently adequate intuitive knowledge).[20]

Let us return now to the *Ethics* and to the concatenation of all things. The *Ethics* is truly a mapless work. First of all, it is notorious for beginning disorientingly and uncompromisingly in medias res. It opens without any introductions, abstracts, prefaces, preambles, or further ado. Rather it catapults the reader amid definitions, axioms, propositions, demonstrations, explanations, corollaries, lemmata, and scholia, whose crystalline clarity as discrete elements is directly proportional to the opacity of the overall project and hence of their import as integral components of the latter. Moreover, not only are contextualizing passages, framing devices, orienting signposts, or expository meta-commentaries absent from the opening pages, such or other types of direct articulations at once of the driving force and of the general trajectory—in sum, of the inherent vector constitutive—of this work are very scarce, if anywhere at all to be found, throughout the entire course of its theorematic deductions. (The deductive progression of this work, to be sure, is punctuated by numerous breaks, caesurae, and excursus, such as, most notably, the scholia; no matter how insightful and illuminating, however, these crucial textual nodes arguably do not play the role of metacommentaries and are implicative rather than explicative, that is, they elaborate the further implications of this work's line of reasoning rather than clarifying why either such a line of reasoning or its implications matter in the first place.[21]) In short, seldom, if ever, in the *Ethics* does Spinoza produce statements indexing directly or explaining explicitly what it is that this work aims to achieve or to express by demonstrating the series of propositions it does demonstrate, what it is in the end that is at stake in its various argumentations. Or, as an exasperated student once put it memorably in class while trying to make sense of the *Ethics*, "I understand what it says but I don't understand what it means"—a sentence that, ironically, did not mean what it said, as I took it to mean, rather, that the student in question understood the signification or meaning of Spinoza's work perfectly well without, however, being able yet to understand its opaque significance, to grasp its elusive sense.

This is why the preceding quoted passage constitutes a remarkable anomaly: it contains possibly as direct, explicit, and concise an encapsulation of the overall project of the *Ethics* as we will find in this entire work, as Spinoza indicates there in passing not only what he is saying and what he means by saying it but also what the sense of meaning it is in the first place. In this passage, Spinoza expresses what sense meaning makes as well as presupposes. He writes, *"quo ipsam explicui,"* that is, "as I have explicated it"—where the *ipsam*, the "it," refers to the immediately preceding *rerum concatenationem*, "the concatenation of all things." But where has Spinoza explicated such a concatenation? Where has he explained how everything is interconnected? If one recalls the exact position of this passage in the text, this question is amenable to only one possible answer: he has explained it in *Ethics* I, which the six-point précis immediately preceding this passage has just summarized. However, there is no mention (literal or otherwise) of such a concatenation either in the précis or in that which this précis summarizes. Spinoza, thus, can mean only one thing here, namely, that what he has demonstrated in *Ethics* I is homologous with the concatenation of things. In this passage, Spinoza states that to demonstrate that God or substance is the immanent rather than transitive cause of itself and of modes is tantamount to asserting that all things are concatenated. Given that the argument regarding God or substance as immanent cause is not only the main thrust of *Ethics* I but also constitutes in effect the transcendental precondition of all other arguments and demonstrations found in the remaining four parts of the *Ethics*, the concatenation of things is being posited here as no less than the axiomatic foundation sustaining the entire theorematic edifice of this work and constituting the sovereign exception to its logical progression and structure. *Deus seu concatenatio*: God or concatenation: such is the pithy postulate of the *Ethics* at once being-as-chain and chain of beings, immanent cause and total relation.[22] To help us make sense of such a postulate—that immanent cause is the concatenation of things by a different name, that all things are related to one another, and indeed are bound and chained together, through that which at once brings them into existence as well as exists only to the extent to which it inheres in them—is precisely Spinoza's project in the *Ethics*.

(Incidentally, it is all the more remarkable and all the more appropriate to find such a fleeting yet crucial metacommentary there where we might expect least to find it. For it is ensconced in a subordinate clause—"..., *quo ipsam explicui*, ..."—which is delimited by commas and dependent on another subordinate clause, which is dependent on another subordinate clause, which is itself dependent on yet another subordinate clause, which is dependent on a primary clause, which is contained within a transitional group of sentences in the body of an appendix bridging *Ethics* I and *Ethics* II.[23] There is nothing particularly exceptional about such syntactical complexity per se, as it is not uncommon of Latin in general and even of Spinoza's fairly clear and relatively uncomplicated Latin in particular. More to the point, rather, is that Spinoza enacts and embeds this revealing aside within a fly-over zone of this work, or at any rate, within an easily overlooked textual enclave, whose primary purpose is to connect two sets of purportedly more significant sections of the work—not only *Ethics* I and *Ethics* II but also the beginning of the appendix consisting of the précis of *Ethics* I and the rest of the appendix consisting of the critique of those prejudices that impede our access to "understanding the concatenation of all things." Put differently, Spinoza posits the articulation of being as chain of things in a passage that not only signifies this meaning but also performs it by virtue of its parenthetical yet connective textual location, as it is positioned ostensibly as a mere link, as it is framed ostentatiously as no more than a chain in a chain of words.)

If absolute immanence is the ultimate signification and meaning of the *Ethics,* concatenation is its ultimate significance and sense. The *Ethics* at one stroke demonstrates absolute immanence as concept and expresses concatenation as sense. More precisely, the propositions comprising the *Ethics* at once *denote* the world as composition of substance and modes without any remainder, *manifest* both adequate and inadequate ways in which the human mode may experience this world, *signify* the concept of this world as absolute immanence, and *express* the sense of such a world as the concatenation of all things. And it is at a moment in this work when the denoting, manifesting, and signifying functions of its propositions are being held momentarily in abeyance that the ubiquitously implicit expressible becomes expressed, that sense leaves its mark on representation and emerges hidden in plain sight. What is unique about the passage in question, in fact, is that here sense is actually materialized and named, here sense finds its proper and adequate name in concatenation. This means that concatenation not only names the sense of the *Ethics* but also names sense as such. If sense is precisely the impossible interface between propositions and (their denoted) states of affairs, the relating nonrelation and conjunctive disjunction between words and things, then the concatenation of *all* things—that is, of all modes, including words and things—is sense par excellence.

Furthermore, as we saw earlier, there is no sense in words without a corresponding event in things. If concatenation is the expressed sense of the propositions comprising the *Ethics,* it is also the attributed event of that state of affairs that those propositions denote. Exactly what state and what affairs are these? A state of affairs may be described as a specific milieu, as a particular organization of stuff, as a determination of networks of relations among things, as a configuration of the world as composition of substance and modes at a certain point in space and time—in short, as a historical conjuncture. The historical conjuncture of the *Ethics* and of its author is well known. Here it might be instructive nonetheless to remind ourselves of a few of the more salient and relevant features of the world of seventeenth-century Amsterdam.

The ebullient, bustling *Stimmung* of this brave new world is captured well by a remark made by the philosopher whose thought was arguably most influential for Spinoza, namely, René Descartes. Around the time of Spinoza's birth in 1632, Descartes writes thus about Amsterdam, the city in which he spent much of his life: "In this large town in which I live, everyone but myself is engaged in trade, and hence is so attentive to his own profit that I could live here all my life without ever being noticed by a soul."[24] Unlike Descartes, Spinoza, for better and for worse, was never to be afforded the luxury of going unnoticed among and by so many profit-making souls—of which, for a time, he was one himself. For Spinoza was intimately acquainted with the ways of profit: he was born and grew up not only in the enthusiastically mercantile city described by Descartes and in its merchant-dominated Jewish community but also in a merchant family whose far-flung import–export business occupied him assiduously for more than a decade; he frequented regularly the Amsterdam stock exchange, which had been instituted recently as the first stock exchange in the world; he lived a stone's throw away from the Amsterdam chamber of the Vereenigde Oostindische Compagnie, the United East India Company, the spearhead of Dutch colonialism that had been founded three decades before his birth as the first joint-stock company in the world (hence as the precursor of our contemporary multinational corporation), whose first shares, exchanged in 1606, in effect brought the Amsterdam stock exchange into existence. (And as fate would have it, yet unsurprisingly, many a member of the council of Jewish notables that pronounced the *cherem*, or excommunication, on Spinoza in 1656, thereby severing his direct ties to the Jewish community as well as to the nascent world of capitalist and colonial enterprise for ever after, happened to be shareholders of the United East India Company.)[25] Moreover, Spinoza was the product of arguably one of the most cosmopolitan and transnational environments on the globe at the time—not only the Amsterdam of the heyday of Mercantilism but also its complex, diasporic, and polyglot Jewish community (at the time composed of recently immigrated Sephardim, primarily Marranos from the Iberian Peninsula, often via France, and to a lesser extent, recently immigrated Ashkenazim, primarily from Germany, Poland, and later Lithuania), whose members were increasingly connected, through chiefly mercantile and familial networks, also with many other parts of the world and especially with the slave-driven economies of the Black Atlantic (and indeed, Spinoza's own personal links to the New World, and to Brazil and the Caribbean in particular, were various and intricate).[26] One need not exaggerate what emerges from this picture to characterize such a state of affairs as the emergent interconnectivity of everything, under the aegis of capitalist exchange relations, on a tendentially and increasingly global scale. *Rerum concatenationem* indeed . . .

Something happened in seventeenth-century Amsterdam. This something must have been very complex, and hence very difficult to comprehend, if one is to judge from, among other things, the myriad volumes that have been and continue to be written about it. If this is something that, evidently, we cannot put to rest, we may rest assured that this something cannot put us to rest either—since it continues to this day as the very opposite of rest. In short, this something constitutes an event whose whole is greater than and irreducible to its parts, an event that is altogether in excess of whatever took place then and there, an event that at once was the cause–effect of a specific state of affairs and yet continues to haunt and to inhere as the cause–effect of our current and ongoing state of affairs, an event that at once is a product of history and yet does not belong merely in history (i.e., does not belong fully either to the history that produced it or to history at all), an event that is not only historical state of affairs but also extra-being or ontological surplus. "Concatenation" is the name of this event in the *Ethics*. Concatenation names at once a sense of words and an event of things, the sense of the *Ethics* and the event of its state of affairs, the sense of its propositions and the event of the state of affairs those propositions denote. The locution *rerum concatenationem* marks virtual sense-event in the *Ethics*.

This is not at all to conflate, however, the concept of absolute immanence, and its attendant and constitutive sense-event of concatenation, with globalizing capitalism as such. Just because the movement of capital lays out a plane of immanence by connecting everything and everybody all over the globe, it does not follow that there is no distinction between capitalism and immanence, between capitalism and the concatenation of all things. Indeed, to draw the (at times fashionable, often tendentious, and always facile) conclusion that, since capitalism and concatenation connect all (the same) things and share in the same logic (immanent causality), they must perforce have the same structure and indeed be one and the same, is not unlike arguing that a diamond, a lump of coal, and a graphite stick inside a pencil—all allotropes of carbon—are the same thing. To put it in more properly Spinozan terms, that there is no potential that is not also actual, and vice versa—one of Spinoza's foundational contentions in the *Ethics*—does not mean either that there is no distinction of any kind between potentiality and actuality or that there may be exclusively and necessarily one-to-one correlations between them (in the sense that that which is potential may manifest itself through one and only one specific mode of actualization).[27] Were such crucial distinctions between potentiality and actuality not to exist, the *Ethics* would constitute indeed not only an explication of the logic that underlies capitalism, among other things, but also an unabashed affirmation and endorsement of capitalism as ontological necessity and as ethical imperative *tout court*. (It is precisely by misrecognizing these distinctions and their consequences in Spinoza that Slavoj Žižek ends up identifying and denouncing Spinozism as the ideology of late capitalism.)[28] In short, capitalism is only one possible modality of actualization of absolute immanence—and a relativizing one, at that. Capitalism constitutes only one possible procedure for concatenating all things, or, which is to say the same thing, only one possible way of materializing surplus.[29]

There is ample reason to believe that Spinoza did not take much stock in capital as the supreme connector of all things. After all, Spinoza's apostatic repudiation of his own milieu—not only of its theological orthodoxies but also of its mercantile cupidity—could have been hardly more vehement. (Even though we may glean such repudiation from his writings, all of which date from the period after the excommunication, it has been argued convincingly that far from constituting a proverbial instance of sour grapes, Spinoza's disillusionment with and dissociation from his milieu well preceded and hence was the cause rather than the effect of his excommunication.)[30] On the opening pages of the *Treatise on the Emendation of the Intellect*, in an uncharacteristic moment of autobiographical introspection verging on the confessional, Spinoza sketches an unsparing portrait of the philosopher as a young man, thereby composing his own bildungsroman. There, while relating the difficulties of his philosophical apprenticeship, he denounces, with passion and in detail, the pursuit of that which human beings, if one is "to judge from their actions," "regard as the supreme good ... namely, wealth, rank, and sensual pleasure [*libidinem*]" (and to his credit, he does not downplay his own initial and considerable resistances to wresting himself away from such pursuits).[31] Later in life, in a letter to a friend, Spinoza rails against a pamphlet he had happened to read recently, in which wealth and rank are posited as the supreme good that must be attained by any means necessary. Spinoza tells his friend that he found this pamphlet "to be the most pernicious work man could devise or invent" and that he considered writing a response in which he would "show the troubled and wretched condition of those who covet rank and wealth; finally proving, by clear arguments and many examples, that the insatiable desire for rank and wealth must bring and has brought ruin to commonwealths."[32] Never one to be captive of the sad passions for too long, Spinoza quickly dispels such angry indignation toward the end of the letter by fittingly invoking Thales of Miletus and his belief that, among friends, all things are in common.[33]

One may object that there is nothing specifically anticapitalist or protocommunist about such jeremiads against money, power, and sex: it could be argued that Spinoza's protestations may apply only or primarily to premodern and precapitalist forms of social relations and that his views here might be more symptomatic, rather, of a somewhat sermonizing, censorious, and possibly even sanctimonious asceticism owing nothing to cognizance of the nefarious novelties of capitalism as such. All this may be the case to a degree. And yet matters become more complicated when considering the exact reasons Spinoza gives for his aversion to the profit-making, power-seeking ways of his world. In the *Treatise on the Emendation of the Intellect*, he also writes:

> The acquisition of money, sensual pleasure, and fame is a hindrance only as long as they are sought on their own account, and not as a means to other things. If they are sought as means, they will then be under some restriction, and far from being hindrances, they will do much to further the end for which they are sought.[34]

Later, in the appendix to *Ethics* IV, he reiterates, modifies, and expands on this point when explaining how human beings need one another—and, in particular, how they need to exchange with one another—not only to survive but also to live well. Spinoza writes:

> But the strength of any one person would hardly be enough to provide [well-being], unless men exchanged services. Money has provided a short cut to all these things, as a result of which its image tends to occupy the mind of the masses [*Mentem vulgi*] very much, because they can hardly imagine any kind of happiness unless it is accompanied by the idea of money as its cause. But this is a fault only of those who seek money, not out of poverty or on account of the necessities of life, but because they have learned the arts of profit [*lucri artes*], whereby they boast most pompously and arrogantly. . . . But those who know the true use of money, and limit their wealth simply to what they need, live content with little.

In these two passages, Spinoza is making a crucial distinction between money as a means to the satisfaction of needs and money as an end unto itself, between, on one hand, money in its exclusively instrumental—and hence limited and limiting—function of medium of exchange and circulation and, on the other hand, money in its limitless, self-referential, self-reproducing, surplus function. Whereas he looks on the former favorably—not only because it facilitates and expedites the process of bringing human beings together in common welfare and in commonwealth but also because it is strictly limited by and subordinate to the satisfaction of needs—he condemns the latter precisely because there is no limit to it and hence is bound to run amok, to become the sole telos of exchange, to elevate itself above, subjugate, and bring ruin to the human commonwealth. In short, Spinoza identifies here the difference between money (as medium of exchange) and (money as) capital. In such scathing denunciations of the "insatiable desire for . . . wealth," the emphasis is placed squarely on the insatiability—namely, on the limitless character—of this desire even more than on the desire per se: it is precisely in such a drive to limitlessness that Spinoza discerns the disastrous, alchemic metamorphosis of money into capital. Spinoza's critique here is already a critique of capitalism, or at the very least, a critique of that always already latent capitalist tendency intrinsic in older forms (and, indeed, in all forms) of mercantile exchange and circulation—a tendency that in his own time was fully emergent, as it was beginning to engulf the globe in its totality and to turn the globe into a totality. No wonder, then, that Spinoza's words echo uncannily in much that Marx has to say on these matters, and especially in the passages quoted at the beginning of this essay. Here is, once again, Marx in *Capital*:

> The simple circulation of commodities—selling in order to buy—is a means to a final goal which lies outside circulation, namely the appropriation of use-values, the satisfaction of needs. As against this, the circulation of money as capital is an end in itself, for the valorization of value takes place only within this constantly renewed movement. The movement of capital is therefore limitless.[35]

My point is not that Marx had read Spinoza: we know that he had (as well as that he had done so largely through the tendentious lens of Hegel's interpretation).[36] The point, rather, is that here, in grappling with the same problematic, Marx and Spinoza share and converge in a common philosophical discourse, namely, the Aristotelian tradition. At the end of the preceding passage, Marx appends a detailed and appreciative footnote on Aristotle's forays into the realm of the economic, found in Book I of his *Politics*. In words—and, more important, according to a logic—that are barely distinguishable from Spinoza's own, Aristotle there famously contrasts two related yet crucially different arts, namely, *oikonomía* (economics) and *chrematistiké* (chrematistics), both of which involve the "art of acquisition" and hence exchange. Economics is the "art of managing a household," namely, the "natural art of acquisition which is practiced by managers of households and by statesmen." For Aristotle, economics is necessary and limited, in the sense that there is a limit to the number of things to be acquired that are "necessary to life, and useful for the community of the family or state." Such things "are the element of true riches; for the amount of property which is needed for a good life is not unlimited." By contrast, chrematistics is the art of acquiring wealth simply for the sake of acquiring wealth.

For Aristotle, chrematistics is unnecessary and unlimited, in the sense that there is no limit to how much wealth can be acquired and that such unlimited acquisition of wealth is not necessary for the management of the household. If these two arts often are confused for one another or thought to be one and the same, Aristotle argues, that is because the "measure" and the "unit of exchange" is the same in both, namely, money. Each of these arts, he writes, "is a use of the same property, but with a difference": whereas the telos of economics is the satisfaction of needs by exchanging money for things or services, the telos of chrematistics is "accumulation" of money—which is why those who confuse the latter for the former think that "the whole idea of their lives is that they ought either to increase their money without limit, or at any rate not to lose it."[37] (Importantly, and unsurprisingly, even more blistering is Aristotle's indictment of usury as the most extreme and "most unnatural" form of chrematistics because "the natural object of" money is "to be used in exchange, but not to increase at interest.")[38] Aside from all the numerous terminological as well as conceptual resonances with Spinoza, it should be noted also that when, in the passage quoted from the appendix to *Ethics* IV, Spinoza refers to the "arts of profit" (as distinct from seeking money because of poverty or to satisfy needs), he uses a locution—*lucri artes*—that is as adequate a Latin rendition as any of the Aristotelian *chrematistiké*. Moreover, such unmistakably Aristotelian echoes in Spinoza are all the more significant if one considers that Spinoza, even though well versed in the Aristotelian and Scholastic traditions, not only did not revere such traditions as dogma but also was at times very critical of them, and even went as far as declaring that Aristotle's authority carried little weight with him.[39] In short, here Spinoza and Marx seize and build specifically on that most prescient aspect of Aristotle's thought that senses (as well as sketches the main contours of) an incipient logic of unbridled growth that is the very logic of capitalism. Spinoza and Marx derive at least two fundamental insights into the realm of the economic from Aristotle, namely, the distinction between money as means of exchange and money as end of exchange, as well as the distinction between the limited circulation of the former and the limitless circulation of the latter.

It is precisely the latter that Marx does not hesitate to call God.[40]

In the *Grundrisse*—whose first chapter constitutes a detailed and complex analytic of money—Marx understands money as having three semiautonomous and at times simultaneous functions: money as measure of value, money as medium of exchange and circulation, and money as money. This last, however, is more precisely defined as the interaction of two mutually determining and mutually negating functions: money as money, namely, money as the "general form of wealth," and money as capital, namely, money as the "material representative of general wealth."[41] In its Janus-headed third function, money sublates the other two and exceeds the process of precapitalist circulation to become the modern, independent, general form of wealth. It is of such a veritable transcendence-in-immanence that Marx writes:

> From its servile role, in which it appears as mere medium of circulation, [money] suddenly changes into the lord and god of commodities. It represents the divine existence of commodities, while they represent its earthly form.[42]

Marx does not elaborate his divine metaphor any further, and hence it is impossible to ascertain exactly what (definition of) God he has in mind here. Such a double articulation of money in its third and properly capitalist function (namely, money-as-commodities and commodities-as-money, exchange value as use values and use values as exchange value, the One as the All and the All as the One), however, does bear more than a passing resemblance to the relation between substance and modes in Spinoza: it is them and they are it—each morphologically different. More important, in the next paragraph, Marx writes:

> Monetary greed, or mania for wealth, necessarily brings with it the decline and fall of the ancient communities [*Gemeinwesen*]. Hence it is the antithesis to them. It is itself the community [*Gemeinwesen*], and can tolerate none other standing above it. But this presupposes the full development of exchange values, hence a corresponding organization of society. In antiquity, exchange value was not the *nexus rerum* [nexus of all things]; it appears as such only among the mercantile peoples [whether in antiquity, in the Middle Ages,

or later], who had, however, no more than a carrying trade and did not, themselves, produce.[43]

The complexity of the relation between Marx and Spinoza is captured exemplarily and in the highest degree by the asymmetrical correspondences between the uncannily similar yet crucially different locutions *nexus rerum* and *rerum concatenationem*. If, earlier, Marx had compared money in its third function to God, here he explains that in mercantile societies, such a God "appears"—at once comes into being, emerges into visibility, and hence enters the field of representation—as the nexus of all things. What Spinoza discovered implicitly and Marx rediscovered explicitly, and what Aristotle was not in a position even to imagine, is that in money-as-capital, all things are bound together, that capital is a form of the nexus of all things, that capital at once materializes and usurps God as concatenation of all things—in short, that capital makes it possible to think the ontological function of God as absolute immanence (thereby also making it difficult yet all the more urgent to distinguish between itself and absolute immanence as such). The unthinkable for antiquity is not exactly capital per se: we have seen how Aristotle—who is well acquainted with the mercantile milieu—anticipates and denounces the structural and definitional features of capital in and as *chrematistiké*. ("Hence," Marx writes, "the wailing of the ancients about money as the source of all evils."[44]) The unthinkable for antiquity, rather, is that the realm of exchange and the realm of metaphysics, that the realm of the economic and the realm of the ontological, could have anything at all to do with one another —let alone overlap to the point of indiscernibility.[45] Such an overlap, thus, might be as good a name as any for modernity itself: distinct yet indiscernible, such are the economic and the ontological in and after modernity.

Yet Spinoza's *rerum concatenationem* is not exactly one and the same with Marx's *nexus rerum*. Whereas the former constitutes the sense-event that, on one hand, corresponds explicitly to the concept of absolute immanence and, on the other hand, corresponds implicitly to the state of affairs of emergent capitalist globalization, the latter constitutes the sense-event corresponding explicitly to both. Or as Marx puts it in the passage from *Capital* quoted at the beginning of this essay, "the tendency to create the *world market* is directly given in the concept of capital itself. Every limit appears as a barrier to be overcome."[46] Spinoza does state, in effect, that the concatenation of all things is directly given in the concept of absolute immanence. Spinoza does understand also the concept of capital as well as its attendant and constitutive logic of limitlessness. If he does not connect explicitly these two distinct lines of reasoning and hence does not articulate these two distinct components of his thought into one explicit conceptual constellation—thereby closing the circuit that will remain open up until Marx—it is because of historical factors rather than conceptual inadequacies. Marx elucidates such factors well by pointing out in the passage quoted earlier that even though in all mercantile societies, money already appears in its properly capitalist function and hence as *nexus rerum*, such societies nonetheless are not yet organized accordingly, in the sense that they have not achieved "the full development of exchange values" because they do "not, themselves, produce" but engage in commercial exchange only. Obviously, Marx is not saying that there is no production of any kind in mercantile societies; rather it is production of a very specific kind he has in mind here. On the same page, he writes:

> It is inherent in the simple character of money itself that it can exist as a developed moment of production only where and when *wage labour* exists; that in this case, far from subverting the social formation, it is rather a condition for its development and a driving-wheel for the development of all forces of production, material and mental.[47]

The "full development of exchange values" and its "corresponding organization of society"—namely, the new "social formation" that emerges from the ruins of ancient commonwealths, much like the phoenix rising from its own ashes—can take place only in the presence of modern industrial production based on the wage, which is the kind of production mercantile societies do not have. And in fact, in the immediately following paragraph, Marx refers to seventeenth- and eighteenth-century Mercantilism proper as the age that precedes "the development of modern industrial society."[48] The point, in other words, is that in the mercantile society Spinoza knows and understands so well, on one hand, money appears already in its capitalist form of *nexus rerum* and, on the other hand, money is not yet really fully the *nexus rerum* (i.e., its potential as *nexus rerum* is not yet completely actualized) because such a society does not function and is not organized according to wage relations.[49] It is this historical as well as ontological discrepancy between a potential and its specific mode of actualization that leads Spinoza to conceive of absolute immanence as *rerum concatenationem* separately from what was at the time its emergent manifestation as well as its conceptual condition of possibility—in short, separately from what was its cause-effect, namely, globalizing capitalism. But it is also such a discrepancy that enables Spinoza to denounce globalizing capitalism without, for this reason, having to throw out the ontological baby with the economic bathwater, that is, without having thus to humiliate absolute immanence as such by denigrating it or retranscendentalizing it. Arguably, since Spinoza, most attempts to critique capitalism have misrecognized the latter as being one and the same with immanence itself and hence have ended up critiquing immanence tout court. Hence the wailing of the moderns and the postmoderns—and especially of the bureaucrats of the dialectic—about immanence as the source of all evils.

It is here—on the plane of immanence—that Marx and Spinoza meet. (Their meeting, thus, is not unlike the infinitely repeated yet always impossible rendezvous between the man and the woman in Alain Resnais's *L'Année dernière à Marienbad*—with Aristotle undoubtedly cast in the role of the jealous husband.) *Marx is the first to discover in the concept of capital that tendency toward the world market that—though not yet fully actual in his own time, let alone in Spinoza's time—constitutes nonetheless the condition of possibility of Spinoza's discovery of that ontological connectivity given in the concept of absolute immanence that manifests itself first and foremost as the very tendency toward the world market Marx discovers in the concept of capital in the first place.* Put differently, Marx's *nexus rerum* constitutes the transcendental precondition of Spinoza's *rerum concatenationem*. To posit thus Marx before Spinoza—namely, to posit Marx as logically prior to Spinoza—constitutes the prolegomena to any future attempt to think these two thinkers together and in common, to think them as sharing not only in common philosophical and political traditions, genealogies, and discourses but also in common philosophical and political possibilities and projects.

On Globalization as Unconscious

If it is the case, thus, that the first and mercantile modality of capitalism becomes legible and intelligible as such in its second and industrial modality, it is also the case that the current, third, fully global, and communicative modality of capitalism may be found encrypted already in the first one to begin with.[50] We have come back full circle here to the contemporary Jamesonian–Althusserian question that opened this essay—undoubtedly itself a question enabled and necessitated by this third modality of capitalism. This is the question—or rather the twin questions—of the inaccessibility by consciousness and in representation, as well as of the purported accessibility by nonrepresentational kinds of knowledge, of that totality that is the capitalist mode of production intended as absent cause immanent in its own effects. It is specifically from the standpoint of this question that I would like now to return to Spinoza's *rerum concatenationem*. And I would like to return first of all to the verb of which this locution from the appendix to *Ethics* I is the direct object: *"rerum concatenationem . . . quo ipsam explicui"*—"the concatenation of all things as I have explicated it." The verb *explicare*—literally, "to unfold," and hence to explicate or to explain—is hardly an innocent term in Spinoza. In *Expressionism in Philosophy*, Deleuze has shown how this verb acquires a particularly charged significance for Spinoza as early as the *Treatise on the Emendation of the Intellect*.[51] More important, Deleuze has shown how in Spinoza, not only *explicare* functions in tandem with another verb, *involvere*—literally, "to envelop," and hence to involve or to implicate—but also how both are to be understood as "the correlates that accompany and further specify the idea of expression."[52] To explicate or explain and to involve or implicate are the two complementary functions of expression.[53]

Before proceeding any further, let me take note of several interrelated matters. First of all, both as a term and as a concept, *expression*, as is well known, constitutes the foundation of Deleuze's epochal interpretation of Spinoza's thought in *Expressionism in Philosophy*. This is an interpretation that starts from and returns over and again to a detailed explication of a crucial passage in the *Ethics* (as well as of its resonances and ramifications throughout the entire Spinozan opus), namely, *Ethics* I, D6: "By God I understand an absolutely infinite entity, that is, a substance consisting of infinite attributes, each of which expresses eternal and infinite essence." (And for our present purposes, it might be useful also to draw attention to at least two of this passage's reverberations, i.e., *Ethics* I, P25C, in which we read that "particular things are nothing other than the affections, i.e. the modes, of the attributes of God, by which the attributes of God are expressed in a certain and determinate way," and *Ethics* I, P36Pr., in which we read that "whatever exists expresses the nature, i.e. the essence, of God in a certain and determinate way.") Deleuze's interpretation of Spinoza, in other words, arises and develops from the fundamental insight that in this thinker expression is a certain way of being, a certain ontological operation or process, that appertains both to substance and to modes, that connects them via the attributes, and that also has important epistemological implications (since for Spinoza, after all, an ideation of any kind is a mode too, specifically, a mode of thought). Second, however, we have encountered expression already in another context. Earlier, I showed that when Deleuze, in *The Logic of Sense,* articulates sense as the expressed or expressible of the proposition, he, in effect, posits expression there as the fourth and foundational function of the proposition constituting the cause-effect of the other three (namely, denotation, manifestation, signification). At that point, I also associated expression with Spinoza's third kind of knowledge, for reasons that will become manifest presently. Third, I believe that these two Deleuzian articulations of expression have very much in common. Even though Deleuze mentions Spinoza only once (and in passing) in *The Logic of Sense,* this work explains what is at stake in the (Spinozan) concept of expression in more direct, explicit, and possibly also more trenchant ways than much of what we read in *Expressionism in Philosophy.*[54] I am arguing, in other words, that in some important ways, *The Logic of Sense* explicates *Expressionism in Philosophy* (which had appeared one year earlier). Fourth, and for our present purposes, most important, as I will try to show in what follows, Deleuze's understanding of expression, in its various modulations across these two seminal works, is crucial for an interpretation of Spinoza as theorist of globalization—and hence another excursus is necessary here, starting from the relation between explication and expression and ending with the relation between expression and representation.

If explication is literally an unfolding of that which expresses itself—for example, an unfolding of substance as it expresses itself in its modes via its attributes—exactly what is it, then, to explicate something? What is involved and implied in explication? What am I and what am I doing, how do I think and how do I know, when I explicate something? In *Expressionism in Philosophy*, Deleuze writes:

> One cannot reduce expression to the mere explication of understanding. . . . For explication, far from amounting to the operation of an understanding that remains outside its object, amounts primarily to the object's own evolution, its very life. . . . Rather than expression being comprehensible in terms of explication, explication in Spinoza . . . seems to me to depend on some idea of expression. . . . It is expression that underlies the relation of understanding between thought and object, rather than the reverse.[55]

Later in the same work, Deleuze adds:

> Expressions are always explications. But the explications of the understanding are only perceptions. It is not understanding that explicates substance, but the explications of substance refer necessarily to an understanding that understands them.[56]

The onto-epistemological implications of such a conception of the relation between explication and expression are radical and manifold. First, there is no breathing room for the ego—and for its narcissistic mirages, specular projections, and imaginary identifications—within the ceaseless explicative unfoldings and implicative foldings of expression. It turns out that whenever I explicate something—that is, if and when I really do so—I am not I. In explication, I am, act, think, and know as other than I, that is, as Other.[57] What a subject may think of as its own explicative understanding of an object is part and parcel of that object: it is, more precisely, that part of the object—that function in its "very life"—that not only refers to but also involves and envelops the subject in the first place. (Undoubtedly, this is another way of saying that so-called subjects and so-called objects are all modes sharing in a common substance that determines both just as it is determined by them.) In short, unlike other, more instrumental, and indeed more Cartesian ways of being and acting, of thinking and knowing, a subject's explication of an object is never a property of that subject—and I do mean *property* here both as quality and as ownership—and hence is never a conquest, mastery, or possession of that object.[58] It is, rather, a feature and a capacity of the object itself. Indeed, in a later commentary on Spinoza, Deleuze puts it even more tersely:

> [Explication in Spinoza] does not signify an operation of the intellect external to the thing, but an operation of the thing internal to the intellect. Even demonstrations are said to be "eyes" of the mind, meaning that they perceive a movement that is in the thing. Explication is always a self-explication, a development, an unfolding, a dynamism: the thing *explains itself*.[59]

I explicate the thing only to the extent to which the thing unfolds and explains itself in me—thereby involving, implicating, and binding us both in a mutually transformative amplexus. The term *dynamism* in this passage indicates what is at stake in Deleuze's formulations: explication is an operation of *dynamis*—the term in Aristotle's *Metaphysics* that is commonly translated as "potentiality." Explication, thus, is an activation of potentiality (in the thing as well as in me). A contingent encounter takes place, say, between the thing and me, such that the thing's capacity to affect me and my capacity to be affected by the thing are activated in such a way that we both turn into something other than what we were prior to our encounter in the first place—and thus contingency turns into (shared, mutual) necessity. Explication constitutes that function of expression that may be described as interference and metamorphosis through common *dynamis*. In explication, expression is revealed as an absolutely impersonal and nonanthropomorphic operation of being and acting, thinking and knowing, that concerns and involves that which is potential in substance and in modes.[60]

Second, all the preceding indicate that something takes place in expression (including in its function of explication) which escapes representation and on which, however, representation feeds and is founded. According to Deleuze, what we think of typically as the explications of our understanding are indeed explications—but not of our understanding! Though they certainly involve our understanding if and when they are understood by it, they are of substance and of modes other than us and hence not of our understanding (which is to say that they are not generated in our intellectual faculties and processes). When strictly of our understanding, in other words, explications are not explications at all: they are, rather, nothing more and nothing less than perceptions, namely, our representational modes of thinking and knowing that which explicates itself in us. In short, explication is not limited to those operations of the intellect that it does involve and that Spinoza designates as the first kind of knowledge (i.e., representational knowledge based solely on sensory perceptions and semiotic systems). Explication always involves representation yet is not defined and exhausted by it. This is all the more so for expression, if it is the case, as Deleuze maintains, that expression is what any explication "depends on" as well as what "underlies the relation of understanding between thought and object, rather than the reverse."[61] In short, expression—in its twin functions of explication and implication, folding and unfolding—enables any representational form of thought and knowledge. Expression constitutes that immanent ground of representation that representation itself cannot represent by definition. Here, in other words, I am reaching through a different procedure the same conclusions I reached earlier, namely, that expression always concerns that which is potential in substance as well as in modes: potentiality qua potentiality, in fact, cannot enter the field of representation even as it makes itself felt there; potentiality qua potentiality constitutes the unrepresentable absolute.

The somewhat tacit primacy of expression over representation in *Expressionism in Philosophy* is pushed to its logical conclusions as well as brought to the fore in an illuminating passage of *The Logic of Sense*. There, while discussing the concept of representation in Stoic philosophy, Deleuze explains how the Stoics, even though they differentiated between sensible representations and rational representations, conceived of both as corporeal, that is, as imprints that bodies leave on bodies.[62] Such corporeal imprints, however, are themselves determined by something incorporeal, namely, by virtual sense-event. Deleuze writes:

Sensible representations are denotations and rational representations are significations, while only incorporeal events constitute expressed sense. We have encountered this difference of nature between the expression and the representation at every turn, each time we noted the specificity of sense or of the event, its irreducibility to the denotatum and to the signified, its neutrality in relation to the particular and to the general, or its impersonal and pre-individual singularity.... But, if sense is never an object of possible representation, it does not for this reason intervene any less in representation as that which confers a very special value to the relation that it maintains with its object.

By itself, representation is given up to an extrinsic relation of resemblance or similitude only. But its internal character, by which it is intrinsically "distinct," "adequate," or "comprehensive," comes from the manner in which it encompasses, or envelops an expression, much as it may not be able to represent it.... For example, the perception of death as a state of affairs and as a quality, or the concept "mortal" as a predicate of signification, remain extrinsic (deprived of sense) as long as they do not encompass the event of dying as that which is actualized in the one and expressed in the other. Representation must encompass an expression which it does not represent, but without which it itself would not be "comprehensive," and would have truth only by chance or from the outside. To know that we are mortal is an apodeictic knowledge, albeit empty and abstract; effective and successive deaths do not suffice of course in fulfilling this knowledge adequately, so long as one does not come to know death as an impersonal event provided with an always open problematic structure (where and when?). In fact, two types of knowledge *(savoir)* have often been distinguished, one indifferent, remaining external to its object, and the other concrete, seeking its object wherever it is. Representation attains this topical ideal only by means of the hidden expression which it encompasses, that is, by means of the event it envelops. There is thus a "use" of representation, without which representation would remain lifeless and senseless. Wittgenstein and his disciples are right to define meaning by means of use. But such use is not defined through a function of representation in relation to the represented, nor even through representativeness as the form of possibility. Here, as elsewhere, the functional is transcended in the direction of a topology, and use is in the relation between representation and something extra-representative, a nonrepresented and merely expressed entity. Representation envelops the event in another nature, it envelops it at its borders, it stretches until this point, and it brings about this lining or hem. This is an operation which defines living usage, to the extent that representation, when it does not reach this point, remains only a dead letter confronting that which it represents, and stupid in its representativeness.[63]

It is in this formidable passage above all that *The Logic of Sense* explicates a crucial aspect of *Expressionism in Philosophy*. This passage reveals how Deleuze's singularly daring, original, and fruitful hermeneutical wager in *Expressionism in Philosophy*—namely, his having spun a reinterpretation of Spinoza's entire philosophical system out of the single term and concept of expression—had been designed to yield a twofold result. On one hand, in producing the (Spinozan) concept of expression, this work had aimed to offer a forceful critique of the (Platonic) concept of representation, namely, that mimetic modality of representation that entertains only an "extrinsic relation of resemblance" with its object, thereby positing (the Idea of) the latter as the original and positing itself as its more or less faithful copy. On the other hand, expression in this work had been put forth not as an alternative to representation, which then would have to be discarded or dismissed altogether, but, on the contrary, as an attempt to salvage representation in extremis by rescuing it from the long history of its Platonic determinations and by refounding it on nonmimetic grounds: the concept of expression had been devised to show that a whole other world of representation is possible, in which representation would entertain intrinsic relations to its object such that it would let itself be marked by something unrepresentable in the object, such that it would let itself be shaped by the object's immanent potential (rather than by its transcendent Idea). This passage in *The Logic of Sense* indicates that *Expressionism in Philosophy* had posited expression as that which enables representation to represent the object not as it is (i.e., in its likeness) but as it could be (i.e., in its capability to be different from what it is). And hence these two works taken together argue in effect (1) that expression is to representation what potentiality is to actuality (and hence that their relation is one of mutual immanence without any remainder) and (2) that representation may relate to the expression it always "encompasses" in two radically different kinds of ways: either by negating it in mimesis (i.e., by foreclosing it altogether, thereby remaining "lifeless and senseless," "empty and abstract") or by affirming it (i.e., by acknowledging it as cause, thereby deriving life and sense from it). For Deleuze, not all representation is mimesis, and mimesis, rather, is what representation becomes when alienated from (its appertaining) expression. For Deleuze, as much as for Spinoza, it is never a question of circumventing or destroying representation altogether. It is, rather, a more complex and more delicate question of distinguishing among different modalities as well as usages of representation on the basis of the different procedures according to which such modalities and such usages give certain, determinate, actual form to the expression of potentiality; it is a question of differentiating among the modalities and usages of representation on the basis of the various procedures according to which they let themselves be formed, imprinted, altered, and guided by potentiality as it implicates and explicates itself, folds and unfolds itself in us all. For both thinkers, it is ultimately a question of reading or mapping the unrepresentable contractions and dilations of being in representation: it is, in short, a question of *making sense.*

We can return now to Spinoza's locution—"the concatenation of all things as I have explicated it"—and reconsider it from the vantage point of such a theorization of expression. First of all, in this locution, Spinoza is invoking a strictly impersonal and nonanthropomorphic operation of being and acting, thinking and knowing: the object of concatenation explains itself here in the grammatical subject that comprehends it; put differently, the concatenation of all things belongs to the order of those phenomena which can be understood and explained by that mode we call the "I" only to the extent to which the latter is able to make sense of how such a concatenation explicates itself in it, thereby involving it and transforming it irreparably in the first place. The verb *explicare* indicates that there is no I witnessing the radically transformative encounter taking place here with such a concatenation or that, if there is an I here, that is so to the extent to which I emerge from that encounter and am constituted by the concatenation of all things. I exist only ex post facto: I come into being only after and as a by-product of concatenation. If there is any mode at all here to which we may refer as subject and as object, that is so to the extent to which expression has already done its job because it "underlies the relation of understanding between thought and object, rather than the reverse."[64] If such an interpretation of Spinoza's use of the verb *explicare* here seems far-fetched, consider the nature of those prejudices that, according to Spinoza, "have had, and still have, the power to constitute a major obstacle to men's understanding of the concatenation of all things as I have explicated it" and that he proceeds to critique systematically and mercilessly in the remaining pages of the appendix to *Ethics* I. Immediately following the passage in question, Spinoza writes:

> All the prejudices that I undertake to point out here depend on one fact: that men commonly suppose that all natural things act on account of an end, as they themselves do. Indeed they think it certain that God himself directs all things towards a certain end, for they say that God has made everything on account of man, and man in order that he might worship God.

Spinoza is unequivocal here: it is impossible to understand the concatenation of all things—which is to say that it is impossible to make real sense of such a concatenation as it expresses itself in us—unless we abnegate all anthropomorphic, anthropocentric, and hence teleological common sense.

Moreover, the verb *explicare* indicates also that when confronted with the concatenation of all things, representation fails, is inadequate, does not suffice by itself. Put obversely, concatenation cannot be merely represented and needs also to be explicated. In short, concatenation operates at the level of expression, and it is only there that it may be found, understood, and made sense of—which is what I meant earlier when I suggested that the locution *rerum concatenationem* constitutes virtual sense-event that defies yet marks representation in the *Ethics*. But let us put this in more specifically Spinozan terms. The concatenation of all things cannot be grasped adequately through the first kind of knowledge, namely, that assemblage of representational knowledge based solely on sensory perceptions and semiotic systems, which, importantly, Spinoza refers to also as "imagination" and "opinion" (*Ethics* II, P40S2). Concatenation cannot be understood fully and distinctly by relying only on the sensorium and its perceptions and images, on the power of the imaginary and its egocentric fantasies, on signs taken for wonders, on common sense or *doxa*. Having said that, however, one would have to add that to state that the first kind of knowledge fails when faced with the concatenation of all things is not saying much yet because for Spinoza failure is constitutive of this kind of knowledge. The onto-epistemological processes comprising representational knowledge are always inherently inadequate by definition: they are, in Spinoza's words, "vague," "mutilated," "confused" (*Ethics* II, P40S2)—which is also to say, however, that they are never completely inaccurate or absolutely false because for Spinoza the false consists in privation of knowledge and hence can never be absolute, while only truth is absolute by definition. In short, for Spinoza, representation always fails and never fails absolutely.

The concatenation of all things, however, constitutes not only a failure of representation but also a failure of reason. For Spinoza, the second kind of knowledge or "reason" is based on "common notions and adequate ideas of the properties of things" (*Ethics* II, P40S2). These are the ideas or concepts that two or more things have in common, including those "ideas . . . which are common to all human beings" (*Ethics* II, P37), because for Spinoza, all things agree in certain, determinate respects, and hence all things have something actually in common (cf. at least *Ethics* II, L2, L2Pr.). (As I will point out, however, there is a world of difference between having in common and being in common, as the former pertains only to actuality, whereas the latter pertains also to potentiality.) For Spinoza, that reason by definition is founded on adequate modes of thought has numerous momentous consequences such as, for example, that reason is conceptual rather than representational[65] as well as that it "is necessarily true" and indeed "teaches us to distinguish the true from the false" (*Ethics* II, P40S2). And yet, even though Spinoza clearly holds reason intended as conceptual knowledge in very high regard, he intimates nonetheless that such knowledge is able to understand the concatenation of all things only by translating it, as it were, into a different language that retains its signification yet loses all its significance in the process: reason is able to come to terms with concatenation not as (expressed) sense but only as (signified) concept. As you will recall, Spinoza states that he has explicated the concatenation of all things there where in fact he had done nothing of the sort, or, rather, there where he had done something quite different, albeit related, namely, demonstrating the corresponding concept of absolute immanence. Reason can signify, demonstrate, and produce concepts but cannot make sense. And without sense, conceptual knowledge remains as "lifeless," "empty and abstract" as representational knowledge: from the standpoint of sense-event and expression, there is no difference at all between the first and the second kinds of knowledge (because they both engage with substance and modes only at the level of the actual).[66] In short, I am suggesting that the concatenation of all things can neither be denoted or manifested as actual representation by the first kind of knowledge nor signified or demonstrated as actual concept by the second kind of knowledge and that, rather, it can be only expressed as virtual sense-event by the third kind of knowledge, by intuitive knowledge. Moreover, I am also suggesting that it is precisely to make sense of concatenation that Spinoza finds it necessary to conceive of an intuitive knowledge that would comprehend yet also go beyond the capabilities of both conceptual knowledge and representational knowledge.[67] The concatenation of all things constitutes the raison d'être of intuitive knowledge.

Genevieve Lloyd has encapsulated the interlocking assemblage of the three kinds of knowledge in an admirably succinct and clear manner:

> The first way of knowing is focused on singular things, but is inherently inadequate. The second is inherently adequate, but unable to grasp the essence of singular things. The third and highest kind of knowledge is inherently adequate and able to understand singular things.[68]

Lloyd is implying that the reason why intuitive knowledge is indispensable, even though conceptual knowledge is just as adequate and truthful in and of itself (cf. *Ethics* II, P41, P42), is that these two kinds of knowledge have radically different aims or ends: whereas conceptual knowledge is concerned with that which things actually have in common, intuitive knowledge is concerned with the essence of things, namely, with that which makes things singular and which, thus, cannot be had or shared in common by definition. (It is crucial to note that Spinoza's concept of essence is a strictly nonessentialist and immanentist one: a singular essence is inherent and appertains to each mode as well as to substance, whose essence, unlike modal essences, is "one and the same" with its existence and hence is to exist necessarily [see *Ethics* I, P20; cf. also n. 84]. In short, no two essences can be shared or can be alike.)[69] More specifically, Spinoza states that intuitive knowledge "proceeds from an adequate idea of the formal essence of some of the attributes of God to an adequate knowledge of the essence of things" (*Ethics* II, P40S2). As Lloyd accurately notes, the definitional object or end of intuitive knowledge is indeed "the essence of things." It seems to me, though, that here it is a question not only of its object but also of its onto-epistemological procedure: what is so indispensable and unique about the third kind of knowledge is not only its end but also its means. The means—that is, the route that is to be followed to approach and to achieve such an end—are just as crucial as the end itself: to conceive of modal essence, this kind of knowledge "proceeds," in effect, from the essence of substance; to be known adequately, in other words, modal essence needs to be deduced from the essence of substance. Intuitive knowledge entails not only understanding that *aliquid,* that certain something, that makes each and every thing singularly what it is but also, and crucially, understanding such *aliquid* by starting from that which necessarily exists in the thing, which is not its essence but the essence of substance. Through a deductive procedure, such knowledge produces a link between the essence of substance and the essence of modes: it reaches and comprehends the singular essence of each and every thing by linking it to the essence of substance that is immanent yet irreducible to it. In short, it is at one stroke that intuitive knowledge understands modal essence and links it to the essence of substance—and hence that understanding and that linking may no longer be distinguished from one another. This is tantamount to saying that intuitive knowledge conceives of modal essence in and as the link to the essence of substance: modal essence is the link between itself and that which causes all modes to exist as linked to one another. It turns out that that which is most singular about each and every thing derives from and consists in precisely its being a link to the link of all links, namely, *nexus rerum* or *rerum concatenationem*. That which is most singular in us all is the manner in which we relate to—that is, the way in which we live—our being embedded in and constituted by the concatenation of all things.

Concatenation is not the taking place of the common, if the latter is intended as the network of relations interwoven by the common notions, namely, by the actual concepts of those actual things that we have in common. Concatenation, rather, is the taking place of the singular. And it is in constituting the taking place of the singular that concatenation does constitute also the taking place of the common: for it is not through that which we have in common that we are in common; it is, rather, in our singularity, in our immanent difference, in our potential to become different from what we are that we are really in common.[70] In what may seem like a paradox, the concatenation of all things is the real being-in-common precisely because it is not the locus of common notions or concepts and because it is instead the taking place of most singular sense-event. And only sense-event can make us different from what we are, only sense-event constitutes the cause–effect of whatever metamorphosis. In a particularly incisive and compelling passage in *Ethics* V, P36S, Spinoza writes:

> The knowledge of singular things, which I have called intuitive, or, of the third kind . . . is more powerful than the universal knowledge that I have said to be of the second kind. For although I have shown generally in Part One that all things . . . depend on God in respect of essence and existence, yet that demonstration—although legitimate and beyond doubt—does not so affect our mind as when it is inferred from the very essence of any singular thing which we declare to depend on God.

In a stunning moment of clarity, this purportedly most rationalist of philosophers tells us that thinking and knowing within the limits of reason alone do not change a thing. Such is the trouble with reason: it is too general, too "universal"—and hence it does not affect us enough. Reason and its concepts lack enough power to move us, to transform us significantly. (Undoubtedly, this is why the critique of ideology, absolutely necessary as it may well be at times, does not suffice to undermine the relations of power and the relations of production that need and produce ideology and on which ideology depends. Undoubtedly, this is also what Spinoza is hinting at in his famous example of our perception of the distance separating us from the sun.)[71] In particular, that which Spinoza demonstrates in *Ethics* I as concept according to the diktat of reason—namely, "that all things . . . depend on God in respect of essence and existence," that all things are embedded in that which at once causes them and inheres in them, that all things are concatenated—is never so powerful as when it makes sense at the level of our "very essence," at the level of our link to the link of all links, at the level of our most singular manner of being-in-common, of being-in-the-world.

The concatenation of all things is the world as plane of immanence, namely, as that which can neither be represented nor be conceptualized and can only be expressed as sense-event or transcendental precondition of both representations and concepts.[72] Strictly speaking, the plane of immanence cannot even be thought. In *What Is Philosophy?*—in a passage that names Spinoza as the "greatest philosopher" owing to his unparalleled ability to engage with the plane of immanence—Deleuze and Guattari write that the plane of immanence is "the nonthought within thought . . . that which cannot be thought and yet must be thought," that which can only be shown as taking place and being there "unthought" in each and every thing.[73] Translated in a slightly different language: *plane of immanence is unconscious*. Elsewhere, Deleuze calls it precisely that. In a remarkable essay on the ethics of the *Ethics*, Deleuze credits Spinoza with the "discovery of the unconscious, of an *unconscious of thought* just as profound as *the unknown of the body*."[74] Crucially, he adds, "The entire *Ethics* is a voyage in immanence; but immanence is the unconscious itself, and the conquest of the unconscious."[75] Immanence is the unconscious *and* its own conquest, just like immanence is substance *and* modes, concatenation *and* things. Far from being a Cartesian conquest—namely, a transcendent triumph of the mind and of its reason over the body and its nonreason—such a conquest is precisely that intuitive knowledge by which things may posit themselves as incorporated in concatenation, by which modes may produce their singular essence as link to the essence of substance, by which we may produce ourselves as sense-event or cause–effect of the unconscious (and Spinoza is adamant that such a knowledge involves equally body and mind; cf. *Ethics* V, P39, P39S). Intuitive knowledge is knowledge of the unconscious or plane of immanence or concatenation of all things. It is only thanks to such knowledge that we may read, map, produce in both reason and representation that syntagmatic and metonymic logic of the geopolitical unconscious that is the world as concatenation of all things.

Intuitive knowledge constituted Spinoza's attempt to provide a radical solution to a novel philosophical and political problem. (And I take it as axiomatic that solutions and problems arise simultaneously by definition, in the sense that a problem comes into being and can be formulated as such only to the extent to which its solution is already in process, unfolding, surfacing—in short, already present in however indeterminate a form.) The problem was how to make sense of a phenomenon that could not be understood adequately either by representation or by reason, namely, that ontological connectivity given in the concept of absolute immanence whose first actual manifestation was beginning to emerge in the early modern era in the form of *nexus rerum,* world market, or globalizing capitalism. Intuitive knowledge was born in relation and as an answer to capital and to its globalizing tendency and totalizing imperative.[76] In fact, it was born, as it were, in competition with and as an alternative to capital, in the sense that both the logic of capital and the logic of intuitive knowledge deal in potentiality. As Marx was the first to discover, in fact, possibly the crucial and defining novelty of capitalism as a mode of production consists in positing potentiality qua potentiality as the object of exchange par excellence: under capitalist relations of production, the worker sells not acts of labor—that is, actual forms of productive activity—but labor power, which Marx famously defines in *Capital* as "the aggregate of those mental and physical capabilities existing in the physical form, the living personality, of a human being."[77] In the *Grundrisse,* Marx writes, "The use value which the worker has to offer to the capitalist, which he has to offer to others in general, is not materialized in a product, does not exist apart from him at all, thus exists not really, but only in potentiality, as his capacity."[78] It is in this sense that capital deals in potentiality: in capital, the production of surplus value is founded precisely on the expropriation and exchange of such incorporeal yet incorporated potentiality (and hence such production cannot be understood, let alone counteracted and combated, if one considers the world only from the standpoint of actuality, namely, within the limits of representation and reason alone).[79] And as we have seen, intuitive knowledge, too, concerns itself with potentiality above all, in the sense that it involves, mobilizes, and complements both reason and representation to seize on that singular-common potential to become different from what we are, which is our very essence and which constitutes our link to the world, to the concatenation of all things.[80] Crucially, this is knowledge from which, according to Spinoza, "there necessarily arises the intellectual love of God"—a love that "is eternal" (*Ethics* V, P33). (And, as Althusser points out, given that for Spinoza intuitive knowledge involves both mind and body, the love that arises from it "is in no way an 'intellectual' love."[81]) Whereas capital mortifies potentiality by extracting it from bodies and actualizing it in and as value, intuitive knowledge glorifies potentiality not only by incorporating it at once as our singularity and as our being-in-common but also by actualizing it as love of the world. Spinoza's wager was that the ontological connectivity he had discovered as concept in absolute immanence and as sense-event in the concatenation of all things could be actualized, materialized, and incorporated as love. This is the question he asks us urgently across the vicissitudes of modernity and that is for us to answer in this third and fully global stage of capitalism: because our globalization is only one possible manifestation of the concatenation of all things, is another globalization possible that would glorify our most singular and most common potential as love? Is it possible to restore our link to and our belief in this intolerable world? Is it possible to love the world today?[82]

Notes

I AM TRULY GRATEFUL to Dimitris Vardoulakis for his incisive and invaluable comments on this essay as well as for his unwavering patience in dealing with the numerous delays in its completion. The essay is dedicated to Jason Christenson—not only because he endured the vagaries of my writing moods with the grace that always distinguishes his love but also because love, ultimately, is what this essay is all about.

All references to the *Ethics* in English are to the following editions: Spinoza, *Ethics*, ed. and trans. G. H. R. Parkinson (Oxford: Oxford University Press, 2000). The Latin edition consulted for all the references is Benedicti de Spinoza, *Opera*, ed. J. Van Vloten and J. P. N. Land (The Hague: Martinum Nijhoff, 1914).

1. Louis Althusser, "Lenin before Hegel," in *Lenin and Philosophy, and Other Essays*, trans. Ben Brewster (New York: Monthly Review Press, 1971), 124.
2. Karl Marx, *Grundrisse: Foundations of the Critique of Political Economy (Rough Draft)*, trans. Martin Nicolaus (Harmondsworth, U.K.: Penguin Books, 1974), 105.
3. During these four decades, there have been (1) thinkers who have written about Marx and Spinoza in separate yet closely related works such as Negri in *Marx beyond Marx: Lessons on the Grundrisse*, trans. Harry Cleaver, Michael Ryan, and Maurizio Viano, ed. Jim Fleming (Brooklyn: Autonomedia, 1991), and *The Savage Anomaly: The Power of Spinoza's Metaphysics and Politics*, trans. Michael Hardt (Minneapolis: University of Minnesota Press, 1991), as well as Étienne Balibar (with Louis Althusser) in *Reading Capital*, trans. Ben Brewster (London: Verso, 1997), and *Spinoza and Politics*, trans. Peter Snowdon (London: Verso, 1998); (2) thinkers who refer implicitly or in passing to the relation between Spinoza and Marx such as Althusser in *Reading Capital* and in his autobiographical writings as well as Warren Montag in *Bodies, Masses, Power: Spinoza and His Contemporaries* (London: Verso, 1999); (3) thinkers whose entire *Weltanschauung* is imbued thoroughly with Spinozan and the Marxian problematics, regardless of whether they acknowledge it explicitly (see, among others, Gilles Deleuze and Félix Guattari in

both volumes of *Capitalism and Schizophrenia*, Michael Hardt and Negri in all their collaborative works, and Paolo Virno in *A Grammar of the Multitude*, trans. Isabella Bertoletti, James Cascaito, and Andrea Casson [New York: Semiotext(e), 2003]); and (4) thinkers who confront the Spinoza–Marx relation indirectly yet significantly via the examination of a third and related thinker (see, e.g., Pierre Macherey's important study *Hegel ou Spinoza* [Paris: Maspero, 1977] as well as Nicholas Thoburn's *Deleuze, Marx, and Politics* [London: Routledge, 2003]). Arguably, among these various and immensely valuable attempts to combine Spinoza's and Marx's systems of thought, the most influential one remains Althusser's pioneering contribution to *Reading Capital,* which, in many respects, is still unsurpassed. All significant differences notwithstanding, what these thinkers share in common is at the very least an understanding of Spinoza's immanentist materialism as a crucial precursor of Marx's philosophical and political project (where *precursor* ought to be understood not only in historical but also in logical terms, in the sense that both Spinoza's and Marx's systems of thought shared the same condition of possibility or cause in the immanent structures of thought and life inaugurated by capitalist modernity rather than one system being the direct and transitive cause of the other). In short, the body of Spinozist Marxism is abundant—yet the literature on Spinoza and Marx is thin. Thin as it is, however, it is notable and significant nonetheless. In particular, I would like to refer the reader to three important exceptions: Eugene Holland's essay "Spinoza and Marx," *Cultural Logic* 2, no. 1 (1998), http://clogic.eserver.org/2-1/holland.html (which discusses some of the works mentioned earlier and cites three earlier precursors, Maximilien Rubel's "Marx a la rencontre de Spinoza," Alexandre Matheron's "Le Traite Theologico-Politique vu par le jeune Marx," and Albert Igoin's "De l'ellipse de la theorie politique de Spinoza chez le jeune Marx," all published in 1977 in the journal *Cahiers Spinoza*); Kiarina Kordela's remarkable study *$urplus: Spinoza, Lacan* (New York: State University of New York Press, 2007) (which constructs a tetradic philosophical structure, whose complementary conceptual personae, as Deleuze and Guattari might call them, consist of Spinoza, Immanuel Kant, Marx, and Jacques Lacan); and Brynnar Swenson's "Multitude, Inc.: Class, Capital and the Corporation," in "The Corporate Form: Capital, Fiction, Architecture" (doctoral dissertation, Department of Cultural Studies and Comparative Literature, University of Minnesota, 2008). For Holland, possibly the most important insight that Spinozist Marxism stands to gain from a direct confrontation between Spinoza and Marx is the eradication of "teleologism from the forces/relation of production model in two ways: there would be no guarantee that forces of production will continue to develop even in the face of restrictive or destructive relations of production; and even if they were to, there would be no guarantee that such development will eventuate in any increase in human freedom." Judging from Kordela's pointed critiques of Hardt and Negri's teleological tendencies, I believe she is in full agreement with Holland on this matter. Kordela, $urplus, 2–5, 127–30. Kordela's project, however, goes beyond the level of critique, as the examination of Spinoza and Marx in her work constitutes an explicit attempt to produce what she refers to as an ontology of *"differential (non-)substance,"* according to which "the registers on which Being needs to be named are the following: *(1) being as the imaginary univocity of abstract thought, that is, as simulacrum (exchange-value or signifier); (2) beings as the multiplicity of being (use-value or physical beings); and (3) the primary, transcendent, yet immanent, differential (non-)substance that at once institutes the above duplicity and is the effect thereof (surplus)."* Kordela, $urplus, 46–47 (this is the culmination of a complex argument, and hence I refer the reader at the very least also to pp. 38–49, in which the intermediary, logical steps leading to this conclusion are taken). Unlike Holland's and Kordela's arguments, Swenson's argument is not only theoretical but also historical, as it shows that both Spinoza's and Marx's systems of thought developed in response to specific developments in the history of the corporate form (whose primary manifestations include the joint-stock company and its contemporary avatar, namely, the multinational corporation). In particular, Swenson argues that it was precisely in response to the incorporeal yet collective character of the corporate form that Spinoza and Marx posited social relations rather than individuals as the starting point for their nonhumanist understanding of politics and economics. I have found Holland's, Kordela's, and Swenson's direct engagements with the Spinoza–Marx relation (as well as the aforementioned indirect engagements) to be provocative, illuminating, and productive: traces of all of them may be found throughout this essay. Last, let me add that as this essay is going into production, a new book on Marx and Spinoza has just been published, which I have not yet been able to consult. Frédéric Lordon, *Capitalisme, désir et servitude: Marx et Spinoza* (Paris: La Fabrique, 2010).

4 Cesare Casarino, "Surplus Common," in Cesare Casarino and Antonio Negri, *In Praise of the Common: A Conversation on Philosophy and Politics*, 1–39 (Minneapolis: University of Minnesota Press, 2008), esp. 30–37. In many respects, this present essay constitutes a further elaboration of some of the arguments articulated in Casarino, "Surplus Common."

5 Marx, *Grundrisse*, 407–8.

6 Karl Marx, *Capital: A Critique of Political Economy*, vol. 1, trans. Ben Fowkes (New York: Vintage, 1976), 253.

7 Ibid., 251.

8 Ibid., 253.

9 Kojin Karatani, *Architecture as Metaphor: Language, Number, Money*, trans. Sabu Kohso, ed. Michael Speaks (Cambridge, Mass.: MIT Press, 1995), 183.

10 Fredric Jameson, *Postmodernism; or, The Cultural Logic of Late Capitalism* (Durham, N.C.: Duke University Press, 1991), 411–12.

11 Ibid., 409–10.

12 Fredric Jameson, *The Geopolitical Aesthetic: Cinema and Space in the World System* (Bloomington: Indiana University Press, 1992), 31. In a sense, this entire work can be understood as an ambitious and largely successful attempt to articulate "the desire called cognitive mapping" as that nonrepresentational kind of knowledge that may detect and register the unrepresentable (totality) within representation. See p. 3, but also all of pp. 1–5, as well as the entire first section on "Totality as Conspiracy," pp. 7–84.

13 The first sentence of the appendix reads as follows: "With this I have explained the nature and properties of God, such as that he necessarily exists; that he is unique; that he exists and acts solely by the necessity of his own nature; that he is the free cause of all things, and in what way; that all things exist in God, and depend on him in such a way that without him they can neither exist nor be conceived; and finally that all things were predetermined by God,

not out of freedom of will, i.e. his absolute good pleasure, but from the absolute nature of God, i.e. his infinite power [*potentia*]." For Spinoza's understanding of substance as immanent cause, see, *Ethics* I, D1, D3, D5, D6, A1, and A2 as well as P18.

14 Translation modified. More specifically, for the purposes of the present arguments, I find it preferable to translate *concatenationem* as "concatenation" and *explicui* as "I have explicated" rather than as Parkinson's "interconnection" and "I have explained," respectively.

15 The Latin *res* in Spinoza has a more extensive meaning than the corresponding term *thing* in English. On this matter, see Seymour Feldman's translator's introduction to Baruch Spinoza, *The Ethics and Selected Letters*, trans. Samuel Shirley, ed. and with an introduction by Seymour Feldman (Indianapolis, Ind.: Hackett, 1982), 24.

16 Gilles Deleuze, *The Logic of Sense*, trans. Mark Lester with Charles Stivale, ed. Constantin Boundas (New York: Columbia University Press, 1990), 14.

17 Ibid., 19.

18 Ibid., 21–22.

19 I am noting here a striking similarity between Deleuze's conception of sense and Giorgio Agamben's conception of a surplus of being (as articulated in Saint Thomas's treatise on halos). Giorgio Agamben, *The Coming Community*, trans. Michael Hardt (Minneapolis: University of Minnesota Press, 1993), 53–56.

20 The first instance of definition and discussion of all three kinds of knowledge occurs in *Ethics* II, P40S2. Spinoza discusses in more detail his theory of knowledge in *Ethics* II (esp. from P13 onward) as well as in *Ethics* V (which is primarily devoted to the third kind of knowledge).

21 Gilles Deleuze has written eloquently on the special role of the scholia in the *Ethics*. Gilles Deleuze, "Spinoza and the Three 'Ethics,'" in *Essays Critical and Clinical*, trans. Daniel W. Smith and Michael A. Greco, 138–51 (Minneapolis: University of Minnesota Press), esp. 145–47 and 151.

22 The late Latin *concatenatio* is a verbal noun morphologically related to the past participle of the verb *catenare*, namely, *catenatus* (i.e., "chained," "bound," "fettered," etc.)—a verb itself related to the noun *catena* (i.e., "chain," "hinge," etc.). Importantly, *concatenatio*

also includes the prefix *cum* and hence means literally "a binding with," "a chaining together," etc.

23 Here is the original passage: *"Porro ubicunque data fuit occasio, praejudicia, quae impedire poterant, quo minus meae demonstrationes perciperentur, amovere curavi; sed quia non pauca adhuc restant praejudicia, quae etiam, imo maxime impedire poterant, et possunt, quo minus homines rerum concatenationem eo, quo ipsam explicui, modo amplecti possint, eadem hic ad examen rationis vocare operae pretium duxi."*

24 This sentence occurs in a letter to a friend, as quoted by Steven Nadler, *Spinoza: A Life* (Cambridge: Cambridge University Press, 1999), 111.

25 Gilles Deleuze, "Life of Spinoza," in *Spinoza: Practical Philosophy*, trans. Robert Hurley (San Francisco: City Lights Books, 1988), 7.

26 Even leaving aside the significant, complex, and global trade networks in which his family firm was involved, Spinoza's more or less indirect connections to the Americas were manifold. First of all, several among Spinoza's close relatives emigrated to the Caribbean: during his lifetime, the younger brother Gabriel, with whom he had managed the family firm after their father's death, and who had taken over the firm after Spinoza's excommunication, moved first to Barbados, and then to Jamaica, where he became a naturalized English subject, whereas shortly after his own death, the sister Rebecca moved with her children to Curaçao. See Nadler, *Spinoza*, 86, 87. Furthermore, Spinoza's childhood teacher, Isaac Aboab da Fonseca, moved to Recife, Brazil, in 1642, to serve as a rabbi in that city's newly established congregation, thereby becoming the first rabbi in the Americas (and, as Spinoza's contemporary and biographer Johan Colerus claims, it was no other than Aboab da Fonseca who, having returned eventually to Amsterdam due to the Portuguese capture of Recife in 1654, read the document proclaiming Spinoza's excommunication in public). See Peter Wiernik, *History of the Jews in America: From the Period of the Discovery of the New World to the Present Time* (New York: Jewish Press, 1912), 38, as well as Steven Nadler, *Spinoza's Heresy: Immortality and the Jewish Mind* (New York: Oxford University Press, 2001), 13. Moreover, before his excommunication, and while head of the family firm, Spinoza is documented as having contributed to charity funds for the Jewish poor of Brazil, possibly as a memorial gift for his dead

father. See Nadler, *Spinoza*, 118. Most famously, perhaps, in a 1664 letter to his friend Pieter Balling, Spinoza mentions being haunted by "the image of a certain black and leprous Brazilian" who appeared to him in "a very unpleasant dream." Benedict de Spinoza, *On the Improvement of the Understanding. The Ethics. Correspondence. Volume 2*, trans. R. H. M. Elwes (New York: Dover, 1955), 325. This letter—and the geopolitical unconscious it indexes—is the topic of another essay on which I am working at present.

27 The immanence of potentiality and actuality without any remainder is affirmed implicitly and explicitly throughout the *Ethics* in a variety of ways and contexts. This may seem to contradict what I have stated earlier. When it comes to God, e.g., Spinoza argues that his "existence and essence are one and the same" (see *Ethics* I, P20). Crucially, he argues also that "the power [*potentia*] of God is his essence" (see *Ethics* I, P34). In short, God's potential is always already actually existent, or God's essence is always already actualized potential for existence. (Or, as he puts it in *Ethics* I, P11S, "God . . . has an absolutely infinite power [*potentia*] of existing, and therefore exists absolutely.") So although the distinction between essence and existence with respect to God is in effect an analytical rather than a real distinction, it is the case nonetheless that their being "one and the same" does not indicate in and of itself *how* they are so exactly. After all, given that God's essence is expressed by an infinity of attributes, and given that each attribute is its own distinct kind (see *Ethics* I, D6, including its explanation), the unity of essence and existence is instantiated in an infinity of distinct kinds. Put differently, that God's always already actualized potential for existence is infinite means that the immanence of potentiality and actuality is subject to infinity. Though, unlike God, modes are relative and finite, and their essence does not involve existence, the immanence of potentiality and actuality holds for them too. In *Ethics* IV, P4Pr., e.g., Spinoza writes, "The power [*potentia*] by which particular things, and consequently a man, preserve their being is the power [*potentia*] of God, i.e. of Nature . . . not in so far as it is infinite, but in so far as it can be explained by actual human essence. . . . So the power [*potentia*] of a man, in so far as it is explained through his actual essence, is a part of the infinite power [*potentia*], that is, of the essence . . . of God, i.e. of Nature." Modal essence, thus, is a

relative and finite degree of God's absolute and infinite potential for existence: it enables modes to "preserve their being"—i.e., to continue to be actualized—for an indeterminate though limited duration. In short, that which is potential in modes—namely, their essence—is always already actualized in and as their existence. In *Expressionism in Philosophy*, Deleuze discusses extensively the question of power (intended as *puissance*, as potentiality) in the *Ethics*. At one point during that discussion, he writes, "The identity of power [*puissance*] and essence means: a power [*puissance*] is always an act or, at least, in action. . . . [A] mode . . . has no power [*puissance*] that is not actual: it is at each moment all that it can be, its power [*puissance*] is its essence." Gilles Deleuze, *Expressionism in Philosophy: Spinoza*, trans. Martin Joughin (New York: Zone Books, 1990), 93. More succinctly, in a later essay, Deleuze writes, "All *potentia* is act, active, and actual." Gilles Deleuze, "Index of the Main Concepts of the *Ethics*," in Deleuze, *Spinoza: Practical Philosophy*, 97, but see also 99 and 101. That for modes all potential is actual, however, does not tell us anything of any sort about what exactly that actual consists of or entails. That potentiality and actuality are strictly immanent for modes does not even begin to address the question of the specific modalities of being of such immanence in the first place. For modes, after all, the plane of immanence is not given a priori: on the contrary, it has to be actively constructed anew each and every time (on this matter, see also n. 72 and 73).

28 Žižek has made this argument repeatedly (largely as a way of critiquing the Anglo-American reception of Deleuze's thought). See, among other works, Slavoj Žižek, *Tarrying with the Negative: Kant, Hegel, and the Critique of Ideology* (Durham, N.C.: Duke University Press, 1993), 216–19. For a welcome and salutary antidote to Žižek's Hegelo-Lacanian reading of Spinoza, see Kordela's Lacanian yet not Hegelian *$urplus* (discussed in n. 3). Incidentally, though I put much emphasis throughout this essay on that work by Deleuze that for Žižek represents Deleuze at his best (i.e., *The Logic of Sense*), I do not share Žižek's veritably Manichean interpretation of Deleuze's philosophical project as split between two irreconcilable logics—a materialist logic best exemplified by *The Logic of Sense* and an idealist logic best exemplified by *Anti-Oedipus*, which Žižek considers to be "arguably Deleuze's worst book." Slavoj Žižek, *Organs without*

Bodies: On Deleuze and Consequences (New York: Routledge, 2004), 21, but see also at least 19–41. In general, even though there are aspects of *Anti-Oedipus* that I do find problematic and at times essentialist (though it should be noted also that these aspects are largely absent from the sequel, i.e., *A Thousand Plateaus*), I find Žižek's outright dismissal of *Anti-Oedipus* and attendant demonization of Deleuze's collaboration with Guattari to be facile, to say the least. For a far more thoughtful and productive engagement with *Anti-Oedipus* and *A Thousand Plateaus*, see Fredric Jameson's "Marxism and Dualism in Deleuze," in *A Deleuzian Century*, ed. Ian Buchanan (Durham, N.C.: Duke University Press, 1999), 13–36. For incisive discussions of Žižek's book on Deleuze, see Daniel W. Smith, "The Inverse Side of the Structure: Žižek on Deleuze on Lacan," *Criticism* 46, no. 4 (2004): 635–50, as well as Eleanor Kaufman, "Betraying Well," *Criticism* 46, no. 4 (2004): 651–59.

29 For related arguments (regarding capitalism as only one possible manifestation of immanence), see Kordela, *Surplus*, 105–8, as well as much of Casarino, "Surplus Common."

30 On this matter, see Nadler, *Spinoza*, 129–38.

31 Baruch Spinoza, *Ethics and Selected Letters*, 233, 234; translation modified. Spinoza, *Opera*, 3, 5.

32 Benedict de Spinoza, *Improvement of the Understanding, Ethics, and Correspondence*, trans. Robert Harvey Monro Elwes (Washington, D.C.: M. Walter Dunne, 1901), 368; translation modified.

33 Spinoza, *Improvement of the Understanding*, 369.

34 Spinoza, *Ethics and Selected Letters*, 235; translation modified. Spinoza, *Opera*, 5.

35 Marx, *Capital*, 1:253.

36 On this matter, see, among others, Étienne Balibar, "The Vacillation of Ideology," trans. Andrew Ross and Constance Penley, in *Marxism and the Interpretation of Culture*, ed. Cary Nelson and Lawrence Grossberg (Urbana: University of Illinois Press, 1988), 204; Maximilien Rubel, *Marx Critique du Marxisme* (Paris: Payot, 2000), 172–73; and Pierre-François Moreau, "Spinoza's Reception and Influence," trans. Roger Ariew, in *The Cambridge Companion to Spinoza*, ed. Don Garrett (Cambridge: Cambridge University Press, 1996), 426.

37 Aristotle, *Politics*, in *The Basic Works of Aristotle*, ed. Richard McKeon,

trans. W. D. Ross (New York: Random House, 1941), 1135, 1137, 1139–40. I have discussed in more detail these passages (as well as related passages of the *Nicomachean Ethics* and *Metaphysics*) in terms of their influence on Marx's thought in Casarino, "Surplus Common," 23–28, 260–64.
38 Aristotle, *Basic Works*, 1141.
39 On this matter, see, among others, Paul Oskar Kristeller, "Stoic and Neoplatonic Sources of Spinoza's *Ethics*," in *Spinoza: Critical Assessments*, vol. 1, ed. Genevieve Lloyd (London: Routledge, 2001), 118, and Nadler, *Spinoza*, 151–53, 167, 210–11. But see also Spinoza's implicit approval of Descartes's critique of certain aspects of Scholastic philosophy in the preface to *Ethics* V—a critique that, Spinoza claims, not even Descartes himself followed properly and to its logical conclusions.
40 I have engaged in more detail with Marx's analytic of money in two other essays (which the following discussion draws from in part as well as takes in different directions): "Time Matters: Marx, Negri, Agamben, and the Corporeal," in Casarino and Negri, *In Praise of the Common*, 235–45, and "White Capital; or, Heterotopologies of the Limit," in Cesare Casarino, *Modernity at Sea: Melville, Marx, Conrad in Crisis* (Minneapolis: University of Minnesota Press, 2002), 63–183.
41 Marx, *Grundrisse*, 233–35.
42 Ibid., 221.
43 Ibid., 223. It is evident from the rest of this page and from the following couple of pages that Marx thinks that what he has just stated in this passage is valid for all mercantile societies, from antiquity up until and including seventeenth- and eighteenth-century Mercantilism proper. Ibid., 223–25.
44 Ibid., 222.
45 As I point out elsewhere, however, there may be some indication in Aristotle of possible relations between the realm of the metaphysical and the realm of the economic. Casarino and Negri, *In Praise of the Common*, 28, 261–62n55.
46 Marx, *Grundrisse*, 408.
47 Ibid., 223.
48 Ibid., 225.
49 It is worth pointing out, however, that even though the wage came

into full fruition with modern industrial manufacture, its historical origins are specifically maritime, as it had been devised first for merchant sea labor during the sixteenth century and hence harks back precisely to the economies of Mercantilism. Whereas in ancient, medieval, and early modern shipping, sea labor was paid predominantly according to the share system—which allotted seamen with a proportional share of the profit—during the sixteenth century a shift to the wage system began to take place as part of larger transformations in property law. See Marcus Rediker's study *Between the Devil and the Deep Blue Sea: Merchant Seamen, Pirates, and the Anglo-American Maritime World, 1700–1750* (Cambridge: Cambridge University Press, 1987), 78–79, 116–52 (esp. 118), 289–91.

50 The third and contemporary stage in the development of the capitalist mode of production has been referred to variously as "global capitalism," "multinational capitalism," "late capitalism," "flexible capitalism," "postmodern capitalism," "post-Fordism," "real subsumption," "biopolitical production," "immaterial production," etc. This is not the place to address the vast literature on such nomenclatures—whose abundance and diversity already attest to the unprecedented complexity of the object they attempt to name. I have discussed these matters in more detail in another essay, "Universalism of the Common," *Diacritics* (forthcoming). A few words on my characterization of this third stage specifically as "communicative," however, are necessary here (and this is a characterization that is compatible with several of the aforementioned designations but that also wishes to highlight what I consider to be a crucial feature of contemporary capitalist globalization). All three stages may be called capitalism because they all share in the production of surplus value (i.e., in the simultaneous expropriation and materialization of surplus in and as the form of value). In each of these stages, however, surplus value is produced in different ways, which is what the attributive qualifiers "mercantile," "industrial," and "communicative" signify. (Obviously, these stages should not be understood only diachronically but also synchronically: the types of production involved in each not only are not necessarily mutually exclusive but also are often spatiotemporally coexistent and are now fully complementary and cumulative.) In communicative capitalism, the production of surplus value is

based primarily on communication—and especially on the communication of thought, language, and affect, in all their myriad forms. From the emergent media network and spectacle society analyzed with much foresight by the likes of Marshall McLuhan and Guy Debord already in the 1960s to the increasingly complex and pervasive production and circulation of the image in its various forms, from the computerization of so many aspects of production and distribution to the internetization of so many (old and new) forms of exchange relations (including social exchange), from online financial transactions to the circulation of knowledge of all sorts, from the call-center phenomenon to customer-satisfaction management, from the swelling of the service industry as such to the growing importance of the service component in all aspects of the entire process of production, the labor involved in communicating forms of thought, language, and affect has become the increasingly dominant and determining form of labor, and hence of exploitation, today. (Importantly, I intend qualifiers such as *dominant* and *determining* in strictly qualitative terms: other forms of labor—such as the labor involved in modern industrial production organized according to Taylorist principles or the labor involved in premodern and precapitalist processes of agricultural production—not only are alive and well but also may well still constitute quantitatively some of the most common forms of labor nowadays; such modern and premodern forms of labor, however, are increasingly determined and dependent on more properly postmodern forms of communicative labor for their continued existence and profitability.) Such an understanding of contemporary global capitalism as fundamentally communicative is particularly germane to Balibar's interpretation of Spinoza's entire philosophical system as "a highly original philosophy of communication." Étienne Balibar, *Spinoza and Politics*, 99 (this entire work concerns itself, directly or indirectly, with the question of communication in Spinoza, but see esp. pp. 95–124).
51 Deleuze, *Expressionism in Philosophy*, 15–16, 353n11.
52 Ibid., 15.
53 More precisely, Deleuze writes, "To explicate is to evolve, to involve is to implicate. Yet the two terms are not opposites: they simply mark two aspects of expression. Expression is on the one hand an explication, an unfolding of what expresses itself, the One

manifesting itself in the Many (substance manifesting itself in its attributes, and these manifesting themselves in their modes). Its multiple expression, on the other hand, involves Unity. The One remains involved in what expresses it, imprinted in what unfolds it, immanent in whatever manifests it: expression is in this respect an involvement. There is no conflict between the two terms. . . . Expression in general involves and implicates what it expresses, while also explicating and evolving it." Ibid., 16. It is in passages such as this one in *Expressionism in Philosophy* that we may already glean the important role that the concept of the fold will come to play for Deleuze two decades later, when he will elaborate this concept further in his monograph on Michel Foucault and, especially, in his monograph on G. W. Leibniz.

54 Spinoza is mentioned in "Lucretius and the Simulacrum"—one of the four appendices to *The Logic of Sense*—which had been written and had appeared earlier as a separate essay. Deleuze, *Logic of Sense*, 273.

55 Deleuze, *Expressionism in Philosophy*, 18.

56 Ibid., 102.

57 I am implying that the onto-epistemological processes involved in expression and explication are at the very least related to Lacan's definition of the unconscious as discourse of the Other (where *Other* indexes radical alterity, as opposed to the ego's always projective and imaginary otherness).

58 I am referring here to that prototypical instrumental reason that Descartes declares to be seeking in *Discourse on Method* and that he defines in the following manner: "a practical philosophy by means of which, knowing the force and the action of fire, water, air, the stars, heavens and all other bodies that environ us, as distinctly as we know the different crafts of our artisans, we can in the same way employ them in all those uses to which they are adapted, and thus render ourselves the masters and possessors of nature." René Descartes, *Discourse on Method and Meditations*, trans. Elizabeth Sanderson Haldane and G. R. T. Ross (New York: Dover, 2003), 41–42.

59 Deleuze, *Spinoza: Practical Philosophy*, 68.

60 Here as well as later, I do not differentiate between being and acting, and between thinking and knowing, because I am persuaded

by Deleuze's argument throughout *Expressionism in Philosophy* that in Spinoza the power of being always involves also the power of acting, and the power of thinking always involves also the power of knowing. See, e.g., Deleuze, *Expressionism in Philosophy*, 120–22.
61 Ibid., 18.
62 In particular, Deleuze has Epictetus and Marcus Aurelius in mind here. Deleuze, *Logic of Sense*, 144–45.
63 Deleuze, *Logic of Sense*, 145–46, but see also 146–47.
64 Deleuze, *Expressionism in Philosophy*, 18.
65 Spinoza is unequivocal regarding the nonrepresentational nature of ideas—which are modes of thought rather than modes of extension like signs and images—and hence of the second kind of knowledge; on this matter, see at least the second paragraph of *Ethics* II, P49S.
66 E.g., as Deleuze notes in the long passage quoted earlier from *The Logic of Sense*, "the perception of death as a state of affairs and as a quality, or the concept 'mortal' as a predicate of signification, remain extrinsic (deprived of sense) as long as they do not encompass the event of dying as that which is actualized in the one and expressed in the other. . . . To know that we are mortal is an apodeictic knowledge, albeit empty and abstract; effective and successive deaths do not suffice of course in fulfilling this knowledge adequately, so long as one does not come to know death as an impersonal event provided with an always open problematic structure (where and when?)." Deleuze, *Logic of Sense*, 145.
67 On the complementary relations among the three kinds of knowledge, see Deleuze, *Expressionism in Philosophy*, 273–320, esp. 298–301, and Genevieve Lloyd, *Spinoza and the Ethics* (New York: Routledge, 1996), 70.
68 Lloyd, *Spinoza and the Ethics*, 67.
69 On the singularity of essence, see *Ethics* II, D2, P10, P10S2, P37. On the relation between essence and existence in substance as well as in modes, see *Ethics* I, D1, D3, D5, D6, D8, A1, A7, P20.
70 Singularity, in other words, is labor power as defined by Marx: I will return to this matter at the end of this essay. On the complementarity of the singular and the common, see Michael Hardt and Antonio Negri, *Multitude: War and Democracy in the Age of Empire* (New York: Penguin, 2004), at least 198, 203–4, 348–49.

71 In *Ethics* II, P35S, Spinoza writes, "When we see the sun, we imagine it to be about two hundred feet distant from us; an error which consists, not in this imagination alone, but in the fact that whilst we imagine the sun in this way we are ignorant of its true distance and of the cause of this imagination. For even after we get to know that the sun is distant from us by over six hundred diameters of the earth we shall still imagine it to be close at hand. For we imagine the sun to be so close, not because we are ignorant of its true distance, but because an affection of our body involves the essence of the sun in so far as the body is affected by the sun."

72 On the plane of immanence understood as the nonconceptual condition of possibility of any concept whatsoever, Deleuze and Guattari write in *What Is Philosophy?* "If philosophy begins with the creation of concepts, then the plane of immanence must be regarded as prephilosophical. It is presupposed not in the way that one concept may refer to others but in the way that concepts themselves refer to a nonconceptual understanding . . . [an] intuitive understanding [that] varies according to the way in which the plane is laid out. . . . Philosophy posits as prephilosophical, or even as nonphilosophical, the power of a One–All like a moving desert that concepts come to populate. Prephilosophical does not mean something preexistent but rather something *that does not exist outside philosophy,* although philosophy presupposes it. . . . Precisely because the plane of immanence is prephilosophical and does not immediately take effect with concepts, it implies a sort of groping experimentation and its layout resorts to measures that are not very respectable, rational, or reasonable. These measures belong to the order of dreams, of pathological processes, esoteric experiences, drunkenness, and excess. We head for the horizon, on the plane of immanence, and we return with bloodshot eyes, yet they are the eyes of the mind." Gilles Deleuze and Félix Guattari, *What Is Philosophy?* trans. Hugh Tomlinson and Graham Burchell (New York: Columbia University Press, 1994), 40–41. Though Spinoza has not been mentioned yet at this point in *What Is Philosophy?*, he is ubiquitous in this passage. E.g., the "nonconceptual" and "intuitive understanding" that appertains to the plane of immanence constitutes a barely veiled reference to Spinoza's intuitive knowledge, and the "bloodshot" "eyes of the mind" (which any sighting of the plane of immanence will cause)

constitute an allusion to *Ethics* V, P23S, in which Spinoza explains that "the eyes of the mind, by which it sees and observes things, are demonstrations." Surely enough, Spinoza appears shortly thereafter in this work as the philosopher who laid out the best plane of immanence (Deleuze and Guattari, *What Is Philosophy?* 60), thereby fulfilling philosophy: "[Spinoza] fulfilled philosophy because he satisfied its prephilosophical presupposition. Immanence does not refer back to the Spinozist substance and modes but, on the contrary, the Spinozist concepts of substance and modes refer back to the plane of immanence as their presupposition." Deleuze and Guattari, *What Is Philosophy?*, 48. Given that Deleuze and Guattari define philosophy in effect as conceptual knowledge, the implication of this passage is that conceptual knowledge finds its fulfillment—that is, its full fruition and highest realization—in that intuitive knowledge whose unique capacity, function, and task it is to engage with the plane of immanence. On this matter, see also Deleuze, *Expressionism in Philosophy*, 296, 298–301.

73 Deleuze and Guattari write, "THE plane of immanence is, at the same time, that which must be thought and that which cannot be thought. It is the nonthought within thought. . . . Perhaps this is the supreme act of philosophy: not so much to think THE plane of immanence as to show that it is there, unthought in every plane, and to think it in this way as the outside and inside of thought, as the not-external outside and the not-internal inside—that which cannot be thought and yet must be thought." Deleuze and Guattari, *What Is Philosophy?*, 59–60.

74 Gilles Deleuze, "On the Difference between the *Ethics* and a Morality," in Deleuze, *Spinoza: Practical Philosophy*, 9.

75 Deleuze, *Spinoza: Practical Philosophy*, 29.

76 It is significant to note in this context that the first concrete (and rather peculiar) example Spinoza gives of intuitive knowledge in *Ethics* II, P40S2, is the almost instantaneous deductive reasoning deployed by merchants in applying the rule of the fourth proportional—an example that, hence, involves money and the exchange relation. So important this example must have been for Spinoza that he uses it already in *The Treatise on the Emendation of the Intellect*. Spinoza, *Ethics and Selected Letters*, 238. Spinoza, *Opera*, 8–9.

77 Marx, *Capital*, 1:277.

78 Marx, *Grundrisse*, 267.
79 On Marx's method as a method of reading for—that is, mapping and producing—potentiality, see Louis Althusser, "From *Capital* to Marx's Philosophy," in Althusser and Balibar, *Reading Capital*, esp. 19–30.
80 On essence understood as potentiality, see n. 27.
81 Louis Althusser, "The Only Materialist Tradition. Part I: Spinoza," in *The New Spinoza*, ed. Warren Montag and Ted Stolze, trans. Ted Stolze (Minneapolis: University of Minnesota Press, 1997), 18.
82 Somebody who has gone far in addressing these questions is Deleuze in those moving pages in which he affirms that the highest political vocation of modern cinema consists precisely in its potential for restoring our link to, belief in, and love of the world. Gilles Deleuze, *Cinema 2: The Time-Image*, trans. Hugh Tomlinson and Robert Galeta (Minneapolis: University of Minnesota Press, 1989), 169–73.

PART III
Spinoza and the Arts

9

Image and Machine: Introduction to Thomas Hirschhorn's *Spinoza Monument*

SEBASTIAN EGENHOFER

I WOULD LIKE TO OUTLINE the topic of the field in which Thomas Hirschhorn's 1999 *Spinoza Monument* is situated as an artwork, as a material locus for the production of a truth. The space in which this topic is inscribed has two primary dimensions: the lateral dimension of extension of the field itself and the vertical dimension of its economic—and that means, following Marx and also Deleuze and Spinoza—its genetic and ontological structure. The phenomenal, imagistic *(bildförmige)* aspect of the works is part of the field's extension. I call the vertical dimension of ontological genesis the dimension of production. Drawing on a few paradigmatic positions, I will try to sketch the relationship between image or form and production in the art of modernity. Within this conceptual and historical framework, I want to determine the relationship between Hirschhorn's *sculpture* (he rejects the term *installation* for his work) and postabstract art since the 1960s. And I want to connect his way of working, and especially the materiality of his works, with the work of another Spinozist, namely, Mondrian. I would like to put the *precarious* materiality of Hirschhorn's works—which stems from the circulation of images and commodities and, above all, from the

Translated by Michael Eldred

evaporative layer of packaging materials, and which, therefore, is explicitly related to today's economic and media reality and also withdrawn from it—into relation to Mondrian's purified image elements, the primary colors and the rectangular grid of lines as the energetic and structural poles of painting that are withdrawn from the space of image *representation* in an equally explicit way.

The field is the space of history and, in particular, the history of art. It covers the publicly exposed reality of the works. If we include the dimension of temporal unfolding, it is already four-dimensional. It is, however, flat because it is the layer of phenomenality and of phenomenalization of the world itself. In Spinozan terms, it is the world as represented within the horizon of the finite mode that the human being is: the apparent world as the collection of imaginings, of perceptual images, under whose form being (the infinite substance) is reflected in the living human body. It is also the public world that is constituted on the basis of the multiply mediated divisibility of these initially radically individuated worlds of images. From a Marxian theoretical perspective, it is the world of products in whose shine the dimension of depth closes itself off, not so much that of the labor currently going into it but rather that of the dead, abstract labor sedimented in the means of production. And it is the world of images produced for the *gaze* that once arose rarely and rigidly from the asphyxiating presence of the infinite in the Eucharist miracle and offered the awaking subject a figure of its self-reflection, and whose inflationary dissemination since the invention of photography on the surface of today's technical image apparatus reveals the movement of capital as their ground and bearer. The artworks with the aspect of their visual form, their phenomenal or aesthetic presence, belong to this world of sensuous illusion, of products formed as commodities and addressed images.

That is the field. It is at least four-dimensional. How can its energetic, economic, and ontological dimension of depth be thought? Within the topic of Spinozan ontology, this is the dimension of infinite substance, of *natura naturans,* in whose productive or expressive movement, as Deleuze has worked out, the finite being (the mode) participates according to the *degree of power* that constitutes its *essence*.[1] This participation is *unconscious*, a structure of being of the finite mode, not of consciousness, which, together with its world of images, is one of the effects, a partial effect of participation. In Henri Bergson's language, which was influential for the thinking of classical modernity on the critique of the images, and which relates precisely to Spinoza in determining the relationship between the infinite and the finite, it is the dimension of *universal becoming*[2] that refracts in the layer of presence[3] into qualitatively differentiated beings exposed in space (is "explicated" and "canceled out," as Deleuze will say in *Difference and Repetition*).[4] To use terminology derived from Kant, it is the presynthetic chaos, the dispersed multiplicity not of sensuous impressions but of the virtual total happening of becoming that only becomes a sensuous impression and thus the raw material of synthetic work in the selective excerpt of affectibility of a living body through which a subject, in this rushing, constitutes an objective world or the order of regularity of nature, *natura naturata*. And finally, apart from subjective–transcendental contemplation of the ontological structure of production that determines both our own and Deleuze's view of Spinoza, it is, in the register of the Marxian analysis of *social* production, the dimension of abstracted past labor accumulated in technical, intellectual, and social means of production and the gravitation and self-movement of this dead labor or of capital that is manifested in the form of marketable and consumable products.

What I call the field is the presence of the objective, imagistic, constituted world. The genetic dimension of depth is that of natural, subjective–transcendental, and social or industrial production. Both philosophically and politically, it is crucial to keep in mind that the dimension of production cannot be made into an image, cannot be objectified. Its *exposition* seals it off and distorts it. It does not belong to reality if reality is the name for the layer of crystallization of what has been produced, for beings or objectivity. Vis-à-vis the ontology of beings, the dimension of production is heterogeneous. It designates a *before* that can only be narrated subsequently as a diachronic sequence of existing circumstances. It belongs to the *heterochronic* time of sedimentation or the absolute past, which stands at odds with the present and also with the sequential happening of present states of affairs that constitute narrative history. It is the *bearer* in a higher dimension of the present and its temporal unfolding into a horizon of memory and planning. The individual and genetic age of the living body, which is the bearer of the presence of consciousness spanning a few seconds, is rooted in this vertical temporal depth. It includes also the in-depth history of the development of means of production that mediate the relationship of a society with indifferent nature. And yet, this dimension *is* not, or it *is* only as the integral of its effects that the presence of beings constitutes, in which, as production, it is already past. According to its formal ontological structure prior to differentiation into natural, transcendental, and social production, production is determined as a folding of the infinite into the finite, of univocal being into the differentiation of beings.[5] Everything turns on this question of translation, which is usually subject to an original forgetting that constitutes the presence of consciousness in its shining and brevity. The artwork, like the human subject, is a place and arrangement of this translation of the infinite into the finite, a double-sided hinge that keeps the relationship between its two sides legible by marking its genetic relationship to the infinite or the dimension of production in the finite, that is, in the form and image.

If I relate works to one another over great historical distances and without regard to biographical relationships or to formal (phenomenal) comparability, then I do this with regard to their specific realization of this general structural relationship between image or form and production, between the finite, present sight, and its crisis, which unbounds it toward production. This structure is not supposed to be understood as a presentation or interpretation of artistic intentions. I am concerned with explicitly situating this casting of a topic of modernity within a broadly conceived ontological framework and also within the history of ideas. Above all, it is a matter of (re)-connecting the "metaphysics" of modernity from the first half of the twentieth century—so strongly rejected by art historians—with the critical discourses dominant since the 1960s. The twofold reference to Spinoza and Marx is a crucial aid for this project.

I do not want to treat the historically real (textual) relationship between Marx and Spinoza and Spinoza's relationship to the golden age of capitalism in the Netherlands, as discussed by Toni Negri.[6] Systematically, Althusser's and Macherey's attempts to substitute seamlessly positive Spinozan determinism for Hegelian concepts of negativity and contradiction as the motor of history to generate a better, nonteleological, subjectless Marxism are the decisive conceptions.[7] It is apparent within the history of ideas or archaeologically that capital and the movement of capital take on the systematic place and function of the infinite substance or the *natura naturans* in Spinoza, whereas the rigidified world of products circulating as exchange values corresponds to the imaginings in whose shape the substance appears within the horizon of the finite modes. The Spinozan imaginary, that is, the perceptual world itself, the illusion of the first kind of knowledge *along with* its sociosymbolic stabilization in the shared obscurantism of superstition, and the Marxian fetishized illusion, Althusser's ideology and Debord's spectacle are structurally congruent. I am concerned with the possibilities that this congruence or, said more carefully, this homology offers for the analysis of the field of art production in modernity. It is a matter of superimposing a classical metaphysical critique of the image, which is initiated as a critique of the finitude of perspectival perceptual consciousness related to a point in space and time and of its deceptive structure, on a critical ideological analysis of the fetishized illusion of the world of commodities in whose perfection the dimension of production is equally contracted, sealed off, and forgotten.

These theoretical and methodological interferences are essential for the history of art in modernity, above all, when this history wants to link the still epistemological work of the critique of representation in the first half of the century, the immanent iconoclasm of the image in abstraction, with the crisis of the presence of the work itself in postabstract installation art. For, whereas a transcendental critique of the illusory structure of consciousness corresponds to that work of critique of the image and representation that finds its model in the perspectival image of the modern age, as Spinoza's theory of knowledge casts in its own way in the second book of the *Ethics*, the destruction of the immediate presence of the work in the art of the late 1960s and 1970s is oriented toward the model of the Marxian critique of the commodity form. This destruction relates the present form and the form of aesthetic presence—which in minimalism, at the concluding moment of the modern critique of representation, has become the pervading element in the existence and constitution of meaning of visual art—to its conditions of production in the economic and political realm.

Put another way, since the complete materialization of the work in its situation, for which minimal art stands, the relevance of the work is established on the ground of its material existence and the form of this existence. It is this form of existence that adds to the merely present or phenomenal form that temporal depth inscribes in it, that *nonsimultaneity* that links the product with the production process, the trace with the moment of its impression. Hirschhorn's expression "precarious"—"limited within time, just as life is"[8]— describes *this* form, which can only be described in adverbial, and not in adjectival, expressions, because here existence has to be understood as the drive for the *happening of the work* and not as the neutral presence-at-hand of a work-object. (This is reflected in the oft-quoted maxim, "To make art politically, and not political art," which Hirschhorn borrows from Godard: the making and the mode of having been made, and thus the mode of existence of art, are political, and not its content or the good or bad conscience put on show.) In view of this *form,* which has stepped out of the ideal space of the image, the frame of reference for the analysis must change from epistemology, which sees in the image primarily a figure of reflection of the subject's relations to the world, to the logic of production, which deciphers in the material object the expression of the relations of production. In both registers of the analysis, that is, in the epistemological register as well, however, as I want to show, the *crisis* of the image (or of the present form) is determined as a relation to production and not to an eidetic transcendence, itself already an *imagistic* infinitude, whether it be the purportedly Platonic realm of ideas to which Mondrian's image-grid could be tied or the power of the institution and the determining contexts to which the increasingly investigative institutional critique of the 1990s ties itself. This solidarity of the infinite with the dimension of production is made clear by the Spinozan framework. Production as the transcendental, ontological genesis of a world of representation whose structure is reflected in the image, and production as the multistage shaping of a material product in the industrial realm, are structurally congruent. Critical theory, which saw the Kantian transcendental subject with its grasping arms (synthesis of apprehension), its serial forms (synthesis of reproduction), and its normative control (synthesis of recognition) always as the figure of reflection of social production, is one of the strongest supports for this interference.[9] Deleuze and Guattari confirm the enforced conformity of nature to industry and the description of the body as part of that universal factory of being from another perspective. I want to sketch these interlinkages as briefly as possible with regard to the art of modernity.

The epistemological work of abstraction is still oriented toward the model of the rational, perspectival image whose transformation and destruction are performed by the painting of modernity—that line of development of painting that leads from Georges Seurat via cubism to Mondrian. The essential steps in this destruction are the energetically differential, and no longer geometrically ideal, determination of *light* as the element for the genesis of the image with Seurat; the splintering of the eye-point, that is, of the pyramidal space of perspectival illusion in analytic cubism; and Mondrian's extraction of the elementary means of production of painting, of the means of production not of the image-*thing* but of the image-*illusion,* and their dynamic integration into the force field of the neoplastic image-surface.

Its execution radiates into the here and now of the image-plane. The new, physiological determination of vision as the work of an eye "made of flesh"[10] in impressionism and neoimpressionism initiates the *incarnation* of the viewer-subject, which leads as far as its bodily enclosure in the theatrical minimalist situation and further to its social and sexual specification in postminimalist installation art. Seurat's atomization of the image's structure and of the production process of painting further produces a new kind of relationship between the space and time of the image—of the scenic, narrative phenomenon—on one hand, and on the other, the space and time of the material production of the image's screen woven from the indices of touches of the brush that technically anticipate the stream of electrons in the magnetic cathode-ray tube. The appearance of the image is constituted as the cavity of spatial ideality in the differential energetic field cut by the material screen. The cubist destruction of central perspective causes the geometrical structure of this cavity to collapse and radically destroys the conformity between the space of the image and the space of representation that perspective art had formalized over five centuries. And Mondrian's abstraction, finally, leads toward a painting of surfaces that localizes the image as a material locus in relation to the real surrounding space and its architectural integration.

All these are moments indicating a new *existential* relation of the image to its *surrounding world*. The increasing incidence of the trace of production is indissolubly intermeshed with the emergence of the *phenomenon* of the painting into the real surface of painting. The modern painting is on the way to becoming an object and therefore necessarily comes more strongly into view with regard to the form of its production and existence—as shown almost anecdotally by Rauschenberg's *White Paintings*, described as "airports for the lights, shadows, and particles."[11] Nevertheless, the epistemological labor of the image's destruction, shown exemplarily by abstraction conceived in this way from Seurat to Mondrian, is linked essentially to the image as a model or analogue of consciousness. Its point of reference is the rational, perspectival image that was conceived as a model of perception and image representation of the subject. In each specific relationship between materiality and phenomenon, between surface, space, and body, between color and drawing in both representational *and* abstracting painting, the structurally analogous relationship between body and consciousness, sensuousness and rationality in the subject's act of perception is reflected and interpreted. The critique of the image in modernity transforms this model in which the subject found the reflex of its sensuous relationship to the world. It thus transforms the concept of subjectivity itself. It is certain, however, that abstract painting does not surrender the epistemological function of the image in favor of a sterile, positivist self-reflection of its mediality as a deeply rooted formalist tradition would like to have it. The abstract image remains determined as the prism of a translation of the infinite into the finite in analogy to the act of the transcendental subject, only with the difference that the determination of the poles of this translation and the structure of the prism in modernity have been radically transformed.

The reference to Spinoza allows us to situate *genetically* within the order of production the structure of this prism itself—the a priori transcendental structures of genesis of the finite phenomenal world according to Kant. The structure of the finite subject, of the hinge between the infinite and the finite, between noumenal being and phenomenal objectivity, is itself thought genetically as a folding of the infinite: as a temporarily stable resonance pattern within the overall happening of becoming.[12] The unconscious life of the body participates in the total process of nature (it is a part of this process in the depth of its individual and genetic age), and it holds up to consciousness concentrated in an ego the mirror of the sensuous fields through which it relates to its (imaginary) objects. To deconstruct the space of illusion of perspectival intentional consciousness can therefore mean two things. The destruction can mean *(more geometrico)* cutting open the perspectival space of representation and relating it to absolute mathematical space, a destruction that shows, according to Spinoza's formula, what the untrue idea of the image *(imago)* is *viewed in itself* or in truth (see *Ethics* II, P32, P33, P35). The aspectual image is related to the plan sections in which its genesis is recorded. It is this critique of the distorted aspectual images of perception by relating them genetically to geometric space without a standpoint as whose paradigm the rational perspective is present in the *Ethics*. However, the destruction can also be performed temporally by relating the images of perception back to the perceiving body in which the presynthetic difference—the outside, becoming, substance—first precipitates as a quality of sensation or as the raw material *for* an objectivity to be synthesized.[13] And it is this model that steps out of the shadows of the paradigm of perspective in the nineteenth century with the discovery of physiological vision and light conceived energetically—and no longer geometrically—and leads to its temporalizing and, finally, to its collapse.

This twofold—spatial geometric and energetic–temporal—topic of the critique of the image is present in classic modernity in various theoretical garbs and formal realizations. Postcubist abstraction as a whole is a destruction of the aspectual image in the name of an infinity that bears various names: Malevich's "nonobjective excitation," Mondrian's "universal," and Duchamp's "four-dimensional bride" point to this dimension, which is translated in the arrangement of their work into the nonetheless finite sight of the form (abstract image or ready-made). Spinoza's ontology is present behind the often manifest and much discussed Bergsonianism and Nietzscheanism. Mondrian's conception here has an exemplary coherence. What Mondrian calls the *universal* is not projected as an eidetic structure beyond the image as the usual Platonizing interpretation of his work would like to have it. The *universal* is preobjective becoming, the flood of intensity which is translated on the screen of the painting as well as in the subject's body into a colored manifestation in an orderly way. The elements of this manifestation are no longer dispersed by Mondrian in such a way that they reconfigure for the gaze, like Seurat's spectral colors, into a scenic, spatial image. After the collapse of the perspectival structure of the image in cubism, Mondrian conceives the painting's surface as the locus for the analysis of those means of production of the illusion of the image that are the *primary*, not further analyzable, and in this sense *elementary* products of the translation of intensity—of the resonance spectrum of light—into an extensive, qualitative phenomenon. Red, yellow, and blue—contained within the structure of the orthogonal linear grid and cut off from one another by the noncolors, white and light gray—are not only the *end products* of abstraction from a natural appearance (of abstraction *from* constituted nature, *natura naturata*) but are above all the primary points of contact or joints between the flood of intensity and a qualitatively chromatic manifestation in the space of representation. Mondrian's critique of individual perspectival image-consciousness, the breaking down of the limitations of the representational image—of the *morphoplastically* limited *form* that corresponds to the localization of finite vision in space—must be connected with its other, no longer geometric, but energetico-economic side that conceives the image as an arrangement of production.

With Seurat, the *laboring* body has been transfigured into the ideal geometric space of perspectival painting as the body whose atomized time of labor precipitates on the screen of brush traces, but also as the bodily eye that reconfigures a scenic phenomenal space from the spectralized dots of color. The screen is still defined as a section through the visual pyramid, but the section is moved forward temporally into the moment when the manifold of resonances of light is still *approaching* the eye, before the reflexes have formed in the perceiving body that are the images in consciousness. Mondrian's work stands in the continuity of this determination of the locus of the image between the energetic constitution of the presynthetic world and the spatial phenomenon. The surface of the painting and the living body—and here I am tempted to call this body *transcendental*—are stretched as a membrane between the *universal* (intensity or the noumenal difference) and the manifestation of the image, which is not perspectival but nevertheless finitely extensive. The energetically conceived infinite lies *this side* of the image, this side of the space of manifestation. On the surface, it is translated into the unsplittable primary colors, the poles of constitution of every possible visibility. The abstract image suspends this translation process at the moment of its primary production. It stops the manifesting primary colors from flowing any further and mixing in phenomenal perspectival space. Mondrian's reference to Spinoza lies in this energetic and dynamic determination of the image as the side of production of (possible) visibility on the edge of noumenal intensity and not in the adoration of the purported stasis of an eternal substance, of a structural eidos behind the change of aspectual images.[14]

I describe this work of classical modernity on a critique of the image as still epistemological because, although it determines the image as the place of production of a visibility in analogy to the living body, in which a confusion of affections is translated into the space of distance and light of the visible world, it realizes this analogy still within the structural and eidetic moments of the image as the form and model of representation and, despite the emissions mentioned, not with respect to its material existence and production. The painting comes into consideration above all as the locus and bearer of a *showing,* not as itself something made and shown under external conditions. But this *is* the case in postabstract art since minimal art. If the work no longer makes available any inner room for play, any zone freed of resistance for the interplay of visual signs and for the constitution of meaning in this interplay, but itself, as an object and material, is such a sign or ensemble of signs exposed to the stream of causality in the profane world, then its material body must become directly the bearer of its constitution of meaning or its production of truth.

Let us firmly note the basic traits of this epochal difference between the painting of the first half of the century and postabstract art since the 1960s. And to be as concrete as possible here, I will compare four positions: Mondrian, Donald Judd, Michael Asher, and Thomas Hirschhorn. The locus of Mondrian's work, of the function of truth of his work, despite the image elements being brought onto the surface and woven with the fine texture of the brush, is the phenomenal space of the painting. Its material conditions of existence and production remain peripheral. The painting's material *subjectile* is covered by the layer of its white grounding. The reverse, the frame, the hanging remain unthematic, despite the envisaged architectural integration. "Plastic art is a free aspect of life," writes Mondrian at the beginning of the Second World War. "*Not being bound* by physical and material conditions, it does not tolerate any oppression and can resist it. It is disinterested; its only function is to 'show.' It is for us to see what it reveals."[15] This freedom of painting is closely related to the painting's ideality. The existence of the painting, its material and economic reality—painting is *cheap* and technically *primitive*—is consumed in the work of *showing*, in the fire of the phenomenon. Abstraction has by no means extinguished this fire, say, to make the concrete, positive materiality of its material means visible. Mondrian's destruction of the image is concerned solely with ensuring that this fire no longer illuminates a perspectival space of depth and memory but the space *this side* of the image-plane, which is structurally the space of the future.

The elements manifesting themselves in Mondrian's image's field—the blocks of pure elementary colors whose *confluence* into the perspectival imaginary space of perception and the image is prevented by the grid of orthogonal lines—are, in minimal art, the shown materials themselves exposed to real space, the Plexiglas and metal plates of Judd's specific objects. The minimal separation between material and phenomenon in the abstract painting has collapsed. The material itself in the tenacity of its existence is what is shown—in the tenacity and duration of its existence and especially, and paradoxically, in the temporal depth of this existence. In a Plexiglas plate by Judd, the abstract labor sedimented in the means of production, and the means of production of the means of production, the "congealed"[16] of past labor, are also exhibited *as invisible*. In the sheer illegibility of the production process, in the radical opacity of the material's presence, we *see* the repressed or truncated dimension of sedimented time itself. Here, therefore, the analysis must change registers, just as perception, although unconsciously, has already changed and therefore, taken in itself, remains aconceptual fascination. Here it is manifestly and explicitly a matter of the conditions and the form of existence, of the material and economic reality of the work, which is not to be produced in a cheap and primitive fashion, but which, already in its phenomenal qualities, in the homogeneity and smoothness of the materials, in the stasis of visual space, presents itself as the incarnation of abstract exchange value.[17] The synchronicity of visual space from which any indication of the sequential time of production has been expelled is the sensuous scheme (in the Kantian sense) of the law of exchange. The tension and openness of the minimalist situation is grounded in its resonance with the fetishism of the commodity form. Its truth is the truth of a symptom.

In his works of the 1970s, Michael Asher opened up this abstract visual reality—the glass of "real space" (Judd) in which the minimalist situation is crystallized—to the dimension of its economic genesis. I name two paradigmatic works: the exhibitions at the Galerie Heiner Friedrich (Cologne, September 4–28, 1973) and at the Galleria Toselli (Milan, September 13 to October 8, 1973).[18] At the Galerie Friedrich, Asher had the ceilings in all the rooms of the gallery—the exhibition spaces, offices, kitchen, and lavatory—painted in the same color as the floor and thus turned a partial function of the gallery, the function of *exhibiting*, against its overall economic function. All the rooms with their contents and practical routines now stretched between the equally large slabs of floor and ceiling, now in the same colors. The abstract visibility, the *emptiness* of the exhibition space which in normal operations is tied to turning toward the object exhibited whose sale compensates the gallery for its product, the emptiness of the space itself, was now guided into all the rooms, canceling their functional separation. This self-exposition of the machine at full throttle transforms the abstract visibility that otherwise is the vanishing mediator in the exchange process into a moment of the happening of the work. The false semblance of autonomy of the work-object—that (incomplete) secularized aura in which the gallery envelops the commodified artwork—turns into a moment of the work's truth-function through an explication of its genesis and economic, no longer liturgical, function.

At the Galleria Toselli, Asher had the walls and ceiling of the gallery, a broad room similar to a garage, freed of the many layers of white paint from past years. Four days' work by four workers with sandblasting equipment exposed the material body of the gallery as the bearer of visibility that has left its impression on the bearer itself. At the moment of its exposition, this bearer becomes an image, an historical image, a narrative about the material history of the place that has been written down in a tableau of legible traces. This image, however, is as a whole a trace or an index of the subtraction of the white paint that otherwise provides the neutral background for the object exhibited in the intermeshing execution of the function of exhibiting and the exchange process. Four days' sandblasting—this time, the aggressiveness of this work and the gallery's economic investment (which financed the work) are stacked up in the empty room and indicated by the absence of the white paint, like Seurat's atomized work in the grains of sand of the spectral colors that occupy his screen. What is shown is this absence. The space of visibility, the *empty* space, has been fitted with a temporal index and defined as a *product*. This is not a dematerialization of the work. The excess of abstract visibility has repercussions for the *totality* of the material situation. Asher's work transforms its place into a sculpture that remains surrounded by the space of its current production, which coincides with the space of its exhibition.

For both of Asher's works, the intricate relationship between time and money in the economic realm is central. Time, counted time, is the drive for the self-exposing machine that his interventions construct on the foundations of the material situation and the historical function of the gallery. With Mondrian, the material existence of the painting is absorbed by the function of *showing*, by the phenomenon of the image and its epistemological meaning. With Judd, the visual phenomenon is stuck together with the existence of the object, and the situation gains its truth in the moment of crisis, that is, in the legibility of the symptom. With Asher, abstract visibility, which in minimalism, has climbed out of the painting and been implicitly put into a homology with an abstract exchange value and hits back at the bearer of its real economic production. In this way, the paradigm of exchange is intermeshed with the *incommensurability* of the work, which withdraws radically from exchangeability and the concept of value by not being a *being*. Asher's work *is* the happening of visibility of the material situation itself, the *strife*, to use Heidegger's word,[19] between the transparency of visual space and the bearer it comes up against, causing it to coagulate into an image and an image-ground. (This applies to the "naked" Galleria Toselli but also to the actions executed in the Galerie Friedrich, which, theatralized by Asher's framing, become a performance.) This strife is coupled with a disturbance to the exchange process. It is driven on or, to use Heidegger's word once again, it is instigated by the inference from the gallery's showing function back to the gallery's body or the material situation. For this inference, the economic determination of the time of the happening of the work is essential. It is *counted* time. It is neither the time of nature, daytime, or the time of year, as in Judd's permanent installations in Marfa in Texas, for instance, his alternative to the exhibition situation in the white cube of the gallery that is amalgamated with the exchange process, nor is it the elastic experiential time of a viewer. It is the time of the duration of an exhibition, the time of the *actual* production of the gallery that both drives and limits the happening of the work. The temporal limitation of the work's happening is therefore an essential part of its conception, of what I call the *form* of its existence. It prevents the work from being mistaken for the mere *appearance* of the situation. Through Asher's intervention, the situation has been transformed into a machine in which the counted time of the exhibition's operation remains short-circuited with its product, the nothingness of visibility. This short circuit constitutes the truth function of the work.

The closer the position in historical time–space, the more difficult it is to delimit the general contours of a concept of the work. So far, I have not sketched any genealogy of Hirschhorn's work. Apart from Mondrian, his points of contact lie elsewhere: in Beuys's plastic work on the borderline between artistic and social form; in Warhol's machinism, which intermeshes the visual form of the work with the structure of productive output, of the permanent and blind work of living—"The machinery is always going. Even when you sleep"[20]—and, from the first half of the century, in the collages by Rodchenko, Heartfield, and Schwitters, turned toward the poles of a hoped-for proletariat and a collapsing bourgeois public sphere.[21] To locate his work within a topic of modernity, its relationship to the simultaneously ascetic and materialist practices of the 1970s nevertheless remains essential, for which Asher's empty rooms stand here as paradigmatic examples.

The precarious materiality of Hirschhorn's work is projected into this empty space, which perhaps most recently posed the question concerning the universal publicness of art this side of the element of spectacle, a question forgotten during the 1980s. I ask myself whether and how his work, through its existence and the form of its existence, although bound to material and transportable but not site-specific objects, has a character of happening analogous to Asher's machinic arrangements, and whether it participates in an analogously determined productivity. Of course, the "poor" materials and the reclaimed primitivity of production as well as the appellative urgency of the references—"help please!! I don't understand that!!"[22]—play a crucial role here. The *strife* which in Asher's work runs through the contours of the situation itself draws in Hirschhorn's work the outline of a material product that nevertheless refuses to take on the ontological solidity and harmlessness of an *object*. How is this refusal defined?

For Hirschhorn today and in the 1990s, it was not the question how the representation or the *imaginary* in the work could be destroyed, so to speak, as a surrogate, as was the case for Mondrian and classical modern art. The element that needs to be dissolved analytically and in which the work has to assert its *form* is today the penetrating visibility of the spectacle. Penetrating but nevertheless touching only one layer of beings—that is the paradoxical structure of the spectacular presence that is constituted in the element of value equivalence as a synchronous relationship of calculability of all points of space. This visibility, which no longer has to be tied to and addressed to an eye, is imposed on the supporting media of technical apparatus whose substantial determination cannot be thought in an anthropological, instrumental way, nor in a technical, medial way, but which has to be conceived economically. (The hardware for making the world into an image and an object is today in its substance above all the capital invested in calculating machines.) The spectacular visibility is assumed in the exemplary moment of minimal art as an element of existence—of the material presence—of the artwork. With Asher—and here his work stands in a wider context of conceptual practices critical of institutions—the spectacular visibility is thematized as this element and, by linking it again to its causes, determined as that which, according to Spinoza's formula, it is in truth or viewed in itself.[23] The matrix of this relinking is obviously no longer geometric space.

Modernity as a whole has made the transition from a mathematical to a dynamic, from a spatial to a temporal, from a geometric to an energetic conception of the element of *representation*. The transformation of Spinoza's *mos geometricus* into Marx's *mos oeconomicus* is only one moment of this epistemological transformation.[24] The general element of calculation in which *images* are inscribed as the expression of correlation of the element's points was, in Renaissance perspective, geometric space. Modernity, and not only modern art, has dynamized this element, has grasped it energetically and economically. Rational perspective has lost its function as the paradigm of artistic production of images and the critique of the image (and returns in this function only mediated by photography) because it no longer works as a *hinge* between the finite imaginary and the new, economically fluidized ground of visibility. In the Renaissance, perspective was a technique *(technē)* for connecting the finite aspectual image with its true causes, thus conceding its subjective untruth as a genetic necessity and hence as objective truth. In this sense, as I have said, for Spinoza, perspective becomes a methodological paradigm. The modernity of the nineteenth century and the first half of the twentieth century has performed, on the path outlined, the materialization and dynamization of the elements of this genesis: energetic light, physiological vision, the neuronal body are determined as the bearers of the imaginary space of the gaze, and to this corresponds a transformation also of the genealogical analysis and critique of the image by leading it back to the energetico-differential constitution of the world *prior* to it forming in the transcendental body into *objectively existing* nature. In the space of the spectacle, in the image and space of the present, the supporting element of the collective imaginary is no longer mathematical space or energetically defined light. The bearer of spectacular visibility is the movement of capital, and the space of the imaginary is the being itself as grasped by the commodity form. The inscription of a resistance into this structure must take other paths than the epistemological critique of the image in classical modern art. The methodological or rather *strategic* paradigm, however, remains the same: the explication of the relationship of the false idea to its cause, the relationship of the product to the dimension of production.

The place of illusion today is no longer the depth of perspectival painting that abandons its means to the pull of illusion of the image and ties the mind to a contemplation of the past, to the paradigm of guilt and mourning. Mondrian's painting is conceived as a resistance against this pull. His lines have raked through the space of retrospective illusion and extracted its pure elements. The presence of the primary colors is asserted *in* the plane of the image as the membrane between the past and the future. Hirschhorn does not have to assert the materiality and presence of his work against the space of representation in this sense. This space has been essentially filled in since the 1960s. Rather he has to assert it in and against the space of spectacular visibility. And this assertion can no longer take the path of a *condensation of value* in the materials. Minimal art understood and staged for the first time the economic substance of the work's presence as the medium of art production. After the conceptual practices of the 1970s, which split this substance and explicated it into a space of happening (for which Asher's work, to my mind, is only the most radical example), it can no longer be a matter of anticipating, in the style of mainstream art of the 1980s, the value condensation in the artwork through its material beauty. (The condensation of exchange value can correspond to the determination of the work as a concentrate of potentiated visibility, but it remains essentially a contingency of speculation.) Hirschhorn's materials are taken from the realm of general production, from the nonspecific, lower layer of this production in packaging materials and mass media images. They remain resistant as these materials in the use made of them. Like Mondrian's colors, they do not *mix*; they are not transformed into the illusion of another existence. On the contrary, the cut and contrastive elements of Hirschhorn's *collages* (for that would be perhaps the proper generic concept also for his three-dimensional works) stick firmly to each other. Their contrast keeps them flat. The edges of the images from which often the contextual embedding has been cut off tear also their referential depth into the present. A pasted press photo is like one of Seurat's brushstrokes or Warhol's silk screen shadows, the trace of the production process, the notch that contact with the real leaves behind, not a documentary opening to historical space. The visible surface of the work is the servant of its contact with the world. This contact *as such* has to be shaped—the outline of the trace, not the form of the product. Only the outline defined in this way as the temporal edge of production gives the material happening of the work the force of resistance to assert itself in and against the spectacular realm of commodified visibility. This resisting force is grounded in the nonsimultaneity, in the heterochrony, of form and production.

This procedure does not negate the fact that *money* is the bearer of this precarious existence, the projected ray that generates the image or the form. This image emerges in its urgency, in its flickering on the screen of a present that cannot be conceived as framed by an institution or even by the historical conditions. At this point, Hirschhorn's work is radically different from the institutional critique of the 1990s and the practices of artists such as Andrea Fraser and Christian Philipp Müller. The place of projection, the place of *exposition*, to use Duchamp's basic term, is the contingency of the situation. Therefore this material image is unstable. Or conversely, it is this *conception* of the structure of production and the product that is indicated in the manifest, *dramatized* instability of the material image. In other words, Hirschhorn's work, like Asher's, is strictly nonarchitectural.

The *precariousness* is therefore not a specific feature of Hirschhorn's work whose existence is restricted in the chronological sense. It is a mode of existence shared by all his works. Precarious form is the name for the temporal outline that incorporates that other side of the visually present form turned toward production. The essential achievement of the *artwork* is this structurally reversed side of the form, for this reversal is not a property of commodity fetishism alone but of every product. The temporally ("minted") edge of every present form is turned structurally toward forgetting; it is the seam between the present and forgetting, just as the spatial outline of *disegno* is the seam between the visible extension of form and visibility without a standpoint. The artwork's achievement is not to undo this seam but to turn it inside out so that evidence is shown of contact with the outside or the incommensurable in the form. Giving a form that is more than design is conceivable only as contact with the formless. It is does not take place in the element of an already smooth, synthetic presence that has been freed of resistance but in contact with the presynthetic, in the experience of resistance from the outside. The precarious form is the form that the artwork has assumed, as

FIGURE 9.1. Thomas Hirschhorn, *Spinoza Monument*, Amsterdam, 1999. Copyright Thomas Hirschhorn.

Hirschhorn says, as a "tool for experiencing reality" in going through this experience. It is not the form of a recognizable object but the blind point of contact of the tool with the real that is only translated into a form and image by going through the experience.

The achievement of the work is to enter this plane of immanence with the formless or the real and to inscribe in it a figure of resistance in which a world and the image's reflections of the world are first constituted. In this structure, there is an affinity with Spinozan thinking, which thinks and affirms the finitude of the *mode* (of finite life) and the imagistic forms under which the infinite substance or the outside shows itself to finite life as an expression of the infinite. In this sense, *all* of Hirschhorn's works have as much and as little to do with Spinoza as the 1999 *Spinoza Monument* realized in a group exhibition, Midnight Walkers and City Sleepers, in the red-light district of Amsterdam (see Figure 9.1). There is no Spinozan influence on Hirschhorn's work, no immediate effect of reading. The affinity lies in the process of formation, in the form of material existence of

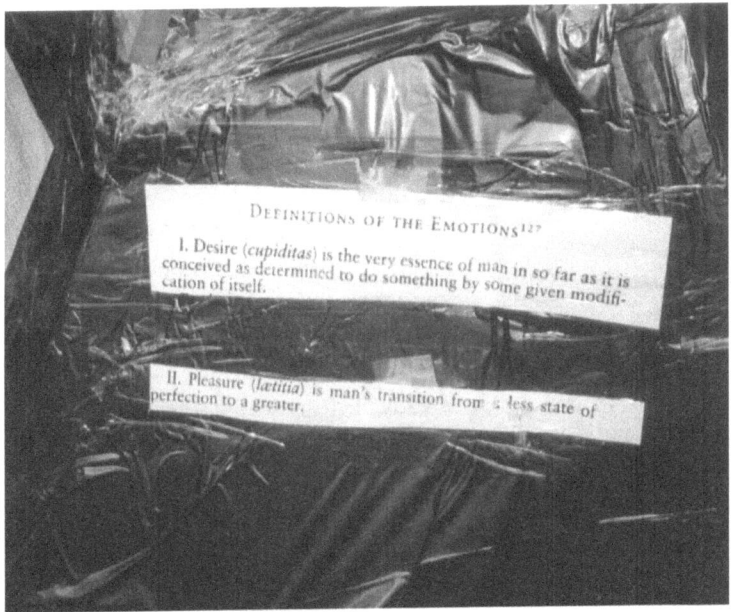

FIGURE 9.2. Thomas Hirschhorn, *Spinoza Monument*, Amsterdam, 1999. Copyright Thomas Hirschhorn.

the works themselves. The *Spinoza Monument* has given this material happening the plastic form that cites in the simplest way the monument's memorial function: statue and name on the rock made of cardboard that emerges from an Amsterdam canal. But the memorial function is put in brackets; it is a ready-made function that the layer of the work's precarious existence slips on. The books in the vendor's tray, the stuck-on excerpts of text, the video in which Hirschhorn reads the *Treatise on the Emendation of the Intellect,* are elements for activating this existence, moments of excess or outflow. The illumination of the statue with integrated neon tubes whose current, like that for the television set, was drawn from a neighboring sex shop underlines this temporal activity and connects the monument to it is actual, current surroundings. Two flags, one red and one green, poles of the battery, bear the labels "DESIRE" and "PLEASURE." Their definitions, derived from "The Definitions of the Emotions" in *Ethics* III, are affixed to the foot of the flagpoles (see Figure 9.2). "I: Desire *(cupiditas)* is the very essence of man insofar as it is conceived as determined to any action from any given affection of itself." "II: Pleasure *(laetitia)* is man's transition from a state of less perfection to a state of greater perfection." In the first sketch for the project, "passion" and "reason" were planned, which would have prescribed a dialectical reading: the critical corrective intervention of thinking into the world of passions and images. This dialectic remains implied in the relationship between desire and pleasure. "The *conatus* with which each thing endeavors to persist in its own being is nothing but the actual essence of the thing itself" (*Ethics* III, P7). Desire is the expression of this endeavor or drive *(appetitus),* insofar that it is "accompanied by consciousness thereof" (*Ethics* III, P9S). The structure of desire is therefore already enclosed within the horizon of the world in which the infinite substance or the outside is reflected in the form of an image. Desire as a drive accompanied by consciousness is directed toward a defined object in which the total movement of finite life—the *conatus* that unconsciously participates in the infinite being of nature—is bound to a particular aim. Only in being bound to the outline of the particular object, to the *imago* of what is held to be *good because* one strives for it (*Ethics* III, P9S), can the subject's finitude drift off into the circuit of illusions and murky passions that succumb to the spell of images. The artwork is an arrangement that conceives this outline in its correlation with the finitude of imagistic representation, that is, of the subject's consciousness and desire, and *turns* this outline *inside out,* relating it to the infinite. It does not destroy the image and desire but displaces the outline into the space of its necessary genesis. It conceives the object of desire once again as the expression of desiring life itself. Pleasure, the "transition from a state of less perfection to a state of greater perfection," is the affect that accompanies this correction, the focusing of the lens and the release of productive life from the image's spell.

Notes

1. Gilles Deleuze, *Spinoza: Practical Philosophy*, trans. Robert Hurley (San Francisco: City Lights Books, 1988), 98ff. "The essence of the mode in turn is a degree of power, a part of the divine power, i.e., an intensive part or a degree of intensity." This quote comes the lemma on power (*puissance* or *potentia*). See *Ethics* III, P7–9. All references to Spinoza's writings are to *Complete Works*, trans. Samuel Shirley, ed. Michael L. Morgan (Indianapolis, Ind.: Hackett, 2002).
2. See esp. the outline within the history of ideas in Henri Bergson, *Creative Evolution*, trans. Arthur Mitchell (Westport, Conn.: Greenwood Press, 1975), chap. 4, where Bergson makes clear the homology of the concept of becoming (*durée* or *élan vital*) with Spinoza's *natura naturans*.
3. This layer of presence is not only the presence of perception and consciousness but presence as such: the limiting layer of the co-actuality of forces in the transition between that which already was and that which is not yet.
4. On the correlation between explication and canceling out (of the noumenal difference in the phenomenon, of intensity in quality and extension), see Gilles Deleuze, "Asymmetrical Synthesis of the Sensible," in *Difference and Repetition*, trans. Paul Patton (New York: Columbia University Press, 1994), esp. 239–40.
5. See Alain Badiou's analysis of structure in "Spinoza's Closed Ontology," in *Theoretical Writings*, ed. and trans. Ray Brassier and Alberto Toscano, 91–93 (London: Continuum, 2004).
6. Antonio Negri, *The Savage Anomaly: The Power of Spinoza's Metaphysics and Politics*, trans. Michael Hardt (Minneapolis: University of Minneapolis Press, 1991).
7. Louis Althusser, *Essays in Self-Criticism*, trans. Grahame Lock (London: NLB, 1976); Pierre Macherey, *Hegel ou Spinoza* (Paris: Maspero, 1979); see also Yirmiyahu Yovel, "Spinoza and Marx: Man-in-Nature and the Science of Redemption," in *Spinoza and Other Heretics*, vol. 3, *The Adventures of Immanence*, 78–103 (Princeton, N.J.: Princeton University Press, 1989), and Eugene Holland, "Spinoza and Marx," *Cultural Logic: An Electronic Journal of Marxist Theory and Practice* 2, no. 1 (1998), http://clogic.eserver.org/2-1/holland.html.

8   "Entretien Avec Thomas Hirschhorn Réalisé Par M. Keïta, S. Keïta, K. Keïta, N. Keïta, Ch. Soumbounou, K. Harra et M. Niakate," *Le Journal des Laboratoires* 2 (June 2004), quoted in *Thomas Hirschhorn Musée Précaire Albinet* (Paris: Éditions Xavier Barral/Les Laboratoires d'Aubervilliers, 2005).

9   See, e.g., Max Horkheimer, "Kants Philosophie und die Aufklärung," in *Zur Kritik der instrumentellen Vernunft*, 203–15 (Frankfurt, Germany: Fischer, 1997), esp. 209. [Translator's note: This is one of the four chapters that were omitted in the English translation of Horkheimer's *Critique of Instrumental Reason*.]

10 Michel Foucault saw this "flesh," which is also the flesh *(chair)* in which the late Merleau-Ponty grounded Husserlian phenomenology, in the blurred image in the mirror of Velazquez's *Meniñas*, which demands a bodily presence in the "place of the king" which was once occupied by the transcendental *cogito*. The eye made of flesh that coagulates in the scientific climate of the nineteenth century around the focal point of perspective painting is the crystallized seed of Foucault's "human being," who entered the stage of the minimalist situation as the viewer–subject in the 1960s (and who, in the meantime, in relational aesthetics, also speaks and eats). The clouding of the space of *representation* runs parallel in the history of painting precisely with the incarnation of the subject in its finite empiricity. See Michel Foucault, *The Order of Things: An Archaeology of the Human Sciences* (London: Routledge, 2002), esp. chap. 9.

11 John Cage, "On Robert Rauschenberg, Artist, and His Work," in *Silence: Lectures and Writings* (Middletown, Conn.: Wesleyan University Press, 1961), 102.

12 See Gilles Deleuze, "Spinoza and Us," in Deleuze, *Spinoza: Practical Philosophy*, 122–30.

13 One's own perceiving *body* is, as Spinoza formulated with pointed emphasis and clarity, "the object of the idea constituting the human mind . . . and nothing else" (*Ethics* II, P13). As he explained further in Part II, the subject does not adequately *recognize* this body that is the bearer of its consciousness (*Ethics* II, P19, P23, P24). The living body is the mirror for the images of the world (and of itself as an object in the world). It *conceals* itself for the subject before these perspectival images that hollow out its mirroring substance and relativize it into a differential of appearances.

14 For more detail on this Spinozan and Deleuzian analysis of Mondrian, see Sebastian Egenhofer, "Die Abstraktion und die Topik des Imaginären," in *Struktur, Figur, Kontur: Abstraktion in Kunst und Lebenswissenschaften*, ed. Claudia Blümle and Armin Schäfer, 271–97 (Berlin: diaphanes, 2007).

15 Piet Mondrian, "Liberation from Oppression in Art and Life," under the earlier title "Art Shows the Evil of Nazi and Soviet Oppressive Tendencies" (1939–40), in *The New Art—The New Life: The Collected Writings of Piet Mondrian*, trans. and ed. Harry Holtzmann and Martin S. James (Boston: G. K. Hall, 1986), 320.

16 Karl Marx, *Capital: A Critique of Political Economy*, vol. 1, trans. Ben Fowkes (New York: Vintage, 1977), 128.

17 The best analysis of Judd's "specific objects" remains Karl Beveridge and Ian Burn, "Don Judd," *The Fox* 2 (1975): 128–42. The general model of a semiology of material that deciphers its hidden historicity—its *economic* reality—can, of course, be found in Roland Barthes, *Mythologies*, trans. Annette Lavers (London: Vintage, 1993).

18 See Michael Asher, *Writings 1973–83 on Works 1969–79*, ed. Benjamin H. D. Buchloh (Halifax, N.S., Canada: Press of the Nova Scotia College of Art and Design), 82–94.

19 Martin Heidegger, "The Origin of the Work of Art," in *Basic Writings*, rev. ed., ed. David Farrell Krell (London: Routledge, 2000), 180ff.

20 Andy Warhol, *The Philosophy of Andy Warhol (from A to B and Back Again)* (San Diego, Calif.: A Harvest Book, Harcourt, 1975), 96.

21 See Benjamin Buchloh, "Thomas Hirschhorn: Lay Out Sculpture and Display Diagrams," in *Thomas Hirschhorn*, 41–93 (London: Phaidon, 2004), and Buchloh, "An Interview with Thomas Hirschhorn," *October* 113 (2005): 77–100.

22 See Thomas Hirschhorn, *Les Plaintifs, les bêtes, les politiques* (Geneva, Switzerland: Centre genevois de Gravure Contemporaine, 1995). (It is Hirschhorn's "atlas," as Buchloh writes in "Thomas Hirschhorn," 52.)

23 See n. 13. On the relinking of the false idea to its causes as the method of Spinoza's epistemological critique, see Deleuze, *Spinoza: Practical Philosophy*.

24 See Yovel, *Spinoza and Other Heretics*, 2:98.

10

Spinoza, Ratiocination, and Art

ANTHONY UHLMANN

SAMUEL BECKETT made use of Spinoza on a number of occasions and copied the following lines into his notes of his reading of Wilhelm Windelband's *A History of Western Philosophy*: "The order of ideas [for Spinoza] is conceived as identical with order of things."[1] It is apparent why such an idea would appeal to a writer: if literature is understood to involve a kind of thinking, to be, that is, a kind of thought, then an immediate connection between events that are described and some process of thinking is attractive.

Yet there is a clear problem when one comes to consider the nature of the interaction between things and ideas in Spinoza, at least from the point of view of literature, which concerns itself with the creation of particular sensual experiences: that is, the problem, at the heart of the *Ethics*, of the nature of the relationship between *natura naturans* and *natura naturata*—the relation between substance, as an infinite being whose essence involves existence, and modes, finite beings whose existence, at least when imagined through the first kind of knowledge given to us by our senses, appears to be contingent.[2]

In attempting to draw out how the problem might shed light on the relationship between literature and thinking, I will consider three interconnected positions from the *Ethics*: first, how the "idea" is defined not to relate directly to words or images but to be, in effect, the process of understanding itself; second, how thinking—that is, the first, second, and third kinds of knowledge—is identified with the idea of the relation, which is also relevant to the existence of the bodies, which are conceived through mutual relations or ratios; and finally, how it becomes possible to develop an understanding of the essence of particular things through the third kind of knowledge, and how this process of development might be understood to involve a kind of creation whose concept sheds light on processes of creation in the arts.

Philosophers such as Edwin Curley, Pierre Macheray, and Gilles Deleuze have long noticed that Spinoza is a philosopher who seems to have a special appeal to nonphilosophers, and to poets and novelists, in particular. Curley lists Novalis, Heine, Coleridge, Wordsworth, Shelley, and George Eliot.[3] On an initial reading, one might wonder why this would be so. There is little direct mention of the arts in the *Ethics*: music is briefly used as an example of an object that might be either good, bad, or indifferent to different people in different circumstances (Spinoza, *Ethics* VI, preface). Yet the circle that surrounded Spinoza formed a group, *Nil Volentibus Arduum*, discussing artistic practice,[4] and this offers evidence of the early recognition of the possible usefulness of his system for the arts.

Still, there are key problems that emerge when one comes to think about art through the *Ethics*. If one believes that works of art function, at least in part, through the production of affects and sensations, that they form beings of sensation that produce affects in us—as Deleuze and Guattari contend in *What Is Philosophy?*, for example—then how can this be reconciled with Spinoza?[5] For Spinoza, affects and sensations pertain to the first kind of knowledge, the imagination, and he clearly states that this kind of knowledge is the sole cause of error (see *Ethics* II, P41). Second, if one wishes to contend that literature develops a kind of thinking, one immediately confronts the further obstacle provided by Spinoza's clear statement in Part II, Proposition 49, to the effect that images and words (which, when one remembers that images for Spinoza involve every kind of sensual material, are necessary to the production of any work of art) only concern the body and are not related to thought:

> Thought . . . does not at all involve the concept of extension. . . . An idea (since it is a mode of thinking) consists neither in the image of anything, nor in words. For the essence of words and

images is constituted only by corporeal motions, which do not at all involve the concept of thought.

Yet, notwithstanding these apparent problems, I would contend that one does not have to read Spinoza against the grain to find material that might be of use to artists.

Ideas are not identified with words or images; rather the idea is the very process of understanding. Spinoza insists on this point, making it more than once, in more than one way, over a number of propositions in Part II. In the Scholium to Proposition 43, he states:

> To have a true idea means nothing other than knowing a thing perfectly, or in the best way. And of course no one can doubt this unless he thinks that an idea is something mute, like a picture on a tablet, and not a mode of thinking, viz. the very [act of] understanding. And I ask, who can know that he understands some thing unless he first understands it? I.e., who can know that he is certain about some thing unless he is first certain about it?

The metaphors are extremely interesting here: a picture on a tablet, a painting, for example, is thought of as "mute," or as Shirley translates it, "dumb" in the sense of mute.[6] Again, such reasoning seems, initially, unpromising for someone interested in art: here the image itself does not speak. Yet it is worth trying to attend to the nature of the contrast. The idea must, in some sense, speak to us directly. It is the very act of understanding, and we immediately understand that we understand. The idea, then, as conceived here, already carries something of the third kind of knowledge: it strikes us immediately and intuitively. Might this mean we do not come to think or learn to think; that rather, insofar as we understand, we are already in thought? This tautological definition is only so helpful.

It would no doubt be possible to attempt to understand Spinoza's point more fully by turning to the ideas of some of those who influenced his own work: the ancient Stoics, for example, whose work Spinoza knew through his reading of Justus Lipsius, who published epitomes of the Stoic doctrines on ethics and physics at the beginning of the sixteenth century.[7] The Stoics distinguished between bodies and incorporeals, and though words are bodies because they pass as sound through the air or are written down, meaning or sense itself is not in the words; rather meaning is attributed to the words and is incorporeal.[8] For Spinoza, the word is not adequate or necessary to the idea; that is, ideas both exceed and precede the human signs that seek to relate them. I would argue that one can link artistic thinking to this very excess: rather than it being the kind of sign system that seeks to link signs as precisely as possible to their intended meanings, like mathematics or an ideal rational language such as that imagined by Wittgenstein in his *Tractatus,* art requires us to understand what is not present in, or goes beyond, the signifier, what is in the idea rather than in the word.[9] Paradoxically, then, rather than this inhibiting someone who writes literature, it might very well be understood to open possibilities: that words might be so related that they invoke moments of immediate understanding in a reader, moments of understanding that are intended to exceed the expression of the words, getting beyond words through words, by making use of the music of language or powerful images, for example. In a famous letter to Vita Sackville-West of March 16, 1926, Virginia Woolf outlines something of her understanding of the process of creation in art:

> As for the *mot juste,* you are quite wrong. Style is a very simple matter; it is all rhythm. Once you get that, you can't use the wrong words. But on the other hand here am I sitting after half the morning, crammed with ideas, and visions, and so on, and can't dislodge them, for lack of the right rhythm. Now this is very profound, what rhythm is, and goes far deeper than words. A sight, an emotion, creates this wave in the mind, long before it makes words to fit it; and in writing (such is my present belief) one has to recapture this, and set this working (which has nothing apparently to do with words) and then, as it breaks and tumbles in the mind, it makes words to fit it: But no doubt I shall think differently next year.[10]

What Woolf is describing comes from sensations and feelings—it is physically sensed. Yet it is also sensed in that it is understood. First, as we will see, feeling is not only involved in the first kind of knowledge but also in the third kind. Second, though Spinoza states that images and words are only related to bodies and not thought, it is nevertheless clear, through his system, that there would necessarily be an idea parallel to an image, an idea parallel to a word. Parallel lines, of course, at least in Euclidean geometry, do not meet. One fails to see how they might be related, unless one understands relation itself to involve the parallel, a gap, a ratio, a proportion that persists and resonates. Pythagoras not only discovered certain mathematical laws through ratios but also immediately applied these to the art of music.

I want to argue that for Spinoza, relation itself is crucial to the generation of any kind of human thought, including thinking in the arts, which, too, proceeds through relations, that is, if we understand relation to involve a kind of linking or connection that proceeds across gaps, urging flashes of insight to emerge, to speak from ourselves to the mute tableau, as a lightening flash leaps from the sky to the ground or a signal jumps across a synapse.

The term *relation* itself is immediately tied to thought in Spinoza: a core meaning of the word *ratio* itself is "reason," or more generally, "thought," as in the English word *ratiocination*. A ratio, in turn, is a relation between things. A definition in scientific terms of *ratio* is "the quantitative relation between two amounts showing the number of times one value contains or is contained within the other" *(Oxford English Dictionary)*. Furthermore, it is the ratio of speeds and slownesses that defines the particular nature of each body; to put this another way, each body has its own logic.

Yet the identification of ratio, or relation and thought, is clarified when we turn to Spinoza's definitions of the three kinds of knowledge. In Proposition 40 of Part II, he states that he can explain each kind through a single example:

> Suppose there are three numbers, and the problem is to find a fourth which is to the third as the second is to the first. Merchants do not hesitate to multiply the second by the third, and divide the product by the first, because they have not yet forgotten what they heard from their teacher without any demonstration, or because they have often found this in the simplest numbers, or from the force of the Demonstration of P7 in Bk. VII of Euclid, viz. from the property of proportionals. But in the simplest numbers none

of this is necessary. Given the numbers 1, 2, and 3, no one fails to see that the fourth proportional number is 6—and we see this much more clearly because we infer the fourth number from the ratio which, in one glance, we see the first number to have to the second.

The use of ratio, or mutual relation, as the material for the example here is not accidental; rather relation, ratio, and proportion inhabit thought itself. The first kind of knowledge commonly involves the association of ideas. Spinoza offers many examples of this when he comes to consider the nature of the affects: we connect, through the imagination, an affect or emotion with an external cause. For example, love is the affect of joy related to the idea of an exterior cause. In the example cited earlier, the merchants might come to the correct answer via the first kind of knowledge because they associate the response to the problem with a formula they have learned by rote (without adequately understanding how it might work). The second kind of knowledge would be made use of by someone who understood common notions such as those described by Euclid in his *Elements*. This person has read Euclid and been convinced by, in Spinoza's words, "the force of the Demonstration"; that is, he or she has, through the intellect, understood a process of causation, and such a process is, in effect, nothing other than a set of necessary interrelations. Through the third kind of knowledge, however, no set of associations needs to be triggered, no logical sequence needs to be traced; rather one understands the relation of terms immediately, with an intuitive understanding that grasps the relations involved as understanding. Intuition, that is, is also a kind of relation, but one in which the related terms—the thing perceived and the thing understood—involve what might almost be thought to be an identification; to put this another way, one is adequate to the other.

It remains to be seen, then, how this notion of thought as relation might be brought into contact with artistic practices. In discussing *Film*, Samuel Beckett's work for cinema, Gilles Deleuze contends that Beckett allows us to recognize key potentials of the filmic medium because he exhausts or negates those elements.[11] The same principle of exhaustion or negation might be seen in Beckett's aesthetic writings, in which he develops the concept of "nonrelation" in art, which he opposes to an artistic tradition that, he states, has always emphasized relation and the power of relation.

In his first novel, *Dream of Fair to Middling Women,* Beckett describes an aesthetic theory that emphasizes the connections or relations between things rather than the nature of those things themselves.[12] In a later letter to Georges Duthuit (written in 1949), Beckett outlines a somewhat different aesthetic understanding, one that emphasizes *non*-relation or the refusal to fully draw connections or relationships. Beckett states:

> As far as I'm concerned, Bram [van Velde]'s painting . . . is new because it is the first to repudiate relation in all its forms. It is not the relation with this or that order of encounter that he refuses, but the state of being quite simply in relation full stop, the state of being in front of. . . . The break with the outside world implies the break with the inside. . . . I'm not saying that he doesn't search to re-establish correspondence. What is important is that he does not manage to.[13]

In "Peintres de l'Empêchement" (first published in 1948), Beckett states that all works of art have involved the readjustment of the relation between subject and object,[14] a relation that he claims has now broken down. He announced this crisis over a decade before and prior to World War II in 1934 in another review, "Recent Irish Poetry," which can also be found in *Disjecta.* Elsewhere I have argued in detail how Beckett moves from making clear links in his works through allusion and other means to occluding the element that would link the terms, while still offering terms that cry out to be related.[15] Such a process of occlusion, or an insistence on gaps, however, differs in degree rather than kind from other modes of artistic thinking.

That is, the insistence on gaps between relatable terms has a long history in art. Stephen Greenblatt, for example, claims that something happens to Shakespeare's artistic method around the time he writes *Hamlet*:

> Shakespeare found that he could immeasurably deepen the effect of his plays, that he could provoke in the audience . . . a peculiarly passionate intensity of response, if he took out a key explanatory

element, thereby occluding the rationale, motivation, or ethical principle that accounted for the action that was to unfold. The principle was not the making of a riddle to be solved, but the creation of a strategic opacity. This opacity ... released an enormous energy that had been at least partially blocked or contained by familiar, reassuring explanations.[16]

One kind of artistic practice, developed to a high degree by Beckett, is to leave gaps between and within the subjects who perceive and the objects that are presented. Such gaps might be understood to involve, to cite Deleuze from his essay on Marcel Proust, the process of leading to thought rather than thinking;[17] that is, in art, the relation still has to be drawn, has not yet been fully drawn, and we need to think in attempting to bridge the gap.

Approaching Beckett's problem of the relation of subject and object through Spinoza, though moving away from Spinoza's terminology, one might consider the first kind of knowledge in Spinoza to be subjective knowledge: Spinoza states that the affections in our bodies and affects in our minds that are caused by external bodies tell us more about the nature of our own bodies than about the nature of the external objects. So, too, again moving away from Spinoza's terminology, the second kind of knowledge, the intellect, which works through common notions that allow us to adequately understand general things but not particular things, might be thought to be objective.

A sophisticated understanding of this relation between kinds of thought (the imagination and the intellect) can be found in ideas attributed to the French post-Impressionist painter Paul Cézanne, who develops the concept of the "sensation" to describe thinking in painting and argues for the possibility of a "logic of organized sensations."[18]

Whereas the idea of an "impression," for the French Impressionists, carries the sense of a passive reflection, with nature impressing its image on the artist, who then faithfully records the moment, "sensation" involves a complex process of interaction that is more active than passive. The sensation is projected by an external nature and is registered by an internal nature; that is, the sensation is both in the image received and in the artist's response to that image.

Furthermore, a sensation analogous to that received from the world is then reprojected by the artist via a process of mental organization or composition and the brushstrokes that correspond to and build up the new sensation on the canvas. The sensations in turn inhere in the canvas, where they are able to be received by viewers. Joaquim Gasquet reports Cézanne as stating that

> the landscape is reflected, humanized, rationalized within me. I objectivize it, project it, fix it on my canvas. . . . It may sound like nonsense, but I would see myself as the subjective consciousness of that landscape, and my canvas as its objective consciousness.[19]

For Cézanne, the artist needs to become un-self-conscious to *be* the subjective feeling of the other. This in turn develops a new interaction of the first and second kinds of knowledge around an understanding of the object:

> There are two things in the painter, the eye and the mind; each of them should aid the other. It is necessary to work at their mutual development, in the eye by looking at nature, in the mind by the logic of organized sensations which provides the means of expression.[20]

There is no lack of thought involved in this concept of sensation; rather the sensation is thought, but not necessarily conscious thought or thought mediated through language.

As we have seen, the problem with the first kind of knowledge is that our affects merely describe the affections of our body, which, in affecting us with joy or sadness, only tell us whether a thing perceived increases or decreases our power of action. It is important to recognize, however, that artistic expression involves a thinking *of,* as much as *through,* the imagination; that is, art attempts to understand what Cézanne calls the "real": the experience of sensation. Reinterpreting a long tradition in thinking about the nature of the relation between the lives of philosophers and their works, Bruno Clément has recently argued that philosophy moves from the particular to the universal; that is, in Spinoza's terms, the affects of the first kind of knowledge are rendered abstract and developed into material that might be manipulated through the second kind.[21] One might argue, again in relation to a long tradition, that art, on the contrary, achieves identification with each reader or viewer in turn affected by the work; that is, an understanding is developed not through an effort to convert things to common notions but by making a particular experience available to others who might adapt it to their own worldviews.

Let us return to the subject–object relation, or gap, again. We see through a cross-reflection between the first and second kinds of knowledge, not only the other as potentially ourselves (which is still only a capacity of the imagination), but the possibility of understanding the nature of the causes that produce that other; that is, we are offered subjective and objective understandings at once: we are allowed to *be* an alien mode while grasping the causes that bring that mode about. Yet this is not done through clear, logical relations; rather the logic of sensations developed in art requires gaps that lead to thought in the effort to bridge the gap.

I will end with one last example. In William Faulkner's novel *The Sound and the Fury*, we are given four narratives with four narrators.[22] The first three of these are first person and recount the thoughts of each narrator, whereas the fourth is a third-person narrator whom Faulkner later identified with himself as author. The first three are Benjy, a mentally disabled man, fixed at a mental age of about two or three, who thinks only by making associations of images and so has no concept of time or the narrative relation this concept allows and who finds only one person, his sister Caddy, who truly loves him; Quentin, his brother, a young man who also deeply loves Caddy and who is riddled with guilt because of the events that lead to her disgrace and who, in consequence, is about to commit suicide; Jason, their brother, who feels intense hatred toward his brothers, Caddy, and Caddy's daughter (named "Quentin," after her uncle, whom some wrongly believe to have been her father) and whose resentment reaches a crescendo through the events he relates. Numerous gaps are left in the narrative, and we are forced to make relations between the different fragments within the story to reconstruct the various lines of causation at play. Some of these connections are made consciously and some are sensed; that is, a system of answering motifs generates resonance and harmony across or through gaps in the relation, creating the sensation of understanding. The work challenges us to understand but does not allow us to understand through the intellect alone. Rather it leads us toward a sense, a feeling, and through the complex interrelations it establishes, it creates a sense of the meaningful, which is identified with a feeling of understanding; that is, we sense the essence of what is at stake.

Feeling does not begin and end with the first kind of knowledge in Spinoza; rather the feeling of understanding is apparent in the intuition that constitutes the third kind of knowledge, an intuition that proceeds from an immediate understanding of elements of the essence of God's attributes to the understanding of any number of other things, including particular things insofar as these are understood to be eternal modes of thinking, or essences:

> Though it is impossible that we should recollect that we existed before the Body—since there cannot be any traces of this in the body, and eternity can neither be defined by time nor have any relation to time—still, we feel and know by experience that we are eternal. For the Mind feels those things that it conceives in understanding no less than those it has in the memory. For the eyes of the mind, by which it sees and observes things, are the demonstrations themselves. (Spinoza, *Ethics* V, P23)

Intuition, then, also involves affect. The adequate idea, the essence, involves a felt identification of a perception and an understanding. Art, in composing relations between the first, second, and third kinds of knowledge, can offer us an image of a particular essence of thinking.

Notes

1. Anthony Cordingley, "Beckett and 'L'ordre naturel': The Universal Grammar of *Comment c'est/How It Is*," in *"All Sturm and No Drang": Beckett and Romanticism, Beckett at Reading 2006*, Samuel Beckett Today/Aujourd'hui 18 (Amsterdam, Netherlands: Rodopi, 2007), 189.
2. All references to the *Ethics* are to the Curley edition: Benedictus de Spinoza, *The Collected Works of Spinoza*, vol. 1, ed. and trans. Edwin Curley (Princeton, N.J.: Princeton University Press, 1985).
3. Ibid., 402.
4. Steven Nadler, *Spinoza: A Life* (Cambridge: Cambridge University Press, 1999), 294.
5. Gilles Deleuze and Félix Guattari, *What Is Philosophy?*, trans. Hugh Tomlinson and Graham Burchell (New York: Columbia University Press, 1994).
6. Benedictus de Spinoza, *Complete Works*, trans. Samuel Shirley, ed. Michael L. Morgan (Indianapolis, Ind.: Hackett, 2002).
7. See Jason Lewis Saunders, *Justus Lipsius: The Philosophy of Renaissance Stoicism* (New York: Liberal Arts Press, 1955); see also Jacqueline Lagrée, *Juste Lipse: La Restauration du Stoïcisme, Étude et Traductions de divers traités Stoïciens* (Paris: Vrin, 1994).
8. Émile Bréhier, *La théorie des incorporels dans l'ancien stoïcisme* (Paris: Librairie philosophique J. Vrin, 1997 [1908]), 15.
9. Ludwig Wittgenstein, *Tractatus Logico-Philosophicus*, trans. D. F. Pears and B. F. McGuinness (London: Routledge, 1995).
10. Virginia Woolf, *The Letters of Virginia Woolf*, vol. 3, ed. Nigel Nicolson and Joanne Trautmann (London: Hogarth Press, 1980), 247.
11. Gilles Deleuze, "The Greatest Irish Film," in *Essays Critical and Clinical*, trans. Daniel W. Smith and Michael A. Greco, 23–26 (Minneapolis: University of Minnesota Press, 1997).
12. Samuel Beckett, *Dream of Fair to Middling Women* (New York: Arcade, 1993 [1932]).
13. Samuel Beckett, "Letter to Georges Duthuit, 9–10 March 1949," trans. Walter Redfern, in *Beckett after Beckett*, ed. S. E. Gontarski and Anthony Uhlmann (Gainesville: University Press of Florida, 2006), 19.
14. Samuel Beckett, *Disjecta*, ed. Ruby Cohn (London: Calder, 1983), 137.

15 Anthony Uhlmann, *Samuel Beckett and the Philosophical Image* (Cambridge: Cambridge University Press, 2006), 36–64.
16 Stephen Greenblatt, *Will in the World: How Shakespeare Became Shakespeare* (London: Jonathan Cape, 2004), 323–24.
17 Gilles Deleuze, *Proust and Signs*, trans. Richard Howard (Minneapolis: University of Minnesota Press, 2003), 94–100.
18 Emile Bernard, as cited in Richard Kendall, ed., *Cézanne by Himself: Drawings, Paintings, Writings* (London: Macdonald Orbis, 1988), 299.
19 Joaquim Gasquet, *Cézanne: A Memoir with Conversations*, trans. Christopher Pemberton (London: Thames and Hudson, 1991), 150.
20 Bernard, as cited in Kendall, *Cézanne by Himself,* 299.
21 Bruno Clément, *Le récit de la méthode* (Paris: Seuil, 2005).
22 William Faulkner, *The Sound and the Fury*, ed. David Minter (New York: W. W. Norton, 1994).

11

An Inter-action: Rembrandt and Spinoza

MIEKE BAL AND DIMITRIS VARDOULAKIS

An (Im)possible Relation

A number of common elements bind Rembrandt and Spinoza.[1] First, Spinoza's materialism can be likened to Rembrandt's realism. In this view, the individuality of the painter's figures would demonstrate the philosopher's insistence on the innumerable modes of being. Second, the psychological depth of the figures' appearance in the paintings can be an expression of man's unity of body and soul. Third, both shared an interest in the relation between actions and passions. Thus Spinoza's dynamic conception of desire could be embodied in Rembrandt's depiction of continuity and change within figures, which he depicted as in a present moment replete with a past and ready to step into the future. Furthermore, Rembrandt's interest in the lower classes might recall Spinoza's grounding of democracy in "the multitude." Also, both shared a keen desire for freedom, neither traveled abroad, and both opposed religious dogmatism. This is the common view of the relation between the two.

Establishing Spinoza and Rembrandt's relation remains fraught with difficulties, regardless of their common elements. On one hand, most attempts to link Spinoza and Rembrandt to date start from the fact they were neighbors. Rembrandt lived in Amsterdam's Jewish quarter, one block away from the young Spinoza, from 1640 to 1656—that is, until the year of Spinoza's excommunication and expulsion from the Jewish community. Such attempts note in addition that Manasseh ben Israel, Rembrandt's friend whose portrait he painted, was also Spinoza's teacher at the synagogue.[2] However, such circumstantial biographical information tends to give rise to fanciful theories, such as Spinoza purportedly having studied drawing under the older master. The inability to find a concrete point of convergence between them, despite their physical proximity, has tempted commentators to reduce their relation to a cliché about the relation between philosophy and art. Clearly, then, their personal biographies are an inadequate starting point for putting Rembrandt and Spinoza into contact.[3]

The affirmation of their relation on conceptual grounds also encounters a stumbling block. This is a passing but significant observation by Deleuze. He describes the infinite abundance of uninterrupted relations that characterize Spinoza's conception of the modes of existence in terms of color relations, whose main feature is the abandonment of any tonal hierarchy. As a consequence, the relation between color and shadow is abolished in favor of continuous interaction between colors: "Modes [in Spinoza], as projections of light, are also colors, *coloring causes*. Colors enter into relations of complementarity and contrast, which means that each of them, at the limit, reconstitutes the whole.... In this way, a difference in kind is established *between color and shadow, between the coloring cause and the effect of shadow*: the first adequately 'delimits' the light, while the second abolishes it in the inadequate." This assertion directly undercuts any conceptual affinity between Spinoza and the "master of chiaroscuro," Rembrandt. Indeed, as Deleuze immediately asserts, "Vermeer is said to have replaced chiaroscuro by the complementarity and contrast of colors . . . and in [this] Spinoza remains infinitely closer to Vermeer than to Rembrandt."[4] The uninterrupted relationality the modes of existence exemplify indicates for Deleuze an intellectual rupture between Spinoza and Rembrandt, a relation that is impossible to affirm.

Instead of privileging the continuous expressivity of the plane of existence, as Deleuze does, however, we lay the emphasis on the points in Spinoza's philosophy where a rupture or interruption is manifest. We are curious to see how such (dis)junctures or hinges affect the thinking of the single immutable substance. From the side of Rembrandt, we seek an analogous rupture or interruption constitutive of his art. In other words, interruption, as a concept and as a praxis, could be used to broach the relation between Rembrandt and Spinoza. In that case, the impossibility of their relation would be nothing more—and nothing less—than the impossible unity between philosophical contemplation and artistic endeavor, the discontinuous relation between the realm of essences and the plane of existence. But then, their relation will not be impossible in any simple sense any longer; rather it will be (im)possible, a possibility that cannot be simply stated. It will rather have to be produced as an *effect* of their shared intellectual outlook—an outlook determined by those points of interruption and discontinuity. It is this (im)possibility that will concern us here.

We will show this relation between Rembrandt and Spinoza first by indicating how the present—the now—is relevant to an understanding of their cultural significance, then by illustrating that significance with reference to Rembrandt's work, followed by suggesting that Spinoza's scant references to art are nevertheless crucial in presenting the cultural politics of his philosophy. This (im)possible relation, then, will display an inter-action between the painter and the philosopher as well as between their respective disciplines.

A Rembrandt for Our Time

Emphasizing the effect of the relation between Spinoza and Rembrandt entails a consideration of how their work is effective. Such a project has to insist on the cultural and political relevance of their work—and that also means the relevance of their work for our time. In *Reading "Rembrandt,"* the case was made that "Rembrandt" is part of popular culture.[5] During the Rembrandt year in 2006, what seemed a persistent project of uglification of Amsterdam seemed to disprove that case because that use or abuse could only turn a lover of Rembrandt's art away from his work. The heading "A Rembrandt for Our Time" might suggest that this would be precisely what these public demonstrations of pride in the past attempt to do: recycle the images for people today. However, just as the ubiquitous Van Gogh sunflowers during the Van Gogh anniversary a few years earlier made us temporarily hate that artist, the only effect of the recurrence on the city streets of the same images—the *Jewish Bride,* the *Night Watch,* and a caricature self-portrait—is to make them cheap, and thereby erase, the potential for actualized meaning of the images that constitute the Rembrandt corpus. A popular-culture Rembrandt would be, rather, art that addresses preoccupations, obsessions, and problems that circulate in popular culture. In other words, to talk of "Rembrandt" as part of popular culture does not mean merely to acknowledge the effect of his images displayed for financial or nationalistic motives; rather, it means primarily to register the effect of living culture in Rembrandt's own work—as well as the reverse, that is, how that culture rewrites, reenvisions Rembrandt's work. Only then will an image be allowed to have its meaning actualized.[6]

The best case for the popular-culture aspect of the images is to be made through Rembrandt's history paintings. For these address popular stories and myths, including the ideologies such stories embody in their various popular manifestations. The recurrence of well-rehearsed stories in culture would, today, be associated with Hollywood cinema, for example, or soap operas on television. In earlier times, the theater would be a place of such recurrence. This is why we will make the case here through the well-worn story of misogyny of Joseph and his attempted seduction and betrayal by Potiphar's wife.

There are two reasons for choosing this story to bring Spinoza into the picture. First, the story is known from the Bible and the Koran and is now transmitted through the medium of painting, so it is useful in showing different ways of connecting, such as those signified with the use of the preposition *inter-*: *inter*-cultural, *inter*-temporal, and *inter*-disciplinary. Spinoza's opposition to dogmatism can easily fit into practices that make an excellent use of this preposition. In the *Theologico-Political Treatise,* for instance, Spinoza argues—with the use of philosophy, biblical hermeneutics, cultural theory, and historiography—that the Bible is not a divinely derived text but a social construct. This not only allows for a comparison between different versions of the same story, for instance, Jewish and Islamic. The different choices and directions taken by an author record those different versions within a text. Thus different versions have a normative significance and thereby disclose the imagination in Spinoza's sense, that is, the culturally determined rules and regulations of a society. Therefore they are indispensable for the construction of meaning.

The second reason for choosing the story of Joseph is the need to revisit the central distinction between image and word drawn in *Reading "Rembrandt"* (see chapter 1 of that volume). As was argued there, paintings like the series depicting Joseph and Potiphar's wife break the relation of illustration, that is, the subordination of the image to the word, or vice versa. There is no simple or immediate way to reconcile the relation between image and word. Conversely, to see their relation as irreconcilably ruptured is indispensable for the actualization of meaning in contemporary culture.[7] This is the constitutive interruption that can be gleaned from Rembrandt's works, as will be shown in the following section. This rupture also stages the relation between painting and philosophy. This is not an attempt to make either Rembrandt or Spinoza exemplars in some kind of common project; rather it shows that art needs thought, no less than thought needs art. What binds Rembrandt and Spinoza is the crucial role they assign to rupture in the production of culture. Ruptures, which allow for cultural, political, and disciplinary inter-relations, are mediated through the rupture between image and word. The split between image and word has the power to produce meaning—a power that is registered in the dynamic articulation of different versions of the same narrative. We will show later how this rupture figures in Spinoza's work—and moreover in ways that make a case for Spinoza's relation to art in general, and to Rembrandt in particular.

For now, we will read closely Rembrandt's different depictions of the Joseph and Potiphar's wife story to show how the actualization of meaning arises when the depiction and the description are productive so long as an immediate or self-evident relation between them is not possible. Meaning is never bestowed immediately, it is not monological; rather it is the interactualization between different versions of the relation between image and word.

Versionings

Rembrandt painted the scene of Joseph's seduction by Potiphar's wife twice. The repetition is generally explained in terms of the theater play after which he painted them, Joost van den Vondel's *Joseph in Dothan*. Halfway during the successful performance of this play in Amsterdam in 1655, the role of the main character changed actress.

FIGURE 11.1. Rembrandt van Rijn, *Joseph and Potiphar's Wife*, oil on canvas, 106 × 98 cm, 1655. National Gallery of Art, Washington, D.C.

For the viewer today, this historical information is not relevant. Instead, on the basis of convention or symbolicity, we propose to read these two paintings in the first place as a comic strip, and hence as a sequence, as if they were subsequent moments or scenes in the episode of the accusation. The first painting (Figure 11.1), now in Washington, D.C., is the first phase. Here the accusation itself is acted out. The second painting (Figure 11.2), now in Berlin, represents Joseph's protestations. This is the gap-filling painting. In the Bible, Vondel's and hence Rembrandt's most likely source, Joseph does not protest. In the Koran, he does. In Vondel's play, he does, too.

Another mode of encouraging narrative reading of paintings is the

AN INTER-ACTION: REMBRANDT AND SPINOZA   283

FIGURE 11.2. Rembrandt van Rijn, *Joseph and Potiphar's Wife*, oil on canvas, 113.5 × 90 cm, 1655. Gemäldegalerie, Staatliche Museen zu Berlin. Photo by Jörg P. Anders.

concentration of several moments at once, as if in a doubly exposed photograph. Rembrandt used a third mode of storytelling, briefly indicated as gesturing hands. We will see that he contributed to the story a vindication of the woman close to the Koran's version. There the woman, who becomes an object of gossip, retaliates by inviting her women friends to a banquet. During dessert, when oranges and very sharp little knives have been distributed, she orchestrates the arrival on the scene of the handsome Yusuf.[8] Stunned by his beauty, the women cut their hands, some of them to the bone, and a genuine bloodbath convinces them that their friend had cause to transgress. Rembrandt contributes to the woman's vindication, even if no little knives wreak bloody havoc in his paintings. The brief reading proposed here was prompted by reading the koranic version.

Both paintings offer a gap-filling and indirect versioning of Genesis—if we assume that Rembrandt was familiar with the biblical story, if not necessarily with the text, and most likely saw the play at least twice but is unlikely to have read the Koran. There are a lot of assumptions here. We only offer them to make what follows a bit less outrageous than it might otherwise be, not to make any historical claims about the paintings. On the contrary, the point is preposterous, that is, contemporary and constructing the past as part of the present, in a rewriting of the past.[9]

According to Genesis, Potiphar is only told about Joseph's alleged attempted assault after the event and in Joseph's absence. Therefore, in terms of Genesis, the presence of Joseph in the paintings suggests a condensation. The scene, then, presents the seduction attempt for which the husband has to be absent together with the later accusation for which Joseph had to be absent. In the Washington painting, Yusuf's position toward the back, on the far left of the picture plane and at the far side of the bed, suggests not only his subordinate position in the house and his subdued position as the accused but also the temporal anteriority of his presence.

Although we will refrain from alleging Rembrandt scholarship, one example of the reasoning in this scholarship might help us understand the difference between the kind of speculation we perform here and the equally speculative reasoning common in art history. The great Rembrandt scholar Otto Benesch claims that in both paintings, Joseph was originally kneeling.[10] This is quite plausible and makes the final decision more meaningful. Yet Benesch's argument that in the Washington painting, this must have been so because the woman's hand is gesturing toward the bedpost is utterly unconvincing. First of all, she is pointing to the red cloth, supposedly Joseph's coat, the evidence of his assault for Potiphar and, for us, of her desire.

While the Washington painting condenses two moments, the

Berlin one takes the aftermath further by expressing Joseph's desperate protestations of innocence. Here we have the seduction attempt, the accusation, and the refutation. Both images position Joseph at the far side of the bed as the earlier moment. In the Berlin painting, Potiphar, at the other side of the bed and closer to the woman, embodies, as listener, the second moment of the accusation but is drawn into the third by Joseph's reply. Thus time is represented by means of space. This we consider a narrativization of the scene. Its move of condensation takes the story further qua narrative. Though the text had to present the events successively, thereby avoiding the meeting of the men, the painting is capable of drawing the three moments together so that this meeting must occur. What the text had to separate, the painting—and the theater—can integrate: two men, one woman.

In the painting from Berlin, the third narrative device, the representation of speech through speaking hands, is integrated. This turns the painting more theatrical. The woman points more explicitly to Joseph than in the other work. In both images, her left hand covers her breast, as if to protect her from the assault while also protesting that she is telling the truth. In terms of the representation of speech, this hand indicates that she is telling Potiphar about Joseph's physical assault on her, and the lively, theatrical manner in which she tells it strengthens the readability of her speech. Moreover, legally, she confirms what Genesis believes and the Koran questions. Potiphar's right hand is resting on the chair, slightly behind the woman, thus creating a sense of intimacy between the two that excludes the accused. Now we have a structure of man-and-wife versus the other man. The Berlin painting is adequate to the mission of telling the story.

The other painting does more. The same semiotic devices are used: sequentiality to symbolically represent narrative time, condensation, and "speaking hands." But the same devices of narrativization are much more ambivalent here as signs. For example, the hand with which the woman supposedly accuses Joseph does point, but not at him. The index is misdirected. It points perhaps to the red garment, the false token—evidence, index—of Joseph's misbehavior: the object that lies. But even that direction is not so clear. And instead of gesticulating theatrically in despair, Joseph, here, is standing still, with downcast eyes. His left hand, which is just a little above his arm, suggests that he was about to say something but has hesitated.

This painting is much more enigmatic than the one in Berlin. For this reason alone, we would like to experiment with a reversal of reading. In the Western tradition, where reading goes from left to right, images tend to be structured in the same way. Rembrandt frequently plays with the tension between compositions on the flat surface of the canvas and the structure of linear perspective.[11] Here a reading from the right side of the bed versions the story in terms quite different from Genesis. Now, on the image seen as flat and from right to left, Potiphar's hand is not so clearly behind the woman but slightly in front of her, as if on its way to grabbing her. The woman protects her breast again but, in combination with the lesser distance between her and Potiphar, his grabbing hand and his determined facial expression, it seems as if, ignoring the biblical story, it is he who is approaching her (sexually?) against her will. Joseph, meanwhile, is just standing there. His passivity, downcast eyes, and darker shape make him now less likely an accused; rather he could be seen as the more desirable, younger, more handsome love object—the woman's fantasy. Yes, this is a preposterous interpretation. Several indications for it, however, can be construed.

First, there is the work of light—one of Rembrandt's signature signs. The light is much more subtle in this painting than in the Berlin one. It falls on the bed and the woman in both paintings, but in the Washington one, Joseph is also very subtly illuminated, whereas Potiphar, in contrast, is almost ghostly. The light produces a pattern in which the young man and the woman are illuminated to the exclusion of the older man. As a ghostly figure, the latter comes to evoke the dead father of Freud's *Totem and Taboo*, who threatens both son and woman. Joseph's face has an intense yet unclear expression. It is hard to decide whether he is anxious, desirous, or admiring. This intense ambiguity points to dreaming, to fantasy. Moreover, he seems here sexually ambiguous. His gender wavers. The curtain, much more clearly indicated in the Berlin picture, as a (realistic) representation of a bed curtain, is here so vaguely indicated that its only function seems to be to set off Joseph as standing in a space, lighter and farther away, *at the other side*.

The most intriguing details are the eyes of each of the three protagonists. Each figure looks intensely but inwardly. No figure looks at a clearly defined object. The woman does not look at her husband; rather she seems to stare at an inner vision—the vision where her desire is staged. The older man does not look at the woman. He, too, may be concentrating on his desire, or from another perspective, he may be looking at nothing; he may already be dead. Joseph's look, not directed anywhere either, is even more inward than those of the two others, while also almost directed at the viewer.

The difference in Joseph's look reinforces the radical separation between Joseph, on one hand, and the couple, on the other. When viewed from the other side of the bed, his image is almost detached, as if it were a portrait on the wall. The lower seam of his garment is the end of him—no legs are attached. Of course, the resulting floating impression of his image will probably have increased over time. Time darkens paint, and thus the dark underside of the embedded image of Yusuf has turned more abstract over the centuries. For today's viewer, this material effect is immaterial, increasing as it does the immateriality effect of he whom the Koran women called "not a man" but "an angel." Visuality, in this way, is pluralized by the different modes of looking so that the figures do not have the same visual status. Joseph is and remains a sign, both for the viewers and for the viewers in the image, the couple. He remains a dream image. Like a portrait on the wall—a projection on a screen—the floating figure of Joseph is itself the inner vision, the object of preoccupation of the two others. When viewed in isolation, Joseph seems full of feeling yet not involved in any event.

Between these three still and intense-looking figures, there is an object that attracts attention, if not from the figures, then at least from the viewer. That is, of course, the red cloth, the garment lying over the bedpost, standing there, erect between the woman and the youth. The color points to the blood that, in the Koran, testifies to the desire of all women—the plural "you" as in "your wiles" of Potiphar's contemptuous generalization. Should the red garment testify here, by the color it shares with blood, to the event the woman is supposed to evoke with indignation as the one that really happened? Or does it represent her desire, her hallucination, that it happened? Between the grounds of iconicity of which, for Peirce, color is the quintessential example, and that of indexicality, where it can point to prior events or desired futures with equal plausibility, the sign should not be split.

All these elements point in the direction of fantasy. But they have led us rather far from Genesis, unless we reprocess Genesis in light of the painting. These are the details that differentiate this painting from its successor in Berlin more radically, say, than they differentiate the painting from the Koran—a text we can presume not to have been Rembrandt's source. With the Koran, it shares the tenderness with which it attends to the woman's desire. The point is one of the two seemingly divergent points of the Koran story, the theological testing of Joseph and the vindication of the woman's desire. Or we may now say that in this painting, the two points are joined, condensed.

The details, or rather, the detailed looking that allows the narrative potential of the picture to unfold, leads to the idea of fantasy. Fantasy, as the uniquely staged projection of a dreamer temporarily split up between the roles of director and actor, is itself held together, albeit tenuously and provisionally, by the intensity of the committed viewer. The latter takes part in the play. This is why fantasy in culture takes on a function that distinguishes it from myth. If myth is the open structure, the screen onto which the cultural *doxa* can make us unreflectively project preconceived opinions about our "others," fantasy, also a projection, engages each of us personally and commits us to looking-with, as in suffering-with: with a commitment to integrate the thrill of sensate vision with intellectual, critical reflection. This distinction between fantasy and myth is important for the conception of the individual within society for Spinoza as well, as we will show later.

Like the Washington painting, the scene in the Koran has the same aspects of intersubjectivity, of lack of limits between subjects, that can be called a "porous" subjectivity. The cutting scene enhances and explains the accusation.

In the Koran, Potiphar commends Yusuf to his wife's care through the invocation of two obligations: hospitality and parenting. In Genesis, Joseph is said to be seventeen years old when he leaves home. This seems a bit old for a child-minding setup. The Koran does not specify his age in numbers but rather in stages. There is no gap but rather a narrative need. For the privileged position he will acquire in the house to be possible, he needs to be hosted like a member of the family. And for this, he must be assumed to be young. This

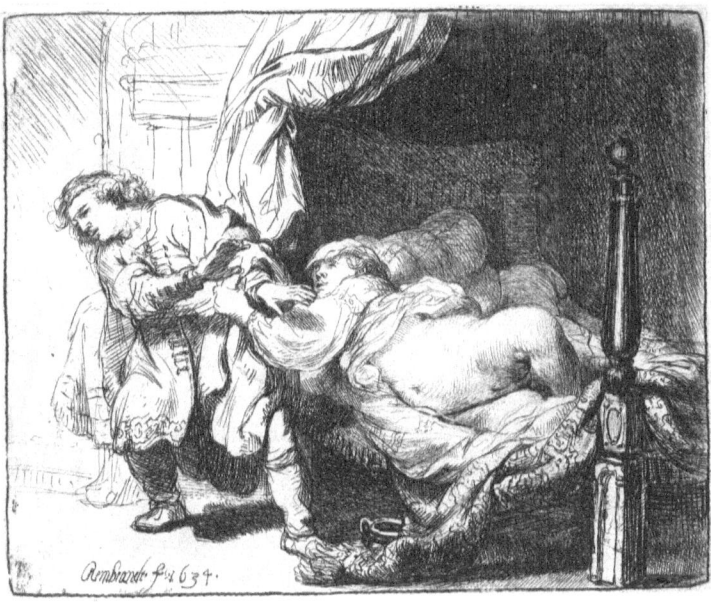

FIGURE 11.3. Rembrandt van Rijn, *Joseph and Potiphar's Wife*, etching, 9 × 11.5 cm, 1634. Teylers Museum, Haarlem, Netherlands.

youthfulness is also required for the story of his temptation. God leads him through the risks of youthful folly. Before any of the mishaps begin, God has already done this: "And when he had reached the age of strength we bestowed on him judgment and knowledge; for thus we recompense the well doers" (12:22).

Transitional age is often symbolized as liminal, from *limen* (threshold). Thresholds and doors represent passages of the life stages. Thus the race of the two characters to the door in Rembrandt's etching of the same episode (Figure 11.3) puts Yusuf and the woman in the same situation, perhaps at the same transitional phase—a race that the Koran mentions explicitly: "And they both made for the door, and she rent his shirt behind; and at the door they met her lord" (12:25). In the Rembrandts, including the Washington painting, the older man's presence on hither side of the bed suggests the door is on the right. In the etching on the same subject, it is on the left. There Joseph still had a choice, but he looked back instead of fleeing. And whereas in the painting, the figure of Joseph has the aura of a fantasmatic projection, in the etching, the woman's distorted body looks less than real. Does this justify the speculation that Rembrandt used the different media of painting and etching to explore two radically divergent versionings? In painting, the medium of commissions and sales, he explored the official version that the *doxa* of his culture prescribed so that, within the margins of socially acceptable behavior, he could only tamper with the scene of the crime enough to turn the accused into a fantasized image.[12]

In the etching, by contrast, we can imagine that he was exploring different possibilities. Now, Joseph is the one hallucinating. What he sees, with that weird back-looking eye, is a distorted, fat belly. He might see in that belly a future in which the woman would bear him children or the chubby belly of a child that could be his sibling. Nothing is too crazy for hallucination. Nor does anyone have to see what this imaginary figure sees-in. That he does do precisely that, seeing-in, seeing more than is there, is what makes him the great visionary, the dream specialist to which the Koran devoted an entire sura, exceptionally.

A man shall not take his father's wife, nor discover his father's shirt, said the end of Deuteronomy 22. There appears to be a link between adultery and transgenerational offence, as there is between the father's shirt and the son's, from the drunken Noah to the tempted Joseph. *Can Christians Believe in the Prophesy of Muhammad?* asked the title of an unpublished text we were able to read.[13] Although it strongly suggests a positive answer, that text ends on a question mark. That is fine with us, for belief is not the issue in this chapter, no more than it was for Spinoza, not because we do not respect or believe other people's beliefs but because we are looking at belief's underside. Fantasy, desire, hallucination, and projection are the stuff that makes belief possible. Clearly Rembrandt suggests, if only through the quietness of his Washington picture of hallucination, that there is no harm in thought or feelings. It is when you begin to believe in what you see that you get into trouble. Joseph, in the etching, sees things that attract and frighten him. No harm done. The woman, in the painting, sees a youthful, handsome beauty. No harm done. The absence of harm is in the eyes of the beholder. Joseph does not look up. His downcast eyes make him the famous visionary, like the blind Homer of old.

Rembrandt's means of storytelling condensed, as we have seen, the two and three key events, respectively, that compose the episode: the attempted seduction against which Yusuf was already protected beforehand, the accusation, and his refutation. In that sense, he also acts like a prophet, for he predicts what was to happen later. But according to both biblical and koranic logic, later is better. The perfectionism implied in the further refinement of creation as well as the relevant exegetical choices retained to make the two points are the perfection of prophecy: to guide humans in the right direction by means of re-citing what will happen. This is the paradoxical performance of prophecy.

Joseph's face in the Washington painting can be seen because he is not God. What is more, it must be seen for the temptation to be possible and to be so generalized that it becomes—let's face it, with God behind it so explicitly—sacred. But he cannot see; he must keep his eyes downcast so that he can "see"—again, like Homer and all those blind sages and prophets who, as Derrida *(Mémoires)*[14] has demonstrated in an exhibition composed of the archives of the Louvre, are the true artists. The paradoxical connection between blindness and insight that sustains the biblical story and becomes radicalized in the semiotic program of the "perfectioned" version of the Koran is in turn conventional. The stakes of this paradox bring us back to the lures and the (im)possibilities of intercultural interpretation. If myths are a cultural necessity—frameworks within which to think—then versionings are the freedom within it. Spinoza's idea of freedom in, or even as, necessity clarifies what rewriters and repainters can do.

This little exercise in constructing such an interpretation helps validate and value different versionings as mutually supportive rather than murderously rivaling. There is little that our time needs more urgently than such a shift in perspective on culture and cultural specificity. The infinite variations Rembrandt brought to the simple materiality of paint help us to understand the many shifts that occur when popular culture takes hold of story matter derived from different sources. The intercultural responsibility that the paintings thus appear to promote can only occur today, in a world in which the past is the responsibility of the present so that the future may survive. And the necessary precondition for assuming such a present responsibility is the distinction between image and word. This means that word and image "do not match, do not overlap; they can neither do with nor do without the other."[15] This rupture in their relation prevents the solidification of myth into a rigid belief and thereby allows for Rembrandt's versionings to acquire an actualized meaning and an intercultural significance.

Art and Culture in Spinoza

The intercultural significance of responsibility for Spinoza can only be understood, as Moira Gatens and Genevieve Lloyd have argued, on condition that responsibility is not reducible to an individual, sovereign subject but rather is dispersed in a collective imagining. Such a responsibility makes both past and future concerns relevant for the present.[16] However, even after realizing that such a notion of responsibility is crucial for Spinoza, there are three further outstanding issues in showing a Spinozist notion of versioning with affinity to the practice of versioning in Rembrandt's work. First, we need to demonstrate what the role of art and its link to responsibility is for Spinoza. Second, we must discover the constitutive rupture or distinction in Spinoza's philosophy that resists the calcification of the image in a rigid interpretation. And third, we have to explain how a Spinozist interpretation against the grain can be allowed—a reading from right to left, so to speak. This is a pressing issue, given that in chapter 7 of the *Theologico-Political Treatise*, Spinoza famously argues in favor of interpreting literally. These three issues are in fact interrelated in such a way, as will be shown, as to elicit the affinity between Rembrandt and Spinoza.

First, then, what is the role of the arts in Spinoza's thought? Spinoza has fascinated practitioners in all art forms perhaps more than any other philosopher. Nevertheless, his philosophy seems oblivious to the arts. References to the arts in the Spinozist corpus are few and far between and do not amount to anything like a developed aesthetic in, for instance, the Hegelian sense.[17] Nor is there in Spinoza an extensive discussion of aesthetic categories like beauty. Spinoza's correspondence contains two references to beauty. Despite their brevity, they are intriguing because they argue that beauty is not a category of a separate realm but rather part of cultural practice. Through looking at the role of beauty, a more general function of the arts in Spinoza can be deduced. At the beginning of his famous 1665 letter about the "little worm in the blood," Spinoza writes to Oldenburg, "It is only with respect to our imagination that things can be said to be beautiful" (Ep. 32). Imagination is Spinoza's first kind of knowledge. As belonging to the imagination in this sense, beauty becomes imbued in the production of cultural norms that bind a society together. The total field covered by imagination also includes the fantasies of the prophets that generated culturally cohesive myths. Spinoza returned to beauty nine years later in a letter to Boxel: "Beauty," he says, "is not so much a quality in the perceived object as an effect in him who perceives" (Ep. 54). The first significant point here is that beauty is not effectuated by the perceiving individual. Spinoza denies that the source of beauty is the individual. But, then, what is the cause of this effect?

It would be too simple to refer back to the letter to Oldenburg to argue that imagination, and hence culture and society, are the cause of beauty because then Spinoza will be forced into an idealist position incompatible with his materialism. Instead, the answer should be sought in the way that the materiality of the object is the cause of beauty, but without thereby making beauty a quality of the perceived object. To put the same point the other way round, the object on its own is not the cause of the imaginative field made possible by its beauty. This leads to an important conclusion for our purposes here. Cultural practice is neither subjective nor objective. Indeed, in the remainder of the same paragraph in his letter to Boxel, Spinoza does not seek to dispel the aporia between the subjective and the objective; rather he further accentuates it: "So things regarded in themselves, or as related to God, are neither beautiful nor ugly. Therefore he who says that God has created the world so as to be beautiful must necessarily affirm one of two alternatives: either that God made the world so as to suit the desire and the eyes of men, or the desire and the eyes of men to suit the world." The regulative term of this aporia is God. The index of ontology—of the "things regarded in themselves"—is the single immutable substance. But the ontology of humans and of things, or of everything created in nature, is different from God's, who is, according to Spinoza, neither a creator nor a purposeful actor.[18] In this sense, Spinoza's substance has nothing do with the God of the dogma and the churches; rather

Spinoza's "god" or substance is the regulative term that guarantees the ontology of being and thought.

Yet the term *aporia* is somewhat misleading in this context. Maybe it would be better to say that God indicates here a principle of rupture or disruption—which leads us to the second issue, about locating that threshold that regulates the relation between images and words. Proposition 7 of Part II of the *Ethics* famously asserts that "the order and connection of ideas is the same as the order and connection of things." This proposition does not assert a parallel between thought and object, as the eighteenth-century interpretation of this proposition emphasized. The corollary makes it clear that the connecting principle here is God. And this means that apart from God, there is a disruption between thought and being. To put this the other way around, that part which disrupts the relation between thinking and existence is God. God's all-inclusiveness makes it necessary that everything else be broken up, ruptured, apart. From this perspective, the connection between things and thoughts is disruptive—or ruptured, interrupted.

It is not possible to explicate in any detail here Proposition 7, which, according to Hegel, contains the whole of Spinoza's philosophy. Rather our aim is to present the repercussions of this disruption for a Spinozist conception of art's cultural significance, in this case, of Rembrandt's work. Indeed, it is significant that Spinoza uses art twice to argue for the importance of another, related rupture, that between essence and existence.[19] These are the two most extensive references to art in Spinoza's corpus. In both cases, Spinoza uses art to argue that the essence and the existence of things are separate. Only in God do essence and existence coincide. Spinoza's God, as already intimated, is not a creator. Essence and existence are, conversely, the attributes of created things. Each mode has its cause in these two attributes. Essence and existence are not related to God as their cause, but rather, as the Proof of Proposition 7 of Part I puts it, the substance's "essence necessarily involves existence." In God, there is no distinction or disruption between them, whereas such a distinction is necessary for all created things.

Erasmus, an interlocutor in the "Second Dialogue" of Spinoza's *Short Treatise*, objects that saying God is not a creator cannot account for the production of anything new without thereby adding to God's essence. Theophilus's reply consists in asserting that creation can occur only if essence and existence are separated: if something new appears, then that is only a part of a whole that remains unaffected. Theophilus offers the following illustration:

> An image-carver has made from wood various forms after the likeness of a human body; he takes one of these, which has the form of a human breast, joins it to another, which has the form of a human head, and of these two he makes a whole, which represents the upper part of the human body; would you therefore say that the essence of the head has increased because it was joined to the breast? That would be erroneous, because it is the same that it was before.

And Theophilus goes on to explain:

> All attributes, which depend on no other cause, and whose definition requires no genus pertain to the essence of God; and since the created things are not competent to establish an attribute, they do not increase the essence of God.[20]

The other side of the assertion that created things—including works of art—necessarily follow the distinction between essence and existence is that there is no absolute novelty in art. An art object is not completely unique. Artistic practice does not consist in the creation of something ex nihilo; rather creation is only ever a re-creation—a repainting, a rewriting, a rephilosophizing. The prefix re- of any creative practice is necessitated by the rupture between essence and existence.

Although Spinoza does not continue to develop a theory of the arts, the way he frames the distinction between essence and existence provides us with the means to do so. Three important inferences follow from it, which concern the work, the artist, and criticism. First, from an epistemological point of view, artistic practice affirms the accidental and the contingent in the work. The rupture between essence and existence prevents the object from claiming for itself a privileged cognitive position, as if it were to offer a perception—an image—whose validity would be universal. As an activity, the art object is material, the product of the artist's chance encounter with matter.[21] Second, the word *chance* does not abrogate the artist's responsibility over the work nor the importance of technique in art practice; rather it indicates that the artist can never have complete control over the material. There is no Artist-Genius who creates his own self-referential—or solipsistic, phantasmagorical—universe. Third, a critical approach to a work is therefore obliged to resist any immediate connection between technical or stylistic aspects of the work and the work's meaning.[22] For instance, no particular color has a meaning in itself, nor can the way that colors are applied on the canvas yield only one conclusion. The play of light and shadow in Rembrandt's use of chiaroscuro is not enough in itself—pace Deleuze's assertion in the citation at the beginning of the present chapter—to form a basis for a critical comparison between Spinoza and Rembrandt. Meaning is actualized only when the form acquired by matter is seen as a productive, dynamic activity open to different interrelations—open to versioning. The production of meaning is also a cultural event, and in this sense, the arts bear an ethical responsibility.

If the arts have an ethical responsibility, it is to be discerned in their resistance to immediacy, in their affirmation of versioning. But this can only occur when artistic practice is understood as the enactment of the rupture of essence and existence. Precisely because the artist *practices* that rupture, Spinoza thinks that the artist is uniquely positioned to demonstrate it, even more than the philosopher who may be lost in intellectual meanderings:

> [*How the distinction between essence and existence is easily learned.*] Finally, if any philosopher still holds doubts whether essence is distinguished from existence in created things, he need not toil away over definitions of essence and existence in order to remove that doubt. For if he merely approaches a sculptor or a woodcarver, they will show him how they conceive in set order a nonexistent statue and thereafter bring it into existence for him.[23]

Art, as a praxis of this rupture, acquires a uniquely didactic and hence ethical significance.

The third issue indicated earlier has to do with Spinoza's insistence on a process of understanding or a hermeneutics which, in Spinoza's phrase, seeks "the literal meaning."[24] Chapter 7 of the *Theologico-Political Treatise* explicitly rejects metaphorical interpretation. This poses a problem about how versioning can become operative within this hermeneutical framework. Artistic categories are culturally significant because of their relation to the imagination, and art's own ethical responsibility is based on its practical aspect. But are not both imagination and responsibility in danger of being canceled out by the positing of a "literal meaning"? Would not such a "literal meaning" grind to a halt the productive force of culture and ethics? We have to show why this is not the case and how Spinoza's notion of a literal meaning in fact tallies with our notion of versioning.

The context within which the argument about literal meaning occurs is important. In the *Theologico-Political Treatise*, Spinoza argues against miracles. The miracles in the Bible are not events that break the laws of nature but rather narrations used by their authors—the prophets—for the purpose of establishing the law or social norms. Therefore a proper hermeneutics cannot start with the acceptance of miracles; rather "the method of interpreting Scripture is no different from the method of interpreting Nature."[25] Just as things in nature display a rupture between essence and existence, so also the interpretation of the events narrated in scripture should incorporate that rupture. An interpretation that allows for the transgression of the laws of nature would amount to nothing but the pure or immediate manifestation of God, an event the occurring of which is immediately related to its essence. But this is precisely what, according to Spinoza, is not possible to see with human eyes or know with the "eyes of the mind." Hence interpretation should find an alternative explanation of such accounts.

Practically, this hermeneutical stance allows "no other principles or data for interpretation of the Scripture and study of its contents except those that can be gathered only from Scripture itself and from a historical study of Scripture."[26] In other words, the laws of the narrative are immanent within the text itself.[27] And this also implies that there is no universal standpoint from which an interpretation can seek its justification. Instead, interpretation is the productive activity of reading a text—a book, a picture, an event. But the text is also actualized through this dynamically productive interpretation. This double movement, or chiasmus, no longer requires an external source of legitimization for the hermeneutical event. Such a literal reading is precisely what we practiced earlier in reading Rembrandt's images of Joseph's seduction. It was the material inherent in the depictions themselves that constructed the terms of the interpretation. For instance, recall the reversal of reading in the Washington painting. Reading from right to left shows Potiphar's sinister undertones. The reversal of the normal reading direction in the West is a literal reading precisely in the sense that it uses what the picture itself presents to the viewer. The law of the picture is immanent in itself. There are no legitimating standards outside it. That is the practical import of reading the literal meaning, in Spinoza's sense.

There is, also, a larger cultural and political aspect alongside the practical hermeneutics. We mentioned earlier that the literal reading of Rembrandt's paintings showed their intimate link to the personal fantasies and cultural myths that were conveyed in the biblical and koranic versions of the story and from which our present interpretation springs—as well as future ones by others. Cultural responsibility is enacted precisely in this scene, where the past and the future collude in the creation of the present. This forms the recognition of freedom within necessity: of freely assuming our responsibility within the constraints that the mythic aspects of society—our cultural imaginings—dictate, without thereby forgetting that this freedom is not absolute but rather constrained by our personal fantasies. According to Spinoza, a metaphorical interpretation of the scripture denies precisely this interplay between myth and fantasy. For instance, to interpret a miracle metaphorically is to give it a universal meaning. The mythic aspect of the miracle, its cultural and political significance, is invested into a new myth. What is abrogated is the interpreter's personal responsibility to offer a critical reflection on the universality of myth as a cultural construct. A metaphorical interpretation imbues the text with a universal significance that eludes its fantasmatic provenance. In other words, the rupture between interpersonal myth and personal fantasy is denied in a metaphorical interpretation. The metaphorical interpreter uncritically legitimates the interpretation myths with the use of personal fantasies.

Spinoza objects to such a forgetting of the fantasy within the myth. His assertion that "all knowledge of the Bible is to be sought from the Bible alone,"[28] is a call to individual responsibility in the construction of culture. As Spinoza clearly states at the end of chapter 7 of the *Theologico-Political Treatise*, "the supreme authority to explain religion and to make judgment concerning it is vested in each individual, because it belongs to the sphere of individual right."[29] A literal interpretation is, on one hand, individual and hence a hallucination linked to the person's desires, and on the other hand, it is a right, part of the mythic construction of law that binds the society together. These two aspects constitute the *inter*-subjectivity that is a necessary result of the rupture between essence and existence in Spinoza's metaphysics. They are also constitutive of the interruption of the immediate relation between images and words in a reading of cultural documents.[30]

An Inter-action

We have examined here three currents in Spinoza's philosophy: the imaginative and hence cultural value of artistic categories, the importance of art in sustaining the distinction between essence and existence, and the way the rupture of essence and existence is indispensable in the actualization of meaning. The interdependence of these three currents announces Spinoza's affinity with Rembrandt. This affinity has nothing to do with any analogy or correspondence between the thought of the philosopher and the art of the painter. It is instead discernible in the way art and philosophy, painting and thought, are positioned at a threshold that indicates a break in their relation. There is no immediate connection between them, nor can one subsume the other. The work of both Rembrandt and Spinoza affirms this rupture.

Simultaneously, their thought and practice strongly affirm that such a lack of immediacy does not posit the creation of separate realms—the kingdom of philosophy versus the kingdom of art. The effective presence of both art and philosophy in the creation of culture means that images and words become productive forces only so long as they are held apart. This has a practical, a political, significance. The rupture between essence and existence has a contemporary cultural relevance only so long as it is practiced—practiced in the present, while being mindful of the past and assuming responsibility for the future. Within this exigency, art and philosophy become of necessity partners so that the rupture between essence and existence can be sustained. And it is as part of this partnership that a condensed, gestural conversation between Rembrandt and Spinoza can unfold. Their relation is (im)possible because it affirms the impossibility of either privileging art over philosophy, and vice versa, or of establishing an immediate connection between them. The (im)possible mediacy between philosophy and art unfolds in the site of the interaction between Rembrandt and Spinoza.

Notes

1. The edition of Spinoza's works cited here is the *Complete Works*, trans. Samuel Shirley, ed. Michael L. Morgan (Indianapolis, Ind.: Hackett, 2002). References to the "Letters" are by letter number preceded by "Ep."
2. See, e.g., A. Wolf, "Introduction," in *Spinoza's Short Treatise on God, Man, and His Well-Being*, trans. and ed. A. Wolf (New York: Russell and Russell, 1963), xviii–xix.
3. W. R. Valentiner, in a monograph on the relation between the two figures, states, "Spinoza and Rembrandt represent two opposing conceptions in the Dutch culture of the seventeenth century: the rationalistic and the intuitive." Valentiner, *Rembrandt and Spinoza: A Study of the Spiritual Conflicts in Seventeenth-century Holland* (London: Phaidon, 1957), 9.
4. Gilles Deleuze, "Spinoza and the Three 'Ethics,'" in *The New Spinoza*, ed. Warren Montag and Ted Stolze (Minneapolis: University of Minnesota Press, 1997), 25–26.
5. See Mieke Bal, *Reading "Rembrandt": Beyond the Word–Image Opposition* (Cambridge: Cambridge University Press, 1991).
6. This double movement is called a *preposterous history* in Mieke Bal, *Quoting Caravaggio: Contemporary Art, Preposterous History* (Chicago: University of Chicago Press, 1999).
7. The terms *image* and *word* are not used here in Spinoza's sense, e.g., in the Scholium to *Ethics* II, P49, where they are set off against ideas or rationality. For a suggestive reading of how this proposition tallies with artistic practice, see chapter 10 of this volume, by Anthony Uhlmann.
8. We have alternated between the biblical spelling of the name as

"Joseph" and the koranic spelling as "Yusuf" to keep track of the context of the references. See also Mieke Bal, *Loving Yusuf: Conceptual Travels from Present to Past* (Chicago: University of Chicago Press, 2008).
9   Cf. Bal, *Quoting Caravaggio.*
10 Otto Benesch, *Collected Writings*, vol. 1, *Rembrandt* (London: Phaidon, 1970), 93–94.
11 This is how Mieke Bal proposed to read two of his major paintings, *Danae* (Hermitage, St. Petersburg, Russia) and *The Blinding of Samson* (Städel, Frankfurt, Germany) in Bal, Reading "Rembrandt," 305–7 and 19–21, respectively.
12 Esther Peeren proposed in *Intersubjectivities and Popular Culture: Bakhtin and Beyond* (Stanford, Calif.: Stanford University Press, 2008) the term *versioning* to suggest a more active relation to the predecessor than the usual term *version*.
13 Paul Heck, "Can Christians Believe in the Prophesy of Muhammad?" (unpublished manuscript, 2005).
14 Jacques Derrida, *Mémoires d'aveugle* (Paris: Réunions des Musées Nationaux and Musée du Louvre, 1990).
15 Bal, Reading "Rembrandt," 34.
16 Moira Gatens and Genevieve Lloyd, *Collective Imaginings: Spinoza, Past and Present* (London: Routledge, 1999), 81–83.
17 James C. Morrison, "Why Spinoza Had No Aesthetics," *Journal of Aesthetics and Art Criticism* 47, no. 4 (1989): 359–65, has even argued that an aesthetics for Spinoza could not have been possible given the terms of his philosophy. Our argument here is the exact opposite: Spinoza's philosophy not only implies but also requires an aesthetics—albeit not in a Hegelian sense but rather as the necessary interrelation between artistic and philosophical practice.
18 One of the best-known places where Spinoza addresses the attribution of creative power and purposefulness to God is the Appendix to Part I of the *Ethics*. Spinoza shows there that the end point of anthropomorphic conceptions of God is indissoluble from political pursuits by men and connected to their creating a good conscience for themselves. "When men become convinced that everything that is created is created on their behalf, they are bound to consider as the most important quality in every individual thing that which was most useful to them, and to regard as of the highest excellence all

those things by which they are most benefited." Spinoza concludes that notions such as beauty—as well as good and bad, etc.—are formed and used as part of such self-interest. (Cf. also chapter 5 of the present volume, written by Michael Mack, for a detailed discussion of anthropomorphism in Spinoza.)

19 The relation between essence and existence is, according to Antonio Negri's contribution to this volume (chapter 12), the major site of philosophical dispute since Hegel's pronouncement of their immediate conciliation in the absolute, at the end of history.

20 One should remember that according to Spinoza, although God has an infinite number of attributes, the only two attributes that could be known are essence and existence.

21 According to Sebastian Egenhofer, "Die Abstraktion und die Topik des Imaginären," in *Struktur–Figur–Kontur: Abstraktion in Kunst Lebenswissenschaften*, ed. Claudia Blümle and Armin Schäfer, 269–95 (Berlin: diaphanes, 2007), Mondrian's abstract aesthetic can be fruitfully related to Spinoza, so long as the artwork is denied such a privileged epistemological position. The artist's perceptions are corporeal and contingent. "*Seine [Mondrians Abstraktion] Macht ist mit der Ohnmacht des Sehenden. . . . Das Bild ist die Falle, die die Falle der perspektivisch-egozentrischen Wahrnehmung verdoppelt und wiederholt.*"

22 For an important study of the rupture between style and the material presence of the work of art, see Andrew Benjamin, *Style and Time: Essays on the Politics of Appearance* (Evanston, Ill.: Northwestern University Press, 2006).

23 "Metaphysical Appendix" to Spinoza, *Principles of Cartesian Philosophy*, Part I, chap. 2.

24 Spinoza, *Theological-Political Treatise, Complete Works*, 469. A thorough investigation of Spinoza's antimetaphorical hermeneutics would have to account for his reception of Maimonides. This would distract us from our objective. For a thorough account of the relation between Spinoza and Maimonides, see Heidi M. Ravven, "Some Thoughts on What Spinoza Learned from Maimonides about the Prophetic Imagination: Part 2, Spinoza's Maimonideanism," *Journal of the History of Philosophy* 39, no. 3 (2001): 385–406.

25 Spinoza, *Theological-Political Treatise, Complete Works*, 457.

26 Ibid.

27 In other words, Spinoza is here propounding the central practical dictum of an "immanent critique" similar to Walter Benjamin's and Theodor Adorno's sense—a critique that finds its conceptual framework within the text at hand. Thus Adorno has also insisted on the importance of a "literal interpretation." Adorno, "Notes on Kafka," in *Prisms*, ed. Samuel and Shierry Weber, 245–71 (London: Neville Spearman, 1967).
28 Spinoza, *Theological-Political Treatise, Complete Works*, 459.
29 Ibid., 471.
30 This intersubjectivity can also be called "transindividuality," following Etienne Balibar, *Spinoza: From Individuality to Transindividuality* (Delft, Netherlands: Eburon, 1997).

PART IV
Encounters about Life and Death

12
Power and Ontology between Heidegger and Spinoza

ANTONIO NEGRI

THE EYE OF THE STORM around which philosophical critique has striven to build and rebuild itself throughout nearly two centuries consists of the fact that in the real—that is, according to Hegel, in the modern—the unity of essence and existence, of the internal and the external, is immediate in the form as well as in the dialectic. It seemed as if Hegel had worked out the problem. And yet, throughout the entire silver age, and even more so in the bronze age of contemporary German philosophy (namely, in the "critical critique" of the nineteenth century and in the great academic philosophy of the fin de siècle), essence and existence, substance and power—by then reconceptualized as *Wirklichkeit* and *Dasein*—are separated increasingly from one another. Substance, first exalted as effective reality, is presented later as command and destiny. Analogously, power, first intended as antagonism, is defined later as irrationality. Little by little, philosophy transforms itself into a sublime effort to exorcise the irrational or, at any rate, into a mystification of power. The furious Hegelian will to fix the dialectical hegemony of absolute substance is opposed by two successive attempts: first, crisis and tragic horizon; later, a repeated call to renew transcendental teleology in more or less dialectical forms. Even though both these attempts hardly survived the scathing

Translated by John Conley and Cesare Casarino

irony of the likes of Marx and Nietzsche, they kept on putting forth increasingly weaker but no less pretentious images of the modern.

It is worth observing that in this way, the hegemony of the relations of production over the forces of production at once disengages its own representation from the Hegelian utopia of the absolute—that is, the Hegelian utopia of the triumph of the modern (capitalist) State—and dons the clothes of reformist teleology. The schemata of indefinite duration, over and against those of dialectical infinity, are renewed as projects in the service of the progressive rationality of domination. The end of history becomes the telos of history.[1] Modernity changes the sheets without getting a new bed. From then on, everything drags along with much difficulty: any capacity for a real renewal of thought is exhausted. Thought devises a thousand tricks to bypass the impoverished as well as illusory, domineering as well as utopian Hegelian intimation of the modern, thereby attempting to substitute it with hackneyed forms of schematism of reason and transcendentality. This process goes on until it wears itself out and projects its own estrangement onto the definition of being itself.

Heidegger is the extreme limit of this process—a process in which he is fully immersed, if it is indeed true that one of the aims of *Being and Time* is to rethink the Kantian theory of transcendental schematism. This is a process, however, that is thrown off track completely at the very moment it sets out along the usual paths. "Our aim in the following treatise is to work out the question of the meaning of *being* and to do so concretely. Our provisional aim is the interpretation of *time* as the possible horizon of any understanding whatsoever of being."[2] However,

> if the interpretation of the meaning of being is to become a task, Da-sein is not only the primary being to be interrogated; in addition to this it is the being that always already in its being is related to *what is sought* in this question. But then the question of Being is nothing other than the radicalization of an essential tendency of being that belongs to Da-sein itself, namely, of the pre-ontological understanding of being.[3]

The theme of the present time, of its relation to being and thus its singular actuality, takes center stage. But here, as opposed to what

Hegel had attempted to build, *Dasein* is a broken temporality that is rediscovered in each and every moment as presence: a presence that is stability, that is a singular rootedness, that is against every dispersiveness and every disorientation of *Man*. History and becoming are now only a destiny of commerce and dejection. Facticity *(effettività)* is no longer the Hegelian *Wirklichkeit* but the crude *Faktizität*. The modern is destiny.

In the final pages of *Being and Time,* when arguing against Hegel's mediation and Absolute Spirit, Heidegger states:

> Our existential analytic of Da-sein, on the other hand, begins with the "concretion" of factically thrown existence itself, and reveals temporality as that which makes such existence primordially possible. "Spirit" does not first fall into time, but *exists as* the primordial *temporalizing* of temporality.... "Spirit" does not fall *into* time, but factical existence "falls," as falling prey, *out of* primordial, authentic temporality.[4]

Here, in this falling, in this being "care," temporality constitutes itself as possibility and project *(autoprogettazione)* in the future. Without ever exposing itself to the insidious dangers of teleology and of the dialectic, here temporality reveals the possibility of the present as the most primordial ontological determination of *Dasein*. Only in presence, therefore, does destiny reopen itself to possibility and to the future. But how is it possible to authenticate *Dasein*? In this tragic entanglement, death is the most proper and authentic possibility of *Dasein*. In this tragic entanglement, death is also the impossibility of presence: the "possibility of an impossibility" becomes, thus, the most proper and authentic determination of *Dasein*.

It is easy to draw the conclusion that the fundamental theme of modernity—the one captured by Hegel, the one of the synthesis of being and time as well of *Wirklichkeit* and *Dasein*—is over. Or, better yet, it is overturned: immediate unity between essence and existence is given in the nothing, in death. The Hegelian claim to the historical determination *(Bestimmung)* of singularity has become resoluteness *(Entschlossenheit)*—deliberation and resolve of the disclosedness of *Dasein* to its own truth, which is the nothing. At the dance of determination and of the transcendental, the music is over.

Between Hegel and Heidegger, thus, we have two opposite experiences of life. Such a situation arises as soon as the bourgeois property of happiness, having highlighted its own possibility of existence in dialectical domination, reveals itself to be insubstantial. Not even the later Heidegger, after the *Kehre*, will modify the situation. The distance between Hegel and Heidegger, which is to say, between Heidegger and the entire course of modern philosophy, could not possibly be any greater. And yet, paradoxically, Heidegger is not so alone.

Heidegger is not merely the prophet of the destiny of the modern; just as he divides, Heidegger is also a window that can open onto antimodernity.[5] Heidegger, in other words, points to a conception of time as ontologically constitutive, which radically breaks the hegemony of substance and the transcendental and opens it onto a certain kind of power. The theoretical decision does not consist solely in affirming resoluteness *(Entschlossenheit)*; it is also related to anticipation and disclosedness, which are truth itself insofar as truth reveals itself in *Dasein*. The discovery of being consists not only in uncovering *(Ent-decken)* the preexistent but also in positing the autonomous stability of *Dasein* over and against the dispersive mobility of *Man*.

By giving itself as finite, *Dasein* is open, and this disclosedness is sight *(Sicht)*: more than sight, however, it is *Umsicht*, an environmental and anticipatory vision. *Dasein* is possibility; it is more than that, however: it is being able to be *(poter essere)*. Heidegger writes, "'We' presupposes truth because 'we,' existing in the mode of being of Da-sein, *are* 'in the truth.'"[6] Moreover:

> But Da-sein is always already ahead of itself; that lies in its constitution of being as care. It is a being that is concerned in its being about its own potentiality-for-being. Disclosedness and discovering belong essentially to the being and potentiality-for-being-in-the-world, and this includes circumspectly discovering and taking care of innerworldly beings. In the constitution of being of Da-sein as care, in being ahead of itself, lies the most primordial "presupposing."[7]

Therefore presence is not only being present in the truth, in the unveiling of being; it is the projection of the present, authenticity, renewed rootedness in being. Time aspires to be power, it alludes to its productivity, it brushes up against its energy. And when it falls back on the nothing, time does not in any way forget this power.

Spinoza reemerges in this articulation and forms a paradoxical relation with Heidegger. *Tempus potentiae*. The Spinozan insistence on presence fills out that which we inherit from Heidegger as mere possibility. The hegemony of singular presence in the face of becoming—a characteristic of Spinozan as opposed to Hegelian metaphysics—reaffirms itself as the hegemony of the ontological fullness of the present as opposed to Heideggerian empty presence. Without ever having entered the modern, it is here that Spinoza suddenly exits from it. Whereas Hegel and Heidegger wanted to condense time in becoming and in the nothing, respectively, Spinoza overturned it in a positively open and constitutive time. In this same ontological condition of absolute immanentism, love takes the place of "care." Spinoza systematically overturns Heidegger: to *Angst* he opposes *Amor*, to *Umsicht* he opposes *Mens*, to *Entschlossenheit* he opposes *Cupiditas*, to *Anwesenheit* he opposes *Conatus*, to *Besorgen* he opposes *Appetitus*, and to *Möglichkeit* he opposes *Potentia*. In this confrontation, presence–antiteleologism–possibility unite that which the different meanings of ontology divide.[8] At the same time, the meanings of being are indeed divided: Heidegger goes toward the nothing; Spinoza goes toward fullness. The Heideggerian ambiguity that wavers over the void is resolved in the Spinozan tension that conceives of the present as fullness. If in both Spinoza and Heidegger, modal presence—that is to say, the phenomenological entity[9]—is released back into freedom, Spinoza, as opposed to Heidegger, also recognizes it as productive force. The reduction of time to presence, therefore, opens in opposite directions: either constitution of a presence that goes toward the nothing or creative insistence of presence. Simultaneously, two constitutive directions open up through the reduction of time to presence: if Heidegger settles his accounts with the modern, Spinoza (who lived in the modern yet never entered modern philosophy) shows the indomitable force of an antimodernity that is completely projected into the future. In Spinoza, love expresses the time of power—a time that is presence insofar as it is the constitutive action of eternity.

Even in the difficult and problematic genesis of Part V of the

Ethics, we see clearly this conceptual process taking shape. First of all, in this process, the formal condition of the identity between presence and eternity is given: "Whatever the mind understands under a species of eternity, it understands not from the fact that it conceives the present actual existence of the body, but from the fact that it conceives of the essence of the body under a species of eternity" (*Ethics* V, P29). All this is reiterated in Proposition 30: "Our mind, in so far as it knows itself and the body under a species of eternity, necessarily has a knowledge of God, and knows itself to exist in God and be conceived through God." Above all, this is explained in the Corollary to Proposition 32:

> From the third kind of knowledge there necessarily arises the intellectual love of God. For there arises from this kind of knowledge pleasure, accompanied by the idea of God as its cause, that is, the love of God; not in so far as we imagine him as present, but in so far as we understand God to be eternal. And this is what I call the intellectual love of God.

Eternity, therefore, is a formal dimension of presence. No sooner has he stated this, however, than Spinoza overturns all of it with the following explanation: "Although this love of God does not have a beginning . . . it has all the perfections of love as if it had come into being"(*Ethics* V, P33S). We must be careful, therefore, not to fall into the traps of duration: "If we pay attention to the common belief of men, we shall see that they are indeed conscious of the eternity of the mind, but that they confuse it with duration and ascribe it to the imagination, i.e. to memory, which they believe to remain after death" (*Ethics* V, P34S). On the contrary:

> This love of the mind must be related to the actions of the mind. It is therefore an action by which the mind contemplates itself, with the accompaniment of God as its cause. That is, it is an action by which God, in so far as he can be explained by the human mind, contemplates himself accompanied by the idea of himself. So this love of the mind is part of the infinite intellectual love with which God loves himself. (*Ethics* V, P36Pr.)

And Spinoza continues:

> From this we understand clearly in what our salvation, i.e. our blessedness, i.e. our freedom, consists: namely, in a constant and eternal love for God, or, in the love of God for human beings. . . . For in so far as it is related to God, it is pleasure. (*Ethics* V, P36S)

And the argument comes to conclusion in the clearest possible terms in Proposition 40: "The more perfection each thing has, the more it acts, and the less it is acted upon; conversely, the more it acts, the more perfect it is."

The time of power is therefore constitutive of eternity, insofar as constitutive action resides in presence. Such a presupposed eternity here is shown as product, as the horizon of affirmation and action. Time is a fullness of love. To the Heideggerian, nothing corresponds to the Spinozan plenitude—the paradox of eternity, of the fullness of the present world, the splendor of singularity. Rather than care, the concept of the modern is burned now by love.

And yet Heidegger and Spinoza had met somewhere. As we have seen, this encounter had occurred with their break from the myth of the modern (and indeed, Nietzsche had staged this encounter already). Such a break with the modern is the common ground between two authors who otherwise could not possibly be further apart. How might this commonality, this passage through a common perception and experience, be expressed? In what way have we come across an irreducible resemblance? The first element of common introspection that Spinoza and Heidegger articulate on the ontological terrain consists in radically affirming being as being-with *(mit-Sein)*: this is the common point at which their opposed philosophies intersect. In both, being presents itself as being-together. Mind you, this *mit-Sein* should not be banalized: it towers over every contingent relation as well as over various figures of linguistic circulation. Neither the weak philosophies nor the philosophies of language have understood it. The realm in which singularities are immersed, the phenomenological fabric of existence, is in fact a fabric of hard relations: one feels as if one is inside a dizzying pre-Socratic experience of being. "Being-with" is disclosed continually, not only toward alterity but toward the abyss: such is the inexhaustible instance that both these philosophies reveal. Already, Husserl had described how this individuality is immersed in that *mit-Sein* from which it was emerging as singularity. Already in Husserl, this dimension was characterized by certain aspects that some would at times call—or even denounce as—vitalist: on the contrary, it is here that the phenomenological condition of immersing oneself in being began to present being as a biopolitical figure. They tell us we should take care when tracing being back to "bios," and indeed there have been too many misunderstandings already regarding this question. I insist, however, that these misunderstandings are the same ones we have already discussed here, namely, the alternative between the void and plenitude, the nothing and power, death and life. Such is the relation between Heidegger and Spinoza: in the latter, being assumes a biopolitical figure when his philosophical project turns toward either "being multitude" *(essere moltitudine)* or "making multitude" *(fare moltitudine)*. Here being is absolute productive immanence. The profoundest abyss becomes the surface of existence.

It is shocking to return to this figure of being. Let us remember Hegel: without radical Spinozism, there is no philosophy. Might we also ask, is there philosophy without Heideggerism? That is what some think, and this contention constitutes the basis of the definitional expression itself as well as of the experience of the postmodern. However, we must go beyond precisely these contentions and have the courage to add that the qualification of being in Heidegger is as scandalous and perverse as it is radically powerful and hopeful in Spinoza. In the latter, being is qualified as ontological capacity for production.

Is Heidegger therefore a reactionary and a fascist, while Spinoza is a democrat and a communist? I am perfectly aware that by putting it in this way, one burdens Heidegger with an undeniable historical responsibility, while attributing to Spinoza improper and historically inadequate affiliations. But it is precisely to explain this historiographical problem when it comes to Spinoza and, on the other hand, to make such a problem explicit with respect to the history that Heidegger interprets in a reactionary manner that we need to take up a few other questions here.

To be in *mit-Sein* is to be in the philosophy of the present. The Copernican revolution in contemporary philosophy happens between Husserl and Wittgenstein. In this great passage, vitalism is translated into two perspectives: it is interpreted mystically in the linguistic analysis of Wittgenstein, and it is constituted ascetically in the philosophy of Husserl. The immanence of being-with *(essere-con)* and of being-within *(essere-dentro)* is established in this alternative. Doing philosophy is to recognize oneself as immersed in time. Doing philosophy is to recognize oneself as immersed in language. Doing philosophy is to recognize oneself as immersed in being. And it is only the relation with the other that relieves us from the immediacy of the immersion of being in time; it is only the meaning of difference (the relation among singularities) that extracts us from that condition. The meaning of difference itself is articulated in the interaction, in the "being-with" and in the "being-within."

In this situation, Heidegger and Spinoza make different choices. Nietzsche, for all the contradictory character of his thought, anticipated all this clearly: it is possible to choose between love of life and allegiance to death, between pleasure of singularity and pleasure of totality; it is possible to mobilize hatred of death against the eternal return, to mobilize the experience of the multitude against the transcendence of the political. What is so astonishing is the extent to which these different choices—made during a period of incredible historical uncertainty—correspond to the historical determinations and political alternatives that postmodernity will present to us. In effect, Spinoza and Heidegger think within the real subsumption of society by capital: if for Spinoza this was a theoretical fiction, an imagination, for Heidegger it was an irreversible tendency. For both, no concrete historical alternatives to this condition exist because their philosophies no longer have an "outside." To be sure, Heidegger often wavers on this matter: he listens to that call of destiny drawing him toward the unknown, he accentuates a mystical current in the experience of being—*amor fati*. To Spinoza, anything of the sort was repugnant: his time and his spirit were open to a democratic revolution, and they drove him toward the choice of freedom and hence of doing *(operare)*, of *praxis,* as well as of the capacity to transform interaction into multiplicity and the multitude into democracy.

It is here that we reach the point at which the two directions of phenomenology (the one of "being-within" the phenomenological context and the one of experimentation with "being-with") intersect, thereby building a contradictory complex that is broken up by different choices. On one hand, we have Heidegger: he understands human activity as abstract labor; he understands human beings as responsible for that subsumption of life under power *(potere)* that annuls the freedom of life by making it a product of destiny. On the other hand, we have Spinoza: he produces a conception of the materialist reappropriation of labor as well as of the rupture of the totality of domination; he prophesizes democratic constitution. For Spinoza, freedom is the very product of desire. If human beings were born free, they would not need good or evil, and there would be neither wealth nor poverty: it is because human beings are born in misery that their desire produces freedom, thereby also defining the good—whereas evil is only the fruit of the privation of freedom. Once again, here Spinoza opposes Heidegger, who says that human beings are born free but that their freedom takes them to the *impasse* of choice, that freedom is always excess, that "being-with" is something that pits human beings against one another, as if they lived in a cage. For Spinoza, *cupiditas* is never excessive because freedom is a surplus of being, because freedom constructs its own measure in constituting itself as history. For Heidegger, freedom is "being-for-death."

Here we are, thus, before the two different forms of phenomenological being inside the exclusive horizon of immanence, of the within. On one hand, reason and affect as construction of this being; on the other hand, *Entschlossenheit* and "care" as experience of subjugation to a being that reveals itself as alienation and nothingness. On one hand is that which is built, that which is project, that which is historically determined; on the other hand is the *Ur*, the unveiling, the knot.

Is there anything that interrupts the postmodern more than this opposition? If Spinoza agrees with Heidegger in positing the phenomenological dimension as fundamental, he is certainly against Heidegger when developing the power of that entity which is within being present—"being within" understood as modality of life. It is interesting to note how Nietzsche had understood the profundity and the power of this alternative. In effect, Heidegger absorbs from Nietzsche above all that "ideological hooliganism" *(teppismo ideologico)*, that flirtation with conservative thought typifying a reactionary choice. No matter what Heidegger says, there is nothing in Nietzsche that pushes toward reaction. There is nothing wrong in opposing Nietzsche and Spinoza, as some have done at times, including myself: the former destructive and ironic, the latter smiling and full of humor—but we should stop there.[10] Irony against humor: on one hand is nature–matter frustrated by necessity and hence tragically open between pressure and (dis)-passion, whereas on the other hand is nature that constructs, rejoices "cautiously," and at times thrusts itself forward with courage. And yet this opposition is so appropriate!

When comparing Heidegger and Spinoza, however, things are quite different. If we take what we have been saying into account, it will not be difficult to discern this great conflict throughout twentieth-century philosophy. In a very real sense, Heidegger and Spinoza provide us with the return to the earth: such a return is to be understood as an exit from any transcendent or transcendental illusion; it is to be understood as recognition of the fact that being is ours, that it is we who constitute it, and that this world is a fabric of human relations. Vitalism? Well, vitalism has various modes of being. The first is that which recognizes vitalism as an environment and a dimension from which to begin the analysis of being, thereby losing itself in the illusion that to be in life is to be in truth as well as in the illusion of truth. The second is that which runs from Dilthey to Husserl and which expresses itself by asserting the necessity for the subject to be immersed phenomenologically in historical being. The latter, however, is perhaps no longer vitalism; rather vitalism is a conception of being in life that seizes the evental and epistemological singularity of *Dasein*. Spinoza had excavated this process of being, whereas Heidegger does everything possible to destroy its meaning.

Up until now, in investigating the possible points of tangency between Heidegger and Spinoza, I believe we have exaggerated far too much the proximity of these two thinkers. The time has come to denounce Heidegger's thought as reactionary, not only because it is probably tied to the vicissitudes of the Nazi movement and fascist politics but also because his conception of being is one that posits destiny as the drowning of life—it is a black snake. Heidegger chokes us. The return to Spinoza allows for a few cautious reflections on that folly of humankind that Heidegger's thought interprets or reveals: such a return allows us to oppose to Heidegger a vision of being together, *mit-Sein*, as the whatever dimension, the strong dimension, of human life. This is probably what democracy needs above all: to proceed with caution in life.

Notes

THIS ESSAY is a translation of "Potenza e ontologia tra Heidegger e Spinoza," a lecture given at the Spinoza Society's conference held in Berlin in 2006. All references to Spinoza are to *Ethics*, trans. G. H. R. Parkinson (Oxford: Oxford University Press, 2000).

As has been often noted, the English term *power* translates two distinct terms in Italian, *potenza* and *potere* (which more or less correspond to the Latin *potentia* and *potestas*, the French *puissance* and *pouvoir*, and the German *Macht* and *Vermögen*). Whereas *potenza* resonates with implications of potentiality, *potere* refers to authority, so much so that the latter has at times been translated into English as "constituted power" or "sovereign power." Unless otherwise noted, all instances of the English term *power* translate the Italian *potenza*.

All the notes are by the translators.

1 In the original: "La fine della storia diviene il fine della storia."
2 Martin Heidegger, *Being and Time*, trans. Joan Stambaugh (Albany: State University of New York Press, 1996), xix (§1).
3 Ibid., 12 (§15).
4 Ibid., 396 (§436); emphasis in Heidegger's original.
5 In the original: "Nel mentre divide, Heidegger é anche una cerniera che può aprirsi sull'antimodernità."
6 Heidegger, *Being and Time*, 209 (§227).
7 Ibid., §228.

8 Throughout the essay, we have translated the Italian *senso* (pl. *sensi*) as "meaning."
9 Here we have translated the Italian *l'ente* as "entity" to register its distinction from *l'essere* (which, we should add, is in this case more aligned with John Macquarrie and Edward Robinson's earlier English translation of *Being and Time*.)
10 Here as well as in the following sentence, *humor* appears in English in the original.

13

A Thought beyond Dualisms, Creationist and Evolutionist Alike

A. KIARINA KORDELA

A COMMON ASSUMPTION in the contemporary reception of Spinoza is that his philosophy is a celebration of pure life, wherein death plays no role on all of the levels that constitute his philosophy: ontology, ethics, and sociopolitical criticism. In this reading, Spinoza's monism is sustained only on the ground of an unspoken fundamental dualism between life and death and the exclusion of the latter. Antonio Damasio's recent interpretation of Spinoza is revealingly symptomatic of this approach, as it unveils that at stake in the underlying opposition between life and death is the psychoanalytic pair of the pleasure principle and the death drive. While Damasio perpetuates the aforementioned dualism by reducing Spinoza's "substance" to the homeostatic principle of pleasure at the exclusion of the death drive, I argue that Spinoza's monism consists in the intertwining and inseparability of not only body and mind but also death and life, and that it is only through this intertwining that Spinoza's ethics can unfurl its potential for social and political criticism.

Body and Mind

In his *Looking for Spinoza: Joy, Sorrow, and the Feeling Brain* (2003), Damasio offers a reading of Spinoza's work informed by neuroscientific evolutionist premises that are both functionalist and teleological.[1] The organizing grid of Damasio's overall argumentation consists of two primary theses.

The first, which will be the subject of this section, concerns the distinction between emotions and feelings, as bodily modifications and their mental representations, respectively, whereby the former precede and cause the latter. Emotions are bodily states caused by "a complex collection of chemical and neural responses" to "an emotionally competent stimulus (an ECS)," all of which come to form "a distinctive pattern" such as "happiness, sadness, embarrassment, or sympathy."[2] Feelings, on the other hand, are "mental representations of the parts of the body or of the whole body as operating in a certain manner"; that is, their "contents consist of representing a particular state of the body" in the mind. Unlike emotions, which pertain to the chemical and neural constituents of the body, a feeling is a mental "representation," a "thought," a "perception," or *"the idea of the body being in a certain way."*[3] If feelings can be distinguished from "other perceptions" or thoughts, even as the former are "just as mental as any other perception," this is so only because "in the case of feelings, the *objects* and *events at the origin* are well inside the body rather than outside of it" because these objects or events are the states of the body itself.[4] What I find really fascinating and properly Spinozan about Damasio's argument is that against the tradition of the opposition between the "thinking brain" and the "feeling heart," it proposes the inseparability between intellect and feelings: the *feeling brain.*

The question, however, is, at least for a reader of Spinozan inclinations, whether Damasio's further line of thought will manage to sustain the Spinozan monistic conception of the inseparability of Body and Mind or whether this distinction between emotions and feelings will eventually slide into the very Cartesian premise that formed the target of Spinoza's criticism: the dualism between body and mind. Far from ignoring this danger, Damasio devotes an entire section to an attempt at negotiating it. His discussion begins with an unambiguous admission that Spinoza's thesis "in the *Ethics,* Part I, that thought and extension, while distinguishable, are nonetheless attributes of the same substance, God or nature," can only entail that "in a strict sense, the mind did not cause the body and the body did not cause the mind."[5] If this is so, then, emotions, too, cannot cause feelings, just as the latter could not be the cause of the former. To surpass this deadlock, Damasio introduces a further dualism, this time one between "an entirely sensible 'aspect' dualism" and what we could call vulgar or "substance dualism."[6] While Spinoza "rejected" the latter, he was nevertheless, Damasio maintains, an ardent advocate of the former. Spinoza's refutation of "substance dualism" postulates that "mind and body would spring in parallel from the same substance, fully and mutually mimicking each other in their different manifestations," but for the "mind [to] spring fully formed from substance on equal footing with [the] body," Damasio speculates, Spinoza must assume "a mechanism whereby the equal footing can be realized."[7] This "mechanism," in turn, "has a strategy: Events in the body are represented as ideas in the mind"; that is, Damasio continues conclusively, "There are representational 'correspondences,' and they go in one direction—from body to mind."[8] In other words, the isomorphism or "correspondences" between body and mind are purely "representational," whereas ontologically speaking, the body precedes the mind and is the latter's cause. Spinoza's monism of substance, Damasio tells us, in truth asserts the ontological primacy of the body—"no body, never mind"—and accords equal footing to body and mind only on the representational or phenomenological level, after the "existence of the body" has caused "the idea of an object in a given mind," in this and only this "one direction."[9] Ultimately, "Spinoza's insight," Damasio states, consists in the following:

> That in spite of the equal footing of mind and body, *as far as they are manifest to the percipient,* there is an asymmetry in the mechanism underlying these phenomena. He [Spinoza] suggested that the body shapes the mind's contents more so than the mind shapes the body's, although mind processes are mirrored in body processes to a considerable extent.[10]

And in the fashion of, at least philosophically speaking, a counterintuitive epistemology, it is surprisingly the empiricist Spinoza whom Damasio assumes to have grasped the truth about the ontology of body and mind, and not the universalizing philosopher, who purportedly remains confined within their phenomenology. Damasio "regard[s] the Spinoza of *The Ethics,* Part I"—"where he addressed the issues of mind and body in general," and about which, Damasio asserts, "the equal footing of mind and body only works in the general description" offered there—"as the consummate philosopher dealing with the whole universe."[11] By contrast, the Spinoza of Part II was one "concerned with a local problem" and did "not hesitate," not unlike in contemporary neurobiology, "to privilege body or mind in certain circumstances" such as "from body to mind when we perceive, and from mind to body when we decide to speak and do so." Moreover, despite the empirical observation that "certain thoughts evoke certain emotions and vice versa," Spinoza was capable of "intuiting a solution he," unlike contemporary neurobiology, "could not specify," namely, that in truth, as in "most of the propositions [from Part II] discussed thus far, the body quietly wins, of course," even as Spinoza may in some cases "privilege the mind."[12] One of the implicit presuppositions in Damasio's argument here is that statistics provides more reliable cognitive access to ontology than speculative philosophy.

In any case, if we accept his position and his further assertion that the "means to achieve the representational correspondences" or this "sort of structure-preserving isomorphism" between body and mind are "contained in the substance," then the substance must guarantee that the mind faithfully mimic, with "proportional" precision "in terms of both quantity and intensity," whatever structures or "modifications of the body" happen to be presented by the latter to the mind.[13]

In short, Damasio's thesis is that Spinoza's magnitude and originality derive from the fact that "perhaps he was not only undermining the traditional notion," also cherished by Descartes, "that the body would arise from the mind, but also preparing the stage for discoveries that would support the opposite notion," feverishly cherished also by neuroscience, in which the mind always arises from the body.[14] The reception of Spinoza as a radical alternative to substance dualism is, Damasio suggests, a massive misconstrual; Spinoza's monism is not a veritable alternative to Cartesianism but merely an inversion thereof, of which neuroscience is the long-awaited realization, capable of providing the vocabulary required "to say for him [Spinoza] what he obviously could not."[15] For, while "of necessity Spinoza knew very little about the brain" (qua organ, as opposed to the mind), we can, "on the basis of the findings from modern neurobiology . . . venture that a vast proportion of the images that ever arise in the brain are shaped by signals from the body-proper."[16]

Now, there is, of course, nothing surprising in the fact that a neuroscientist would claim the causal primacy of the body over the mind, but the question is, can Spinoza be invoked to support this case? Can his theory justifiably be read as just an inverted Cartesianism, as we know it not only from neurobiology but generally from the tradition of positivistic sciences since the Enlightenment? Or is it an unambiguously monistic theory in which the mind (or, for that matter, the body) needs no strategy, graciously offered by its other (body or mind, respectively), to be able to stand on equal footing with it?

Let us begin by examining the passages from the *Ethics* on which Damasio himself draws to make his case. The key passage for him is "The object of the idea constituting the human Mind is the Body."[17] Damasio also sites "other propositions" in which this "statement is reworded and elaborated, such as "the Mind does not have the capacity to perceive ... except in so far as it perceives the ideas of the modifications (affections) of the body," or more accurately, in Edwin Curley's translation, "the Mind does not know itself, except insofar as it perceives the ideas of the affections of the Body [*Mens se ipsam non cognoscit, nisi quatenus Corporis affectionum ideas percipit*]."[18] Worth citing is also the following reformulation of this basic thesis: "The human mind is capable of perceiving a great number of things, and is so in proportion as its body is capable of receiving a great number of impressions," or, again in Curley's translation, "the human Mind is capable of perceiving a great many things, and is the more capable, the more its Body can be disposed in a great many ways [*Mens humana apta est ad plurima percipiendum, & eo aptior, quo ejus Corpus pluribus modis disponi potest*]," and as Damasio puts it, "perhaps most importantly," "the human Mind does not perceive any external body as actually existing except through the ideas of the modifications (affections) of its own body [*Mens humana nullum corpus externum, ut actu existens, percipit, nisi per ideas affectionum sui Corporis*]."[19]

In the last of these formulations, Spinoza states that the human mind can perceive an external body as actually existing not directly through *"the modifications (affections) of its own body,"* that is, following

Damasio's own distinction, not through the body's *emotions*, but only through *"the ideas"* thereof, that is, through *feelings*, which, as Damasio has been arguing, are themselves perceptions or thought. And the same is, of course, true of Proposition 23, which states that the mind would not know its own existence if it did not have *ideas* of affections, that is, feelings or thoughts. As far as the human mind is concerned, if these thoughts are not in it, neither itself nor external bodies would exist. Far from supporting the causal primacy of the body, the cited passages, including the "perhaps most important" proposition, seem rather to indicate: no mind, never body.

Moving to Proposition 14, it is precisely the concept of "proportion," and the "statements in which Spinoza finds ideas 'proportional' to 'modifications of the body,'" that lead Damasio to deduce "some sort of structure-preserving isomorphy" between mind and body presupposed in Spinoza's scheme.[20] But far from implying any direction between the two parts, isomorphy entails that if the mind is more capable the more its Body can be disposed, then the inverse must also be true, so that the more the mind is capable, the more ways there are in which the body can be disposed. Why, then, one could object in support of Damasio's thesis, doesn't Spinoza add explicitly that the inverse is also always necessarily the case? Because, as he stated already in Part I of the *Ethics*, "*God is the immanent, not the transitive, cause of all things*" (*Ethics* I, P18), which is also to say, as he states in the preface to Part IV, if "God, *or* Nature . . . are one and the same [*Deus, seu Natura . . . una, eademque est*]," without the one preceding the other, then the real cause of something is its immanent, and not some contingent transitive, cause. In short, the real cause is itself effected by its own effects, in a synchronicity whose force reduces to sheer falsity either the Body's or the Mind's claim to causal precedence.

As far as Spinoza is concerned, both the Cartesian idealistic primacy of the mind and the positivistic, including the vulgarly materialistic, primacy of the body are the ostensibly true and false manifestations of the proper truth. For, as he states in a passage in the *Ethics,* in which, not accidentally, he returns to "questions" about which he has shown the "causes of falsity . . . most clearly from P19 to P35"—that is, in the very propositions invoked by Damasio—

"truth is the standard both of itself and of the false" (*Ethics* II, P43S). Depending on one's predispositions, the mind may appear to be the cause of the changes in the body as much as the body may appear to be the cause of the changes in the mind, but this switch in perspective is itself possible only because, Spinoza teaches us, in truth, "thought and extension" stand "on equal footing," as the empirical modes of "a single substance," just as (the) itself (of the truth) and the false stand on equal footing, as the empirical modes of truth.[21] And this is the foundation of proper materialism.

Spinoza's thesis is that, if we want to understand how the human body and mind work, we must not assume the causal primacy of either.

Evolutionism and Psychoanalysis

The second primary thesis in Damasio's argumentation concerns the subjection of life to the evolutionist principles of the best possible self-preservation, adaptation, and development toward ever more complex and functional forms of life. Damasio links the principle of the best self-preservation to Spinoza's concept of *conatus* and, indirectly, via his reference to "homeostasis," to Freud's concept of the pleasure principle.[22] The "homeostatic mechanism," Damasio writes, strives toward the "maintenance" of the "organism's structure" and "chemical balance" and is thus, not unlike Freud's pleasure principle, a "principle of constancy," an "apparatus" that "is subsumed as a special case under Fechner's principle of the 'tendency towards stability.'"[23] Jacques Lacan also affirms the identity of the Freudian pleasure principle as a homeostatic mechanism:

> The organism already conceived by Freud as a machine, has a tendency to return to its state of equilibrium—this is what the pleasure principle states. . . . This restitutive tendency . . . [or] pleasure principle is explained in the following way—when faced with a stimulus encroaching on the living apparatus, the nervous system is as it were the indispensable delegate of the homeostat, of the indispensable regulator, thanks to which the living being survives, and to which corresponds a tendency to lower the excitation to a minimum.[24]

On the basis of the assumption that "in the course of evolution the innate and automated equipment of life governance—the homeostatic machine—became quite sophisticated," Damasio proceeds to procure a hierarchical list of homeostatic functions, from "the lowest branches" or the "bottom" of the "organization of homeostasis" to the levels "higher up" until we reach "the top," to conclude eventually:

> The entire collection of homeostatic processes governs life moment by moment in every cell of our bodies. . . . First, something changes in the environment. . . . Second the changes . . . can constitute a threat to [the organism's] integrity, or an opportunity for its improvement. . . . Third, the organism detects the change and acts accordingly, in a manner designed to create the most beneficial situation for its own self-preservation and efficient functioning.[25]

There is not the slightest trace of hesitation in Damasio's spontaneous equation of the homeostatic "maintenance" of the organism's "chemical balance" with the attainment of its "most beneficial situation for its own self-preservation and efficient functioning." This automatic association derives its license from the aforementioned evolutionist premise that evolution—change and differentiation in life—proceeds in a hierarchical way, from lower forms of life to higher ones. For if this is the principle guiding life in general, shouldn't also the life of each individual organism be guided by the same principle so that each organism strives to its higher, most efficient functioning and beneficial situation for its own self-preservation?

Here, however, we evidence the abyss that separates evolutionist from psychoanalytic thought. Having concluded the earlier cited summary of Freud's conceptualization of the pleasure principle as the homeostatic "tendency to lower the excitation to a minimum," so that the organism sustains, as Damasio would put it, its balance, Lacan pauses to ask, "*To a minimum,* what does that mean?"[26] How is the balance or the minimum of energy within an organism to be defined? It is only on the basis of the evolutionist, hierarchical and functionalist, thought that it can be presumed to entail necessarily the "most beneficial situation" for the organism's "self-preservation."

For his part, Lacan continues to address the question beginning with the following observation:

> There is an ambiguity here. . . . The minimum tension can mean one of two things, all biologists will agree, according to whether it is a matter of the minimum given a certain definition of the equilibrium of the system, or of the minimum purely and simply, that is to say, with respect to the living being, death.[27]

It is due to this ambiguity inhering in concepts such as "minimum" or "balance" that, as Lacan—after a long series of analytic authors who have been puzzled by the relation between the pleasure principle and the death drive—remarks, "at first sight, this restitutive tendency is not clearly distinguishable, in Freud's text, from the repetitive tendency," that is, the death drive, the very concept that Freud is introducing, while attempting to define the pleasure principle as the latter's beyond.[28] Lacan continues his syllogism to equate eventually, on one hand, the pleasure principle with the first law of thermodynamics, regarding the conservation of energy, and, on the other hand, the death drive or repetition compulsion with the second law of thermodynamics, regarding entropy, while stressing that "these two tendencies are strictly inseparable. No notion is less unitary than that."[29]

Thus the specific "definition of the equilibrium of the system" for psychoanalysis is given on the basis of the law of the conservation of energy—according to which, "if there is something at the end, just as much had to be there at the beginning," regardless of how beneficial or well functioning this state of the organism may be for its own self-preservation.[30] Insofar as excitation entails an increase in the organism's amount of energy, it follows that in the last analysis, the "pleasure principle—the principle of pleasure—is that pleasure should cease."[31] The validity of this law applies within "the limits of the human in the organic sense of the word"; yet this law is inseparably intertwined with the death drive, as "an incontestably metaphysical category," which is a tendency toward disequilibrium.[32] By contrast, in Damasio's evolutionist neuroscientific model, the pleasure principle or the homeostatic machine is conceived as a mechanism infallibly intended toward maximum pleasure and benefit, while having as its sole enemy factors external to the organism itself. If this were Spinoza's *conatus*, then, contrary to Damasio's own assertion, Spinoza would not "have had an important influence on Freud."[33]

Beyond this smooth sliding from the concept of homeostasis to the teleological, non-value-free, and self-interested notion of the organism's unmitigated striving toward ever more pleasure and profit for itself, Damasio's thought operates on the assumption that also the passage from chemical processes to the symbol, that is, to thought (including, of course, feelings), is equally smooth so that he can unimpededly infer:

> From chemical homeostatic processes to emotions-proper, life-regulation phenomena, without exception, have to do, directly or indirectly, with the integrity and health of the organism. Without exception, all of these phenomena are related to adaptive adjustments in body state and eventually lead to the changes in the brain mapping of body states, which form the basis for feelings. The nesting of the simple within the complex ensures that the regulatory purpose remains present in the highest echelons of the chain.[34]

Given these two central smooth paths that allow for Damasio's tireless comings and goings between animate life and speaking animate life, it is no surprise that his reading of Freud allows him to align him with Charles Darwin as the "two thinkers who dedicated their work to studying the diverse influences of the innate and the acquired from below stairs," with Darwin focusing on the fact "that we have humble origins" and Freud on the fact "that we are not full masters of our behavior."[35] Interestingly, Lacan's reading of Freud leads him to a radically different conclusion:

> The idea of living evolution, the notion that nature always produces superior forms, more and more elaborated, more and more integrated, better and better built organisms, the belief that progress of some sort is immanent in the movement of life, all this is alien to him [Freud], and he explicitly repudiates it. . . . It is his experience of man which guides him. . . . It allowed him to locate the register of a certain kind of suffering and illness, of fundamental

conflict, in man. To explain the world with a natural tendency to create superior forms is quite the opposite of the essential conflict such as he sees it played out in the human being.[36]

The "essential conflict" to which Lacan is referring is specifically that between the pleasure principle and the death drive.

Evolutionism and Spinoza

But, one might rightly argue, even if we grant that Damasio profoundly misreads Freud's pleasure principle, the primary emphasis of his book is the connection not between Darwin and Freud but between Darwin and Spinoza. What if Spinoza's *conatus*, psychoanalysis notwithstanding, indeed supports Damasio's evolutionist conceptualization of the "homeostasis machine"?

At first sight, this hypothesis seems indeed plausible, particularly given that it is supported by certain other theoreticians who are considerably familiar with Freudian and Lacanian psychoanalysis, including the subtleties involved in the pleasure principle and its relation to the death drive.

The French philosopher Alain Badiou, whose work addresses and draws on various philosophical systems and French contemporary theories, such as Deleuze and Derrida, including Lacanian psychoanalysis, states unequivocally that "the ordinary behaviour of the human animal is a matter of what Spinoza calls 'perseverance in being,' which is nothing other than the pursuit of interest, or the conservation of the self," that is, the homeostatic mechanism of the pleasure principle.[37] And though the "perseverance of being" falls under the law of the pleasure principle, its *beyond*, which obeys the laws of the death drive, as Slavoj Žižek, the Lacanian and Marxist philosopher and cultural critic, argues, seconding Badiou, is entirely incompatible with Spinoza's theoretical edifice. In Žižek's words:

> What is unthinkable for [Spinoza] is what Freud terms "death drive": the idea that *conatus* is based on a fundamental act of self-sabotaging. Spinoza, with his assertion of *conatus*, of every entity's striving to persist and strengthen its being, and, in this way, striving for happiness, remains within the Aristotelian frame of what good life is.[38]

Is it indeed the case, as both Badiou and Žižek maintain, that there is no room for the death drive in Spinoza's theory? The basic principle of Spinozan monism is that human beings and everything else that exists (all modes of substance, in Spinoza's parlance) embody the attributes of the one substance (God) in the same degree of perfection as it. In Gilles Deleuze's words, "the same attributes are affirmed of the substance they compose and of the modes they contain."[39] It follows that if God or Nature "has no end set before it, and . . . all final causes are nothing but human fictions" (*Ethics* I, P36, Ap.)—if, in other words, one of the attributes of God is this radical absence of will or entelechy—then, according to Spinoza's own system, this should also be true for all existing beings (modes of substance); that is, all existing beings must be marked not only by the tendency to increase their power and pursue their interests—something which, being a goal, a "final cause," must necessarily be based on a fiction—but also by a complete indifference toward their own power and interest, up to and including the opposite impulse, namely, to undermine their power and interest. The Spinozan adamant elimination of will in God or the One substance and the corollary principle of the univocity of the substance's attributes and its empirical modes make it impossible that the fiction of self-preservation will have the last word.

Given that indifference in itself cannot lead to action, the attribute of God's radical indifference, the fact that God or Nature has no end, can manifest itself empirically only in two antinomic modes, as the intertwining of two opposed tendencies: the tendency to self-preservation and the self-sabotaging impulse we know as the death drive. This is why, as Deleuze puts it, the death drive is "not the exception to the [pleasure] principle but . . . its '*foundation*.'"[40] To return to Lacan's words, the "incontestably metaphysical" presupposition or foundation of the pleasure principle—the latter being the law that governs only the domain of the living organism or "the human in the organic sense"—is the death drive, which is therefore "a category of thought" and, as such, irreducible to neurobiology, even as the latter can explain how thought may occur in the brain chemically speaking.[41] Recalling again Spinoza's dictum that *"truth is the standard both of itself and of the false,"* it follows that the death drive and the pleasure principle are the truth and the false modes in which the attribute of the truth of God's radical nonwillfulness or indifference manifests itself empirically.

Far from making the death drive a concept "unthinkable" in Spinoza's thought, his own ternary conception of truth, as the standard both of itself and of the false, constitutes one of the earliest and most succinct ways of articulating the relation between the pleasure principle and the death drive as necessarily supplementary rather than opposite tendencies of which one could accept the one and expel the other from one's theory of human life.

Let us unpack the relation between the pleasure principle and the death drive in more comprehensive Spinozan terms. What Lacan and Deleuze refer to as the "metaphysical" level or the "foundations" corresponds to what Spinoza calls the "third kind of knowledge." This he defines as a "kind of knowledge [that] proceeds from an adequate idea of the formal essence of certain attributes of God to the adequate knowledge of the [NS: formal] essence of things."[42] The use of the word *formal* here already indicates that the object of the third kind of knowledge does not concern the contingent and particular accidents (in the Aristotelian sense of the word) but the immutable and universal forms constituting the essence of the things examined. Indeed, Spinoza offers an elaborate explanation of this knowledge of formal essence, which is the object of the third kind of knowledge, which we shall pursue presently.

In the same scholium, Spinoza had already defined the "first kind of knowledge" either as deriving "from singular things which have been presented to us through the senses in a way that is . . . without order for the intellect," in short, a "knowledge from random experience," or as a knowledge deriving "from signs, e.g., from the fact that, having heard or read certain words, we recollect things, and form certain ideas of them, which are like them, and through which we imagine the things" on the level of a knowledge that is "opinion or imagination." The "second kind of knowledge" consists of our "common notions and adequate ideas of the properties of things." While the first kind of knowledge pertains to imagination and "is the only cause of falsity," "knowledge of the second and third kind is necessarily true," with the second pertaining to reason and the third forming what Spinoza calls "intuitive knowledge" (*Ethics* II, P41,

P40S2). In the fifth part of the *Ethics*, Spinoza returns to the "third kind of knowledge" to say that it "depends on the Mind, as on a formal cause, insofar as the Mind itself is eternal" (*Ethics* V, P31). In this context, Spinoza introduces a crucial distinction between "duration" and the "species of eternity," or what, in poststructuralist terms, we could call the distinction between diachrony and synchrony: "Whatever the Mind understands under a species of eternity, it understands not from the fact that it conceives the Body's present actual existence, but from the fact that it conceives the Body's essence under a species of eternity" (*Ethics* V, P29). Spinoza proceeds to demonstrate this proposition: "Insofar as the Mind conceives the present existence of its Body, it conceives duration, which can be determined by time, and to that extent it has only the power of conceiving things in relation to time. . . . But eternity cannot be explained by duration. . . . Therefore, to that extent the Mind does not have the power of conceiving things under a species of eternity" (*Ethics* V, P29, Pr.). To follow further Spinoza's reasoning, we must now go backward to the second part of the *Ethics,* where he advances avant la lettre the Kantian position that—given that God is Nature, that is, everything existent, including the Mind—"the very necessity of God's eternal nature" entails that it "is of the nature of Reason to perceive of things under a certain species of eternity," and hence "to regard things as necessary, not as contingent." This also means that "the foundations of Reason are notions . . . which explain those things that are common to all, and which . . . do not explain the essence of any singular thing" but of the universal, which therefore "must be conceived without any relation to time, but under a certain species of eternity" (*Ethics* II, P44C2 and Pr.). Going forward now again to the fifth part, and the conclusion that the Mind, in its capacity of conceiving the Body in time, cannot explain eternity, Spinoza continues:

> But because it is of the nature of reason to conceive things under a species of eternity . . . and it also pertains to the nature of the Mind to conceive the Body's essence under a species of eternity . . . and beyond these two, nothing else pertains to the Mind's essence. . . . This power of conceiving things under a species of eternity pertains to the Mind only insofar as it conceives the Body's essence under a species of eternity, q.e.d. (*Ethics* V, P29, Pr.)

The third kind of knowledge is concerned only with the universal under "a species of eternity," wherein there is no time and the Mind conceives the Body as eternal. The third kind of knowledge, therefore, addresses not the empirical life as we conceive it within time but the metaphysical presuppositions of this empirical life. And it is precisely in this sense that the death drive is the metaphysical presupposition of the pleasure principle—which is also why, contrary to a common misunderstanding, it does not designate any tendency to die within the linear temporality of our biological existence.

What is more, Spinoza's understanding of the Mind's essence as conceiving of all things and its Body's essence under a species of eternity has portentous consequences on his conception of the Body, up to and including death. It follows directly from Spinoza's monism—and therein lies the crux of the matter—that the inseparability of body and mind would necessitate a radical reconceptualization of death, given that *"the Mind itself is eternal"* (*Ethics* V, P31). Spinoza is very explicit about the fact that by death, he does not mean necessarily biological or clinical death. In his own words:

> I understand the Body to die when its parts are so disposed that they acquire a different proportion of motion and rest to one another. For I dare not deny that—even though the circulation of the blood is maintained, as well as other [signs] on account of which the Body is thought to be alive—the human Body can nevertheless be changed into another nature entirely different from its own. For no reason compels me to maintain that the Body does not die unless it is changed into a corpse. And, indeed, experience seems to urge a different conclusion. Sometimes a man undergoes such changes that I should hardly have said he was the same man. (*Ethics* IV, P39S)

Death can be seen only as a subcase among all possible instances in which the Body can "be changed into another nature entirely different from its own" so that one "should hardly have said [it] was the same [Body]." A trauma, for instance, whether due to biological or psychological reasons, can be said to involve death in the Spinozan sense, insofar as the person concerned may be an entirely different person after the traumatic experience. Let us call this nonbiological death "symbolic death," but let us also keep in mind that whenever "death" appears in Spinoza's text, both meanings should be taken into account.

Furthermore, whether death, or the threat thereof, manifests itself as biological or symbolic death, Spinoza is again very explicit about the fact that the self-preservation of the human being is not, and, a fortiori, should not be, the primary principle guiding human life. Again in his own words: "What if a man could save himself from the present danger of death by treachery? Would not the principle of preserving his own being recommend, without qualification, that he be treacherous?" (*Ethics* IV, P72S). Spinoza responds to his question in an emphatically negative way, comparing the logic of this claim to one that would maintain that a free man could act deceptively:

> If a free man, insofar as he is free, did anything by deception, he would do it from the dictate of reason (for so far only do we call him free). And so it would be a virtue to act deceptively . . . and hence . . . everyone would be better advised to act deceptively to preserve his being. . . . But this is absurd. (*Ethics* IV, P72, Pr.)

Therefore "a free man always acts honestly, not deceptively" (*Ethics* IV, P72). Similarly, with regard to using treachery to save one's life, biological or symbolic, Spinoza tells us:

> The reply to this is the same. If reason should recommend that, it would recommend it to all men. And so reason would recommend, without qualification, than men make agreements, join forces, and have common rights only by deception—i.e., that really they have no common rights. This is absurd. (*Ethics* IV, P72S)

However, "absurd" or not, I will maintain that this is exactly what happens when one sustains that the homeostatic mechanism is the ultimate principle of human life. All the more so when one raises it to an ethical principle, which is what Damasio does in his book. This brings us directly to the field indicated by the title of Spinoza's major book, *Ethics*, which will be the subject of the next section.

For now, let us examine some further passages from the *Ethics* regarding a specific kind of death: suicide. Once again, Spinoza makes it amply clear that by death, he always means also symbolic death, as is evident in the following list of examples for reasons to commit suicide:

> Someone may kill himself because he is compelled by another, who twists his right hand (which happened to hold a sword) and forces him to direct the sword against his heart; or because he is forced by the command of a Tyrant (as Seneca was) to open his veins, i.e., he desires to avoid a greater evil by [submitting to] a lesser; or finally because hidden external causes so dispose his imagination, and so affect his Body, that it takes on another nature, contrary to the former, a nature of which there cannot be an idea in the Mind. (*Ethics* IV, P20S; brackets in the original)

In the last example, the Body does not necessarily undergo biological death; rather the suicide consists in assuming "another nature, contrary to the former," of which "there cannot be an idea in the Mind" so that the person becomes a new person both in Body and Mind, as was the case of that "Spanish Poet who suffered an illness," and "though he recovered, he was left so oblivious to his past life that he did not believe the tales and tragedies he had written were his own" (*Ethics* IV, P39S).

Drawn to its logical conclusion, this conception of death leads, of course, to a fundamental psychoanalytic position, which Spinoza foresaw, even as he shrank before his own thought, stating, "But rather than provide the superstitious with material for raising new questions, I prefer to leave this discussion unfinished" (*Ethics* IV, P39S). The terrifying answer that Spinoza refuses to give, possibly because he suspects it, responds to the question he raises immediately after the example of the "Spanish Poet":

> If this seems incredible, what shall we say of infants? A man of advanced years believes their nature to be so different from his own that he could not be persuaded that he was ever an infant, if he did not make this conjecture concerning himself from [NS: the example of] others. (*Ethics* IV, P39S)

What in psychoanalysis is known as castration, that is, the entrance of the infant into the symbolic order (language), is precisely a death, in fact, the first symbolic death of the human being, out of which emerges the (speaking) subject, the subject as a member of the symbolic order. And as Žižek reminds us, this death takes place as a sacrifice in the form of a forced choice, that is, to repeat Spinoza's words, a sacrifice motivated by the "desire to avoid a greater evil by [submitting to] a lesser," whereby there is only one "right choice" if one is to become a member of the symbolic community in the first place. In Žižek's words:

> The fundamental insight behind the notion of . . . symbolic castration . . . is that a certain "sacrificial situation" defines the very status of man *qua* "parlêtre," "being of language." . . .[43] The entire psychoanalytic theory of "socialization," of the emergence of the subject from the encounter of a presymbolic life substance of "enjoyment" and the symbolic order . . . [is] the description of a sacrificial situation which, far from being exceptional, is the story of everyone and as such *constitutive*. . . . [That is,] the "social contract," the inclusion of the subject in the symbolic community, has the structure of a *forced choice*: the subject supposed to choose freely his community (since only a free choice is morally binding) does not exist prior to this choice, he is constituted by means of it. The choice of community, the "social contract," is a paradoxical choice where I maintain the freedom of choice only if I "make the right choice": if I choose the other of the community, I stand to lose the very freedom, the very possibility of choice (in clinical terms: I choose psychosis).[44]

Because the subject enters the symbolic community through the paradoxical path of this forced choice, which as such is not a free choice, in truth the choice of the symbolic community by the subject is not ethically binding "since only a free choice is morally binding." This, as we shall see in the next section, is not without consequences for the issue of ethics.

Read against the background of this concept of castration or the "social contract"—no less operative because tacit in Spinoza's text—as the human's first symbolic suicide, and specifically as a forced and hence ethically nonbinding choice, Spinoza's commentary on suicide reveals itself as a radical social critique, already advancing the thesis that "people don't commit suicide, it is society that suicides people"—if it so happens that society is so profoundly contrary to their nature. In Spinoza's words:

> No one ... unless he is defeated by causes external, and contrary, to his nature, neglects to seek his own advantage, *or* to preserve his being.... Those who do such things are compelled by external causes, which can happen in many ways.... But that a man should, from the necessity of his own nature, strive not to exist, or to be changed into another form, is as impossible as that something should come from nothing. (*Ethics* IV, P20S)

No person would commit suicide if external reality were not contrary to the person's nature. To remain close to home, given the external causes, the specific sociohistorical circumstances of Spinoza's own life, his self-preservation required at least two suicides. Spinoza wouldn't have led either the Christian or the Jewish community to excommunicate him if they were not contrary to his nature. Conversely, remaining within either community would amount to losing both his freedom and his virtue, which, for Spinoza, would be worse than biological death. For self-preservation is for Spinoza the preservation not of just nature or life but of a *specific* nature or life—which no neurobiological conception of evolution could ever specify.

In a footnote to his translation of the *Ethics,* Edwin Curley remarks that "it is true that Spinoza does not condemn suicide, but neither does he regard it as an act which could ever be virtuous, much less paradigmatically free."[45] It goes without saying that suicide cannot be a virtuous act for Spinoza, given that "virtue ... is nothing but acting from the laws of one's own nature," and if people commit suicide, biologically or symbolically, they do so because of "external causes" that are "contrary" to their nature (*Ethics* IV, P18S). Similarly, it is impossible that suicide could ever be a "paradigmatically free" act, given that one could never find oneself in a society that is contrary to one's own nature by one's own free choice—one finds oneself there through the paradox of "forced choice." The issue, therefore, is not simply that, in Curley's words—unlike Caillois's position, according to which, even on the issue of suicide, "Spinoza is a Stoic"—Appuhn is correct in arguing that Spinoza's "treatment of suicide marks an important point of difference from the Stoics" just because Spinoza, unlike the Stoics, did not praise suicide as a virtuous or free act. What is more, Spinoza differs radically from the Stoics in this point also insofar as his entire theory—as is also evident in other of his works, particularly his two treatises—is an acute, however subtle and self-censored, critique of his contemporary society.

Homeostasis, Joy, and Ethics

It is time to return to the crucial moment in Spinoza's argumentation at which reason decisively dictates that one contributes to one's own death by persisting in not committing treachery. We can imagine this scene as much in a torture chamber as in a bourgeois salon—torture and death come in various modes—though it is more likely that Spinoza had biological death in mind with regard to this example, and as far as Damasio's argument is concerned, death taken here only in the biological sense suffices to indicate that Spinoza gives unambiguous priority to reason over self-preservation as understood by Damasio.

Spinoza's thesis derives directly from his conceptions of freedom and virtue and is corollary to his overall social critique. If virtue dictates that one conducts one's existence according to the laws of one's own nature, and if external conditions oppose this nature, then there is no reason to preserve this existence that is detrimental to one's own nature. There are cases in which this requires a biological suicide and others in which it entails a symbolic suicide, but in both cases, it is a matter of a choice between evil and lesser evil. If treachery is against reason, then it is contrary to the nature of the free person (i.e., the person of reason), and hence the latter will choose to die. Here we have the repetition of the primary choice involved in the entrance of the subject to the symbolic order, the difference being that whereas that choice was forced (one must choose the right choice to be able to choose in the future), here one is free to choose either, that is, to choose either to remain free or to lose one's freedom. It is therefore on the level of such choices that the ethical dimension is opened up.

Given that death, too, biological or symbolic, is an alteration of human nature—arguably, in fact, the most radical—the crucial question arising here is, how is it possible that death can, under certain circumstances, be a lesser evil compared to any other evil? To respond to this question, which constitutes the core of ethics and generally the conduct of human life, we must first pursue further the proper domain of ethics as one which, contrary to Damasio's designation of it as the domain of the homeostatic principle of self-preservation, is defined precisely as its beyond.

Despite what I see as his misreading of Spinoza, Badiou is right in arguing that "the composition of a subject of truth," that is, of an ethical subject—a subject who knows what is good or not beyond the question of the mere "conservation of the self"—"does not fall under this [homeostatic] law" of the pleasure principle that determines "the ordinary behavior of the human animal."[46] Similarly, his reading of Spinoza notwithstanding, Žižek is also right in arguing that "what is outside [the] scope" of the homeostatic principle, and hence presumably outside Spinoza's scope, "is what Kant refers to as the 'categorical imperative,' an unconditional thrust that parasitizes upon a human subject without any regard for its well-being, 'beyond the pleasure principle.'"[47] Both statements refer to the domain Lacan has designated as the "between two deaths," that is, that "point of view" from which "life can only be approached, can only be lived or thought about, from the place of that limit where . . . life is already lost, where [one] is already on the other side," from where one "can see [life] and live it in the form of something already lost."[48] In other words, in our ethical dimension, we are in a realm beyond "the historical drama [one] has lived through," at "the limit or the *ex nihilo*" outside the confines of time, where, as it were, death and immortality coincide.[49] To put it in Spinoza's terms, the possibility of ethics in human life emerges out of the Mind's essence, its characteristic of conceiving the Body under a species of eternity. The ethical dimension, therefore, opens up on the level of the third kind of knowledge, which means that ethics is a purely metaphysical human modality.

The crucial point is that, as Spinoza writes, "whatever we understand by the third kind of knowledge we take pleasure in." For if, as we have seen, the Mind's essence is to think in terms of the third kind of knowledge, then "from this kind of knowledge there arises the greatest satisfaction of Mind there can be . . . Joy" (*Ethics* IV, P32 and Pr.). This is how it is possible to experience the threat of death as lesser evil, in fact, as the sole possible Joy, if all other alternatives oppose one's nature. In fact, Spinoza writes as much fairly explicitly in the context of his discussion of the third kind of knowledge: "death is less harmful to us, the greater the Mind's clear and distinct knowledge" (*Ethics* IV, P38S).

It is this metaphysical pleasure or joy, deriving from the third kind of knowledge, to which Lacan refers with the term *jouissance* (enjoyment), the very concept he introduces in his attempt to formulate a theory of ethics that goes beyond the entirety of a tradition "from the origin of moral philosophy" to Damasio and beyond, in which "all meditation on man's good has taken place as a function of the index of pleasure . . . along the paths of an essentially hedonistic problematic."[50] Spinoza's ethics is clearly an exception to this tradition, placing at the center of his investigation metaphysical Joy, a pleasure beyond any pleasure and consideration the Mind and the Body may have within time.

There is more to be said about this Joy. In the first part of the *Ethics*, Spinoza had introduced God's own pleasure as nothing other than his radically indifferent will: "this opinion, which subjects all things to a certain indifferent will of God, and makes all things depend on his good pleasure, is nearer the truth than that of those who maintain that God does all things for the sake of the good" (*Ethics* I, P33S2). In the fifth part, we come to understand that God's pleasure is the very pleasure or Joy we experience through the third kind of knowledge, which is why, as Proposition 33 continues to state, "*our pleasure is accompanied by the idea of God as a cause,*" which has as its corollary that "from the third kind of knowledge, there necessarily arises an intellectual Love of God. For from this kind of knowledge there arises . . . Joy, accompanied by the idea of God as its cause, i.e., Love of God, not insofar as we imagine him as present . . . but insofar as we understand God to be eternal. And this is what I call intellectual love of God" (*Ethics* V, P32, Pr. and C). Here I am tempted to state that the true formula of atheism is not "God is dead" but "God is not that which we imagine to be present but that which we understand to be eternal." For his part, and having in his repertoire a concept unavailable to Spinoza in this specific sense, Lacan states that "the true formula of atheism is not *God is dead* . . . [but] *God is unconscious.*"[51] Albeit cast in the terminology of another century, Lacan's thesis remains in absolute accord with Spinoza's position that God is the cause of our metaphysical pleasure, the very pleasure we derive from the ethical state opened up to us by the third kind of knowledge, insofar as, again in Lacan's words, "the status of the unconscious is ethical, not ontic."[52] In other words, if the third kind of knowledge is the realm of metaphysics and ethics, their cause is the unconscious (Spinoza's God).

That the unconscious is not ontic also means that, as Freud already knew, it operates outside the categories of space and time that predicate the empirical or ontic world. Spinoza is equally explicit that his entire discussion of the third kind of knowledge and the joy we derive from it, up to the intellectual love of God, do not concern objects in time and space. First he advances the by now obvious to us thesis that *"there is nothing in nature which is contrary to this intellectual Love, or which can take it away"* (*Ethics* V, P37). I say this is obvious given the example of the free man who chooses death rather than treachery: even death cannot conquer the man's intellectual Love for God, as the former takes place within time, whereas the latter takes place under a species of eternity; a fortiori, it is precisely the choice of death, postulated by Reason, that allows for this intellectual Love of God in the first place. Nevertheless, Spinoza proceeds to demonstrate his position in his usual geometric manner, wherein he argues that "this intellectual Love follows necessarily from the nature of the Mind insofar as it is considered as an eternal truth, through God's nature" (*Ethics* V, P37, Pr.). One implication here is that nothing in nature could destroy this intellectual Love of God because it is eternal, and therefore there is nothing that can be greater, whether in extension or power, and hence capable of destroying it. Earlier, however, Spinoza had posed the axiom that "there is no singular thing in nature than which there is not another more powerful and stronger. Whatever one is given, there is another more powerful by which the first can be destroyed" (*Ethics* IV, A1). Sensing the possibility of a perceived (ostensible) contradiction on the part of his reader, Spinoza adds the following Scholium immediately after the demonstration of Proposition 37: "[part] IV [axiom] A1 concerns singular things insofar as they are considered in relation to a certain time and place." Hence this axiom has no validity within the timeless realm of the third knowledge.

For the effect of stark contrast, it is worth citing extensively, without interruption, Damasio's thesis on both "institutions involved in the governance of social behavior" and ethics:

> The ultimate goal of those institutions . . . is precisely the regulation of life in a particular environment. . . . The ultimate goal of these institutions revolves around promoting life and avoiding death and enhancing well-being and reducing suffering. . . . This was important for humans because automated life regulation can only go so far. . . . Without the help of deliberation, pedagogy, or formal instruments of culture, nonhuman species exhibit useful behaviors that run from the trivial—finding food or a mate; to the sublime—showing compassion for another. But look, for a moment, at us humans. We certainly cannot dispense with any part of the gene-given innate apparatus of behavior. Yet it is apparent that, as human societies became more complex . . . human survival and well-being depended *on an additional kind of nonautomated governance* in a social and cultural space. I am referring to what we usually associate with reasoning and freedom of decision. . . . Nature has had millions of years to perfect the automated devices of homeostasis, while the nonautomated devices would have a history of a few thousand years. . . . Social conventions and ethical rules may be seen in part as extensions of the basic homeostatic arrangements at the level of society and culture. The outcome of applying the rules is the same as the outcome of basic homeostatic devices such as metabolic regulation or appetites: a balance of life to ensure survival and well-being. . . . The constitution that governs a democratic state, the laws that are consonant with that constitution, and application of those laws in a judicial system are also homeostatic devices. . . . All of these institutions can be seen as part and parcel of the tendency to promote homeostasis on a large scale. Along with the good results they often achieve, however, these bodies suffer from many ills and their policies are often informed by deficient conceptions of humanity that have not taken into account emerging scientific evidence. . . . Proposition

18 in part IV of *The Ethics* . . . reads: ". . . the very first foundation of virtue is the endeavor (conatum) to preserve the individual self, and happiness consists in the human capacity to preserve its self." . . . How does Spinoza move from oneself to all the selves to whom virtue must apply? Spinoza makes the transition relying again on biological facts. . . . The biological reality of self-preservation leads to virtue because in our inalienable need to maintain ourselves we must, of necessity, help preserve *other* selves. . . . The essence of this transition can be found in Aristotle, but Spinoza ties it to a biological principle—the mandate of self-preservation. So, here is the beauty behind the cherished quote [Spinoza's earlier cited proposition], seen from today's perspective: It contains the foundation for a system of ethical behaviors and that foundation is neurobiological.[53]

Several questions, rhetorical or not, come to mind when reading the preceding line of argument against the background of Spinoza's work. Even forgetting that Spinoza's concept of self-preservation is so vastly wider than its neurobiological counterpart (to the extent that the former can turn against the latter and demand suicide)—even forgetting this—how is neurobiology going to consider the human body and mind under a species of eternity, which is Spinoza's very precondition of any discussion of ethics? The constitutive postulate of neurobiology is to examine living beings precisely under the categories of space and time. The law Damasio mistakes for the foundation of ethics, the homeostatic principle of self-preservation, can at most be valid with regard to the survival of animal life, and even there, it fails to explain all of it, as his own examples, from the self-sacrificial "bonobo chimpanzees to various other nonhuman species," demonstrate,[54] let alone when reason enters the picture, with its postulate of conceiving the universal under a species of eternity. No matter how much time passes, the neurobiological organism cannot enter the realm of eternity.

It is no accident that when it comes to the issues of eternity and the intellectual love of God, Damasio devotes to them no much more than one page in his book, framing his discussion with the qualification that here we are entering something "complicated and difficult to tease apart."[55] Nevertheless, this does not prevent Damasio from quickly concluding that the point of the intellectual love of God is that through it the individual "achieves the most desirable kind of joy in Spinoza's canon, a joy that is perhaps best conceived as pure feeling almost liberated for once, from its obligate body twin."[56] So the culmination of the entire *Ethics* is a state, the intellectual love of God, at which the Mind is, "for once," liberated from the Body. Then we will have to infer that, appearances to the contrary, deep down, Spinoza was, after all, a crypto-Cartesian. But there is good reason why Damasio is misled to this conclusion, namely, that neurobiology cannot conceive eternity, the liberation from time, but as a liberation from the Body because neurobiology can address the body only as an object in time.

As for the institutions that govern human behavior, the bitter truth is that, however anti-Spinozan (false) Damasio's presentation of the ideal function of institutions might be, it is a more or less accurate (true) description of the actual institutions that throughout history have attempted to regulate human life, as is evident in the fact that Spinoza himself had to commit the said suicides. For it is precisely insofar as the homeostatic mechanism constitutes the institutions' founding principle and ideal (however asymptotically or only in appearance) that they exclude the realization of ethical human beings—unless, of course, one is willing or forced to exit them, whether as a passive outcast or to fight back against the nature of the institutions. Reason does not recommend this choice, but the decision to raise the homeostatic machine to the universal ground of the institutional regulation of social life entails with necessity and, to repeat Spinoza's words, "without qualification, that men make agreements, join forces, and have common rights only by deception—i.e., that really they have no common rights." And given that in history, "the mass of mankind," and hence of their institutions, "remains always at about the same pitch of misery," this must be about as true today as it was in the time of Spinoza.[57]

Notes

1 Antonio Damasio, *Looking for Spinoza: Joy, Sorrow, and the Feeling Brain* (Orlando, Fla.: Harcourt, 2003).
2 Ibid., 53.
3 Ibid., 85.
4 Ibid., 91.
5 Ibid., 209.
6 Ibid.
7 Ibid., 209, 212.
8 Ibid., 212.
9 Ibid., 213.
10 Ibid., 217; emphasis added.
11 Ibid., 214.
12 Ibid., 71, 14.
13 Ibid., 212–13.
14 Ibid., 216.
15 Ibid., 213.
16 Ibid., 213–14.
17 Baruch (Benedict de) Spinoza, *Ethics*, in *The Collected Works of Spinoza*, vol. 1, ed. and trans. Edwin Curley (Princeton, N.J.: Princeton University Press, 1985), *Ethics* II, P13; cited in Damasio, *Looking for Spinoza*, 211. Unless otherwise noted, all cited passages from *Ethics* are from Curley's edition of the *Ethics*, and all brackets in citations are mine. Latin citations of Spinoza's *Ethics* are from the following edition: *Die Ethik (Lateinisch und Deutsch)*, trans. Jakob Stern (Stuttgart, Germany: Reclam, 1990).
18 Damasio, *Looking for Spinoza*, 211; *Ethics* II, P23.
19 *Ethics* II, P16, P26; Damasio, *Looking for Spinoza*, 212.
20 Damasio, *Looking for Spinoza*, 213.
21 Ibid., 209.
22 Ibid., 30.
23 Ibid.; Sigmund Freud, *Beyond the Pleasure Principle*, trans. and ed. James Strachey, with an introduction by Gregory Zilboorg and Peter Gay (New York: W. W. Norton, 1961), 6.
24 Jacques Lacan, *Book II: The Ego in Freud's Theory and in the Technique of Psychoanalysis, 1954–1955*, ed. Jacques-Alain Miller, trans. Sylvana Tomaselli (New York: W. W. Norton, 1991), 79–80.

25 Damasio, *Looking for Spinoza*, 30–35.
26 Lacan, *Book II*, 80.
27 Ibid.
28 Ibid., 79.
29 Ibid.
30 Ibid., 81.
31 Ibid., 84.
32 Ibid., 79.
33 Damasio, *Looking for Spinoza*, 260. I address extensively the profound relation between Spinoza and psychoanalysis in A. Kiarina Kordela, *$urplus: Spinoa, Lacan* (Albany: State University of New York Press, 2007).
34 Damasio, *Looking for Spinoza*, 49.
35 Ibid., 49, 161.
36 Lacan, *Book II*, 79.
37 Alain Badiou, *Ethics: An Essay on the Understanding of Evil*, trans. Peter Hallward (London: Verso, 2001), 46.
38 Slavoj Žižek, *Organs without Bodies: On Deleuze and Consequences* (New York: Routledge, 2004), 34.
39 Gilles Deleuze, *Spinoza: Practical Philosophy*, trans. Robert Hurley (San Francisco: City Lights Books, 1988), 52.
40 Gilles Deleuze, *Masochism: Coldness and Cruelty* (New York: Zone Books, 1994), 113.
41 Lacan, *Book II*, 79.
42 *Ethics* II, P40S2. "NS" refers to *De Nagelate Schriften van Benedict de Spinoza*, "the contemporary Dutch translations which appeared in the other posthumous edition [of the *Ethics*] in 1677." Edwin Curley, general preface to Spinoza, *Collected Works*, x.
43 *Parlêtre* is a neologism coined by Lacan to designate the speaking being in one word made up from the words *parler* (to speak) and *être* (to be).
44 Slavoj Žižek, *Enjoy Your Symptom! Jacques Lacan in Hollywood and Out* (New York: Routledge, 1992), 74–75.
45 Spinoza, *Collected Works*, 557n15.
46 Badiou, *Ethics: An Essay on the Understanding of Evil*, 46.
47 Žižek, *Organs without Bodies*, 34. In one of his discussions of ethics in this work, Žižek writes, "According to Kant, if one finds oneself alone in the sea with another survivor of a sunken ship near a

floating piece of wood that can keep only one person afloat, moral considerations are no longer valid. There is no moral law preventing me from fighting to death with the other survivor for the place on the raft; I can engage in it with moral impunity" (38n44). In a footnote elsewhere, I took Žižek's recapitulation of Kant's position at face value, as my concern was more the internal consistency within Žižek's own argument (see Kordela, $Surplus$, 2007, 147n8). Assuming that Žižek's account of Kant is right, then we could say that Spinoza's ethics goes far beyond the "Kantian rigor" Curley detects in Spinoza's comment on the issue of treachery, that "if reason should recommend that, it would recommend it to all men." Spinoza, *Collected Works*, 587n37, and *Ethics* IV, P72S. Certainly this statement intimates Kant's postulate that the ethical imperative should be universalizable, but Spinoza's primacy of virtue over self-preservation would have no equivalent in the Kantian ethic, as Kant would seem to subject everything to the ultimate law of self-preservation. Žižek does not give bibliographical reference to the passage in which Kant is supposed to have advanced the preceding argument. The sole relevant passage I have found argues effectively the opposite, indicating, other major differences notwithstanding, a convergence between Spinoza and Kant with regard to the subordinate role of self-preservation in ethics: "There is no *casus necessitatis* except in a case where duties, namely an *unconditional duty* and a (perhaps very important yet) *conditional duty,* conflict with each other, e.g., if it is a matter of preventing some catastrophe to the state by betraying a man who might stand in the relationship to another of father and son. This prevention of trouble to the former is an unconditional duty, whereas preventing misfortune to the latter is only a conditional duty (namely, insofar as he has not made himself guilty of a crime against the state). One of the relatives might report the other's plans to the authorities with the utmost reluctance, but he is compelled by necessity (namely, moral necessity)—but if it is said of someone who, in order to preserve his own life, pushes another survivor of a shipwreck from his plank, that he has a right to do so by his (physical) necessity, that is quite false. For to preserve my life is only a conditional duty (if it can be done without a crime); but not to take the life of another who is committing no offense against me and does not even *lead* me into the danger of losing my life is an unconditional duty." Immanuel Kant, *Practical Philosophy*, ed. and trans. Mary J. Gregor (Cambridge: Cambridge University Press, 1999), 299n. Albeit largely in a context of a political position starkly different than that of Spinoza, Kant's general position on this matter is thoroughly Spinozan: "a right of necessity *(ius in casu necessitatis)* . . . , as a supposed *right* to do *wrong* when in extreme (physical) need, is in any case an absurdity." Ibid., 299.

48 Jacques Lacan, *Book VII: The Ethics of Psychoanalysis, 1959–1960*, ed. Jacques-Alain Miller, trans. Dennis Porter (New York: W. W. Norton, 1992), 270, 280.

49 Ibid., 279.

50 Ibid., 221. There are, of course, innumerous implications regarding the ideological function of enjoyment, or Spinoza's Joy, which are, however, irrelevant to this line of argument here, but I address some in Kordela, $urplus, 2007. To avoid confusion, note that *enjoyment* may also indicate the "presymbolic life substance" referred to by Žižek in a passage cited earlier.

51 Jacques Lacan, *The Four Fundamental Concepts of Psychoanalysis*, trans. Alan Sheridan, ed. Jacques-Alain Miller (New York: W. W. Norton, 1981), 59.

52 Ibid., 34.

53 Damasio, *Looking for Spinoza*, 166–71.

54 Ibid., 167.

55 Ibid., 276.

56 Ibid.

57 Benedict de Spinoza, *A Theologico-Political Treatise and A Political Treatise*, trans. and with an introduction by R. H. M. Elwes (New York: Dover, 1951), 5.

14

A Matter of Life and Death: Spinoza and Derrida

ALEXANDER GARCÍA DÜTTMANN

For Robert Savage

IN PROPOSITION 67 of Part IV of his *Ethics,* Spinoza states that there is one thought that almost never crosses the mind of the free human being.[1] Thoughts cross our minds more or less frequently. Whoever proves to be free, however, thinks of death least of all. The British philosopher Stuart Hampshire warns us against making light of this statement by reducing it to "rhetorical ornament" and ignoring its importance for a Spinozan sense of "objectivity."[2] The American philosopher Steven Nadler speaks of a "proclamation" and thereby suggests that Spinoza is taking a stance rather than just stating a thought. In the manner of a forerunner to and herald of the Enlightenment, Spinoza would be arguing against the "superstitious multitude who, moved by hope and fear, worry about what is to come in an alleged hereafter."[3] It is as if the very idea of freedom were tied up intimately with the infrequency or even absence of the thought of death, or as if the quantity denoted a quality, a necessary irrelevance. When we are free, death almost never comes to mind, and this is necessarily so because of the irrelevance of the thought of death, not for the dubious kind of freedom that renounces the arduous and often disappointing endeavor of thinking but for the kind of freedom that expresses itself, and must express itself, in thinking, in a certain understanding of things and their necessity, in a grasping of the laws that govern nature. In other words, the thought of death is not even a thought or is a thought awaiting further qualification.

Doubtless the philosopher might have something to say about death, or in the case of Spinoza, about the mortality of the body. Spinoza says that there is no reason why the actual transformation of the body into a corpse should be the only occasion for speaking of death. Each time the rule that determines the relationship between rest and movement is altered, the disposition of bodily parts is transformed. When this happens, it can be difficult to ascertain whether a human being is still the same being we have encountered before (*Ethics* IV, P39S). The first example Spinoza provides is of an unnamed Spanish poet afflicted with amnesia and hence unable to recognize the works he has written as his own. Spinoza's second example seems to imply that the causes for the evolution of the body and the mind are not merely internal. It refers us to the changes that take place during the passage from childhood to maturity. To the extent that the mind is the idea of the body, that thinking forms an idea of whatever affects the body, and that our self is "the idea that we have of our body and of our mind insofar as something has an effect on them," as Gilles Deleuze puts it,[4] it is clear that these transformations have a bearing beyond the exteriority of bodily parts. The German philosopher Theodor W. Adorno, not much of a Spinozist, claims in his "Meditations on Metaphysics" that the "biological" dimension of death encompasses not only the physical existence of people of old age but also their selves, everything that once made them into human beings. People of old age appear to disintegrate, to fall apart, to crumble away, even though they might not be prone to illness or "violent intrusions."[5] In a lecture course from the late 1970s and early 1980s, Deleuze reminds us that for Spinoza, death is always something that hits us from outside, as it were, and that no thought could be more alien, more external to Spinoza's views, than the thought of a death drive.[6]

Thus there is little doubt that Spinoza has something to say about death. Yet the thought of death itself results from an affect of fear and is more like the idea of an uncertain image or of the unfathomable way in which our bodies will be affected externally. Whoever thinks of death, and does so frequently, has an axe to grind. It is not surprising that Spinoza dismisses suicide, to which the recurring thought of death may point, by denouncing the lack of power of those who contemplate the possibility of putting a willful end to their lives. The semblance of willfulness obfuscates that the suicide is entirely overwhelmed by "external causes" opposed to his nature and its necessity (*Ethics* IV, P17S). He is a slave to fear. I may turn into a being that bears little resemblance to the being I was before. I may lack an awareness of who I was up to the moment in which I became a different being. But this becoming is not inscribed in the necessity of my nature. Suicide gives way to the "law of the other,"[7] to use an expression from Pierre Macherey.

One could be tempted to push the argument further and maintain that the thought of death recurs frequently precisely because it is not simply a thought, an insight dependent solely on itself, but remains determined by a fear of dying. Both the inability to subsume things under the laws of nature and the inability to comprehend their essence intuitively lead to a necessity different from the necessity of the substance. It is the necessity of destiny that manifests itself in the fear of dying, in the uncontrollable frequency with which the thought of death recurs. As long as it is not related to the substance whose existence stems from itself, the law always splits into two, into the law of one's own and the law of the other. Such an interpretation of Spinoza's proposition would entail that the fear of dying is in a sense exemplary of the affect of fear, of a diminishing of the same power that, when increased, liberates us from destiny by eliciting a rational conception of cause and effect and an intuitive comprehension of essence.

Two negative and two positive conclusions can be drawn at this point. On the one hand, it would make no sense to consider the vanishing of the thought of death from the free man's mind as the result of a *decision* to think of death only occasionally, just as it would make no sense to assume that the free man contents himself with following some moral device or prescription that tells him that it is better not to think of death all too often. On the other hand, freedom must be considered as an act of liberation that allows human beings to wrest themselves from the sway of affects, or passions, and the illusory necessity of destiny, just as it must be assumed to be a comportment of the mind toward life after the liberating effort has succeeded. At the very end of his *Ethics,* Spinoza stresses that freedom is never a given and that, to begin with, we are not free. In the part on human bondage, he even quotes a line from the *Metamorphoses*: I can see what is better, acknowledge it, and keep adhering to what proves worse. A successful liberation from affects, however, engenders a form of wisdom that consists in reflecting upon life rather than death and disclosing the existence of a law, or a necessary link, where unpredictable contingencies used to hold the reins. This form of wisdom is free inasmuch as it is not guided by a preceding fear. The free and wise man thinks of the preservation of his being, of ways of acting that will work out to his advantage and prevent him from succumbing to whatever might impede the recognition of the law's necessity and cloud the intuition of the essence of things, diminishing, as a consequence, his power to exist. Spinoza insists on our ignorance in the face of the body's capacity for acting. He is adamant that bodily affections can be related to the idea of God. But although the body is never entirely destroyed and its idea always subsists through the fatal encounter with "external causes," the mind is able to relate to necessity in a way in which the body cannot. The wise man exists without ever ceasing to be. He has freed the law from the other and touched on reality or being itself. When Schelling, in the lectures of his *Philosophy of Revelation*, dismisses Spinoza's doctrine for conceiving of the necessity of being in logical terms alone and thus lacking an answer to the question, why is there something rather than nothing? it is this sense of reality that he, too, has in mind.[8]

The claim that the fear of dying is in truth a fear of life can be found in Macherey's extensive commentary on the fifth part of the *Ethics*.[9] We are now in a position to understand this claim and to render the statement or the proclamation concerning the frequency of the thought of death more intelligible. Indeed, it would be impossible to decipher the fear of dying that triggers the recurrence of the thought of death as a symptom of a fear of life and hence as a resistance to life itself, if freedom did not consist in an act of liberation *and* in a form of wisdom. This distinction entails that the act of liberation from affectivity, the transformation of passions into affects of self-affection and self-determination, must contain some trace of the wisdom yet to be attained and that, conversely, no wisdom can be achieved without a preceding liberation. Only if I am already on the way toward achieving wisdom will my fear of death be a fear of life, and only if my fear of death is a fear of life will it be a fear of death in the first place. Jacobi, who started the famous debate on Spinozism in German philosophy, anticipates Schelling's critical arguments by charging Spinoza with remaining caught up in the sphere of the logical or philosophical and neglecting the heterogeneity between the positive and the negative, between faith and the fatalism inherent in all reasoning. "How can we strive to obtain certainty if we are not acquainted with it from the beginning?," Jacobi asks.[10] Yet, in a sense, it is this very structure of presupposition, a kind of hermeneutic or performative circle, that Jacobi shares with Spinoza in the moment that he rejects his doctrine. Freedom that did not consist in a preceding act of liberation, that was not something to be accomplished, would not deserve its name, at least not if it is to qualify a behavior or a comportment toward the world. As a given, it would be indiscernible and coincide with mere necessity. The freedom of the substance is not the freedom of its finite mode, of a mode that comes close to the substance's freedom only when it has liberated itself from the "law of the other." Thus freedom must presuppose itself, just as understanding must, for instance, in the guise of faith. In Spinoza, the presupposition of freedom and the presupposition of understanding are one. Turning to an apparently trivial remark can elucidate the point further. Very few people, Deleuze observes in his lecture course, are complete idiots, for everybody understands something.[11] This remark supplements and completes the picture of eternal life that Deleuze draws in the final pages of his study on Spinoza's concept of expression. The one who fears death has a reason for doing so.[12] He has not wrested himself from the sway of passive affects and still has something to lose, for once the relationship of the extensive parts of his body has changed so radically that the transformation has amounted to a destruction, he will no longer be able to suffer and will maybe have an affect such as fear. In Michael Powell's and Emeric Pressburger's film *A Matter of Life and Death*, the scenes set in heaven are shot in black and white. Heaven is represented as a legalistic hell, hardly a view of Spinozan inspiration given that, in the *Ethics*, God, the one substance, is certainly not a legislator, a supreme judge, or the president of a court of law who could inflict the most terrible punishment on men and make them fear a death worse than death. But the idea that a human being who has died is granted a second chance and allowed to return to his or her former life seems like a humorous echo of the idea that a free person almost never thinks of death, at least if we take this idea to mean that men have a task to accomplish.

The act of liberation by which men gain a sense of reality that makes them think of death least of all ultimately puts an end to the law's splitting into the law of one's own and the law of the other. It is as if the law were restored to the infinite nature of the substance from which it follows. In the chapter of his *Theological-Political Treatise* that discusses the divine law and establishes a difference between the laws of nature and the laws posited by mankind, Spinoza notes that Christ had an intellectual understanding of revealed contents and perceived them by means of pure thinking, not by way of words and images. He distinguishes those who, incapable of such an understanding, have access to revealed contents in the shape of a law to be obeyed from those who can see these contents as eternal truths and are thus free of the "law's bondage."[13] There is a difference between knowing the law and knowing its letter. To know the law, a knowledge that Macherey interprets as an active engagement or comportment toward the world rather than a form of contemplative intellectualism, is to have an insight into its necessity. The one who has such an insight is not subject to it anymore without, however, suspending its validity and exempting himself from the law. The free man is not an anarchist. Does he not think of death least of all because he can relate knowingly to the law inscribed within his nature and because his knowledge can restore it to the infinite nature of the substance?

In the beginning and at the very end of his long essay *H.C. for Life, That Is to Say . . .* , Jacques Derrida writes that the difference between him and the work of his friend Hélène Cixous lies in that he has always been said to side with death, whereas she has always chosen to side with life: "Between her and me it all seems to be a matter of life or death."[14]

Of course, Derrida does not simply mention this view, or return to it, in order to confirm and ratify it. Early on in the essay, he shows that in truth, it is impossible to discriminate between life and death as if they were two sides that can be opposed to each other or two opposite shores that face one another. When it comes to death, there is no side we could prefer to some other side. We cannot take sides here and hence find ourselves deciding each time in favor of life, regardless of how important, how serious, how grave the decision might be. Does Derrida imply in this context that even suicide is a decision for life, though probably a decision that does not know itself? It is precisely because life is not the opposite of death that it does not remain untouched. In *Of Grammatology*, Derrida characterizes the organization of life as an economy of death. In his essay on Cixous, he refers to his definition of *différance* in *Speech and Phenomena* when he claims that life is infinite, without some other side that could be opposed to it, and yet finite, that is limited by one side only, the side that it itself forms, as it were. It is as if death had a double effect on life, making it form a side or create a shore and allowing it at the same time to stretch infinitely. A conventional decision requires a number of identifiable alternatives. But where it is all a matter of life and death, there is no alternative, no option that can be privileged over a different option. Does the fact that every decision must be a decision in favor of life mean that no decision can ever be made? From a Spinozan point of view, the answer would be affirmative. The freedom of will, to which decision making belongs, proves to be an illusion, a lack of knowledge with regard to causes. We cannot make a decision because we are always already on the side of life, whether we know it or not. However, such a point of view would also entail that life can appear to be infinitely finite only from the limited perspective of the man who still thinks too much of death because he has not attained the freedom and understanding conferred by the second and third kinds of knowledge. The side of life is not a side. For Derrida, then, the necessity of a decision being essentially a decision for life does not invalidate the possibility and the necessity of making decisions—quite the contrary. *Life,* like *différance,* designates undecidability itself,[15] the relationship to something that interrupts all relations and that, for this very reason, again and again calls for a relation or a decision. We must take sides where, by definition, no side can be taken, not because there are no sides but because we are already on one side and cannot be on any other side. Ask why we need to keep insisting on the notion of a one-sided border here, a shore-facing nothingness, in Kantian terminology, a barrier and not a limit, and you may well be on the way toward becoming a Spinozist.

To maintain that life is finite in its boundlessness or that the essence of finitude lies in infinite *différance* amounts to maintaining that a decision is the expression of an irreducible undecidability and that undecidability renders decision making possible in the first place, just as life allows for experience, assuming that experience is always the experience of a border, the crossing of borders that forever stays on a border, not, as a Spinozist would claim, the experience of eternity. In short, Derrida does not conceive of life as substance, whether in a Spinozan or a Hegelian sense.[16] It is unavoidable to have an axe to grind, though in the instant we want to rely on our agenda, we will discover that there is none, that it keeps vanishing, because to live means to corroborate or to revoke decisions in ever-shrinking time intervals, especially it being all a matter of life and death, an urgent matter of life *or* death, decisions as to who we are. In the end, perhaps, a Derridian can rely on an agenda as little as a Spinozist can, though in one case, the lack will be interpreted as a sign of knowledge, even wisdom, and in the other case, not so. On the one hand, we give in to death if we do not make decisions constantly, harass others and ourselves; on the other hand, we give in to death, think of it too many times, if we continue to believe that we can and that we should make decisions or that anything truly relevant will depend on such behavior. Both for the Spinozist and the Derridian, it is all a matter of life *or* death rather than a matter of life *and* death. One could say that the act of deciding is a false act of liberation that leads to the thought of death becoming entrenched even deeper in our being. Derrida does not use the concept of freedom often, if at all. It could be argued, however, that for him, freedom would consist in the necessity of making a decision in the absence of a set of reliable criteria, outside a given framework and without another side to which one could turn for further orientation. The celestial court in the film *A Matter of Life and Death,* to which unlimited resources are available, is not a place for decisions or resembles too much an earthly court for its own good.

To the extent that the thought of death can recur, we can relate to life, that is, we can seek to "live truly," as Macherey phrases it when he tries to speak the "last word of Spinozan ethics."[17] To the extent that, as an economy of death, the organization of life exceeds any attempt at grasping its law, and that grasping its law would entail the possibility of crossing over to some other, opposite side or border, or of crossing back and forth between shores facing each other, we can relate to life, "prefer life to death," and try to live on in the "most intense possible manner," as Derrida says in the last interview he gave before he died.[18] To the same extent, however, to the extent that life cannot be opposed to death because it is constitutively in excess of itself, finite in its infinity, we cannot relate to life and "prefer life to death" or choose death over life. The moment we relate to something that interrupts the relationship and in doing so calls for us to relate to it nonetheless, we already live, we are already alive and in the midst of life, on its side, trying to catch up with ourselves while running along the shores.

Now, if we take into account that Derrida depicts the law as a "forbidden place,"[19] a place to which we have no access, and that he explains how the law must be forbidding and command respect for it to function as the law, withdrawing when we try to grasp and understand it, having the effect of the law only inasmuch as it remains an essentially unrecognizable cause, we will be in a position not simply to draw a structural analogy between life and the law as necessarily interrupted relationships but to identify the law and life on the grounds of their ambiguity. The law, Derrida writes, forbids us to access it, to understand fully why it makes the claims it makes or why it states whatever it states, by contradicting itself and placing human beings in a contradiction, in a situation of double bind. This seems to hold true for the law as an ethical or legal instance. In nature, one could assert that, in the wake of Derrida's discourse and against the background of Spinoza's claims, the explanation of a law refers us back to another law, to another cause, to another condition that has not been understood yet, in a regression that forestalls totalization. The law, which necessarily contradicts itself, creates or provokes undecidability. It confronts us with demands that are incompatible, whether because one demand excludes the other or because one demand is recognizable and the other carries us beyond what we can recognize. This is how, in "Force of Law," Derrida describes the relationship between the law [le droit] and justice, between the law that has been posited or laid down in a historical development and the law that addresses itself to us without allowing for a deduction, a justification, or, possibly, a transformation. Thus, in the end, the law remains a forbidden and forbidding place as it hovers between a relative recognizability and a relative unrecognizability. It escapes our grasp because it gives us something, lets us relate to it, and does not leave us with nothing. We *live* under the law. Liberation from its bondage would render the very notion of life meaningless. Yet, although the law accords us some freedom, the freedom to comport ourselves toward life through decisions we make, it also bars us from ever touching on necessity itself, that is, on reality or being. So it is not astonishing to hear Derrida say that he never feels more haunted by the "necessity of dying" than in "the instants of happiness and pleasure."[20]

You use the concept of necessity, but you deprive yourself of the means of conceiving of necessity in the first place. You cannot *really* understand what necessity, or the law, designates because you believe that by introducing a distinction between two sides, a temporal and an eternal aspect, you can explain finitude with respect to the infinity of the substance, one enveloping the other, and control the thought of death. You compromise necessity by comprehending it, as it were. In our gigantomachia, you are the idealist, for to *really* understand what it means to speak of necessity, or the law, I must acknowledge that I cannot touch on reality or being itself.

For you, the point at which the validity of the law is both confirmed and suspended is a point of self-contradiction and hence of turmoil at which it proves impossible to touch on reality or being. The law reaffirms itself in its very exteriority. For me, this point is the point at which my intelligence and the affect that I call the intellectual love of God allow me to touch on reality or being, that is, to stop relating to the law as something that I can only obey, to cease thinking of death and to look at life under the aspect of eternity. When I succeed in looking at life under the aspect of eternity, my individuality, too, is both confirmed and suspended, confirmed in that I am never more active and self-determining than at this stage and suspended in that I come to know the whole of nature, or something of it, and feel united with it. Now I would like to ask you the following question. We both side with life in a diverging manner. Can this decisive divergence between you and me be a matter of decision, as if, having reached the same point as I appear to have reached, you had decided to subordinate the aspect of eternity to the aspect of temporality? I wonder whether you are not a secret idealist. Do you not shrink away from your own courage when you conceive of the law as continuously holding back and keeping itself in an unattainable reserve? This would explain why you still think of death, why you do so in the instant in which you experience life at its most intense, to use your own words. To conceive of necessity *really* must mean to set oneself free. Although you claim on several occasions that there is no metalanguage, for example, in your essay on Cixous, and that metalanguage is nothing but an effect, you do after all formulate the law of the law. To put it differently, you do formulate the necessity of remaining under the forbidden, forbidding, contradictory law, without understanding it. Thus you claim an understanding of the law, at least implicitly. You cannot relate to the law in the same way as before once you have understood that the relationship to it is, by necessity, an interrupted one. And do you not, in the film that bears your name as its title, refer to an experience during which something imposed itself on you as self-evident, in a moment of enlightenment and understanding in which you did see things under the aspect of eternity, if you do not mind me resorting to my own vocabulary? You had finished writing a long text, which you then included in *Of Grammatology*. Perhaps all you did was to shout yes! silently or audibly. I understand you.

Notes

1. The edition of Spinoza's works used here is *Complete Works*, trans. Samuel Shirley, ed. Michael L. Morgan (Indianapolis, Ind.: Hackett, 2002).
2. Stuart Hampshire, *Spinoza and Spinozism*, rev ed. (Oxford: Clarendon Press, 2005), 126, 128.
3. Steven Nadler, *Spinoza: A Life* (Cambridge: Cambridge University Press, 2001), 349.
4. Gilles Deleuze, *Spinoza et le problème de l'expression* (Paris: Minuit, 1968), 131.
5. Theodor W. Adorno, *Negative Dialektik* (Frankfurt am Main, Germany: Suhrkamp, 1975), 364.
6. Gilles Deleuze, *En medio de Spinoza* (Buenos Aires: Cactus, 2003), 150.

7   Pierre Macherey, *Introduction à l'éthique de Spinoza—La cinquième partie: les voies de la libération* (Paris: Presses Universitaires de France, 1997), 56.
8   F. W. J. Schelling, *Philosophie der Offenbarung* (1858), repr. *Ausgewählte Werke* (Darmstadt, Germany: Wissenschaftliche Buchgesellschaft, 1990), 1:242.
9   Macherey, *Introduction*, 195.
10 F. H. Jacobi, *Über die Lehre des Spinoza* (Hamburg, Germany: Meiner, 2000), 113. On Jacobi's misunderstanding of Spinoza's doctrine, see chapter 4 of Eckart Förster, *Die fünfundzwanzig Jahre der Philosophie* (Frankfurt am Main, Germany: Vittorio Klostermann, forthcoming) (English trans. to be published by Harvard University Press).
11 Deleuze, *En medio de Spinoza*, 145.
12 Deleuze, *Spinoza et le problème de l'expression*, 297.
13 Spinoza, *Theological-Political Treatise*, in Spinoza, *Complete Works*, chap. 4.
14 Jacques Derrida, *H.C. pour la vie, c'est à dire . . .* (Paris: Galilée, 2002), 136 ; see also p. 36.
15 Ibid., 46.
16 Hegel disagrees with Spinoza on matters of life and death. In his mind, it is not enough to acknowledge that next to a "substance which proves to be empty and dead," there is "a world of determinations which lives off its own negativity." Pierre Macherey, *Hegel ou Spinoza* (Paris: Éditions La Découverte, 1990), 143.
17 Macherey, *Introduction*, 187.
18 Jacques Derrida, *Apprendre à vivre enfin. Entretien avec Jean Birnbaum* (Paris: Galilée/Le Monde, 2005), 55.
19 Jacques Derrida, "Préjugés. Devant la loi," in *La faculté de juger* (Paris: Minuit, 1985), 121.
20 Derrida, *Apprendre à vivre enfin*.

Contributors

Alain Badiou is professor at the École Normale Supérieure and also teaches at the Collège International de Philosophie. His many books translated into English include *Manifesto for Philosophy*; *Deleuze: The Clamor of Being* (Minnesota, 2000); *Ethics: An Essay on the Understanding of Evil*; *Infinite Thought: Truth and the Return to Philosophy*; *Saint Paul: The Foundation of Universalism*; *Handbook of Inaesthetics*; *Being and Event*; *The Century*; *The Concept of Model*; *The Meaning of Sarkozy*; *Logics of Worlds: Being and Event, Volume 2*; and *Theory of the Subject*.

Mieke Bal is Royal Netherlands Academy of Arts and Sciences Professor based at the Amsterdam School for Cultural Analysis. Her areas of interest range from biblical and classical antiquity to seventeenth-century and contemporary art and modern literature, feminism, and migratory culture. Her many books include *A Mieke Bal Reader, Travelling Concepts in the Humanities, Reading Rembrandt: Beyond the Word-Image Opposition, Loving Yusuf: Conceptual Travels from Present to Past,* and *Narratology*. Mieke Bal is also a video artist. Her experimental documentaries on migration include *A Thousand and One Days, Colony,* and the installation Nothing Is Missing. She is currently making her first fiction film, *Mère folle*. Her feature film *A Long History of Madness* is being exhibited internationally. Occasionally, she acts as an independent curator.

Cesare Casarino is professor of cultural studies and comparative literature at the University of Minnesota. He is the author of numerous essays on literature, cinema, and philosophy as well as the monograph *Modernity at Sea: Melville, Marx, and Conrad in Crisis*

(Minnesota, 2002). He is the coeditor (with Saree Makdisi and Rebecca Karl) of *Marxism beyond Marxism* and coauthor (with Antonio Negri) of *In Praise of the Common: A Conversation on Philosophy and Politics* (Minnesota, 2008). At present, he is working on a book manuscript on Gilles Deleuze's two-volume study of the cinema as well as a book manuscript on Spinoza and Marx.

Justin Clemens has published extensively on philosophy and psychoanalysis and is the coeditor of many scholarly anthologies, including *The Work of Giorgio Agamben* (with Nick Heron and Alex Murray) and *The Praxis of Alain Badiou* (with Paul Ashton and A. J. Bartlett). He is also the coeditor of *The Jacqueline Rose Reader* (with Ben Naparstek) and *Alain Badiou: Key Concepts* (with A. J. Bartlett). He teaches at the University of Melbourne.

Simon Duffy is lecturer in the department of philosophy at the University of Sydney (Australia). He is the author of *The Logic of Expression: Quality, Quantity, and the Intensity of Spinoza, Hegel, and Deleuze*, and he is the editor of *Virtual Mathematics: The Logic of Difference*. He has published articles in the *International Journal of Philosophical Studies*, the *Journal of the British Society for Phenomenology*, *Paragraph*, and *Angelaki: Journal of the Theoretical Humanities*. He has also translated a number of Gilles Deleuze's "Seminars on Spinoza," which are available online at http://www.webdeleuze.com/.

Alexander García Düttmann is professor of philosophy and visual culture at Goldsmiths, University of London. His most recent publications include *Philosophy of Exaggeration*; *Visconti: Insights into Flesh and Blood*; and *Derrida und ich: Das Problem der Dekonstruktion*.

Sebastian Egenhofer is Laurenz Professor for Contemporary Art at the University of Basel and member of the NCCR eikones / iconic criticism in Basel. His interests include contemporary art and theory, nineteenth- and twentieth-century modernism, the theory of perspective in early Renaissance Italy, Hercules Segers, and the emergence of Dutch landscape painting. Recent publications include the monograph *Abstraktion–Kapitalismus–Subjektivität: Die Wahrheitsfunktion des Werks in der Moderne* and several articles such as "Die Abstraktion und die

Topik des Imaginären" in Claudia Blümle and Armin Schäfer, eds., *Struktur–Figur–Kontur* and "Figures of Defiguration: Four Theses on Abstraction" in *Texte zur Kunst*.

Arthur J. Jacobson is the Max Freund Professor of Litigation and Advocacy at the Benjamin N. Cardozo School of Law, Yeshiva University. With Stephen B. Smith, he has edited *Spinoza's Law,* a volume of conference papers on Spinoza's legal theory. Among other books, he is the author (with Bernhard Schlink) of *Weimar: A Jurisprudence of Crisis*. He has published articles in legal theory.

A. Kiarina Kordela is professor of German and cultural studies at Macalester College, Saint Paul, Minnesota. Her publications include *$urplus: Spinoza, Lacan* and several articles on a broad variety of subjects ranging from German literature, such as Goethe (in *Modern Language Studies*) and Kafka–Corngold (in *Literary Paternity–Literary Friendship*), to philosophy, psychoanalysis, critical theory, sexual difference, film, and biopolitics—with a focus on Spinoza, Kant, Marx, Lacan, Foucault, and Deleuze—in collections and journals such as *European Film Theory, The Dreams of Interpretation, Angelaki, Cultural Critique, Parallax, Rethinking Marxism,* and *Political Theory*.

Michael Mack is reader in English studies and medical humanities at Durham University. He has published two books: *Anthropology and Memory: Elias Canetti and Franz Baermann Steiner's Responses to the Shoah* and *German Idealism and the Jew: The Inner Anti-Semitism of Philosophy and German Jewish Responses,* the latter of which was short-listed for the Koret Jewish Book Award 2004. He has published over thirty articles in international journals across the disciplines of English, history, philosophy, theology, anthropology, and critical legal studies. He is completing a book manuscript on Spinozist self-preservation and self-destruction titled *Thinking with Spinoza: Toward an Inclusive Universalism*. He also has a forthcoming book, *How Literature Changes the Way We Think*.

Warren Montag is professor of English and comparative literature at Occidental College in Los Angeles. His books include *Louis*

Althusser and *Bodies, Masses, and Power: Spinoza and His Contemporaries* as well as the edited volume (with Ted Stolze) *The New Spinoza* (Minnesota, 1998).

Antonio Negri, who has taught at the University of Padua and the University of Paris, is the author of more than thirty books, including *Empire* and *Multitude: War and Democracy in the Age of Empire* as well as *Labor of Dionysus* (with Michael Hardt, Minnesota, 1994). He has published two books on Spinoza, *The Savage Anomaly: The Power of Spinoza's Metaphysics* (Minnesota, 1990) and *Subversive Spinoza: (Un) Contemporary Variations,* while Spinoza's thought informs much of his other writings such as *Time for Revolution* and *Insurgencies: Constituent Power and the Modern State* (Minnesota, 1999). Other recent books in English are *The Porcelain Workshop: For a New Grammar of Politics* and *Political Descartes: Reason, Ideology, and the Bourgeois Project.*

Christopher Norris is Distinguished Research Professor in Philosophy at the University of Cardiff, Wales. He has written numerous books on various aspects of philosophy and the history of ideas, among them *Spinoza and the Origins of Modern Critical Theory.* More recent works include *Quantum Theory and the Flight from Realism*; *Philosophy of Language and the Challenge to Scientific Realism*; *Language, Logic, and Epistemology*; *On Truth and Meaning*; *Platonism, Music, and the Listeners's Share*; and *Fiction, Philosophy, and Literary Theory.* His latest are *Alain Badiou's Being Event: A Reader's Guide* (2009) and *Re-Thinking the Cogito: Naturalism, Reason, and the Venture of Thought* (2010). His books have been translated into ten languages, and he has also taught and lectured at many universities around the world, including periods as visiting professor at the City University of New York, the University of Santiago de Compostela in Spain, and the School of Criticism and Theory at Dartmouth College.

Anthony Uhlmann is professor in the Writing and Society Research Group, University of Western Sydney. He is the author of *Beckett and Poststructuralism* and *Samuel Beckett and the Philosophical Image* and coedited *The Ethics of Arnold Geulincx* (with Han van Ruler and Martin Wilson). His new book, *Thinking in Literature*, was published in 2011. He is the editor of the *Journal of Beckett Studies.*

Dimitris Vardoulakis is senior lecturer at the University of Western Sydney. His publications include *The Doppelgänger: Literature's Philosophy*. Other edited or coedited volumes include *Benjamin and Heidegger*, *Kafka's Cages*, *The Political Animal*, and *After Blanchot*. He is the author of numerous articles published in English and Greek, and he has translated two books into Greek. His book *Sovereignty and Its Other* is forthcoming.

Index

Adorno, Theodor, 110–14, 303n27, 352, 361n5
Aesop, 68
Agamben, Giorgio, n87n11, 222n19
Althusser, Louis, xv, 4, 6, 9, 13–15, 18, 22, 26–27, 29, 32n4, 33n24, 35n33, 37n63, 39, 128n1, 164, 166, 176n7, 179–80, 217, 218n1, 219n3, 234n79, 234n80, 234n81, 240–41, 259n7
Anaximander, 67, 87n13
Antisthenes, 68
Appuhn, Charles, 340
Apuleius, 86n10
Aquinas, Thomas, 67, 87n13, 105–6
Aristotle, 16–17, 42, 67, 68, 82, 86n9, 87n13, 132n40, 196–97, 199, 201, 205, 226n37, 227n45
Armstrong, D. M., 35n50, 94n34
Asher, Michael, xxi, 247, 259–52, 255, 261n18
Augustine, 105–6
Augustus de Morgan, 67
Aurelius, Marcus, 231n62

Austin, J. L., 17
Averroes, 67, 88n13, 89n17, 114

Bachelard, Gaston, 26, 36n62
Badiou, Alain, xvii–xviii, xxxi, 9, 51, 79, 91n28, 259n5, 331–32, 341, 348n37, 348n46
Bal, Mieke, xxii, 300n5, 300n6, 401n8, 401n9, 401n15
Balibar, Étienne, xv, xxvin2, 4, 6, 11, 18, 21–22, 26–29, 32n1, 33n5, 35n29, 35n33, 35n49, 92n29, 99, 112, 123n1, 131n32, 218n3, 226n36, 229n50, 234n79, 303n30
Barthes, Roland, 161n17
Bayle, Pierre, xii, xiii, 79, 92n30
Beckett, Samuel, 263, 268–70, 274n12, 274n13, 274n14
Beeckman, Isaac, 83
Benesch, Otto, 284
Benjamin, Andrew, 302n22
Benjamin, Walter, 69, 70, 87n11, 303n27
Bennett, Jonathan, 5–8, 10, 13, 18, 30, 33–35, 37n68

Benton, Ted, 37n64
Bergson, Henri, 76, 239, 259n2
Bernard, Claude, 129n15
Bernard, Emile, 275n18
Beuys, Joseph, 251
Beveridge, Karl, 261n17
Bible, the, xx, 103–4, 132, 141, 150, 163, 166, 170, 172, 280, 282, 284–86, 288, 297–98
Bieser, Frederick C., xiii, xxvin4, 32n3
Bird, Graham, 37n71
Blumenberg, Hans, 115, 132n40
Blyenbergh, William van, 119
Borges, J. L. 86n3
Borradori, Giovanna, 131n30, 134n55
Bourbaki, Nicolas, 88n15
Boxel, 293
Bréhier, Émile, 274n8
Bresson, Robert, 88n15
Buchloch, Benjamin, 261n21
Buridan, Jean, xviii, 66, 67, 82–85, 87n13, 95n43, 95n44
Burn, Ian, 261n17
Burton, Robert G., 90n20

Cage, John, 260n11
Caillois, Roger, 340
Caird, John, 78, 91n25
Canetti, Elias, 110, 131n29
Carroll, Lewis, 67
Casarino, Casare, xx, 221n4, 226n29, 227n37, 227n40
Cassin, Barbara, 84n3
Cassuto, Philippe, 175n17
Cavaillés, Jean, 39
Cézanne, Paul, 270–71, 275n18
Chalmers, David J., 36n60
Christenson, Jason, 218
Cixious, Heléne, 356–57, 361
Clemens, Justin, xviii, xix

Clément, Bruno, 271, 275n21
Coleridge, Samuel Taylor, 264
Colerus, Johan, 223n26
Colie, Rosalie L., 174n2
Cordingley, Anthony, 274n1
Cottingham, John, 66, 84n2, 91n25, 100, 128n6, 129n7
Crane, Tim, 35n50
Curley, Edwin, xv, xxvi n10, 34n22, 264, 325, 339–40

Damasio, Antonio, xvi, xxiii, xxvin17, 7, 28–29, 34n17, 37n67, 102, 128n14, 133n45,n52, 321–31, 336, 340–42, 344–37, 347n1, 347n2, 347n3, 347n4, 347n5, 347n6, 347n7, 347n8, 347n9, 347n10, 347n11, 347n12, 347n13, 347n14, 347n15, 347n16, 347n18, 347n19, 347n20, 347n21, 347n22, 348n25, 348n33, 348n34, 348n35, 350n53, 350n54, 350n55, 350n56
Dante Alighieri, 67
Darwin, Charles, 102, 129n15, 330–31
Davidson, Donald, 6, 19–23, 25, 31, 33n8, 35
Debord, Guy, 229n50, 241
Deleuze, Gilles, xii, xviii, xx, xxvi n11, 4–6, 9, 11, 15, 18, 21, 26–29, 33n5, 35–37, 39–64, 7– 82, 88n16, 90n22, 92n29, 93n34, 94n40, 95n41, 99, 102, 118, 121–22, 128n1, 233n46, 135n48, 180, 185–86, 202–9, 215, 218n3, 222n16, 222n17, 222n18, 222n19, 223n25, 225n27, 225n 8, 226n28, 229n51, 229n 52, 229n53,

230n53, 230n54, 230n55, 230n56, 231n60, 231n61, 231n62, 231n63, 231n64, 232n72, 233n72, 233n73, 233n74, 234n82, 237–38, 289, 243, 259n2, 259n4, 260n12, 261n23, 264, 268, 270, 274n11, 275n17, 278–79, 296, 300n4, 331–33, 343n39, 343n40, 352, 355, 361n4, 361n6, 362n11, 362n12
Democritus, 18
Derrida, Jacques, xxiii–xxiv, 6, 16–17, 34n15, 35n38, 35n39, 35n40, 73, 87n12, 88n16, 111, 123, 291, 301n14, 331, 356–60, 362n14, 362n15, 362n18, 362n19
Descartes, René, xviii, xix, 2, 7–8, 11, 31, 44, 46, 80, 83, 84n3, 100–120, 128n6, 130n19, 130n24, 132n40, 132n44, 133n44, 133n48, 191, 227n39, 230n58, 324
Dilthey, Wilhelm, 317
Donagan, Alan, 6, 10, 13, 33n8, 34n27, 35n31
Donaldson, Margaret, 36n51
Duchamp, Marcel, 245–55
Duffy, Simon, xviii, xxi, 62n3, 64n34
Duhuit, George, 269
Durant, Will, 65
Düttman, Alexander Garcia, xxiii

Egenhofer, Sebastian, xxi, 261n14, 302n21
Eldred, Michael, 237
Eliot, George, xvi, xxvin18, 264
Epictetus, 231n62
Epicurus, 18
Epimenides, 70
Erasmus, Desiderius, 294

Euclid, 86n8, 268
Ezra, Ibn, 165

Faulkner, William, 272, 275n22
Fechner, Gustav T., 327
Feiner, Shmuel, 130n18
Feuer, Lewis Samuel, 28, 32n1, 37n66
Fichte, Johann Gottlieb, xiii
Fonsecca, Aboabde, 223n26
Foucault, Michel, 230n53, 260n10
Fraser, Andrea, 255
Freud, Sigmund, 102, 129n15, 286, 327–31, 244, 247n23

Galileo Galilei, 83
Garret, Aaron V., 127, 134n58, 134n59
Garrett, Don, 33n8, 128n3
Gaswuet, Joaquim, 271, 275n19
Gataker, Thomas, 67
Gatens, Moira, xvi, 32n3, 132n42, 292, 201n16
Gebhardt, Carl, 156n1, 156n2, 156n3, 156n4, 156n5, 156n6, 156n7, 156n8, 156n9, 157
Gersonides, 156
Ghazali, Al-, 67, 88n13
Gillespie, Michael Allen., 115, 132n41
Gillespie, S., 92n28
Godard, Jean-Luc, 292
Gödel, Kurt, 91n28
Goodchild, Philip, 130n27, 134n55
Greenblatt, Stephen, 269, 275n16
Grene, Marjorie, 33n8, 36n54, 215, 218n3, 219n3, 226n28, 232n73, 233n72, 233n73
Guattari, Félix, 35n37, 243, 264, 274n5
Guéroult, Martial, xiv, xxvin9, 39
Guyer, Paul, 37n71

Hacking, Ian, 36n54
Hampshire, Stuart, 5, 30, 33n8, 37n69, 351, 261n2
Hanna, Robert, 37n72
Hardt, Micheal, xvi, xxvi n14, xxvi n15, 219n3, 220n3, 231n40
Heartfield, John, 251
Heck, Paul, 301n13
Heidegger, Martin, xxii–xxiii, 250–52, 261n19, 308–18, 319n8, 319n9, 319n10, 362n16
Heine, Heinrich, 69, 86n10, 264
Heraclitus, 68, 86n9
Hirschhorn, Thomas, xvi, xxi, 237, 242, 247, 251, 254–56, 260n8, 261n22
Hobbes, Thomas, xviii, xix, 77, 79–80, 83, 87n11, 93n31, 93n33, 94n34, 112–15 120–21, 124n49, 124n50, 131n35, 132n35, 132n36, 132n37, 162
Hölderlin, Fredrich, xiv
Holland, Eugene, 219n3, 230n3, 259n7
Homer, 290–91
Horkheimer, Max, 110, 260n9
Hume, David, 12
Husserl, Edmund, 17, 314–15, 317

Igoin, Albert, 219n3
Isaiah, Rabbi Abraham ben, 158n53
Israel, Jonathan, xx, 27, 32n1, 33n5, 35n28, 37n65, 92n30, 103, 130n25, 161–63, 166, 174, 175n1, 175n4, 176n13
Israel, Manasseh ben, 278

Jacobi, Friedrich Heinrich, xiii, 355, 362n10
Jacobson, Arthur J., xix, xx
James, Susan, 100, 128n5

James, William, 129n5
Jameson, Fredric, 179, 182, 221n10, 221n11, 221n12, 221n28
Janouch, Gustav, xxiv, xxvi n19
Judaism, 93, 99–100
Judd, Donald, xxi, 247–48, 251, 261n17

Kafka, Franz, xxiv–xxv, 34n18, 303n27
Kant, Immanuel, 8, 11, 16–17, 30–31, 67, 99–101, 114–15, 128n10, 161, 219n3, 239, 244, 341, 348–50n47
Karatani, Kojin, 181–83, 221n9
Kaufman, Eleanor, 226n28
Kaye, S.M., 85n5
Kierkegaard, Søren, 73, 88n16
King, Peter, 67, 85n5
Kolakakowski, Leszek, 32n3
Koran, the, 280, 282–85, 287, 288–90
Kordela, A. Kiarina, xxiii, 94n40, 219n3, 220n3, 225n28, 226n29, 349n47, 350n50
Koyré, Alexandre, 82, 95n42
Kristeller, Paul Oskar, 227n39

La Fontaine, Jean de, 68
Lacan, Jacques, 84n3, 219n3, 230n57, 327–33, 341–44, 347n25, 248n26, 248n27, 248n28, 248n29, 248n30, 248n31, 248n32, 248n36
Lagrée, Jacqueline, 91n24, 274n7
Lautréamont, Comte de, 49
Lee Rice, Douglas Den Uyl, 175n3
Leibniz, Gottfried W., xxvn2, 30, 69, 74, 76, 230n56
Lenin, Vladimir, 179
Leo X, 106

Lessing, G. E., xiii
Levi, Primo, 87n11
Levine, Michael P., 129n17
Levy, Benny, 39
Lipsius, Justus, 265
Lloyd, Genevieve, xvi, xxvi n6, 32n2, 33n8, 132n42, 212–13, 227n39, 231n67, 292, 301n16
Locke, John, 161–62
Lord, Beth, xxvin4

Macdonald, Cynthia, 35n50
Macherey, Pierre, xviii, xxvin6, 11, 12, 26, 29, 33n4, 90n23, 175n4, 219n3, 240, 259n7, 264, 353–46, 358, 362n7, 362n9, 362n17
Mack, Michael, xix, 218n2, 131n28, 131n31, 132n43, 302n18
Magris, Claudio, 86n10
Maimondides, Moses, xix, 135, 138–55, 159, 164–67, 173, 176n8
Malcolm, Noel, 93n31
Malcolm, Norman, 35n50
Malevich, Kazimir, 245
Marion, Jean-Luc, 105, 130n20–21
Marx, Karl, xiv, xx, 4, 15–16, 27, 39, 46, 56, 69, 179–81, 184, 196–201, 216, 218n2, 218n3, 219n3, 220n3, 221n3, 221n4, 221n5, 221n6, 221n7, 221n8, 226n37, 226n40, 226n41, 226n42, 226n43, 226n44, 226n46, 226n47, 226n48, 226n49, 231n70, 233n77, 223n78, 223n79, 223n80, 237, 240, 253, 261n16, 308
Matheron, Alexandre, 219n3
McAdam, James I., 89n20
McDowell, John, 31, 37n74
McLihna, Marshall, 229n56

McShea, Robert, 33n5
Mendelssohn, Felix, xiii
Merleau-Ponty, Maurice, 260n10
Mondrian, Piet, xxi, 237–38, 242–48, 251, 254, 261n14, 261n15, 302n21
Montag, Warren, xv, xiv, xx–xxi, xxvi n13, 33n4, 132n42, 218n3
Montaigne, Michel de, 67
Moore, F. C. T., 85n4, 89n18, 90n21
Moreau, Pierre François, xxvin3, 175n4, 226n36
Morrison, James C., 301n17
Muller, Christain Philipp, 255
Mundle, C. W. K., 36n52

Nadler, Steven, xxvn1, 32n2, 35n28, 100–101, 129n8, 129n9, 130n25, 134n49, 223n24, 224n26, 226n30, 227n39, 274n4, 351, 361n3
Negri, Antonio, xv–xvi, xxii–xxiii, xxvi n14, xxvi n15, 9, 11, 26–27, 29, 34n24, 35n29, 39, 40, 90, 102, 128n1, 175n4, 180, 218n3, 219n3, 220n3, 221n4, 231n70, 259n6, 302n19
Nietzsche, Friedrich, xiv, 16–17, 68, 308, 313, 315, 317
Norris, Christoper, xviii, 32n1, 33n7, 34, 37, 39, 51
Novalis, xiv–xv, 18, 264
Nussbaum, Martha, 99, 102, 128n1

Ockham, William of, 67, 84n4, 86n5, 116, 119
Oldenburg, Henry, 121, 176n15, 293
Olivi, Peter John, 67

Parkinson, G. H. R., 33n8, 36n54

Paterson, Sarah, 35n50
Pautrat, Bernard, 42
Peeren, Esther, 301n12
Peirce, C. S., 287
Pironet, Fabienne, 95n44
Plato, 17, 42, 85n4, 87n13, 103
Pollock, Frederick, 5
Pope, Alexander, xvi
Popkin, Richard H., 33n6
Powell, Michael, 355
Pressburger, Emeric, 355
Preuss, Samuel J., 32n2
Priest, Stephen, 36n51
Proust, Marcel, 270
Pythagoras, 267

Rabelais, François, 67
Ramond, Charles, 40, 51, 62n2
Rauschenberg, Robert, 244
Rediker, Marcus, 228n49
Reichenbach, Hans, 35n25
Reid, Thomas, 67
Rembrandt, xxii, 277–84, 286, 288–89, 290–92, 294, 296, 298–300
Renais, Alain, 201
Rescher, Nicholas, 67, 75, 86n6, 87n13, 88n17, 89n19
Rodchenko, Aleksander, 251
Rorschach, H., 16
Rorty, Richard, 36n52
Rosenthal, David M., 36n51
Rossetti, Dante Gabriel, 85n4
Rousseau, Jean-Jacques, 17
Rubd, Maximilien, 219n3, 226n36
Russell, Bertrand, 5, 30

Sackville-West, Vita, 266
Saunders, Jason Lewis., 274n7
Schelling, F. W. J., xiv, 354–55, 361n8
Schlegel, K. W. F., xiv

Schmitt, Carl, 87n11
Schneewind, Jerome B., 114–15, 131n33, 132n39
Schopenhauer, Arthur, 67
Schumpeter, Joseph, 68, 72, 86n7
Schwitters, Kurt, 251
Scotus, Duns, 67 86n5, 114, 116, 119
Segal, Gideon, 32n1
Sellars, Wilfrid, 31
Sen, Amartya, 68, 72, 88n15
Seneca, 337
Seurat, Georges, 243–46
Shakespeare, William, 69, 269
Shelley, P. B., 295
Shirley, Samuel, 168, 171, 265
Skousen, Mark, 72, 88n14
Smith, Daniel W., 226n28
Smith, Steven B., 32n2, 101, 128n4, 129n11, 129n12, 129n13
Socrates, 85n4
Spinoza, Baruch: *The Correspondence of Spinoza*,133n47, 135n51, 256; *Ethics*, xi, xiv, xvii, xviii, xix xx, xxiii, xxv n1, 5–7, 11–13, 15, 17–19, 35n44, 35n45, 39–54, 57–58, 61–63, 65–78, 80, 84n1, 90n21, 90n22, 90n23, 90n24, 90n25, 90n26, 95n38, 99–102, 104, 107–9, 112, 116–18, 120–26, 128n13, 130n35, 132n44, 133n49, 162–63, 166–67, 173, 184–85, 187–90, 218, 222n14, 224n26, 224n27, 226n31, 226n 32, 226n34, 227n39, 231n65, 231n68, 232n71, 232n72, 233n24, 226n31, 226n32, 226n33, 226n34, 226n35, 227n39, 231n65, 231n66, 231n67, 231n6, 232n71, 232n72, 233, 241, 245, 257–60,

263–64, 273–74, 294, 300n7, 201n18, 311–13, 318n1, 322–27, 332–37, 339, 342–46, 247n17, 247n18, 247n19, 248n42, 349n47, 351–55; *Treatise on the Emendation of the Intellect*, 36n53, 36n55, 78, 92n27, 193–94, 202, 256; *Political Treatise*, xi–xii, xvi, xxv n2; *Principles of Cartesian Philosophy*, xxvi n3, 302n23; *Short Treatise on God, Man, and His Well-Being*, 294; *Theological-Political Treatise*, xi, xii, xix, xxv n1, 9, 13–15, 33n6, 79–80, 93n30, 93n31, 94n35, 94n35, 94n36, 94n37, 94n38, 94n39, 104, 142, 156–59, 161, 163–66, 168–74, 176n9, 176n8, 176n9, 176n10, 176n11, 176n12, 176n13, 176n14, 176n15, 176n16, 177, 266, 280, 350n57, 356, 362n13
Stoics, 76, 132n44, 133n44, 206, 265, 340
Stolze, Ted, xv, 33n4
Strauss, Leo, 33n6, 114, 131n35, 132n37, 132n38
Strawson, P. F., 37n70
Styron, William 87n11
Suarez, F., 105, 110, 112, 114
Swan, David, 24
Swenson, Brynnar, 219n3, 220n3

Taylor, Kenna C., 72, 86n7, 88n14
Thales of Miletus, 194
Theophilus, 295
Thoburn, Nicholas, 219n3
Torah, the, 142, 145, 146, 148, 150–54, 176n8

Uhlmann, Anthony, xxi, 275n15, 300n7

Valentiner, W. R., 300n3
van Gogh, Vincent, 279
van Velde, Bram, 269
Vardoulakis, Dimitris, xxii, 156, 218
Velázquez, Diego, 260n10
Verbeek, Theo, 32n2, 93n32
Vermeer, Johannes, 278
Vernière, Paul, 175n2
Vesey, G. N. A., 35n50
Viesel, Hansjörg, 87n11
Villon, François, 67, 84n4
Virno, Paolo, 219n3
Vodel, Joost van den, 281
Vopa, Anthony J. La, xxxvi n7

Warhol, Andy, 251, 254, 261n20
Weil, Simone, 91n24
Wienpahl, Paul, 32n1
Wiernik, Peter, 223n26
Windelband, Wilhelm, 263
Wittgenstein, Ludwig, 36n52, 40, 74, 76, 266, 274n9, 315
Wolf, A., 300n2
Wolff, Christain, 67
Wolfson, Harry Austryn, xiv, 77–78, 90n22
Woolf, Virginia, 266, 274n10
Wordsworth, William, 264

Yovel, Yirmiyahu, xiv, xxvi n6, 32n1, 32n2, 259n7, 261n24

Zac, Silvain, 33n6
Zadeh, Khodja, 67
Zeno, 70
Žižek, Slavoj, 193, 225n28, 226n28, 331–32, 338, 341, 348n48, 348n44, 348n47
Zupko, Jack, 95n43, 95n44

www.ingramcontent.com/pod-product-compliance
Lightning Source LLC
Chambersburg PA
CBHW032015230426
43671CB00005B/88